SCOTLAND SINCE 1707:
THE RISE OF AN
INDUSTRIAL SOCIETY

SCOTLAND

SINCE 1707

The Rise of an Industrial Society

R. H. CAMPBELL

Professor of Economic History,
University of East Anglia

BARNES & NOBLE, INC · NEW YORK

PUBLISHERS · BOOKSELLERS · SINCE 1873

Published in the United States
in 1965
by Barnes & Noble, Inc.
105 Fifth Avenue
New York, New York 10003

PRINTED IN GREAT BRITAIN

CONTENTS

v

PART THREE

Economic Pressure, 1870's to 1939

Introduction

DURING the last two hundred and fifty years the economic history of Scotland has turned full circle. From being an insignificant part of a nascent international economy, Scotland emerged to a position of leadership, which has since been lost. The record of the growth of Scottish industrial society, with opportunities, lost and taken, and problems, solved and unsolved, is the backbone of Scottish history, especially since the end of the country's parliamentary independence in 1707.

The Union of the Parliaments of Scotland and England in 1707 did not provide the first impetus towards the evolution of the modern Scottish economy, because attempts to follow English ways were evident in the seventeenth century, but, by removing both the possibility of indiscreet economic action by the Scots and of peevish reprisals by the English, it did lead to an environment in which such efforts were more likely to succeed. But the Scottish economy was not immediately able to meet all rivalry from England and overseas. For three-quarters of a century thereafter the struggle for economic advance, which had started before 1707, continued, and, though frequently arrested in the eighteenth century by the chronic poverty of the country, it was attended by solid, and cumulative, gains. During that period the country was still an agrarian and trading economy; such industry as it possessed was only a portent for the future.

Around the 1780's the industrial successes were consolidated, and there began a century of notable economic expansion, when the industrial society which is modern Scotland was formed. The basis of success lay at first in the growth of the cotton industry until it was displaced from its position of supremacy through the rapid development of iron production from the 1830's, but, whatever the basis, the 1780's to the 1870's was a period of economic achievement, when Scotland emerged as an industrial power without rival in some fields. Though the society which then evolved was riddled by squalor and unrest, its economic foundations seemed so lasting that they bred complacency and self-satisfaction, which contrasted with the efforts and struggles of the eighteenth century, and which served Scotland ill in later years.

From the 1870's the industrial successes continued, but became progressively less dazzling, chiefly because Scotland was no longer immune from the pressures of international competition. The cotton industry first suffered its effects before the middle of the nineteenth century, but the changes and warnings it implied were then overshadowed by the resounding successes of the expanding iron industry. From the 1870's similar warnings became more numerous, but the extent of the decline of Scotland from a position of international economic leadership was rarely appreciated before 1914, because of the continued expansion in the allied fields of shipbuilding and steelmaking. Their success ensured that Scottish industrial society remained relatively prosperous, though increasingly specialized, until 1914, and it was their collapse in the inter-war years which plunged the economy so completely, and, it seemed to many in the 1930's, so irrevocably, into depression. Yet that was the culmination of a trend which had been evident for at least fifty years. In the 1930's, therefore, Scotland reaped the bitter fruit of a degree of specialization which, though once highly successful, had led to a failure to exploit the newer industries which other countries, and other parts of the United Kingdom, possessed. Scotland had then to tackle the problem of economic adjustment, made more intractable, yet more pressing, by its long neglect.

Part One

ECONOMIC STRUGGLE
1707-1780's

I

A CHANGING SOCIETY
The consequences of 1707

ULTIMATELY the Union of 1707 had a sweeping influence on Scottish life, but it did not represent the first infusion of a new and wider culture. Even earlier, Scottish experience was expanding through contact with 'the broadest river in European culture, the Stoic-inspired Roman jurisprudence, carried practically throughout Europe on the broad currents of Roman and Canon Law'.[1] This intellectual background had its most fruitful impact on the Scottish educational system, which, though not developed as its founders had planned, was still superior to any in Europe in the eighteenth century. The country's five universities,[2] especially those of Glasgow and Edinburgh, were leading European institutions at a time when England's two were moribund. They attracted students from overseas, and from England came the nonconformists who found the doors of their own universities barred against them. The universities were among the active pioneers of a new society in Scotland. They transformed their own teaching methods when,

[1] A. L. Macfie, 'The Scottish Tradition of Economic Thought', *Scottish Journal of Political Economy*, vol. ii, no. 2, p. 87.

[2] At Aberdeen, King's College and Marischal College were still separate institutions.

B   I

following the example of Francis Hutcheson, Professor of Moral Philosophy at Glasgow, the Latin 'dictates' were replaced by lectures in English, and were supplemented, especially in certain science classes, by 'examination hours', or sessions for discussion and tutorial teaching. More important, the scientific investigation carried out in the universities had a practical implication, frequently relevant to economic development. In the eighteenth century the Scottish universities ensured the full application of scientific method to agricultural and industrial problems. William Cullen (1710–90), who taught at both Glasgow and Edinburgh, was probably second only to Hermann Boerhaave of Leyden in the fields of medicine and chemistry. He reformed the pharmacopoeia and led in the study of soil science. Francis Home (1719–1813), Professor of Materia Medica at Edinburgh, pioneered the chemistry of bleaching to assist the improvement of Scottish linen production, investigated plant nutrition, and recommended the boiling of water as a precaution against epidemics. Contact between the universities and industry and agriculture was not only one way: while the academics helped the industrialists, the industrialists moved happily within the universities. The greatest example of such co-operation was in the 1760's at Glasgow between Joseph Black, the Professor of Chemistry who discovered the principle of latent heat in 1758, and James Watt, the mathematical instrument maker within the university precincts. Their work in repairing the old Newcomen engine used in the natural philosophy class of John Anderson (who by his own bequests did much to forward scientific education, and, in particular, co-operation between science and industry in the west of Scotland) marked the beginning of a new age. Though the idea of the separate condenser, which was the basis of the new and successful steam-engine, was Watt's, the discussion and co-operation with others in the university was a necessary prelude to the accomplishment. In this way the origin of the steam-engine, with all its subsequent implications for industrial growth, was the outcome of Scotland's intellectual abilities and interests in the eighteenth century. And when Watt attempted commercial production he received help first from John Roebuck, an Englishman, but a typical, though financially unsuccessful, product of the Scottish educational system.

To distinguish the contribution of the scientist from that of the industrialist in Scotland in the eighteenth century is unrealistic. The divergence between the two groups, which became more characteristic of Scotland in the nineteenth century, and which had unfortunate repercussions on the country's international economic competitiveness, was not evident earlier, when both worked happily together in a common effort to apply their special abilities towards the promotion of Scotland's economic welfare. At the time of the Union, Scotland's economic backwardness, especially when compared with England, made the need for such co-operation and effort essential. Yet recognition of that backwardness, and the consequential imitation of English achievements, were not the products of the Union of 1707 but were current even in the seventeenth century. It is wrong to stress the extent to which the increasing contact established after 1707 engendered the desire to copy English economic ways. The desire was already present. Economic policy derived, therefore, from the same motives both before and after 1707. Yet the Union did effect a difference sufficient to classify it as an epoch-making event in Scottish economic history. The difference lay in the means by which the same aim, emulation of English economic achievement, was to be reached. It had two new aspects, one external, the other internal. The external factor was the confirmation of the reorientation of Scotland's trading links from Europe to England, and so to America, and their increasing fruitfulness.[1] Though to some the attempts to re-establish closer links with France through the rebellions of 1715 and 1745 were valiant endeavours to maintain Scotland's earlier independence from England, to the majority of Scots, especially to those promoting and profiting from the reorientation of economic contacts, the rebellions were unfortunate interruptions, the tragedy of which was not that they failed, but that they ever happened. The Union of 1707 effected an internal change in the means of remedying Scotland's economic backwardness by ensuring that Scottish economic policy aimed at rivalling the achievements of the English economy through complementary rather than competitive action. Before 1707 the incomplete political union led in a mercantilist environment to attempts at competitive rivalry of a stronger economic power in the fields of its success. Such efforts inevitably came to little unless supported by a protectionist policy, while even high protection failed to save those ventures, especially cloth production, which were directly competitive with English manufactures. The industrial successes lay only in sectors, such as sugar refining, which were not competitive but complementary to the English economy. After 1707 political union ensured that, once and for all, attempts at economic development in Scotland had to follow complementary lines.

[1] See below, pp. 41–2.

Emulation of English ways and achievements inevitably implied a social transformation before modern industrial techniques could be applied, or the wider stresses of a trading community assimilated, but it was one which was achieved more easily through the traditional leaders of the old society becoming the first leaders of the new, and through their willingness to absorb others into their own ranks. The unquestioned leaders of Scottish society at the time of the Union were the landowners, whose social prestige derived from their political power. Parochial authority rested in a balance, not always clearly defined, between the kirk session and the heritors, who were the proprietors of land within the parish to the extent of at least £100 (Scots) of valued rent appearing in the land-tax books. Heritors were responsible for the upkeep of church, manse, school and school-house and shared with the session the responsibilities for poor relief. The landed interest still maintained its authority in the wider spheres of county administration, in which the two chief bodies were the Justices of the Peace and the Commissioners of Supply for the shire. Justices were chosen by the sovereign but the office was confined in effect to landowners. Commissioners of Supply, appointed originally from among those paying the land tax, and charged with its collection, came to include most of the landed proprietors. Since the higher administration always remained rudimentary neither body dislodged the parochial authorities.

The need for landowners to use the power and influence they possessed for the development of the Scottish economy was more necessary after 1707 than it had been before, because the abolition of the Scottish parliament and privy council meant the end of an effective Scottish administration. Though from 1709 to 1746 a third secretary was added to the United Kingdom's existing two, and charged with responsibility for Scottish affairs, the office was frequently vacant. After 1746 the Lord Advocate and, until 1827, unofficial Scottish 'Managers', the leading Scottish politicians of the day, were responsible for the administration. As a result there was no really effective Scottish administration from the Union until the institution of the Scottish Office in 1885. Under such conditions any failure by the landowners to encourage economic development could not easily have been made good. Fortunately, there was no such failure. The landowners discharged their responsibilities, especially when there was an infiltration into their ranks of new men, ready to use the privileges of their status to effect the social and economic transformation which

Scotland required. In this respect the experience of the Highlands and Lowlands differed. In the Highlands the ancient landowners retained their privileged position longer, but in the Lowlands successful bankers, lawyers and merchants were readily accepted as landed proprietors. They purchased their way into social position with a speed and completeness less easily achieved by their nineteenth-century counterparts, because assimilation was easy in the eighteenth century, when many of the successful lawyers, merchants and bankers were themselves scions of ancient landed families and so were returning to their heritage, and when many of the landowners participated in industrial enterprises so long as these remained subordinate to their normal rural activities. Until the nineteenth century there was no sharp distinction between the successful commercial men and the landowners, since the interests of both were complementary. The two groups moved easily together, as did both with the intellectuals. But the new landowners brought a unique contribution to the social and economic influence of their class in Scotland in the eighteenth century. While they used their possessions to obtain social prestige, the new landowners also regarded them as a means of obtaining further commercial advance. The estate had to be a good investment, commercially as well as socially. All the economic opportunity implied in its possession, and in the accompanying social prestige, were exploited, and so the traditional power of the landowners, which could have been a restraining, if not an opposing force, became the chief support of social and economic reform in Scotland in the eighteenth century.

Though the ultimate benefits of the social changes of the eighteenth century cannot be disputed, they were not all immediately apparent. Social stress, though perhaps less than has been thought, appeared in two fields: in the failure of provision for poverty and distress, and in movements of population.

Such provision as the poor law then made for social distress in Scotland rested on the successful working of the parochial system. Many of its alleged defects—notably the refusal of relief to the able-bodied and the reliance on financing by voluntary means, especially by church collections—were less harmful in a well-conducted parish. But of the operation of the parochial system we know little in detail. To judge by modern standards of liberality is misleading, as are the more critical remarks of those who suffered from the disciplinary activities of the kirk session. A suitably balanced kirk session and heritors could provide an answer to the problems of poverty. That they did not always do so is not a necessary condemnation of the entire system, the conditions necessary for the successful functioning of which were clearly enunciated in the words of one of its later critics.

'In a perfectly simple, and at the same time educated and civilized state of society . . . where all the higher orders who are to give, and all the lower orders who are to receive, are aware of their duties, and are known to one another, and, as long as the proprietors are resident, of charitable disposition, and attentive to their duties, the burden may be sufficiently equalized among the former, and the benefits sufficiently secured to the latter, without intervention of the law; or if the law interfered, it will be only to sanction, or sometimes to define, and partially extend the present practice.'[1]

In some areas the social changes of the eighteenth century ensured that these conditions no longer applied even before the advent of modern industry. The improving movement in agriculture, which drew so much of its first initiative from the landowners, was symptomatic of the change. It aimed at making the best use of the estate. Parochial responsibilities had to meet the more stringent tests of minds versed and trained in the ways of business. A beneficial effect which followed was the greater assurance that these duties would not be ignored or neglected, as they had sometimes been earlier; the harmful effect was the beginnings of the destruction of the possibility of landowners retaining an intimate personal knowledge of their parish. Some began to leave matters increasingly to their agent, while the larger became more interested in the social and political life of Edinburgh and London. Landowners began to lose their personal interest in parochial school and parish church, as English ways attracted them, and so the fine balance between heritors and kirk session was destroyed. A novel distinction began to appear in Scottish society. Generosity and a conscientiousness in the discharge of parochial duties, sometimes greater than in the past, could never be an exact substitute for personal interest. The interest was maintained mainly in the areas of small proprietors, but their concern was often exercised more towards the restriction of expenditure. That attitude did not encourage the fuller and proper functioning of the poor law.

The disintegration of the traditional social structure was demonstrated in its influence on the movement of population from the

[1] W. P. Alison, *Observations on the Management of the Poor in Scotland* (Edinburgh, 1840), p. 58.

countryside, both to the areas of new opportunities within Scotland and overseas. The sequence of change was conspicuous in the Highlands, which supplied most of the permanent emigrants of the mid-eighteenth century, and where a conflict between two sets of ideas and customs appeared. On the one hand were those derived from the earlier society of the clan, when strategy rather than economy dominated Highland life. Hence came the recognition of the binding obligations of kinship, and the attachment of the Gael to the land. On the other hand were the new, primarily economic motives, acceptable in an industrial society but not in one ruled by custom. The new standards began to be applied in certain areas, notably on Campbell lands, even before the rebellion of 1745. Afterwards in all districts the landowners who remained in possession of their estates became more concerned with economy than with strategy, and, wherever the ancient landowners lost their estates, the Commissioners for the Forfeited Estates made the change for them. In the eighteenth century such an ideological clash alone was sufficient to rend Highland society. Its results were only worsened by the contemporaneous population increase in an area of limited natural endowments. Consequently, some of those who left the Highlands in the mid-eighteenth century, though departing unwillingly, sailed overseas, not because of economic failure, but in an attempt to maintain lost social prestige. In this category fell the tacksmen, generally kinsmen of the chief, who were an essential part of the old strategic system, and who were supported by the difference between the largely nominal rents they paid for the tracts of land they held on lease (tack) from the chief and the rents at which they let that land to sub-tenants. The tacksman's function collapsed with the end of the old system, and only from many of his attempts to organize emigration is it possible to speak realistically of emigration from Scotland being a movement before the 1770's.

Since the initiation of such emigration came from changes in the social order, especially from those which followed the 1745 rebellion, its explanation was frequently assumed to lie in the landlords' demands for higher rents, as they tried to raise their standard of living to conform with new conceptions of their status. Though the demand for higher rents was a common complaint of those who emigrated, it is not easy to substantiate the accusation that the landlords were forwarding their own ends selfishly at the expense of the welfare of their tenants. Retaining everyone's younger sons on the land implied wretched tenantry. Since by about mid-century few people, landlords or tenants, were willing to accept that implication any longer; emigration was a means of avoiding it. By forcing him to emigrate a landlord was, therefore, frequently only forcing a tenant to act as he would have had to do eventually. Yet, though in the long run there was probably no other alternative, and so landlords, like tenants, were the victims of economic forces over which they had little control, they did not accept the position easily. In the eighteenth century few landowners advocated emigration openly; many opposed it. Indeed some policies consciously adopted by landlords frequently aimed at restraining emigration, even though the new social relationships of the time encouraged it. Under such circumstances movement could not be extensive, and became so only later in the eighteenth, or, in some cases, only in the nineteenth, century.

The financial crisis of 1772 provides a convenient break in the pattern of emigration, since, though there are no adequate statistics, it certainly increased from the 1770's and was then the consequence of more specifically economic influences. Movement from the Lowlands, previously insignificant, grew, especially when, following an example set at Wigtown in 1773, a number of associations were formed to provide assistance to those anxious to go. In that year, pamphlets describing the attractions of St. John's Island (where leases were offered at rents rising during seven years from 2d. to 2s. an acre 'and never after to be raised') were causing alarm among the landed proprietors of Ayrshire, who feared the information would encourage their tenantry to follow those who had already gone from Ulster and Argyll. To many landlords the restriction placed on emigration in 1775—mainly in an effort to prevent accessions to the ranks of the rebels in America—was, therefore, welcome. The movement from the Lowlands was encouraged by the adverse economic conditions of the early 1770's, and, even more conspicuously, by those of 1782 and 1783. In the Highlands, too, at the same time, similar economic forces began to reinforce the existing social tensions that made for emigration, but their influence was more fully experienced in later years, especially in the nineteenth century. The one economic factor relevant in the Highlands even before 1800, the increasing openings offered in the Lowlands, led to movement only within Scotland. Seasonal demand for agricultural labour and for special grades of industrial labour, as in the bleachfields of the Vale of Leven, was of long standing; until the large-scale influx of the Irish in the nineteenth century, it was met in most areas, except the southwest, which always relied on the Irish, from the Highlands. To that seasonal demand a permanent demand was added as the growth of modern Scottish industry was accelerated from the 1780's. Such economic opportunities in the Lowlands led to a greater exodus from the south and east of the Highland area. Though less dramatic than the emigrant ships which sailed from remote parts with those who could no longer be assimilated into Highland society, this exodus was more important. But the emigration of the 1770's and 1780's, in both Highlands and Lowlands, is not remarkable by comparison with that of the nineteenth century, but only by comparison with what had gone before. The incentive, or compulsion, to move, to countries overseas or to the towns of Scotland, was to become yet greater. Hence the balance of Scotland's population was not radically altered before the 1780's. Scotland was still a rural society, but one in which transformation was clearly imminent.

The people and their way of life

It is notoriously difficult to explain population trends before the modern system of vital statistics appeared. In England attempts to do so have been made from the information which may be culled from parish registers and bills of mortality. In Scotland it is virtually impossible to do likewise. The parochial registers of Scotland, now far from being all extant, were commonly used and were fairly complete until 1783 when a tax of 3d. an entry was imposed. In consequence, since registration was optional, it was generally dropped. Even earlier there were difficulties. The register of baptisms omitted those baptized privately at home, and the increasingly important group of seceders; the register of marriages was really one of the proclamation of banns, which led to duplication through recording in the parishes of both bride and bridegroom; lastly, the register of burials sometimes missed those buried outside their usual parish of residence and, most important of all, only those using the parish mortcloth, or pall, were included. Hence the vitally important age group of under ten was missed. Even in places where more detailed records were kept, such as Edinburgh or Glasgow, the information was similarly defective.

For the first reasonably accurate estimate of the population of Scotland in the eighteenth century it is necessary to turn, therefore, to the census carried out by Alexander Webster, Minister of the Tolbooth,

Edinburgh. Webster's figures, supposedly relating to 1755 but probably to some years earlier, were subject to a possible serious error by being based only on the number of 'examinable' persons in each parish. Those under six years of age, and in some parishes even older children, were, therefore, excluded. To compensate for this omission Webster added two-ninths to the number of those examinable and so reached his total of 1,265,380 persons. Webster also detailed the distribution of the population and its religious affiliation. His simple ecclesiastical census, distinguishing protestant from papist, showed a distribution of denominational affiliation since radically altered by Irish immigration. In contrast to the later position, Lanarkshire had only two Roman Catholics; Ayrshire and Wigtownshire had none. The distribution of the population among different counties also differed from later experience, as it was shortly afterwards permanently altered by industrial development. In 1755 the population of Lanarkshire was exceeded by those of Aberdeenshire, Midlothian and Perthshire and almost equalled by that of Fife.

TABLE I. DISTRIBUTION OF THE POPULATION, 1755

County	Population	Roman Catholics	County	Population	Roman Catholics
Aberdeen	116,168	2,288	Midlothian	90,412	263
Angus	68,883	35	Moray	30,604	90
Argyll	66,286	4,329	Nairn	5,694	—
Ayr	59,009	—	Orkney	23,381	—
Banff	38,478	3,150	Peebles	8,908	22
Berwick	23,987	—	Perth	120,116	194
Bute	7,125	—	Renfrew	26,645	3
Caithness	22,215	—	Ross and Cromarty	48,084	29
Clackmannan	9,003	2	Roxburgh	34,704	—
Dumfries	39,788	35	Selkirk	4,021	—
Dunbarton	13,857	—	Stirling	37,014	8
East Lothian	29,709	2	Sutherland	20,774	—
Fife	81,570	8	West Lothian	16,829	—
Inverness	59,563	5,664	Wigtown	16,466	—
Kincardine	23,057	17	Zetland	15,210	—
Kinross	4,889	—			
Kirkcudbright	21,205	349			
Lanark	81,726	2	Scotland	1,265,380	16,490

Source: J. G. Kyd, Scottish Population Statistics. Scottish History Society Publication (3rd series), no. xliii (1952).

Though there is some uncertainty about the number of people, the conditions in which they lived are more abundantly documented. Webster showed that the towns were small. The parishes of Edinburgh, Canongate and St. Cuthbert's, then Scotland's biggest conurbation, had only 47,570 inhabitants. But it was in the towns, small as they were, that conditions of living were particularly degrading, and by the early eighteenth century their housing had earned the reputation of being Europe's worst. In Edinburgh the earlier, but by the eighteenth century the out-dated, necessity for defence had led to very few houses being built outside the city gates. The largest part of the population lived in the typical high tenement stone buildings, as much as ten storeys high at the front and fourteen storeys high at the rear. By each floor being let to a different family, Scotland followed a European tradition. As Adam Smith pointed out, 'a dwelling-house in England means every-thing that is contained under the same roof. In France, Scotland and many other parts of Europe, it frequently means no more than a single storey'.[1] Social distinctions were not determined by the part of a town in which one lived, but by the layer of the tenement rented. In Edin-burgh it was socially desirable to have a flat in the middle, about the fifth floor, while the higher and lower flats were let to those less elevated socially. Even when the defensive reasons, which had dictated its adoption, had ceased to be relevant, the old method of living was continued, partly because it was preferred, until its attractions were outweighed by the appearance of a desire for more healthy living in the later eighteenth century. The classic instance of such a change was in Edinburgh, where housing conditions were at their worst, not only because defence considerations had forced building upwards within the old city walls, but because of strict geographical considerations. The Castle, Holyrood, the Nor' Loch and the Burgh Loch effectively encircled the city except for a small piece of land to the south. In the long run these physical limitations proved beneficial as they forced the construction of the New Town, where the foundation-stone of the first house was laid in October 1767. James Craig's plan for the New Town of Edinburgh aimed at preventing some of the old difficulties and defects. An Act of 1771 limited the height of houses on the main streets to three storeys, inclusive of basement, and to two storeys in other, intermediate, streets. The completion of Charlotte Square, designed by Robert Adam, in 1800 marked the conclusion of this early essay in town planning, though one arrested and restricted by the

[1] A. Smith, *Wealth of Nations* (Cannan edition), vol. i, p. 119.

difficulty of acquiring land from the Corporation, which was apprehensive of the falls in value in the old town. Nevertheless the overall effect of such building was slight. The magnificence and satisfactory construction of the New Town of Edinburgh was comparable with the contemporary magnificent seats of some of the nobility—Hopetoun, Mellerstain, Culzean—often built to the designs of the Adam family. These new constructions provided accommodation for only a fraction of the Scottish people. Until well beyond this period, consequently until well into the age of industrialism, little was done to improve their lot and so the adverse effect of the new economic conditions on housing was intensified. Hence the extent of the adverse consequences of industrialism on public health. Hence also the explanation of the continuing problem of overcrowding in Scotland.

Overcrowding was not confined to the towns. In the burghs considerations of defence, of geography, and of policy, sometimes forced construction to take place within restricted limits, but in the countryside, where it was often physically possible to spread the construction of houses over wider areas, it was frequently financially impossible to do so. The construction of houses was often solid, but was determined, as in any poor country, by the materials available locally. Bricks were everywhere uncommon and in the Highlands were unknown. In the country the usual cottage was built of undressed stones and divots, or sometimes of mud walls, or, especially in the Highlands, of turf only, with walls about five or six feet high. The roof was kept in position by branches of trees over which straw and turf were laid to try to keep the house watertight, a method which frequently meant only a reduction to drops of sooty water in wet weather and to falling of worms in dry weather. Chimneys were uncommon and the smoke escaped, when it did, through a hole in the roof. A desire for heat, as potent a factor as poverty in determining the construction of Scottish houses, militated against windows. Upper storeys were rare, so that the family had only a damp soil floor on which to sleep, though a few did possess a recess above the rafters, to which access was obtained by a ladder, and which provided the normal sleeping-place for the male members of the family. Families and cattle lived together, though some rural houses had triple partitions, the byre being separated from the kitchen by a low partition of wattle and the kitchen from the spence, or parlour, generally by the box-beds, two of which were placed lengthwise from the walls. The outside door was often common to both man and beast, and the entrance and mud-floor inside were so churned up that the laying of fresh turf was an unavailing task. Outside was the midden, a chief source of disease.

Higher up the social scale certain improvements could be noted, but in degree rather than in kind. Even in the laird's house conditions were cramped. The distinction between living-room and bedroom was neither exact nor rigid, understandably in the cramped quarters of the old town of Edinburgh, and in some parts of the Highlands, where until after 1745 it was still thought a mark of social distinction to have a large retinue of followers. Thus the great hall of some West Highland castles became at night the sleeping-chamber of the gentlemen dependants of the family. Again, furniture was not a necessary element, not even in the houses of the Highland gentry; but, where it did exist, it was usually neither extensive nor beautiful. Though the previous century had witnessed some notable improvements in furniture manufacture, it was only later in the eighteenth century that the increasing wealth of the country led to the purchase of greater quantities of mahogany furniture and the opening of shops in Edinburgh by the London manufacturers. The record of the Countess Marischal's furniture in 1722 is a depressing catalogue of broken pieces. In all the household plenishings—in high and low estate—only linen was in ample supply, but throughout the century there appeared an increasing spread of articles indicating greater wealth and the drawing of supplies from a wider area, and their use spread down the social scale.

The bad construction of Scottish housing was complemented by lack of sanitation. That the filth of Edinburgh was jettisoned out of all the windows at the sound of the 10 o'clock bell from the High Kirk to the warning cries of 'Gardyloo' is well enough known. John Wesley in 1761 could write feelingly: 'How long shall the capital city of Scotland, yea, and the chief street of it, stink worse than a common sewer? Will no lover of his country, or of decency and common sense, find a remedy for this?'[1] Even in Glasgow, then commended by many for its charm and beauty, a statute of 1696, which tried to stop the throwing of filth out of windows by day or by night, failed to do so. As with improvements in housing, most of those in sanitation were also delayed until the later eighteenth century. The magistrates made some efforts to improve Edinburgh's unenviable reputation towards the end of the seventeenth century, but all types of penalties failed to secure adherence to the provisions. Though the first Inspector of Cleansing was appointed in 1700, a major change in the public's attitude came only by

[1] J. Wesley, *Journal* (Everyman Edition), vol. 3, p. 54.

the middle of the eighteenth century; in 1771 an Act was obtained for the cleansing of the southern suburbs, and this was extended later to the whole city. Probably in all Scotland no single factor was more important for better sanitation than an improvement in the water supply. The quantity was generally adequate at the public wells or conduits in the main streets, except in a town such as Edinburgh, with an increasing and concentrated population, or in a few places— Auchterarder was one—where the water supply frequently dried up in summer. Quality was much less satisfactory. Since few houses had independent supplies, water had to be carried to most, a formidable task in tall tenements, as in Edinburgh, where water was brought to houses by full-time, but inefficient, caddies. Once again the improvements began in the second half of the century, when an increasing number of towns laid down metal pipes for conveying water supplies. Thereafter it was easier to have water led into houses, but the practice remained uncommon until well into the nineteenth century.

Under such conditions it is not surprising that, when Webster used his census to provide an estimate of the expectation of life for the actuarial basis of annuity schemes, an indication of the shortness of life and of the extent of infant mortality was given. Less than 75 per cent of those born survived their first year; 50 per cent survived only to their tenth year; only 25 per cent survived beyond their forty-eighth year. It is possible to confirm Webster's conclusion on the high death rate of early years from the mortality bills of a few Scottish towns, not representative in any way except that they possessed well-kept records for some years before the *Old Statistical Account*. In the parish of Kettle in Fife there were 625 deaths in a period of over 20 years. Of these 140 were of children under six. In Tranent, in East Lothian, during a period of 30 years, 586 deaths out of a total of 1,620 were of children under six. In Torthorwald, in Dumfriesshire, conditions were better, with an expectation of life at birth of 49·64 years and at age five of 54·69 years. In Kettle the expectation of life in infancy was 40·6 years. On the basis of these figures Sir John Sinclair felt entitled to assert that 'there is no country in Europe, whose inhabitants are more distinguished by their healthiness—their longevity—or the inconsiderable number of the diseases to which they are liable, than those of Scotland',[1] but his assertion rested on the basis of an analysis of the statistics for such unrepresentative places as Torthorwald. Even there the incidence of

[1] Sir John Sinclair, *Analysis of the Statistical Account of Scotland* (Edinburgh, 1831), p. 110.

child mortality was heavy; the expectation of life rose for those who survived their first five years.

The level of child mortality was the key to so many social problems, especially in the large towns. In 1791, for instance, of 1,508 deaths recorded in the City Parish of Glasgow 46 per cent were of children under two and 63 per cent of all deaths were of children under ten. Any large-scale improvement came only after the middle of the nineteenth century. In 1861 42 per cent of all deaths were still of children under ten. If child mortality was a major factor ensuring the maintenance of a high death rate in the eighteenth century two chief explanations of its fluctuations may be offered. First, in Scotland the margin of subsistence remained small. Malthus regretted the lack of full information on this topic in the *Old Statistical Account*, because he believed it would have provided him with grounds for asserting that population had a chronic tendency to increase beyond the limits of subsistence. Further information may well have disappointed him. Agricultural developments, in some cases from early in the eighteenth century, more generally from mid-century, removed the spectre of famine from Scotland for the first time. The lean years of the end of the previous century were still recalled with horror in agricultural reports of the later eighteenth century, but they never recurred. There were still occasional years of scarcity, or periods of intense local shortage, especially in such areas as the Highlands, where the margin of subsistence was least, and where poor communications made it less easy to relieve local shortages. Hence there were years of want in 1740, 1772, 1782, 1783 and 1793, when scarcity directly increased the death rate in what was still predominantly an agricultural society. But by the end of the eighteenth century it became increasingly evident that dearth, and its consequences, came to many Scots less through the direct effect of failure of food supplies than through a failure of industrial employment.

Epidemics were the second, and more important, factor leading to variations in the death rate. They were not so violent as they became in the congested conditions of the towns, and in the eighteenth century, if a Scotsman survived his childhood, he had a reasonable chance of living to a good age. Sir John Sinclair's adulation of the healthiness of the Scot rested on this assumption. Hence, when dealing with the medical history of adults, he could assert more truthfully that, 'excepting cold and rheumatism, occasioned by inattention, and often by poverty, there is no disease that can be called peculiar to Scotland;

neither are the distempers, by which we are sometimes visited, more frequent, or more fatal and violent, than in other countries, which are esteemed highly salubrious'.[1] Rheumatism became increasingly prevalent throughout the eighteenth century, but, though it greatly decreased industrial and agricultural efficiency, and was the cause of much discomfort, it was not a major cause of death. That was the role of the 'distempers', which, as Sinclair stated, did not come to Scotland often, but, when they did come, came with disastrous effects.

Even among these more violent diseases some did not take their tolls in the eighteenth century. The plague, for instance, had not reappeared in Scotland since the 1640's, but the greatest scourge of the time was smallpox. Sinclair was justified in putting it at the head of the diseases with which the country was then affected. Highland parishes suffered particularly, but its consequences were more dramatic in the cities, and among children, especially in the latter case if it was accompanied by whooping cough. Thus in Edinburgh from 1740 to 1742, years of general dearth, 2,700 out of a total population of 40,000 died from smallpox, and of these more than half were children under five. In the twenty subsequent years 10 per cent of all deaths in Edinburgh were from smallpox. In the last quarter of the eighteenth century Glasgow was even more unfortunate as almost 19 per cent of all deaths, and more than half of those of children under five, were due to smallpox. The disease was first attacked with some success by inoculation, first tried out in Aberdeenshire in 1726, but used extensively only towards the middle of the century. Though in 1754 the College of Physicians of Edinburgh declared inoculation to be 'highly salubrious to the human race', it was not accepted without severe criticism. Its early use in Aberdeenshire was discontinued because of fatalities; it was thought to tamper with divine laws; many parents objected to the temporary upset it caused to their children; some objected to the cost. The last objection led to the cost of inoculation sometimes being borne by the heritors or by the kirk session. But inoculation had one important and real defect, though not one so readily recognized by those contemporaries who attributed much saving of life to the practice. Because those inoculated became carriers, smallpox, instead of occurring at long and relatively infrequent intervals, appeared frequently, especially, of course, among children. The real change had to wait on vaccination, which appeared only in the last few years of the eighteenth century.

Whatever was done to mitigate the ravages of smallpox other

[1] Sinclair, *op. cit.*, p. 120.

diseases remained rampant. Reports of 'fever' throughout the eighteenth century are frequent, but various types were not distinguished, in part because clinical diagnosis is not easy in any case. But Sinclair noted a difference over the century. In the earlier part 'the pleuristic and inflammatory kinds' were common, but later these gave way to 'low, lingering and nervous' types. Two diseases which certainly showed a variation in incidence were ague or malaria, and tuberculosis. The ague was previously so common, especially in spring and summer, that it sometimes interfered with agricultural operations. By the end of the eighteenth century it had become much more infrequent, not only because of enclosure and drainage of land, which was the explanation of contemporaries, but because the indigenous mosquito was attracted from its breeding ground in human habitations to cattle houses, which it prefers, by the increased survival of the cattle in the winter-time. On the other hand an unfavourable change during the eighteenth century was the increasing incidence of consumption. The Western Isles, later to suffer so severely from the scourge, were relatively immune from it throughout most of the eighteenth century. There were sufficient explanations for the independent increase in consumption, especially the effects of Scottish housing, without Sinclair's suggestion that 'where the ague has ceased to exist, consumptions are apt to become prevalent in their room'.[1]

---

[1] Sinclair, *op. cit.*, p. 138.

C

II
AGRICULTURE

The old system and its methods

In the eighteenth century the physical influences of a harsh climate and a poor soil provided many of the problems of Scottish farmers. Agricultural operations were frequently late and protracted, especially on the west coast, where rain fell on about two-thirds of the days of the year. Inadequately drained, and consequently sour, soils prevented much early sowing, so that harvests were late, frequently lasting until November. Sometimes crops, rarely adequate even in the best of weather, were lost through rain, and even snow. The soil did not offset the adverse influence of climate. With few exceptions the hill land was uncultivated. The most barren area, then as now, was in the north and west, where the vagaries of climate were at their most potent. Further south and east the adverse influence of the physical forces became only less pressing. Wresting a living from such an environment was difficult.

The history of Scottish agriculture is largely concerned with attempts at mitigating the physical adversities. Drainage prevented the land from becoming as sour as in the past; shelter belts of trees, and afforestation generally, mitigated the severity of winds; a greater variety of crops helped to stagger agricultural operations, heightening the probability of obtaining the benefit of good weather when most required; mechanization speeded operations. The way for improvements was paved through changes in land tenure, and through changes, sometimes but not always, consequential, in methods of cultivation.

Three forms of land tenure were of special importance in Scotland before the agricultural improvements of the eighteenth century. The first was steel-bow tenure, comparable to the French métayage. Its chief feature, the assumption by the landlord of responsibility for the provision of some working as well as fixed capital, made it attractive in a country as poor as Scotland and ensured its continuation. The second characteristic tenure, and one more common in the Highlands in the eighteenth century, was that of the tacksman, the merits and demerits of which stemmed from its military character. The advantages accrued to the tacksman, who held the land cheaply, but was able to

18

sub-let it at a much higher rental, even when he required additional military obligations from his sub-tenants. So long as a strategic, not an economic, criterion was being applied to landholding, the tacksman's position was unassailable, as it assured a military following to the head of a clan. The disadvantages were mainly economic, since the strategic necessity of using the land primarily to maintain a military retinue inhibited agricultural improvement. When an economic criterion came to be applied, as it was increasingly in the eighteenth century, the tacksman had to go, but his departure implied social upheaval.

The third, and most important, characteristic tenure was that of holding land in different rigs, or strips, the system known as runrig. A farm was frequently leased by a number of joint-tenants, who comprised the inhabitants of the very small rural villages, the fermetouns, of the period, but it was divided into rigs, generally of from a quarter to half an acre, which were held in turn by different tenants. At the beginning of the eighteenth century the system was almost universal, but as agricultural improvements spread, runrig was replaced by new forms of consolidated tenure. By the time of the *Old Statistical Account* and the agricultural reports of the late eighteenth century, runrig was already a system of the past in some areas—Ayrshire, Berwickshire, Lanarkshire, East Lothian and elsewhere—while in others—Perth, Argyll, Inverness, and the Islands—the system continued into the nineteenth century. The strips, or rigs, were generally allocated annually, though sometimes for longer periods, and sometimes, when the system was in decline, the allocation became permanent.

The defects of the older system of land tenure were re-enforced by inefficiencies in the method of cultivation, the general pattern of which —though with local variations—was reasonably clear. The arable and meadow land was separated from hill pasture by the head-dyke, a unique Scottish feature, continuous from Rhu to Thurso, which indicates the limits to which cultivation was then driven in an effort to maintain a small population at a low standard of living. The basic characteristic of the cultivated land was its division into the infield and the outfield of the farm or township. The infield, the land adjacent to the farm steading, was under constant cultivation, and generally comprised about one-fifth of the total arable average. On it a rudimentary rotation was commonly followed. Each year one-third, which was given all the dung available, was sown with barley, or bere, and in the two following years, until the rotation of the infield was completed, two unmanured crops of oats were taken from it. The variations on the

basic pattern took different forms. In more fertile areas, as in the Carse
of Gowrie, or where the arable acreage was limited, the infield exceeded
one-fifth of the land cultivated; more unusual rotations, often improvements on traditional practice, were found in the more advanced
agricultural districts, as in Ayrshire, where an occasional fallow year
interrupted a rotation of oats, oats and barley; and, usually in less fertile
regions, attempts were made to cultivate crops, no matter how poor,
from the same plot of land for as many successive years as was possible
without much, or any, manure.

Unlike the infield the larger outfield was not in continuous cultivation. Part was cropped, generally with oats, for a number of successive years, probably about four or five. When the return no longer
justified the effort (and standards of judgement were low) the cultivation of that section was abandoned for some years and its place taken
by another, which had regained some fertility through resting. Otherwise little attention was given to the outfield. Local variations in its
cultivation, mainly in manuring and in the number of successive crops
taken, were less marked than with the infield. Even the best manuring
practice of folding cattle on parts of the outfield for short periods,
sometimes at night, sometimes during the middle of the day, was
grossly inadequate. The number of successive crops taken off the same
part of the outfield varied according to the physical environment and
to the degree of agricultural enlightenment: in the north-east sometimes five times as many were taken off a patch of the outfield as were
taken from a similar piece of land in the south-west.

The implements used in cultivation were primitive and inefficient.
The old Scots plough, a mouldboard plough, was about thirteen feet
long and, apart from the share, coulter and bridle, which were of iron,
was made entirely of wood. Because of its weight it was a useful implement for breaking up rough, and especially stony, ground, but could
be drawn only with considerable power. Common practice was to use
a team of eight oxen, but again there were local variations. In Aberdeenshire as many as twelve oxen were used; in the Lowlands the team was
frequently a combination of six oxen and two horses; in Ayrshire it was
often formed entirely of horses. Such unwieldy power, linked to an
unwieldy instrument, could be controlled only by a band of men,
which the prevalence of joint tenancies provided. One man urged the
animals forward; another, or sometimes a woman, removed stones;
another ensured that the plough made a furrow of a correct depth; yet
another followed behind to remedy the defects and deficiencies in the

ploughing with a spade. Such effort ploughed perhaps half an acre in a day.

The plough left an indelible imprint in the ridges into which Scottish arable land was formed. Ridges were not unique to Scotland. Partly they were the result of ploughing from the centre to the outside; partly they were formed by design, because—of minor importance—in a system of intermixed strips an individual could then preserve his soil from spilling over to his neighbour's ridge, and—of major importance— because they provided an elementary form of drainage. But the old Scots plough ensured that these ridges, sometimes five hundred yards or even more in length, were crooked. To guarantee straightness the head ridge would have had to be of enormous breadth to allow the huge plough team to turn, but a deflection at each end enabled the team to draw the plough out on a moderately broad head ridge. Whatever advantages the ridges possessed were outweighed by their disadvantages. It was difficult to apply modern methods of cultivation to land covered with ridges, which were 'almost universally broad, high, crooked and of unequal and irregular breadths, and frequently had strips of uncultivated land between them, named *baulks*, some- times of considerable breadth, which were overgrown with brush- wood and weeds, and filled with every kind of rubbish gathered from the cultivated land'.[1]

The use of the old Scots plough was wellnigh universal. Lighter ploughs were used mainly in the Highlands: the ristle, or restle, to break up ground prior to ploughing with the heavy plough; the better- known *cas chrom*, or foot plough, still used within the last century, to turn over patches of arable ground roughly. The implements used in subsequent agricultural occupations were equally primitive. Harrows, like most of the old Scots ploughs, were sometimes made of wood, especially in more backward areas, so that teeth were easily broken. Frequently they were tied to a horse's tail, and in some areas in the Highlands and Islands, even into the twentieth century, were man- or woman-handled. The sickle was used, again in some cases until the twentieth century, to reap the crops; the flail was a major means of threshing them.

'Under the system of management . . . even that part of the lands of Scotland which is capable of good cultivation could produce but little in comparison of what it may be capable of producing.'[2] The range of crops was, therefore, limited. Oats and barley were most

---

[1] Sinclair, *op. cit.*, p. 356.   [2] Smith, *op. cit.*, vol. i, p. 221.

commonly cultivated. The former was of two types: white or grey oats, which gradually gained ground in the Lowlands and in the better land in the Highlands, and inferior, small, grey or black oats, the cultivation of which persisted in some areas because its lightness enabled it to withstand the ravages of wind and rain better than the heavier white oats. Bere, an inferior type of barley, was grown for the same reasons as the black oats. It thrived on land of poor quality, was less liable than barley to be affected adversely by wet weather, and it matured more quickly. The acreage sown with bere or barley was only about half that of oats but other crops were of much less importance still. Rye was grown, sometimes as a mixture with oats, but not extensively, as it was considered an impoverishing crop, though with the compensating reputation of grinding more economically than oats. Wheat was cultivated in the best infield lands of the Lothians, the Merse, the Mearns, Ayrshire and elsewhere. Flax was grown generally only for domestic use, and, though its importance increased in the eighteenth century, its main contribution was to industrial rather than to agricultural improvement. Finally, though the potato was cultivated in Scottish gardens by the time of the Union, its major contribution to Scottish agricultural development came only later in the eighteenth and in the nineteenth centuries.

In the early eighteenth century an adequate supply of good pasture was more important than any of these crops, because in many areas, especially where physical conditions of soil and climate were most adverse, as in the Highlands, agriculture depended more on the rearing of livestock than on arable cultivation. Beef cattle were most important, because they gave the greatest surplus for sale off the land; sheep ranked next, and in some areas, notably the southern uplands, were the major agricultural product. Both suffered from undernourishment in winter, especially if there was much snow, and from disease. Sheep suffered particularly, because, as a means of combating maggots, the animals were smeared with a mixture of tar and butter which ensured that the wool was of a poor quality, as effectively as disease and inadequate feeding ensured the inferior quality and inadequacy of the mutton. In the long run the growth of arable and livestock production could not be separated. The maintenance of additional stock required improvements in arable cultivation, even though some increase was always possible without improvements, as happened in Galloway in the 1720's; or, more important, through the very old and international practice of transhumance, followed most extensively in the Highlands, by which a large part of the community moved with most of their animals to the shielings in the hills where there were plentiful supplies of summer grass. In the early eighteenth century such a practice was essential for the growth of the cattle trade in the Highlands, because the cattle returned from the summer grazings to conditions approaching starvation. In this the Highlands were only worse than the rest of Scotland. Until the late eighteenth century the use of artificial grasses and the making of hay to provide fodder directly by arable cultivation, were unknown. The meadow land was therefore, in effect, those parts which were so defective that they could not be used for arable cultivation. Swampy or stony ground produced little for grazing and less for hay, which was, therefore, only of the poorest quality. Since survival was not easy in some areas even in summer, unless the cattle were removed to more succulent hill pasture, it was often impossible in winter. Cattle existed, if at all, on straw, dry rushes or thistles, boiled chaff and similar non-nutritive foodstuffs. Estimates of mortality vary, partly because of regional differences, but in some areas it may have been at times as high as one in five, while those animals which survived were in such a poor condition in the spring that they were hardly able to persist in the active research necessary to locate the scanty fodder available. Scientific breeding was irrelevant under such conditions; the supply of fodder had first to be increased.

The significance of livestock production in Scotland in 1707, and for some years thereafter, had one unfortunate feature. Its importance in the country's agriculture arose only because arable cultivation was so unattractive. It was, therefore, a reflection of the country's poverty. Yet that very poverty inhibited the development of both better arable cultivation and of livestock. In the first half of the eighteenth century, and earlier, before the Union, even within the old structure of Scottish agriculture, improvements were effected. The infield was extended and limed, especially in the Lothians, and implements lighter than the old Scots plough were used. Combined with relatively better weather, these developments explain why famine was much less common in the fifty years after the Union than it had been in the fifty years before. But such improvements within the old structure were inadequate to support an increasing population with a higher proportion engaged in non-agricultural pursuits. Though the change in the structure of the Scottish economy which began in the first century after the Union, and was completed in the second century after, led to a diminution in the relative importance of agriculture, its absolute contribution to the national product had first to undergo a radical transformation.

The improving movement

The action necessary for agricultural improvements required changes both in methods of land tenure and of agricultural production. Certain aspects of the former were unique to Scotland, where, though cultivation was sometimes communal, the limits of an individual's ownership or tenancy were precisely determined. A partial exception was in some of the grazing areas, where, especially on the poorer hill land, something akin to common pasture had appeared through proprietors failing to determine their rights. Hence in Scotland in the eighteenth century, while provision was necessary to ensure the division of such few commons as existed, much more urgent was the need for some provision for the consolidation of strips held in runrig and for ensuring that enclosure, fencing, hedging, or walling of land could be implemented without opposition from difficult proprietors.

Acts of the previous century provided for action in all directions. An Act of 1695 authorized the division of all commons, except those belonging to the king or to royal burghs, by a process in the Court of Session. Commons, including mosses and peat bogs, were to be divided among proprietors in proportion to the valued rents of their existing holdings. A subsidiary provision recognized that owners of land adjacent to a common might have acquired rights to its use by custom. Though a legal process of rouming and souming could limit the number of animals which could be grazed (by reference to the land rents of the farms using the common and to the number of cattle which each could support with his own winter fodder), the right, if it had been exercised without dispute for forty years, was continued after division by the burden of it being placed on one proprietor who had his share of the divided common increased accordingly. A second Act of 1695 authorized sheriffs to divide lands held in runrig. As in the divisions of commons, allocations had to be of land adjacent to the proprietor's dwelling-house. Though the effectiveness of the Act was limited by the exclusions from its provisions of the lands of incorporations, which included burghs, it was extended to cover intermixed holdings, even when they were not lying separately in rigs. Lastly, a series of Acts of 1661, 1669, and 1685 provided for the erection of fences along the boundaries of different holdings—for enclosure in the literal sense—by a process before the sheriff in which a proprietor could ensure that his neighbours paid half the cost of erecting fences, and that boundaries were straightened wherever necessary.

The legal provisions for division, consolidation and enclosure were important in facilitating the introduction of new methods of agricultural production, the changes in implements, rotations and crops which were so notable in the eighteenth century. The old Scots plough was replaced chiefly by a light plough designed by a Berwickshire man, James Small, in 1763. Small's plough was the most notable innovation in farm implements in the eighteenth century, as it replaced the worst and most cumbersome of the old. Complementary to it were a variety of other improvements: iron teeth took the place of wooden ones in harrows generally; stone, and later cast-iron, rollers replaced mallets as means of smoothing out rough patches on the ground; leather straps and iron chains replaced twisted hair or heather as harness and implements ceased to be attached to horses' tails. In addition there were a few more radical changes, comparable with the introduction of Small's plough, as in the second and ultimately successful threshing machine of Andrew Meikle in 1786. The new implements were the means by which the ground was prepared in new ways—levelling, draining, manuring, liming—all preparatory to the introduction of new rotations. Throughout Scotland rotations varied, but the four-fold, turnips, barley, clover and wheat, of Norfolk was the norm, except that in Scotland oats generally replaced wheat. By the late eighteenth century grain was alternating with grass and green crops throughout all the arable land of Scotland. Though oats remained the most important crop, with the white oat increasingly displacing the grey oat, except in the Highlands, the most characteristic crops of the new order were the turnip and the potato. Their contribution to Scottish agricultural development differed. The turnip became the basis for the rearing of much fatstock, especially the higher-grade animals of the north-east and of other livestock-rearing areas. A poor season in 1782 gave a special encouragement to its introduction, and also to that of many kinds of artificial grasses, in some of the areas in the north which had resisted them longest. The potato, on the other hand, augmented human diet, especially in those regions where the margin of subsistence was low. It was a crop suitable for areas of less generous natural endowments, because, as well as giving acceptable food, it could be grown easily. Though suited to drill cultivation, the potato, unlike the turnip, did not require it, but could be grown by the 'lazy-bed' method, particularly suitable for wet land. Thus the potato's most important contribution was to the agriculture of the Highlands and, even more so, of the Islands, unsuited as they frequently were for the cultivation of almost anything else. The potato first reached the Islands at South Uist in 1743, and though initially planted in Lewis only in 1753, by 1764 the potato had taken the place of bread in the diet there for about six months in the year.

Many of the improvements were adopted only later in the eighteenth century. Even land held in runrig was not brought to an end quickly, and, perhaps because its worst defects were circumvented by the permanent allocation of the strips, the system survived even in districts with improving lairds. By the middle of the eighteenth century the transformation was common, but, as is evident in every volume of the *Old Statistical Account*, it became widespread in the second half of the century and was eliminated only after the Napoleonic Wars. Enclosure proceeded more slowly except where, as in Galloway in the 1720's, it was necessary to effect a change in agricultural production. In general it was a development of the late eighteenth and early nineteenth centuries, consequently one of the later improvements to be carried out. It is important, therefore, not to stress unduly the availability from the late seventeenth century of legal provision adequate to enable a transformation of Scottish agriculture to be effected. In any event some of the Acts were less important in Scotland than they would have been in other countries. For example, the importance of the Act relating to the division of commons was lessened by the rights of landowners and tenants being already clearly defined in Scotland, since the feuing movement established definitive, rather than customary, tenure in the sixteenth century,[1] while in the Highlands the retention of the military tenure of ward-holding prevented the evolution of a new structure until its abolition in 1747. Consequently, in the Lowlands and in parts of the Highlands, those on the land at the time of the Union were either tenants, with clearly defined, and usually short-term, rights and obligations, or landlords, whose power, within the limits of the fairly short-run leases they granted, was absolute. Even where farms were let to several tenants, the lease was normally short-term, and, when its course was run, the landlord could then consolidate the various holdings to farm them or to lease them to anyone he wished. In Scotland, therefore, if landlords wished to consolidate or enclose, they could not easily be hindered. Difficulties arose only where a number of individual

[1] For further information see I. F. Grant, *Social and Economic Development in Scotland before 1603* (Edinburgh, 1930), pp. 265 ff.

proprietors held strips in runrig, or where adjoining proprietors were unwilling to share the costs of enclosure. In both cases opposition could be overcome, in the first by the second Act of 1695, which gave power to sheriffs to divide land, and in the second by the Acts of 1661, 1669 and 1685, which required expenditure on enclosure to be shared. The unique legal position of Scotland was not, however, without some important implications. First, since the legal basis for many tenurial changes had existed even before the Union of 1707, such rural unrest as arose in the eighteenth century, though much less than in England, cannot be traced to the appearance of new legal procedure. It is significant that it was most noticeable only in those areas where the type of agricultural production changed. The first conspicuous example was in Galloway, where the rise in cattle prices after the Union encouraged the conversion of arable land to pasture. The proprietors' legal right to evict tenants to effect the change was not disputed, though in the 1720's the evicted tenants objected so vigorously to the landlord's moral right to do so, that they threw down the dykes built to retain the cattle. Even better-known, though later, examples come from the Highlands, where the conversion of arable land to sheep-walks and, later still, to deer-forests, was enacted on the same legal basis, without any legal redress, but with the same social upheaval. When social unrest appeared in the Scottish countryside, it indicated change, usually drastic change, in the type of agricultural production, though even the influence of this factor was limited in most areas of Scotland, apart from the Highlands and southern uplands, by arable cultivation remaining the common type of agricultural production, or, as in the north-east, by it being only partly displaced by stock-fattening.

Second, though changes in the legal framework in themselves failed to provide an adequate incentive for improvement, they provided the environment within which other influences could be effective. The environment was particularly conducive to action by the landlords whose social and political power and prestige is a key to understanding the success of the agricultural improvers. Their failure to exploit immediately the favourable legal provisions, especially those on enclosure, indicated the need for additional influences to be brought to bear even on them for their legal privileges to be fully utilized. Nevertheless, since they already enjoyed a favourable position by law, the speed of agricultural improvement was increased when they, more than others, were subjected in the later eighteenth century to the new influences which encouraged improvement. But even when they made contact with other areas, especially with those in England where the new agricultural methods were being applied, some remained limited in their ability to apply the new methods through possessing only entailed estates. Since it was estimated that about one-third of the country was entailed, a statute was passed in 1770, permitting various minor actions to facilitate enclosure, such as the exchange of small parcels of land, and the granting of longer leases, contingent on the tenant agreeing to effect certain enclosures, and including an important provision to allow proprietors of entailed estates to charge to his heirs three-quarters of the money spent on enclosure and other agricultural improvements. Since demand for agricultural products was increasing at the same time, the incentives to effect improvement then became more effective.

The initiative for the improvement of Scottish agriculture in the eighteenth century came from relatively few individuals though from all levels of landowners. Perhaps the best known of all was John Cockburn of Ormiston in East Lothian, whose background demonstrates the formative influences common to many agricultural improvers. The eldest son of a Lord Justice-Clerk, he represented the new element then being infused into the landed interest, and, as Member of Parliament for Haddington, had sufficient opportunity to observe the new practices of English agriculture. His improvements, more notable for scale than for their uniqueness, took the common form of long leases, enclosure, the planting of trees, the growing of new crops, such as barley (for which he considered East Lothian ideally suited), turnips (though he was probably not the first to introduce them to Scotland), artificial grasses, clover, potatoes, and so on. Cockburn's efforts were more remarkable in extending from the introduction of several commendable but isolated improvements to an attempt to achieve a complete and radical reorganization of his estate. This was the hall-mark of the leading improver. Thus in 1734 he rebuilt the village of Ormiston and, combining industrial with agricultural improvement, tried to encourage the linen industry by importing skilled labour from Ireland and forming a bleachfield. Other improvers were of the same stamp. Sir Archibald Grant of Monymusk in Aberdeenshire was the son of a Senator of the College of Justice, Lord Cullen, who had purchased the estate in 1713, and so regretted the purchase that three years later he handed its management to his son, then aged twenty. When the son died, in 1778, the entire estate had been transformed. Lord Kames was

probably the most important improver among several in the College
of Justice itself. His contribution was more interesting than many,
because he carried out improvements in different environments; first
in Berwickshire, where he probably introduced turnips in drills for
feeding cattle and the cultivation of potatoes with the plough; second
in Perthshire, at Blair Drummond, which he inherited through his
wife, and where, though then aged seventy, he added to the usual
improvements a major attempt to clear the Moss of Kincardine, a
venture which could have been undertaken only by someone not
requiring, or not demanding, an immediate capital return. In addition,
Kames spread his knowledge by means of his writings in a way few
other improvers did. The contribution of such improvers among the
minor landed gentry, and especially among those of the first or second
generation of those who had entered their ranks from the professions or
merchanting, was of major importance as it was found throughout
Scotland except in the extreme north and west. In Kirkcudbrightshire
was William Craig of Arbigland; also in the south-west at Arkland in
Dumfriesshire worked Robert Maxwell; on the east coast were Robert
Barclay of Ury in Kincardineshire, and Lord Gardenstone, another
Senator of the College of Justice, at Laurencekirk. Beside the contributions of the lesser gentry must be set those of the greater lairds, whose
influence also stretched throughout Scotland; from the estates of the
Earl of Stair in the south-west, as well as in the Lothians, to those of the
Earl of Marchmont and the Earl of Haddington in the south-east, and
to those of the Earl of Findlater, improved greatly by the sixth earl
while still only heir as Lord Deskford, in the north-east.

The strength and common identity of the landed interest ensured a
degree of uniformity in the methods of the improving movement, but
two major influences prevented uniformity in its impact. First, though
individual experience varied, improvements were apparently rarely
profitable to the improvers themselves. Any accurate estimate of the
gain from them is exceptionally difficult to judge, because so many of
their benefits accrued only after an exceptionally long period, and were
social rather than private. Whatever the benefits to Scotland, the
improvers only rarely saw tangible reward in the form of increased
profits for their efforts. So it was with Cockburn of Ormiston, who
had to sell out to the Earl of Hopetoun in 1748, and, more strikingly,
because he was perhaps the greatest improver of all, though of a later
generation, with Sir John Sinclair of Ulbster. Such failure to gain
extensive or quick rewards made it more than ever important for the

improvers to have adequate financial resources personally or be able to obtain adequate assistance from the banks or elsewhere. For many, the Entail Act of 1770 was a major help, yet none, except perhaps a handful of the most affluent of landlords, could have undertaken such expenditure on improvement, even with the help of the banks, if financial considerations had been a significant determinant of their actions. In sum, the improvements cannot properly be explained from a financial standpoint. The Scottish improvers were activated by other motives, if not in the first initiation of their actions, then at any rate in their continuation. On the other hand financial stringency, especially in such a poor country as Scotland, limited the implementation of these ideas and so made the influence of the improving movement less uniform. The limitations were lessened only by the interest of the wealthier elements of society in the improvements. Their resources ensured that the movement continued without interruption through a variety of conflicting economic disturbances in the eighteenth century, even when individual improvements failed to bring the returns anticipated.

The second factor making for lack of uniformity in the improving movement were the variations in the extent to which the new ways were copied. The improvers were notable by being exceptional, but emulation was essential for any lasting legacy on Scottish agriculture to be possible. In one respect it was more difficult to propagate such new ideas generally than in Scottish industry, where the virtual absence of any effective modern industrial basis implied the existence of fewer prejudices to be broken than in agriculture, in which the bulk of the population worked according to customary routine and to practice not easily altered. But the major limitation on radical and general agricultural improvement in the eighteenth century was that, even within the old system, considerable improvements were effected, such as intaking from the waste, so that dearth became much less common than it had been. In such circumstances many saw no need to follow the improvers at least in the more radical and more expensive fields of enclosure, road-building and large-scale drainage. It was easy to regard the new practices as expensive and not always profitable hobbies to be followed by those with outside incomes, but not to be emulated by others, not at least until the rise in prices in the later eighteenth century made them less risky ventures. Consequently conservative arguments against any form of change were advanced well into the century, as, for instance, the suggestion that hedges encouraged undesirable number of birds, but the major deterrent was the real one of the country's poverty. Tenants were particularly affected by it and by the shortness of some leases. Since the benefits from enclosure, in particular, could be reaped only over a long period, few tenants could afford to risk being refused compensation for such improvements. A lease considered sufficiently long to encourage other improvements was considered inadequate to encourage enclosure. Even on their own estates proprietors found difficulty in obtaining fullest co-operation and emulation because of the opposition of many tenants to any alteration to customary practice. When Cockburn and Grant changed land use, both encountered opposition similar to that experienced by the Galloway proprietors. At Monymusk objections to afforestation, because it reduced the area available for grazing, were so strong that tenants met it by the destruction of trees and of fences. Though opposition could be combated in some cases by such compulsion as the insertion of restrictive clauses in new leases, or, by following the ways of Sir Alexander Grant, and using the powers of the Baron Court, a form of persuasion was necessary for the full benefits of the improvements to be dispersed throughout Scotland.

Three methods of persuasion were most effective in Scotland. The first, similar to that followed by some industrialists when faced with a similar problem, was to introduce Englishmen to teach new and better ways to the Scots, sometimes by using English materials. Grant of Monymusk had an English manager and used English horses and ploughs. Cockburn introduced English farmers to Ormiston and sent his tenants' sons south to learn English ways. Hutton, the geologist, also an important improver in Berwickshire, studied agriculture in Norfolk for a time and returned home with a Norfolk ploughman and English implements. The Earl of Findlater likewise introduced an English manager. From such centres of enlightenment a cumulative influence spread in turn throughout Scotland. Sir James Hall of Dunglass sent three of his 'most knowing tenants to Ormiston where they have learned more of labouring and improving their grounds in two days than they have done in all their life'.[1]

The second method of persuasion was by placing in influential positions those tenants converted to the new ways and able to exploit them. A major social effect of the changes in tenure in the eighteenth century was to give rise in many parts of Scotland to a new type of tenant, the full-time professional farmer. He differed from some of his predecessors and from those of his contemporaries who continued in

[1] Historical Manuscripts Commission, vol. 67. Polwarth MSS., vol. v, 208.

the old ways by being no longer completely absorbed in the same everyday work of his employees, though he differed from the improving lairds and proprietors by being engaged full-time in agricultural pursuits and by being wholly dependent on them for his livelihood. This type of tenant farmer was not unknown before the second half of the eighteenth century on the estates of improving lairds, especially in the south-east, but after about 1750 his influence spread and he made a major contribution, supplementing that of the lairds, to the improving movement. Many of the more successful lairds realized the importance of allowing such tenants to devise their own form of improvements. Giving them freedom produced more satisfactory results than an improving lease which, because of its rigidity, was not always most suitable for a particular farm. The possibilities of such co-operation were illustrated most strikingly by the progressive Wight family, tenants of Cockburn of Ormiston. Robert, who tenanted Muirhouse, first co-operated with Cockburn, but the partnership was strengthened greatly by his son, Alexander, who maintained a correspondence with Cockburn when the latter was in London and, with Charles Bell, the gardener at Ormiston, who was the executor of many of the laird's ideas. Alexander's son, Andrew, later made a major contribution to the improvement of Scottish agriculture, and to our knowledge of it, when in 1778 to 1784, on Lord Kames' suggestion, he visited every county on the Scottish mainland, except Argyll, and wrote reports on the improvements which had been made in their agriculture. Though such a family of tenants did make a major contribution to the improvement of Scottish agriculture, the social and legal structure of the period, with the initiative in the hands of the landed proprietors, and with the need for adequate financial resources to back improvements, meant that tenant farmers could achieve little on their own, Equally, since co-operation between laird and tenant was essential, the influence of tenants of the stamp of the Wights was as important as the influence of lairds of the stamp of Cockburn. In each area of successful improvement examples of co-operation similar to that of Cockburn and Wight can be cited. Successful improving lairds realized the need for such tenants by fixing long leases, sometimes for thirty years or more, often with the same, satisfactory family, and by taking smaller monetary rents in order to get an acceptable tenant. The Earl of Findlater leased one farm to a father and son for nearly a century, while Barclay of Ury once declared that he never acted more selfishly than when he refused a rent of £71 and chose instead to take one of £60 from someone he considered would be a good tenant, at the same time offering that tenant an interest-free loan of £200.

The third method of ensuring co-operation was by disseminating agricultural information at all levels, geographically and socially. The methods were various, but notable among them were the use of literature, local discussion groups, and national societies. Agricultural literature in the eighteenth century was of all kinds and came from all sources. Sometimes the writers were simply observant men with no practical experience of agriculture, sometimes they were improvers (Sir Archibald Grant published pamphlets and Lord Kames was a notable writer), and sometimes they were the inevitable armchair critics. The form of the literature differs before and after about 1770. Before then most writers were encouraging Scots to follow the ways of others. After about 1770, when the pace of improvement in Scotland increased, there were sufficient examples of improved practice in Scotland to provide adequate illustrations of the way enlightened men should travel. The progress of Sir Archibald Grant's pamphlets confirms the point. In sum, in Scotland fifty years or so after the Union the new agriculture was no longer simply a theory but an established practice in some places among some people. When the literature could be compared with successful practice, its effect among tenants was greater. The agricultural discussion clubs had an equally varied influence. Many were never formally organized, many never kept records, fewer still of these records have survived. One of which the records do survive, the Farming Club at Gordon's Mill, was limited to fifteen members, and, since six of these were members of the University of Aberdeen, its influence was restricted. The Club met fortnightly outside Aberdeen, the members recording and discussing agricultural improvements, especially those in the neighbourhood. Though apparently limited in its influence, the great advantage of such a club was that it could sift the experience of other areas to find what was most applicable in a particular locality. In this way the local groups made the influence of the national bodies more effective. The first of all the agricultural societies was a national one, The Honourable the Society of Improvers, founded in Edinburgh in July 1723. Though it lasted only until 1745 the Society of Improvers had a major influence in propagating the new methods, especially since membership of the Society was fashionable. Its three hundred members contained most of the peerage, the landed gentry and the leading professional men. When the society had an exceptionally active secretary in Robert Maxwell of

D

Arkland, it had the necessary stimulus to ensure that its great potential power as an improving agent in Scottish agriculture was not lost. The Society discussed all the innovations of the time and by publication and encouragement ensured their adoption. Local societies were founded to carry on its work, as by Cockburn at Ormiston in 1736. In the second half of the century, with the more widespread adoption of the new methods, the local societies became more numerous. The demise of the Society of Improvers in 1745 did not end its work and a decade later another society, formed from the Select Society founded a year earlier by Allan Ramsay, the painter, with similar, though wider, objects, was formed to carry on the work. Known as the Edinburgh Society, the new body encouraged the arts, sciences and manufacturers in Scotland, and so included agriculture. The financial crisis of the early 1760's brought its end in 1764. For twenty years, until 1784, no similar body took its place, but in that year the Highland Society was formed. Its activities relate to a later period, but the apparently more restricted concern of this society is significant. By that time improvements in agriculture had been introduced in many parts of the Lowlands, and a non-agricultural sector was rapidly growing in its economy. Conditions were different in the Highlands. Thus it was to this area that many of the nobility in Scotland felt they should direct their energies. Just as the Lowlands had started to emulate England and other areas successfully in the three-quarters of a century after the Union, so it was felt the Highlands should be encouraged to emulate the Lowlands.

The Highlands and the cattle trade

The introduction of the new methods of agriculture in the Highlands required social change to provide the initiative necessary for improvement. Such social transformation was taking place before the rebellions of 1715 and 1745, but was accomplished more effectively after the latter, especially when the heritable jurisdictions and ward-holding were abolished in 1747. Then, those lairds who had remained loyal found the scope for imitation of Lowland examples increased, and on the lands of attainted lairds, where the urge to retain the old society was often strongest, the Commissioners for the Forfeited Estates were given the opportunity to implement the new ideas. As some of the

Lowland improvers sat as Commissioners—Lord Kames was one—the aims they set for their own estates were applied in the Highlands. In this way the official agency of the Commissioners for the Forfeited Estates in the Highlands must be set against the individual agency of the improving lairds in the Lowlands as the major source of initiative in the transformation of Scottish agriculture in the eighteenth century.

The Commissioners' influence began only in the second half of the eighteenth century, but earlier, even in those regions of the Highlands where the influence of improving lairds was not experienced, the form of agricultural production had been affected by the Union. As Adam Smith pointed out, the Union had an immediate effect on the cattle trade.

'Had the Scotch cattle been always confined to the market of Scotland, in a country in which the quantity of land, which can be applied to no other purpose but the feeding of cattle, is so great in proportion to what can be applied to other purposes, it is scarce possible, perhaps, that their price could ever have risen so high as to render it profitable to cultivate land for the sake of feeding them. . . . Of all the commercial advantages . . . which Scotland has derived from the union with England, this rise in the price of cattle is, perhaps, the greatest. It has not only raised the value of all highland estates, but it has, perhaps, been the principal cause of the improvement of the low country.'[1]

Even before the Union large numbers of Scottish cattle were driven south, providing for some Highland areas virtually the only export to the Lowlands and to England. The trade to England was frequently interrupted by political factors. In 1705 it was resolved by the English Alien Act, though the decision was never implemented, to prohibit the importation of Scottish cattle to England. With the removal of such political restrictions after 1707 the trade stood to gain, but it gained much more by the rising demand for food in England and by the Navy's need of salted beef, especially during the series of wars in which Britain was involved throughout the eighteenth century. Consequently prices rose with only minor interruptions until 1815. About the time of the Union the average price of cows in Scotland was about 20s. to 27s.; in 1794 the average price of the animals sold at the Falkirk Tryst was £4.

[1] Smith, *op. cit.*, vol. i, pp. 219–20 and 222.

Two factors limited the growth of the cattle trade in the eighteenth century. The first was the difficulty of fattening cattle in unimproved pastures in Scotland so that Scotland was concerned more with cattle-breeding than with cattle-rearing. The second factor, a related one, was that the only method of transport available in the eighteenth century—making the animals walk—did not bring them to the consumer in the best possible condition. The Scottish system of cattle droving developed out of this situation. The drovers were not usually men of substance, though they sometimes worked in co-operation with those who were, but their transactions were frequently helped by the ease of obtaining credit in Scotland, and, in particular, by the willingness of some banks to discount their bills freely. Owners parted with their cattle to the drovers in return for only a small payment in cash, taking the remainder in bills of exchange. Cattle from the Highlands were taken to the trysts, first at Crieff, then at Falkirk, while those from Galloway went to Dumfries. Because of the inadequacy of the pastures on which they had been fed, the cattle were in such poor condition that they were then driven further south to fatten on English pastures. Though the numbers passing south are unknown, and estimates are subject to a wide margin of error, it seems that before the Union about 20,000 head went south annually. In the middle 1720's about 30,000 cattle were sold annually at the Crieff Tryst, and by the end of the eighteenth century, when the trade was gaining from the stimulus of the price rise during the Napoleonic Wars, about 100,000 cattle were exported every year from Scotland.

These great sales were beneficial to the Highland economy, but the stimulus envisaged by Adam Smith was even more conspicuous in the north-eastern counties. In the Highlands the rise in cattle prices in the eighteenth century, but particularly during the Revolutionary Wars, retarded the change, by enabling an anachronistic economy to continue to exist still longer. The incentive to change was greater in the north-east where cattle-raising, by the use of artificial as well as natural grazing, began to replace the old system of arable cultivation. This was exactly the effect Smith stressed. Consumers preferred the cattle from the north-east and so the trade from Aberdeenshire, Moray, and Angus grew more rapidly and grew from a cattle-breeding into a cattle-fattening trade. Complete success then required that the condition of cattle should not be allowed to deteriorate through having to walk to markets in the south. The north-east breeders were, therefore, ready to exploit to the full the advantage of the better methods of transport when they appeared in the nineteenth century. The drovers' activities were then extinguished, but not the cattle trade. A more efficient one appeared, but, since it was concentrated in the north-east, it combined with the new openings in sheep-farming, to spell ruin to the cattle trade of the Highlands.

III
TRADE AND TRANSPORT

The Union and trade

THE pattern of foreign trade provides an indication of Scotland's economic structure and of its deficiencies. The major imports were manufactured goods, especially the luxuries which became the symbol of the rise in the standard of living in the eighteenth century. The exports were chiefly raw materials, or manufactured goods of coarse or inferior quality. From the Low Countries came velvets, lace, cambrics and imitation Indian goods, though the industrial expansion in Scotland later in the eighteenth century led to a decline in imports of fine linen and later of cambrics. From France, frequently smuggled, came the wines and brandies so necessary for the standard of living many then sought. From England came an even greater variety of manufactured goods, as is evident from the long list of commodities which Patrick Lindsay enumerated in 1733.

'From England we are served with broad Cloths of all Kinds, from the best *Spanish* wooll Superfines, to the lowest pric'd Yorkshires; with *Norwich* Goods of all Kinds, with Silk-hose of all Kinds, and large Parcels of fine woollen Hose; with Silks and Silk-stuffs of all Kinds and Prices; Mohair-goods, Cotton-goods; fine Hats; Gold and Silver Laces, and Twist, with all the Toy-trade and all Sorts of Iron-Mongers Ware, and Cutlery ware, Drinking-glasses and Mirrors, and fine Furniture of various Kinds; Indian Goods that pay Duty at the Port of *London*, of all Sorts, with many other Goods of lesser Value, all for Home-consumpt, which to enumerate would be endless.'[1]

Imports were by no means wholly of manufactured goods. Raw materials and foodstuffs entered the country too, coming frequently from economies even less well developed than Scotland. Ireland sent raw hides and oatmeal in times of famine; from Norway came timber; the Baltic exported iron.

[1] P. Lindsay, *The Interest of Scotland* (Edinburgh, 1733), pp. 101–2.

To pay for the imports Scotland exported grain to Norway; coal to Ireland; coal for the Rotterdam breweries; coarse woollen goods, smelted lead and lead ore to the Low Countries; fish to France; sheepskins, dressed and undressed, tallow, eggs, fresh salmon, lobsters and, above all, linen and cattle to England. The trade with England was always of special importance both before and after 1707, and, since it was kept well in surplus by exports of linen and cattle, the English threat to stop imports of these commodities in the Alien Act of 1705 was an effective means of exerting economic pressure on Scotland. After 1707 the need to maintain the surplus was not diminished. Rather emotively Lindsay pointed out a further strain that became increasingly evident in the balance with England in the eighteenth century.

'To all this we have to add another very heavy Article against us, in the Balance of our Trade with *London*, our Expense there; that the Persons of Quality who have the best Estates here, live for the most Part at *London* and have all their Rents sent thither in Specie, or by Bills of Exchange; and are there consumed.'[1]

A more important reason for maintaining the surplus with England after the Union was that it could be used to offset imports from other countries with which Scotland had a trading deficit, such as France. Triangular trade had been a feature of the Scottish economy before 1707. It remained so afterwards.

Towards the promotion of trade with England, and of Scottish foreign trade generally, the Union made important contributions. There were short-run benefits, such as the profits obtained through selling in England imports made to Scotland before duties were raised to the higher English rates, or through the inferior organization of the Scottish customs enabling the Scots to be better smugglers; but the major contribution came from inclusion within the privileges of the Navigation Acts, the restrictions of which had previously barred Scottish trade with the English colonies. The Scots fully appreciated the benefits which they could obtain under the Acts' protection and tried in the negotiations before the Union to secure their privileges for the maximum number of ships. It was proposed that all vessels belonging even only in part to Scottish subjects, whether built at home or overseas, should be counted ships of Great Britain if registered within twelve months of the Treaty of Union. Against this all-embracing

[1] Lindsay, *op. cit.*, p. 102.

provision, which, especially through the possibilities of part-ownership, would have opened the closely preserved English trade to a multitude of outsiders, the English rebelled and insisted that only ships registered at the date of the Treaty, and wholly owned by Scots, should be included. Substantially the English had their way, except that the privileges of the Acts were extended to ships wholly owned by Scots at the date of the ratification of the Treaty. Nevertheless, inclusion within the privileges of the Navigation Acts was not so completely responsible for the growth of Scottish trade as has sometimes been assumed. First, the Navigation Acts did not inhibit entirely the growth of trade before 1707, because it was possible to comply with their terms by trading—as was done—through Whitehaven. Second, an illicit trade grew up, helped by the presence of many Scottish servants (exempt, with victuals and horses, from the restrictions of the Navigation Acts) in the plantations. This trade before 1707 helped to account for the first rise of the west, and of Glasgow in particular as a trading centre. Nor did the Union, and the consequential privileges of the Navigation Acts, immediately confirm the supremacy of the west of Scotland, because it was not till about 1740, when Scottish imports of tobacco, then equal to about 20 per cent of total British imports, began to rise rapidly after some years of stagnation, that Glasgow began to achieve its final and complete triumph over Whitehaven, Liverpool and Bristol. The lag may be attributed simply to the time taken to break the rivalry of other ports, or, until the others found the slave trade, in which Glasgow did not participate, more profitable; but the existence of the lag meant that the legal privileges of the Navigation Acts had to be supplemented by greater efficiency, or by a more favourable geographical situation, to give Glasgow the place it eventually occupied. Certainly contemporary Scots did not look on the Union as having first opened up such trade to them. Since they had already traded, illicitly of course, with the English colonies, so after 1707 they were continuing an established practice. Legality helped especially in leading towards a more extensive trade, but alone it was not enough, and its benefits were certainly not immediate.

It is much more difficult to judge what effect the trade had on indigenous industrial development. One point, perhaps obvious, must be stressed. The trade which grew up successfully in Scotland was an entrepot trade, requiring relatively few Scottish products for export and requiring relatively few markets in Scotland for the disposal of its goods. In 1771, just before the interruption of the financial crisis of the following year, 46,000,000 lbs. of tobacco, the principal commodity of trade, entered the Clyde and 44,000,000 lbs. were re-exported, most of it being sent to the Farmers-General of the French Customs. The vessels which carried the tobacco to Europe were then loaded with European manufactured goods, sometimes took wine on board at Madeira, perhaps called at the West Indies for rum and sugar before returning to the North American colonies. Only a minority of ships did go directly from Scotland to North America with the typical variety of manufactured goods which the colonists required—linens, leather goods, pots, pans, axle bushes, hoes, shovels—but this demand was not necessarily a demand for Scottish products, because part was met through the export of goods made in England. The connection can be tested by reference to the linen industry. Its progress, especially in increased sales to foreign markets, was discouraged immediately after the Union when, in 1711, a new export duty was laid on Scottish linen exports. Though the tax did not ruin the industry, Scottish manufacturers had difficulty in meeting competition in colonial markets from German and Austrian cloth re-exported through London until after 1742, when bounties were paid on exports of British linen. Production of linen, which was stable at about 4,500,000 yards annually in the decade before 1742, doubled in the subsequent decade and fell only with the removal of the bounties between 1754 and 1756. In these years the continuing competitive weakness of the industry was confirmed by pleas that, if the bounties were not received, no drawbacks should be given on foreign goods re-exported and duties on imported foreign yarn removed. Consequently, even from the mid-1750's, when information on Scottish exports first becomes available, until the mid-1770's, perhaps only about 10 to 15 per cent of production was exported. Unfortunately a statistical difficulty makes it impossible to reach any conclusive judgement on the effects of the Union in stimulating demand for Scottish products. After 1707 goods sent to England were no longer included as exports, but it seems that the major benefits of the Union came from the opening of English markets, especially to imports of Scottish linen and cattle, which the Alien Act had threatened to stop.

Even if the direct stimulus of the Union to trade and to the development of the Scottish economy may be minimized, the indirect effects of the Union on the pattern of Scottish trade cannot be. The Union's greatest contribution lay in providing a final confirmation of a change in Scotland's international relationships, a change which, without such final constitutional confirmation, could not have been as effective as it became. It is as a confirmation of an established trend that the Union of 1707 must be interpreted. It was not in itself an economic watershed at all comparable to the constitutional watershed, because even before 1603 Scotland was turning to England for economic contacts. James VI and I's rapid departure for the south was, therefore, perhaps that sovereign's wisest action for his own country, as his ideas on economic integration were valid in the long run, through assuring contact with the most rapidly expanding markets of the time for the Scottish economy. The reasons for the changing Scottish connections in Europe at this time were various. The importance of the French connection to Scotland was declining for strictly economic reasons as well as because of cultural and religious factors, but, whatever the explanation, its decline placed the Scottish economy in a superior position to reap the gains from international trade. The connection with foreign markets, which the link with England ensured would be maintained, meant a link with continually growing foreign markets. Freer access to English markets was only the first and most evident outcome of the new connection and the gains were conspicuous in the few cases, such as the cattle trade, where Scotland could exploit the opportunities offered without any further developments—even though the exploitation was less efficient than it might have been. In short, the Union provided the best environment for sales, an environment necessary for success when low-cost production became characteristic of Scottish industry later in the eighteenth century. When after the 1780's the Scottish economy was resting on a basis laid by achievements apparently its own, it was in reality resting on a foundation established through Union with England.

The tobacco trade

The success of the Scots in the tobacco trade, indubitably the most successful branch of foreign trade in the eighteenth century, has been attributed to many factors: by English merchants, displaced by Scottish successes, to fraudulent ways; by the Scots, to their greater frugality and efficiency. Though the Scottish trade was not uniquely organized to guarantee absolute efficiency, it did have some characteristic features. In the early eighteenth century planters normally consigned their tobacco to British merchants. The planter retained ownership of the tobacco, though the merchant was completely responsible for the cargo after its arrival in Britain, for unloading, paying customs duties, warehousing and, ultimately and most important, for selling it. The merchant used the proceeds to purchase such manufactured goods as had been ordered by the planter and was remunerated by a percentage of the price obtained for the tobacco and any profit he made on the goods exported. Generally the Scots did not adopt the consignment system for the large-scale expansion of trade. They first traded with America in the most primitive form, by a merchant either taking himself, or sending a supercargo with, a cargo of manufactured goods which were bartered for tobacco. The method of bartering was confined to the early days of the trade. With its expansion the merchants appointed resident factors, who purchased tobacco outright and sold goods exported from Scotland. Initially each merchant or firm had a single store but soon, especially with the rapid expansion of the trade in the middle of the eighteenth century, some firms, notably the Cunninghames and John Glassford, began to have several stores scattered throughout Virginia and Maryland. Though the merchants had suffered much criticism under the old consignment system, the new store or factoring system gave rise to much more. Under it the merchants received all the opprobrium reserved for middle-men, especially when they tried, not always successfully because of the number of merchants engaged in the trade, to fix the prices at which the tobacco should be bought. The Scottish merchant became one of the most disliked members of colonial society, the man at whom non-importation agreements were aimed, and one cause of the Revolution.

The two systems differed in ways which favoured the Scots. First, the American planter was in chronic need of credit, at least seasonally, but frequently for much longer periods. Loans to American planters were rarely self-liquidating as the annual sale of the tobacco crop did not always pay off the debts. Though, in theory at any rate, the consignment system should not have led to the granting of credit, it did through the planters buying more from the merchants than could be paid for by the proceeds of the tobacco which they had sent for sale. Under the store system the separation of the purchasing of tobacco and the sale of the goods imported led to a direct grant of credit, though one that had often to be paid for by planters generally in the form of higher prices. The store system, therefore, required greater credit resources on the part of the merchants, though in practice the difference was less marked because of the extent to which sales of tobacco under the consignment system did not cover the planters' purchases of goods. The merchant had to be able to purchase the tobacco outright and carry some stocks in his stores in the plantations. The Scottish merchants were more able to supply such capital because their intimate connection with some of the new banks in the west of Scotland gave them privileged access to financial resources, but even this institutional advantage did not overcome the overall scarcity of credit in Scotland. The more efficient organization of the banking system in the eighteenth century was, therefore, vitally important to the merchants because it enabled them to draw more freely on the greater resources of the London capital market, especially when the Scottish banks stabilized the exchange on London. That reason probably explains a peculiar aspect of Scottish economic history in the eighteenth century, that, while the merchant's need for credit was probably greater than that of the manufacturer, his complaints about not receiving it were less. The organization of Scottish banking helped to provide him with it more efficiently than it did to the manufacturer.

A second feature of the store system worked even more distinctly to the advantage of the Scots. Under the consignment system a merchant tended to have only a few customers in the colonies, whereas under the storage system he had a large number. Consequently, though the total debt owed to the Scottish merchants was often considerable, it was usually composed of a large number of small accounts. One computation suggests that in the early 1770's about 31,000 individual accounts were due to 112 stores in Virginia belonging to 37 Glasgow firms. The disadvantage of such a system, where, as the debtors were so numerous, some had frequently only limited resources, was more than outweighed by the overriding advantage that the total debt could be more easily reduced than under the consignment system. This was to prove important to the Scottish merchants when the tobacco trade collapsed.

The first signs of impending difficulties for the tobacco merchants came with the non-importation agreements, the settlers' way of meeting the Stamp Act, when the value of Scottish exports to North America fell from £270,548 in 1763 to £185,733 in 1765. In 1767 the value rose again to £274,610. The distribution of the population and the absence of large trading centres placed difficulties in the way of the enforcement of the Acts, but in any case the presence in the colonies of the loyal Scottish factors required by the store system provided a vitally important link in ensuring a continuation of imports, and so in ensuring that the effects of the non-importation agreements were less detrimental to the Scottish than to the English merchants. The effects of the non-importation agreements, and of the restrictions on credit following the financial crisis of 1772, were much less important than the crisis of 1776. The collapse of the tobacco trade in that year is well known. Imports of tobacco in 1775 were nearly 46,000,000 lbs.; in 1776 they were almost 7,500,000 lbs.; in 1777 they had fallen to less than 300,000 lbs. Re-exports fell too. In 1775 they were over 30,000,000 lbs.; in 1776 nearly 23,500,000 lbs.; in 1777, 5,500,000 lbs.; in 1778 about 2,300,000 lbs.

The merchants were not ruined by this collapse, because it did not come as a surprise to them and they did everything in their power to minimize its impact. The reports from the factors, with their intimate knowledge of colonial conditions, prepared the way for remedial action. From 1774 some factors were sending home warnings of possible insurrection. In 1775 the *Caledonian Mercury* was circulating reports—apparently false, but symptomatic of the feelings of the time —that the Navigation Acts were being openly infringed by vessels trading directly from Virginia to Dunkirk. In light of these warnings the Scots adopted two methods of cutting their prospective losses. First, they pressed their factors to obtain payment for all debts, the smallness of most of which, combined with the presence of the factors, made collection easier, though it did not enhance the reputation of the merchants among the settlers. Second, the factors were urged to try to buy as much tobacco as they could in the years immediately before the Revolution, with the expectation, which was realized, that these exceptionally heavy imports would later be sold at inflated war-time prices. Thus the average annual imports of about 44,000,000 lbs. were maintained from 1770 to 1775, though during the same period re-exports were falling. The Scottish tobacco merchants were therefore well organized when the blow, which they had expected and which they had anticipated, duly struck. There was, therefore, no immediate collapse, though the traders had to face the problem of replacing the system on which they had built their reputation. In the short run this was difficult, and the fortunes of Scottish traders fluctuated during the war. The colonists began to send their ships directly to Europe; the harvest was poor in 1777; in 1778 war with France precipitated a run on the banks. The result was a number of failures in the next two years, relieved only by both exports and imports rising from the low level to which they had fallen on the outbreak of the Revolution. Then the

Scots traders began to take measures for a revival of trade. That was achieved only in a later period.

The success of the Glasgow tobacco trade has led to much stress being placed on its contribution, and indeed on that of foreign trade generally, to the development of the Scottish economy. Yet care must be exercised in judging how relevant the growth of foreign trade was to the internal growth of the economy. The tobacco trade, which formed such an important element of the country's trade, was an entrepot trade and probably made an even less important direct contribution than in comparable economies. The Scottish economy was too backward to take immediate advantage of the new overseas demand which the trade opened up. The demands of the merchants were not immediately met by Scottish manufacturers, nor did the merchants themselves become industrialists. Even after the collapse of the tobacco trade in 1776 there is little evidence to support the traditional belief of a large-scale movement of resources from trade to industry, and especially to the nascent cotton industry. There are a few examples of such transference: James Dunlop took over the Clyde ironworks; Robert Dunmore, described as a 'Virginia Merchant', but by that time also laird of Ballindalloch and Ballikinrain, built the mill at Balfron; one of the Bogles took an unsuccessful interest in promoting cotton-spinning in the Highlands, and John Glassford, who was to be found at that time in most economic ventures in Scotland, helped to found works for the manufacture of cudbear, a powder used for dyeing. But these are isolated examples. The Glasgow tobacco lords' greatest contribution to the economic growth of Scotland was not by becoming industrialists.

The contribution of foreign trade to economic development is of a more general and indirect kind. First, merchants generally, but especially those engaged in foreign trade, were among the leading promoters of the new banks, especially in Glasgow. The Ship Bank was first floated under the title of Colin Dunlop, Alexander Houston and Company, names of tobacco lords, Second, foreign trade brought wealth to a few Scots, some of whom had gone to the colonies in lowly positions, but who returned to Scotland with sufficient wealth to set themselves up as landed gentry and, more occasionally, as industrialists. A notable example, who probably provided the prototype for Mr. Cayenne in John Galt's *Annals of the Parish*, was Alexander of Ballochmyle, whose settlement as a landed proprietor was matched by other successful merchants in the same district of central Ayrshire at the same time, such as the Hamiltons, in their various branches, of Bourtreehill, Pinmore, Sundrum, Rozelle and Belleisle. Alexander was notable only for his industrial interests. On the other hand the number of Scots who made good in this way was not great. Many went out, few lived to come back at all, fewer still came back with adequate wealth, and of those who did so succeed many were blood relations. Though the power and authority they enjoyed as landowners heightened their influence, it was still confined mainly to their lands, spreading only indirectly to other sectors of the economy.

Yet an evaluation of the indirect contributions might simply confirm the fundamental importance of the direct effects. It is true that Scottish foreign trade did not absorb an overwhelming part of Scottish industrial production, and that the failure of the Scottish linen industry to respond readily or completely to the new demand indicates the importance of some other limitations on the country's industrial growth, which had to be removed before overseas demand could have its main impact. But Scottish overseas trade still provided a continuing demand for Scottish products, which, though not absorbing a large part of Scottish industrial production, was of crucial importance in some cases. This was so with Carron Company: from the earliest days the Glasgow merchants were among its most important customers and such they remained, so that just before the American War no less than seventy-five Glasgow merchants were on the Carron books. In short in the eighteenth century Scottish overseas trade opened up a new demand for Scottish manufacture. It was a new challenge. Though the Scots could not satisfy the new demand at once, its existence was a necessary prerequisite for subsequent developments, but before it could be fully exploited, additional changes were necessary, and towards these foreign trade made some contribution through the men and the finance it produced.

In looking for these additional contributions it is necessary to move from concentration on the activities of the merchants engaged in foreign trade to those who participated primarily in the country's frequently neglected domestic trade. The most important of this group were associated with the organization of the linen trade and with ensuring the maintenance of its external connections, either to obtain raw materials or to sell the finished product. Because of the domestic, dispersed, and, at least in the early years of the century, the part-time nature of the various operations in the industry, there were thrown up a number of people with some capital and, as important, with the ability to organize their workers. The need for such large-scale organization did not arise from the new techniques of manufacture introduced later in the eighteenth century; it was only changed, sometimes indeed, through their greater concentration, in a way which made the task easier. These merchants, with their interests rooted primarily in domestic industry, rather than the foreign merchants, made the most direct contribution to the new industry which appeared after the 1780's. This is the contribution of trade which must be stressed.

Communications

Though extensive trade, domestic and foreign, required improved communications, Scottish producers always had the advantage of being sited in close proximity to their domestic market in central Scotland, especially in Glasgow and Edinburgh. Though the population of Scotland was more evenly distributed throughout the country in the eighteenth century, income was not, and, of particular importance, Scottish merchants were not. Scottish producers had, therefore, the advantage, short term though it was, of a market relatively sheltered by transport costs from English competitors. Hence transport improvements were less important for the industrial growth of Scotland in the eighteenth century than they were for the development of the heavy industries and the full exploitation of the country's natural resources in the nineteenth century.

Topographically there are few more obvious locations for a canal than central Scotland, especially since the sea passage around the northern coast is long, dangerous, and virtually impracticable for small vessels at certain times of the year. The first serious survey of the route, made in 1762, proposed a canal from the Yoker Burn to the river Carron at Abbotshaugh, about two miles from where it joins the Forth. The Board of Trustees for Fisheries and Manufactures was interested in the venture and in the following year commissioned John Smeaton to make another survey. In 1764 Smeaton reported to the Trustees on two possible routes. One, not seriously considered until the 1920's, was along the Forth for some miles above Stirling, then across to the Endrick into Loch Lomond, finally by the Leven into the Clyde at Dumbarton. The second route, which became the basis for future serious discussion, was 'from the River Carron, by way of the Bonny, through the Bog of Dolater into the Kelvin and from thence into the Clyde by way of the Yoker Burn'. Smeaton thought the first route would require only seventeen miles of artificial cuttings against twenty-seven miles for the second route. On the other hand the greater elevation of the first offset any economies through less artificial cutting. In any case, whichever method was going to be adopted, the canal would obviously be expensive. For one seven feet deep on the second route Smeaton estimated that the cost would be about £80,000.

The implications of these financial requirements must be appreciated to understand much of the subsequent discussion on the canal and, in addition, the light it throws on the economic problems of contemporary Scotland. The resources required were so substantial that some assistance from public funds was thought necessary. There were precedents in road-building and in other subventions to industry and, in addition, the Board of Trustees had been sufficiently interested to commission an early survey. Hope centred on the Commissioners for Forfeited Estates, but, when they refused to supply funds, the need to raise the necessary capital by public subscription was recognized. To some concerned with the venture this placed the whole project in a different light and a lengthy and pointed debate ensued. Probably Smeaton had suggested the route that was technically, perhaps in the long run even economically, superior, but his opponents were more concerned with what they considered to be the virtual impossibility of raising £80,000 privately in mid-eighteenth-century Scotland, more especially in the mid-1760's, and with the location of the canal. The rivalry was most acute between Glasgow and Edinburgh, the interests in the former campaigning for a smaller and, to their way of thinking, more realistic canal. Eventually a compromise was effected and an Act of 1768 authorized a seven-foot-deep canal from Grangemouth to Dalmuir (later altered to Bowling), with authorized capital of £150,000 and power to raise another £50,000 if necessary. There was still much opposition from the defeated Glasgow interests, especially from Samuel Garbett, who even brought James Brindley, the engineer, to make a further survey in 1768, but with no effect, as the Act of 1768 provided the basis on which the canal was built.

It is easy to criticize the Glasgow interests as short-sighted, but their fears of the possible recklessness of the financial proposals proved to rest on good grounds. While the advocacy of a large canal, sufficient to accommodate subsequent developments, seemed to indicate vision and foresight, it displayed much more the characteristic of being too

E

elaborate and capital-consuming. Such schemes frequently run into financial disaster. So it was with the Forth and Clyde canal.

Construction began at the east end in July 1768, reaching Kirkintilloch in 1773 and Stockingfield in 1775. Expenditure exceeded estimates, so, though parliamentary sanction was sought for raising additional funds, it proved impossible to continue and work stopped in July 1775. The Glasgow interests rescued the venture in part by raising sufficient funds to complete a cut in 1777 from Stockingfield to Hamilton Hill, which remained the Glasgow terminus until a larger basin, Port Dundas, was built in 1790. Nine years later the financial implications of the venture, which had been so easily neglected, had to be tackled, and this time along the lines the Glasgow interests had originally thought necessary, by appealing for support to the government. In the end the belief held in Glasgow, that such a venture was beyond the limits of private resources, was proved right. In 1784 an advance of £50,000 was authorized from the Forfeited Estates to allow the canal to be completed, which was finally achieved in the summer of 1790.

The Glasgow interests may thus be complimented for their common sense, especially their financial common sense, rather than accused of their lack of enthusiasm. On the other hand the Glasgow interests were more concerned with the expansion of international rather than inter-regional trade in the late eighteenth century and so were less anxious to establish contact with the east of Scotland. Apart from their obvious lack of interest in a canal which entered the Clyde only at Bowling, they did not see this waterway offering them all the prospects it might have even a short time earlier. By the time the construction of the canal was an actuality, their trade was firmly rooted to the west. Consequently, of greater importance to them was the deepening and widening of the Clyde, the second main transport improvement in Scotland of the eighteenth century.

The beginnings of the need for such development go back to the seventeenth century. Though the Broomielaw was long used for loading and unloading small vessels, its first quay was built in 1663. Five years later, when it could acquire land at neither Greenock nor Dumbarton, Glasgow purchased land in the parish of Kilmacolm where Port Glasgow eventually appeared. Improvements began in 1755, when John Smeaton reported on the possibilities of deepening the Clyde, and in 1759, when an Act of Parliament was obtained for this purpose. The plan followed was that of John Golborne, who, after a survey in 1768, proposed building jetties at intervals along the river, so confining it to a narrower channel, which could be deepened by dredging. From 1799 to 1806 the jetties were linked by parallel dykes to secure a continuous uniform channel. Since then improvements have been continuous. The Clyde was in the favourable position of having a bed which could be deepened, but the success of this enterprise, especially when compared with the restricted achievements of the Forth and Clyde Canal, confirmed the accuracy of the emphasis Glaswegians chose to place on transport developments at the time.

The desirability of better waterways was increased through the deficiencies of roads. Though a study of the maps of the *Military Survey of Scotland*, carried out by General Roy around 1755, might seem to indicate a fairly comprehensive network, most tracks did not have made surfaces and were quite unfit for wheeled vehicles. In some areas, such as west of the Great Glen, roads were non-existent. Elsewhere they were inadequate, as, for instance, from Selkirk to Edinburgh, where the carrier sometimes found the channel of the Gala Water safer than the road. The statutory basis for the upkeep of roads was laid down in a series of Acts, chiefly of the seventeenth century. In 1719, when another Act completed the provision, Justices of the Peace and Commissioners of Supply were authorized to appoint overseers to ensure that the roads were properly maintained by six days' compulsory labour required annually from tenants and others, while, to provide necessary funds, they were permitted to tax heritors to an amount not exceeding 10s. in the £100 Scots of valued rent. The effectiveness of these provisions varied. In some counties, such as Ayrshire, Commissioners and Justices did not co-operate; in others, such as Lanarkshire, the Justices had to act alone. Heritors objected to paying any levies and tenants objected to the compulsory labour. Improvements could be effected, therefore, only in areas where a major landowner was able and willing to direct improvement, as in Banffshire under Lord Deskford, the father of the improving Earl of Findlater. Even there opposition continued, and, in any case, knowledge of road-making was so elementary that no lasting improvement of surfaces could be effected until satisfactory road-making techniques were evolved through the work of several engineers, including John Loudon McAdam, who built a stretch of road from his own property to the highway in Ayrshire in 1787.

Improvements in roads and canals were limited, therefore, fundamentally by the same reasons, especially by lack of funds. There was, however, one major difference between the two. The improvement of local roads, and minor bridge-building, could be undertaken on a much more limited scale than was feasible in the construction of any waterways or major roads. In the eighteenth century many Scottish landowners engaged actively in such minor improvements as an effective means of bettering their estates. Sometimes they worked independently; at other times they tried to force their fellow Commissioners of Supply to take action. In 1754 Grant of Monymusk was endeavouring to 'rouz gentlemen to serious thought and application' to improvement at the next meeting of the local Commissioners.[1] But many in Scotland would not be roused, partly through the inadequacy of the resources at their disposal, partly because improved roads were, with some justification, not always considered of vital importance for many economic enterprises in Scotland in the eighteenth century. Consequently, since roads were built in Scotland only if some special factor brought extraordinary support for their construction, the co-ordination of action necessary to promote any major improvement could also be engendered only through the operation of exceptional circumstances. Only the influence of the improving movement on the landed interest was adequate to lead to effective private action, but its influence was frequently confined to restricted areas. For a wider impact the prospects of profitable improvement through the turnpike trusts, which enabled the trustees who constructed the roads to levy tolls at the gates, or turnpikes, was necessary. The first turnpike Act, for Midlothian, was passed in 1714, the next only in 1751. Though their main contribution came with the use of better methods of road construction in the late eighteenth and early nineteenth centuries, they had important effects from the 1770's especially in the developing areas. Most striking was the bridge-building in which some Commissioners of Supply displayed great interest in the 1770's. In Lanarkshire some fine bridges were built during the decade—Roberton reputedly in 1769, Hyndford in 1773, Thankerton in 1778—all improving the access from Clydeside to the south. As construction of roads and bridges grew, even on the local level that was characteristic of most years of the eighteenth century until towards its close, easier communication was brought to many places which had previously been accessible only by pack-horses. Internal trade was facilitated and concentrated. In 1740 there were fifteen fairs in East Lothian; in 1796 there were only six.

A more striking, and co-ordinated, group of road improvements,

[1] H. Hamilton, *Selections from the Monymusk Papers* (1713–55). Scottish History Society Publication, vol. xxxix (third series) (Edinburgh, 1945), p. 162.

though with much less economic significance, was carried out at the public expense chiefly in the Highlands, the result of the official policy of attempted pacification. They fell into two main phases. The first, between 1726 and 1737, was when General Wade built about 250 miles of road and 40 bridges. The second was after the '45 Rebellion, when about 800 miles of roads and 1,000 bridges were built. Direct military labour was used in these cases and the aim was frankly strategic. Only in the nineteenth century were attempts made to bring roads with more peaceful purposes to the Highlands at public expense.

IV
INDUSTRY AND FINANCE

The Union and the linen industry

THE fortunes of Scottish industry were not transformed by the Union of the Parliaments. After 1707, as before, the country's industries required a new basis of processes and products to enable them to rival producers in other countries, above all in England; but such an industrial renovation required a level of capital investment for which Scotland did not have the resources, until increased wealth, at a time of technical development for which Scotland was particularly suited, eventually provided a solution. Until that period, around the 1780's, Scottish industry was only struggling towards the successes that were to follow. When it is stressed that, in spite of the economic achievements of the seventy-five years after 1707, it was still the next three-quarters of a century which witnessed the main industrial developments in Scotland, then the rise of Scottish industry cannot be explained simply as the product of political union, delayed perhaps by rebellion. Shortly after 1707 such a proposition seemed self-evident to many Scots who considered the Union caused industrial dislocation through the removal of Scottish protective barriers, and the consequential freeing of trade with England, leading to the collapse of some Scottish industries. The belief was prejudiced. The only notable failure was of the cloth industry, but before 1707 it had survived with decreasing success even behind protective barriers. As an export industry the finer cloth industry had declined before 1707, while, on the other hand, the coarse cloth industry survived the Union even to the extent of being able to send some cloth to England to be finished in the 1720's. The industries which collapsed were, in short, only those which had been stimulated by the seventeenth-century economic policy, which had encouraged industries in direct competition with superior English production. Such a policy could not survive a union. Its collapse, with some inevitable adverse effects in a few industries, was not an example of a vindictive English policy towards a growing competitor (Scotland was far from being able to claim to be such) but was necessary to ensure that Scotland finally surrendered her seventeenth-century attempts to prosecute industries, such as the manufacture of cloth, in which it had a comparative cost disadvantage, and concentrated instead on those in which it had a comparative cost advantage.

In such an indirect way the Union ensured that industrial expansion in Scotland was of a type which could be maintained. To industrial growth the financial provisions of the Treaty of Union made a more direct contribution. The inevitable equalization of customs and excise duties in the two countries normally implied an increase of duties in Scotland and, further, that part of the revenue raised in Scotland after the Union was utilized in helping to service the larger national debt which England had incurred before 1707. Compensation for the assumption of this burden involved refined discussions of equity before it eventually assumed two forms. First, Scotland received a payment of £398,085 10s., 'the Equivalent', the capitalized value of the existing revenue-yield which would help to service the English national debt, and, second, an 'Arising Equivalent', which could not be calculated at the time of the Union, but which was to be a continuous compensation from revenue raised in Scotland. The second, or Arising Equivalent, was to consist of the entire increase in Scotland's customs and excise revenue for the seven years after the Union and of such part of the increase as would be used to meet payments on the English debt thereafter. Article XV of the Treaty of Union stipulated that the various funds of the Equivalent were to be used for a variety of purposes— payment of Scotland's own national debt; provision of compensation for those who lost through standardizing the coinage of the two countries and for investors in the Darien Company; lastly, assistance, of £2,000 a year, for the woollen industry and other economic projects.

The history of the Equivalent provides the key to an understanding of the effect of the Union on Scottish finance. Economic projects received little immediate benefit because a large part of the funds available was absorbed in meeting the various demands of Scottish aristocrats and high officials. The Scots assumed that the Equivalent would solve many of their pressing financial problems. It failed to do so after the Union because, while Scottish revenue was insufficiently buoyant to provide the additional compensation anticipated under the Arising Equivalent, the English saw no reason why they should provide any subventions. Payment of the Equivalent, no matter how tardy, was considered to have given the British parliament the right to tax Scotland as it wished, and the assertion of that right was at bottom the source of the most popular dissatisfaction with the Treaty of Union from 1707 to 1760. There is no doubt that during this period the Scots failed to obtain the financial benefits they had anticipated from the Union. After 1707 they were more conscious of the additional taxes they had to pay: the new export duty on the Scottish staple export of linen in 1711; the increased salt tax, disastrous to the Scottish fishing industry which relied on salt imported from overseas, in 1712; and, most controversial of all, the malt tax in 1713 and 1725. Though even such additional taxation failed to provide the increased revenue the Scots hoped for under the second, or Arising Equivalent, it is equally clear that lack of buoyancy in the revenue, not English domination, was the basic reason why it became necessary to impose additional taxation rather than provide additional expenditure after 1707.

Of the major sources of revenue only the land tax, or cess, which Article IX of the Treaty of Union made a fixed proportion of the English land tax in the ratio of about 40 : 1, produced a substantial remittance to London. Practically all raised in Scotland, apart from various allowances for the apprehension of deserters, was sent to Westminster. The land tax was the exception. The salt tax provided for only one small remittance, of over £1,500, in 1716. Of the customs revenue only about 5 per cent went south in the eight years from the Union until 1715. Thereafter nothing was sent until 1747-8 when irregular, but fairly small, remittances began. But it is the experience of the excise duties which is most interesting, because they included the more controversial, especially the malt tax. Immediately after the Union few charges against excise revenue in Scotland allowed considerable remittances to be made to London, but as the charges, especially the cost of maintaining the Scottish courts, grew, the remittances declined and ended after 1717. In this decade, from the Union till 1717, the excise had a sufficient surplus to enable about 27 per cent of its gross produce, or 40 per cent of its net produce, to go south. The chief cause of the inability to meet the higher expenditure in Scotland and maintain remittances to Westminster was the failure of the malt tax.[1] Its net produce to the Scottish Exchequer in 1717–18, the year in

[1] There is some confusion on when the malt tax was imposed in Scotland. The proposal to impose the duty of 6d. a bushel on malt in 1713 was considered to be a direct contravention of Article XIV of the Treaty of Union, which prohibited any malt tax during the war, which was still not quite over, and brought universal opposition culminating in a proposal to dissolve the Union. For this reason some authorities state that the tax, though duly authorized, was never

which remittances south ended, was less than £1,500. In 1724–5 its net produce was negative. In this situation Walpole's decision to levy a tax of 6*d*. a barrel on ale may be understood, but it was certainly not by the Scots. To them it was the ultimate indignity to be inflicted by the Union and the opposition was so strong that Walpole abandoned a tax on ale and substituted a duty of 3*d*. on every bushel of malt with the additional assurance, regarded by many contemporaries as 'a blind to make the tax go down',[1] that any revenue in excess of £20,000 would be used for the encouragement of Scottish manufactures. Until 1737–8 the malt duties provided the £20,000 for remittance to London, as had been planned, with a small surplus available for expenditure in Scotland. Thereafter, as its net yield fell below that level for some years, so did remittances. When yield recovered, so did they. In short, both were roughly similar until 1760. Until 1760 then, during the period when most disputes were over taxation, remittances to the Exchequer at Westminster were provided mainly by the land tax and the malt tax. They ensured that for fifty years after the Union about 15 to 20 per cent (but very rarely any more) of revenue raised in Scotland went south. Consequently, in spite of all the objections made, then and now, to the higher taxation which emerged in Scotland after 1707, the Union was not such an expensive political venture that it prevented a solution of the financial problems which lay at the root of Scotland's inability to exploit to the full the opportunities it provided; though perhaps equally important is the point contemporary Scots stressed, the financial provisions of the Union did not provide a ready-made solution.

Nevertheless the Union did help towards a solution in two ways at least. First, it gave readier access to capital in the richer south. Little moved north until political confidence was engendered by the Union, and later by the defeat of the Jacobite rebellions. Not only private English capital came to Scotland. The Scottish banks used London agents as lenders of last resort and so had to hold less extensive liquid reserves in Scotland, a privilege which in later years proved a source of much annoyance to English financial interests. Second, and more immediately, the policy of complementary development was made more effective after the Union by being officially sponsored. Whereas

enforced (P. Hume Brown, *History of Scotland* (Cambridge, 1909), vol. iii, pp. 150–1). Nevertheless the records of the Scottish Exchequer record revenue from the malt tax from 1713.

[1] Robert Wodrow, *Analecta* (ed. Maitland Club, 1842), vol. ii, p. 281.

before 1707 such official aid as was given was directed, consistently and purposely, towards competitive rivalry with England, after 1707 it was continued but directed to more complementary aims. Confirmation is found in the records of expenditure from the Scottish Exchequer from the revenue from customs and excise. A large proportion of the revenue raised was, of course, absorbed by the costs of doing so. Thereafter almost all the customs revenue was used to meet various bounties or debentures. (The only major exception began shortly after 1715 when allowances were granted to the Equivalent Company, into which the holders of various obligations which should have been met by the Equivalent, but were not, had been incorporated.) Excise revenue was used for more varied purposes. The largest single item of expenditure was for the maintenance of the courts and other civil purposes. In addition excise duties financed a steady stream of assistance for economic projects complementary to English efforts: bounties for fish and flesh exported, which, as one contemporary remarked, 'is an encouragement for exporting the product of the Country not known before the union';[1] grants to the S.P.C.K., concerned with propagating educational and economic, as well as Christian, knowledge; and, from 1727 throughout the century, a steady income, especially in some years from any surplus of the malt tax above £20,000, was given to the Board of Trustees for Fisheries and Manufactures, which was set up in 1727 to administer the funds provided by the Equivalent for economic development. The policy of the Board of Trustees provides the most conspicuous example of economic action after the Union, and was probably the Union's most beneficial, though delayed, consequence. The benefits were most clearly demonstrated in the development of the linen industry.

Before 1707 linen production was the branch of manufacturing industry most successfully prosecuted in Scotland, so successfully that its exports to England were sufficiently important for their threatened exclusion by the Alien Act of 1705 to be an effective means of exerting economic pressure on Scotland. Nevertheless, by contrast with later achievements, the linen industry had many inadequacies at the time of the Union, and their removal was its main concern throughout the eighteenth century. Possibilities of improvement appeared at all stages of production: at one end the flax, frequently a by-product of unimproved agriculture, was of poor quality; at the other end part-time efforts of spinners and weavers could not ensure a good finished product.

[1] Scottish Record Office, *Clerk of Penicuik Muniments*, 2703.

So long as the production of Scottish linen remained subsidiary to agriculture and was aimed primarily at supplying a highly localized market, frequently indeed only family needs, the limitations of inferior workmanship were less restrictive. They became so only with attempts to expand sales in wider markets, in England or overseas. Then the linen industry faced the need to reform its manufacturing processes. This problem pressed even more heavily against other less successful branches of Scottish industry in the eighteenth century, confining them in consequence to the domestic market. The linen industry was, however, the first to succeed in the task of renovation, but not for some time after 1707. There were grave difficulties in the path of improvement. It was ineffective to urge, as did the Convention of Royal Burghs, that parliament should try to enforce higher standards of production, because any such attempts were unlikely to succeed when the Union had deprived Scotland of her indigenous administration. The only body which could take any action on a national level was the Convention of Royal Burghs itself, but by then it represented only a small group of vested interests and was frequently more interested in the preservation of existing rights and privileges than in branching into new ventures. The creation of the Board of Trustees for Manufactures in 1727 provided a more efficient means of effecting improvement. Since the Board was unattached to any particular vested interests, though its members were generally the more enlightened landowners, it was more able than the Convention to venture into new areas. Its willingness to pioneer new methods rendered a contribution to the renovation of the linen industry as important as the limited financial aid it could provide. Of the £6,000 available for the Board's expenditure in its first year, £2,600 each was earmarked for the linen industry and for the herring industry and £700 for the manufacture of 'coarse tanned wool'. Precept and example became the Board's chief weapons to effect improvement.

The direct encouragement to technical improvement took various forms. First, distinguished Scottish scientists, such as Home, were encouraged to investigate the industry's problems. Second, the Board tried to introduce superior foreign skill and knowledge to Scotland in the hope that the natives would be taught better ways. Dutch bleachers and French cambric weavers were attracted to Scotland, the latter setting up their school in what has since become known as Picardy Place in Edinburgh in 1729. Third, the Board sent representatives overseas to learn secrets there, probably the most important instance being in 1728, when, in one of its earliest actions, the Board despatched a man to the Continent to study the difficult processes of scutching and heckling. From his experience he was able to invent a scutching machine which was adapted for waterpower at Bonnington Mills, Edinburgh. Technical ability was thus improved at a difficult juncture in flax preparation. Indirectly the scutching machine made an even more radical contribution to industrial change by beginning the break from the domestic, and frequently part-time, nature of the industry. After the success of Bonnington Mills similar lint mills increased throughout the country and by 1772 there were 252, stretching from Caithness to Dumfries, in which scutching was carried out by specialists. General implementation of the examples so provided was encouraged by spreading knowledge of new discoveries and by financial reward. At the Board's behest Home gave a course of lectures on the chemistry of bleaching; subsidies of 15s. an acre were granted to growers of flax willing to follow the Board's instructions on its cultivation; prizes were awarded for all sorts of special performances; more expensive processes were given special aid, as in the offer of £50 an acre to those who laid out bleachfields up to 40 acres in extent.

The success of these various efforts to improve the quality of the product was limited by the difficulty of diffusing its message of better methods. In 1743 the Board of Trustees had to come to the help of the French cambric weavers by advancing £845, arranging supplies of yarn at prime cost, and by fitting up additional looms, but in 1755 it reported that its attempts to establish the manufacture of French cambric in Edinburgh had failed. The undoubtedly fashionable nature of the spinning schools, or the high social evaluation of the ability to spin, could break the general technical incompetence only by encouraging an influx of capital and finance to the industry. More efficient means of production required more expensive methods, machines and buildings. This was one of the lessons of the Bonnington Mills. Moreover, even under the traditional methods and organization of production certain processes were skimped or neglected, not wholly by choice but because of the financial burden of implementing them properly. Bleaching was a case in point, as bleachfields absorbed considerable capital. In short, lack of adequate finance frequently limited the application of improved methods. Others could have echoed the wail of one pioneer, Alexander Mackenzie of Coul, when he found in 1751 that in his efforts to encourage spinning '£200 credit would perfectly answer and put the Business on a certain good footing'.

'I am very unwilling to drop an undertaking of such consequence to my Country and so Creditable to myself. Yet without more ready Money than I can spare my Undertaking must Languish, that is to say it must be creeping not walking.'[1]

The total funds made available to the Board were never sufficiently generous that it could make a contribution to the easing of such financial stringency. Significantly, in 1752, the year after Mackenzie of Coul's plea, the diminution in the revenue of the malt tax, any surplus of which over £20,000 went to the Board, forced a reduction of salary on many of its officers. But some of its critics queried whether even such expenditure as the Board made was always in ways that were most effective. The prizes were often simply rewards for special, but not typical, performances, which left little permanent legacy. Among the subsidies, that to the growers of flax was certainly even more misconceived, because, as one pertinent commentator put it, 'we do not want to raise flax so much as we want to raise good flax'.[2] Whatever the exact validity of these criticisms, they confirmed the financial needs of the industry if its renovation and expansion were not to be restricted. An important contribution towards the provision of more adequate credit came in 1742 with the foundation of the British Linen Company, which in due course became the British Linen Bank. At first the Company, which had a nominal capital of £100,000, did not conduct banking business but provided credit to the dispersed spinners and weavers then engaged in the industry, and Mackenzie of Coul found that the Company helped to alleviate his financial stringency by giving him credit on the flax he bought for spinning. But the Company's activities were various. To quote one observer:

'they import flax from abroad, the best lint-seed, pot and weedashes for bleaching, and sell them on credit to proper hands, then buy the yarn and linen all at reasonable prices; which linen, particularly the sort corresponding to Osnaburghs, etc., fit for America and the West Indies, they keep in large ware-houses, both here and at London, where they are sold for exportation.'[3]

[1] Scottish Record Office, *Clerk of Penicuik Muniments*, 5924. Alexander Mackenzie of Coul to Sir George Clerk, 8th November 1751.

[2] Lindsay, *op. cit.*, p. 171.

[3] M. Postlethwaite, *The Universal Dictionary of Trade and Commerce* (4th edition, London, 1774), vol. ii. Article on Scotland.

In these ways the British Linen Company performed the function which was later to be assumed by individuals whose leadership was vitally important in the growth of Scottish industry. The British Linen Company was their precursor.

The variations in the effectiveness of the Board's policy limited the extent of the industrial renovation it achieved. Certainly the Trustees recognized that their efforts were not immediately and spectacularly successful, when they asserted, a decade after their first appointment, that their method of encouraging renovation in the industry would prove to be of more lasting success only slowly. But an indication that the delay in the appearance of a large increase in output was due to factors not easily surmounted was the inability of the Scots to break German and Austrian competition in the plantations, which, with their important contingent of Scots-born residents, were potentially the most favourable markets for Scottish linen products. Such competition was possible because in the early eighteenth century German and Austrian cloth, when re-exported through London by British merchants, was allowed a drawback on most of the import duty which had been paid on it. To the Scots this was a scandal and throughout the 1730's petitions for help poured into parliament from Scotland. Eventually in 1742 the Bounty Act subsidized exports, and provided a stimulus to increased output. Its contribution was confirmed on the cessation of the bounty in 1754, when the Board of Trustees recorded a drop in the linen produced—'by much the greatest alteration for the worse that has happened at any period since his Majesty was graciously pleased to take the Linen Manufacture under his Royal Care'.[1]

Though the industry was, therefore, still vulnerable, especially to competition from other producers, its lack of security compared unfavourably only with the secure international standing Scottish industry acquired in the late eighteenth century. Compared with the failures of earlier years, improvements were steady, especially after the 1740's, when the major increases in output began. In 1728 output was 2,200,000 yards; in 1742, the year of the Bounty Act, it was 4,500,000 yards; in 1750, 7,575,000 yards; in 1760, 11,750,000 yards; in 1770, 13,000,000 yards. In addition an unrecorded quantity was produced for domestic consumption. The only flaw was that the greatest physical increase in output was in coarse cloths, produced chiefly in the east of Scotland, which retained leadership in the manufacture of the coarser fabrics,

[1] Scottish Record Office, Records of the Board of Trustees, *State of the Annual Progress of the Linen Manufacture, 1727 to 1754*, p. 135.

until the industry gave way, except in Dunfermline, to concentration on more specialized lines: to jute in Dundee and to linoleum in Kirkcaldy. The more valuable branch, producing fine-quality goods, was in the west, where, though in some years, notably in 1742, the Board of Trustees recorded improvement, expansion was less marked until the mid-eighteenth century. Then the west of Scotland, above all Paisley, began to make a reputation in the manufacture of fine linen fabrics, represented most strikingly by the introduction of the manufacture of silk gauze to Paisley in 1759. Though this interest was but temporary, the Paisley weavers quickly rivalled those of Spitalfields, whose products they displaced even in foreign markets. A more permanent specialization came from attempts to imitate French lawns and cambrics, but doing so required imports of French and Flemish yarns because of two continuing defects in the Scottish linen industry. First, though scutching and heckling became specialized processes in the various lint mills and heckleries which appeared in the later eighteenth century, and though many of the mills were engaged in processing flax which was imported from Europe, the dressed flax remained of an inferior quality. Second, the increased supply of dressed flax was often spun incompetently, so that the yarn was inferior, and was also inadequate for rapid expansion of weaving. Though weaving became a man's job and a full-time occupation, spinning remained the concern of women and still a part-time activity, interspersed with others, both domestic and agricultural. Though imports of flax and yarn helped to offset the restrictions of an inadequate supply of flax and of inferior spinning, the greatest success of the achievements in weaving in the west of Scotland came only when the technological changes in textile production later in the eighteenth century removed them. With these changes came the successful establishment of the cotton industry in the west of Scotland.[1]

The iron industry

The textile industries eventually provided the basis of Scottish economic success later in the eighteenth century, whereas the iron industry became a staple industry only in the nineteenth century. But even while its numerical significance, measured by employment or output, remained slight, the iron industry was the scene of moves, sometimes

[1] See Chapter 6.

abortive, towards more modern ways. In one respect the environment of the iron industry in the eighteenth century favoured such experiments. The modernization of the linen industry was restricted by the domestic environment in which it had first become Scotland's staple: not so the foundation of the modern iron industry. But the renovation of both was limited basically by its expensive nature.

Though the foundation of the modern iron industry in Scotland is frequently identified with the foundation of the Carron ironworks in 1759, iron was manufactured in Scotland before then. For long it had been smelted in primitive conditions, but the first modern blast furnace in Scotland was at Invergarry. The works there, founded in 1727 and first in operation in 1729, could more properly be regarded as an off-shoot or outpost of the iron industry of England than as truly indigenous to Scotland. They were founded, and directly controlled, by a Lancashire concern, the Backbarrow Company, which was attracted to the west of Scotland because of the difficulties in which the English iron industry found itself as supplies of timber suitable for making charcoal, then required to smelt the iron, became increasingly limited in the iron-producing areas, if not throughout the country. Smelting and refining were forced to go to the timber necessary for charcoal. That was the only reason which led to the foundation of the Invergarry works, and it was one which proved fully advantageous. At Back-barrow the cost of charcoal in the production of one ton of pig iron was 50s. 3d.; at Invergarry it was 28s. 9d. Practically all other considerations warranted a different location. The ore, brought from Lancashire to Corpach, mainly by vessels going on to the Baltic, was then taken along a road constructed by the Company to Loch Lochy, at the north end of which it again traversed a new road to the furnace. The result was that the cost of the ore offset the savings on the charcoal. At Backbarrow it was 27s. 10d. per ton of iron produced; at Invergarry it was 54s. 6d. Desperately, but unsuccessfully, the Company looked for local resources, not only on the mainland but in Islay and Jura. Other costs tended to be higher in Scotland too. Skilled labour had to be imported from England and charcoal burners from Ireland, while the local labour did not always prove suitable even for unskilled tasks. Finally, the pig iron was not consumed locally but was sent south. Some went to Lancashire to be used in the forge at Furness, some to Scarborough, but most went to Bristol. Yet in spite of the additional costs, the quality of the Scottish iron was so inferior that, while Furness iron sold at £8 a ton, it sold at only £5 10s. a ton. In these circumstances it is not surprising that the life of the Invergarry works was unsuccessful and short. It came to an end in 1736.

The background to two other concerns was exactly comparable. The Bonawe or Taynuilt furnace, built in 1753, was first in the hands of Richard Ford and Company and later belonged to Harrison, Ainslie and Company, both Lancashire concerns. Another Lancashire concern, the Duddon Company, or Jonathan Kendall and Company, built a furnace at Inverleckan, later renamed Furnace, on Loch Fyneside in 1775. The latter furnace remained in blast until towards the end of the Napoleonic Wars but the Bonawe furnace was more successful. It came to an end only in 1874. As at Invergarry both works imported their ore, sent most of their pig iron to the parent concern in England, and both suffered from similar problems. In particular, the reduction in charcoal costs which they experienced was counterbalanced by an increase in the cost of ore. At Richard Ford and Company's English works charcoal and ore costs were respectively 66 per cent and 12 per cent of total costs of production of iron; at Bonawe they were 33 per cent and 30 per cent respectively. The problem of such early ironworks was, therefore, clearly one of trying to reduce costs of production. The most probable way of doing so seemed to be the utilization of native ores. An early but unsuccessful attempt to do so was made at the York Buildings Company's ironworks at Abernethy. It started operations about 1730, used ore brought by pack-horse from Tomintoul about twenty miles away, but lasted only for about ten years. The successful exploitation of Scottish natural resources was first pioneered only at the Carron ironworks.

Carron Company differed from the other concerns in size and in the technical processes adopted. When it was founded, the existing ironworks in Scotland were only small charcoal-burning ventures. But an early memorandum detailing the projected size of the Carron works listed four blast furnaces, plus ancillary equipment, a forge of three fineries and hammers, a boring mill, a slit mill and at least four air furnaces. A works of this magnitude was constructed at the outset and it quickly earned the reputation of being the chief foundry in Europe. In production methods too Carron Company was revolutionary, not only in succeeding, where the Abernethy works had failed, in the use of native ore, but in its decision to be the first concern in Scotland to smelt with coke, a process first used successfully fifty years earlier but not widely adopted. Carron Company thus became the first firm to take full advantage of the Scottish coal measures.

F

Unlike the earlier ironworks Carron Company was dependent, therefore, on the natural resources which later provided the basis for the success of Scottish iron production, but initially it was plagued with difficulties both technological and financial. So long as the Company confined itself to the casting of simpler goods, pots, girdles, axle bushes and so on, it was successful. Tributes to the usefulness of these soon came from customers overseas as well as from those at home. The difficulties began with more advanced work, notably with ordnance, the Company's most famous product. Skilled gunfounders were introduced from Sussex and in 1761 the first gun was cast, from a pattern taken at Edinburgh Castle. Then in 1764, by a sharp and risky price cut, the Company obtained orders from the Board of Ordnance against opposition from the usual suppliers, chiefly in Sussex. Success was fleeting. In 1771 the Board of Ordnance objected that the number of Carron guns bursting was excessive, and, in spite of a worried search for remedies (and excuses), the unfavourable trend continued. After two proofs at Woolwich in May 1773, when 36 of 133 Carron guns failed to pass, the Company was peremptorily ordered to cease casting guns for the Board, the removal of Carron guns from all naval ships was ordered, and the Board's original suppliers, whom Carron Company had supplanted with its sharp price cut, stepped once more into their previous position.

The basic fault was that Carron Company could not guarantee absolute precision, a fault of increasing consequence in the new industry. So in the new industrial structure, of which Carron Company so obviously was trying to be a part, the Company was at a severe disadvantage. Its cylinders could not compete against those from Coalbrookdale when used for the older type of engine; they could not provide James Watt, as he found to his cost, with sufficiently precise work for his early experiments with the steam-engine, and later, when he and Matthew Boulton found that John Wilkinson could give them the precision they wanted, Boulton always refused to allow Carron Company to bore any cylinders, not even for the Company's own steam-engine. The technical problems were not insurmountable, but their removal involved additional cost. In particular, as at other early ironworks, skilled labour and some of the constructional materials had to be brought from the south. The builders of the furnaces, the skilled men to operate furnace and forge, colliers, nailmakers, and others, were brought from England. Again, in common with the experience of other works, Carron products were not immediately superior to those of rivals in the south, so the prices that could be obtained for them were no higher either. Consequently profits proved elusive and the technical difficulties were frequently outweighed by the financial. The original contract of co-partnery provided for a capital stock of £12,000 with provision for its increase to £24,000, an amount soon shown to be inadequate. Ten years after the foundation over £150,000 had been spent on the works, so much more than the partners had envisaged that two of the three founders became bankrupt, and the other had to surrender other important interests to support Carron Company. Assistance was gratefully taken from any source. Like so many concerns in late eighteenth-century Scotland the Company was on a precarious financial footing, so that any interruption to the flow of funds was liable to arrest its growth.

In the nineteenth century other concerns were as successful as Carron Company became after the introduction of its famous product, the carronade, in 1778, but for a time it remained unique. Since Carron Company consumed its own pig iron in foundry and forge, and since the west coast furnaces sent most of their produce south, the growth of production of pig iron in Scotland provided little stimulus to the foundation of either foundries or malleable ironworks to process iron further. Imported bar iron from Sweden and Russia was used in the two most extensive malleable ironworks, Smithfield and Dalnotter, in and near Glasgow, and even Carron Company imported for use in its forge and in its slitting-mill at Cramond. Since there was no immediate growth of dependent or rival concerns, Carron Company remained the outstanding economic enterprise in Scotland for some time, but its experiences were not unusual. Until the 1780's most Scottish industry was still striving towards the success and security it later achieved. Even official help, as in the linen industry, or dynamic entrepreneurship, as in the case of Carron Company, was inadequate to ensure security. The industrial renovation that was required was known by some, the difficulty was in persuading others that it was absolutely necessary. The problem was not simply one of propaganda. Even those who were convinced of the need often found the financial implications of such renovation onerous. Scotland's traditional poverty exerted its influence strongly once more.

Banking and finance

The collapse of many early attempts at industrial development through the inadequacy of financial provision highlights the importance of any efforts made to provide more adequate credit in the early eighteenth century. Virtually all eighteenth-century commentators accepted the fact of the poverty of Scotland, and it is an appreciation of this problem, even if not an acceptance of its overriding importance, which has led many subsequent commentators to stress the prominence of Scottish banking and the form of its development at this time.

The foundation of the Bank of Scotland in 1695 marked the beginnings of the framework of Scottish banking. The Bank was given a monopoly of Scottish banking for twenty-one years but it was broken in 1727 with the foundation of the Royal Bank of Scotland. The Royal Bank's origins were peculiar. Among the many claims which the Equivalent was to meet were the payment of the Scottish national debt, deferred pay and pensions. Since most of the Equivalent was used for other purposes, debentures were issued to these creditors, but, in spite of prolonged efforts by their holders, the debentures were not repaid. In due course, as many of the debentures were eventually sold to English speculators, the holders found difficulty in collecting the interest, as it was payable in Edinburgh, and so formed themselves into the Society of the Subscribed Equivalent Debt, the chief object of which was to purchase Equivalent debentures, receive the interest in one sum, and divide it among its members. A similar society for Scotland was founded in Edinburgh shortly afterwards. After spreading their activities to making loans to members and others on the security of debentures and other stocks, and to speculating in lottery tickets, the Societies tried to obtain full banking powers, but were effectively baulked in England by the opposition of the Bank of England, while in Scotland the Bank of Scotland looked with disfavour on a proposed amalgamation with them. Then in 1724 the holders of Equivalent debentures were incorporated as the Equivalent Company, the Society of the Subscribed Equivalent Debt subscribing its holding, as did others, with the exception of those holding debentures to the value of £1,474, which remained unclaimed for ever. The possibility of conducting banking operations in Scotland was soon raised, but the directors, in doubt whether they were formed as an English or a

Scottish corporation, were uncertain of their powers. Though convinced that banking business was certainly prohibited only in England, they made their position sure in 1727 by obtaining a separate charter, carefully vetted by the law officers, and granted under the Great Seal of Scotland, permitting members of the Equivalent Company to subscribe their stock to the Royal Bank of Scotland. One of the first deposits was the payment by the government of the £20,000 which was to provide the income for the encouragement of industry and fishing by the Board of Trustees. It is fruitless to speculate on whether or not the Jacobite proclivities of the Bank of Scotland facilitated the granting of this charter to the Royal Bank and so the break in the Old Bank's monopoly, but the New Bank's foundation did lead the structure of Scottish banking to develop in a way that contrasted sharply with England, where the Bank of England long and actively maintained its exclusive privileges. No breach of principle was involved, therefore, when the British Linen Company, incorporated in 1746 'to do everything that may conduce to the promoting and carrying on of the linen manufacture', spread its activities to banking.

In contrast to the structure of English banking, dominated by the Bank of England at the top and with a host of smaller private banks beneath, the structure of Scottish banking consisted in due course of a few large joint-stock banks with branches. Two leading advantages could be claimed for the Scottish structure. First, the greater resources of the larger Scottish banks, especially their investment by branch banking over a wider area, gave the entire network a much greater degree of stability than was the case in England, where the resources of the private banks were usually limited and also highly localized. Second, from the foundation of the Royal Bank, the highly competitive relationship between the senior banks, though with its discreditable episodes, augured well for many future Scottish borrowers, especially when a variety of means of aiding the borrowers, notably cash credits, were extensively used in Scotland. To some extent the two advantages claimed, stability of the banking structure and easy lending facilities, contradicted each other, and the constant struggle of the banks to maintain a balance between them quickly led to the criticism that the established banks followed insufficiently liberal lending policies. Sometimes it was alleged that the lending was insufficient in total, sometimes that it was inadequate in direction, sometimes that it was inadequate in certain geographical areas. Such criticism must be stressed because, paradoxically, it was directed against the policy which ensured the stability of Scottish banking and so against the policy which has been frequently claimed to be one of the country's most commendable features. Stability of the banking structure prevented the worst cumulative effects of financial collapse, which were more common in England. But stability is more obviously beneficial in the long run, and especially in retrospect.

The two possibly contradictory policies, stability of banking structure and easy lending facilities, could not easily be reconciled, but it is not certain that the quest for stability was necessarily the more desirable policy for the time, because it lessened the provision of risk capital, which, in a country such as Scotland then was, could arrest economic growth. Scotland desperately required supplies of such capital for her new industrial undertakings. Care must therefore be exercised in discussing the contribution of the banks and the criticism made of it. The banks' own argument, that their greatest contribution lay in ensuring financial stability, forgets two important points. First, financial collapse was not completely avoided in Scotland, though it may be suggested that it would have been if the policies advocated by the chartered and private banks had been followed whenever any difference of opinion arose. Second, and probably of greater relevance, stability was much less necessary in Scotland then than now. The basic defect in any commendation of the policy of the established banks is that it judges the merits of the two possible strands of banking policy from a modern standpoint. Financial collapses were less important in arresting industrial growth in eighteenth-century Scotland than the country's desperate need for capital, especially for capital willing to run great risks. The consequences of even the most dramatic of the century, that of 1772, were confined mainly to the commercial and banking world of Edinburgh. It had little impact on Glasgow and the city's growing commerce continued virtually without interruption. If a commercial panic did not have widespread adverse repercussions, it was not so with the need for capital. In sum, it must not be assumed that the stability of the banking structure was the greatest contribution the Scottish banks could make to the country's economic growth, if stability could be achieved only by following more conservative lending policies than were necessary for the country to fulfil the industrial and commercial opportunities then appearing. This was the nub of the criticism against the policy of the established banks.

The criticism was perhaps most valid over the geographical inadequacy of Scottish banking, especially the failure to provide adequate facilities in Glasgow. The first country bank in Scotland was the Banking Company of Aberdeen, founded in 1749, but more important were the beginnings of banking in Glasgow. In 1750 Dunlop, Houston and Company, known as the Ship Bank, was started and helped by credits from the Bank of Scotland. Also in 1750 the Royal Bank encouraged the foundation of Cochran, Murdoch and Company, known as the Glasgow Arms Bank. The Edinburgh banks encouraged these ventures to forge connections with the Glasgow merchants, who were the leading projectors of the banks, but the merchants' policies soon became too independent, and there appeared a divergence of policy, which was to reappear frequently as a dispute between Glasgow and Edinburgh. Independence of policy could not be tolerated, whether in Glasgow or in Aberdeen. In Aberdeen an agent had been employed by the Edinburgh banks to try to collect the notes of the Aberdeen Banking Company and by presenting them at the bank's office embarrass it through its lack of coin. In 1753 the Aberdeen Bank succumbed to the pressure. Similar action was adopted in Glasgow later in the 1750's, but in this case the withdrawal of the credits granted by the Bank of Scotland and the Royal Bank a few years earlier failed to lead to a stoppage of business. The resources of the Glasgow banks were greater and both survived: the Ship Bank until it amalgamated with the Glasgow Banking Company in 1837 as the Glasgow and Ship Bank, becoming part of the Glasgow Union Bank a year later, and the Arms Bank until its failure in 1793.

The inadequacy of the geographical spread of banking facilities was lessened by the growth of branch banking, which, though one of the more important features of Scottish banking, was not extensive until the later eighteenth and early nineteenth centuries. The Bank of Scotland was quickly, though only temporarily, in this field. In 1696 it had branches at Glasgow, Aberdeen, Dundee and Montrose, but they lasted for only a year. In 1731 the attempt was repeated though not at Montrose, and the branches lasted for two years. In 1774 a third and successful attempt was made by the Bank of Scotland at Dumfries and Kelso, a year later at Ayr, then at Kilmarnock, Inverness, Aberdeen and Stirling, though only in 1804 at Glasgow. The Royal Bank opened a Glasgow branch, with David Dale as its agent, in 1783, but actively promoted branch banking only after the failure of the Western Bank of Scotland in 1857, when it took over many of its agents and branches. The peculiar origin and organization of the British Linen Bank enabled it to convert some of its agencies to branches. But the British Linen

Company only gradually became a bank. In 1750 it began issuing notes, but even in 1765, when the British Linen Company finally withdrew from commercial operations, its banking business was more akin to that of the private bankers. Yet even taken together these efforts added up to very little. Until after the Napoleonic Wars branch banking remained unimportant, and so the extension of banking facilities in the middle eighteenth century, when it was so greatly needed, was not provided on a large scale by the older chartered banks. It was left to the Commercial Bank of Scotland to pioneer extensive branch banking among its many other revolutionary ideas in the decade from 1815 to 1825, though its activities were then matched by those of the British Linen Bank. Hence this particular aspect of Scottish banking was chiefly a phenomenon of the nineteenth century and was particularly the work of some of the critics of the existing structure. The Commercial Bank pioneered the new conception of national instead of local banking and that is the key to any successful prosecution of branch banking. Only later did others follow its lead.

The criticism of the failure of the banks to spread geographically, or the inadequacy of branch banking, is best regarded as an example of the more fundamental criticism that the banks were insufficiently liberal in their lending policies. One certain fact in the economic life of Scotland was the existence of an unsatisfied demand for credit. Since credit was usually granted by discounting bills of exchange rather than by advances, commercial interests could more easily obtain legitimate accommodation than industrial interests. A possible solution for those thus thwarted in their search for credit was to issue accommodation bills, that is bills which purported to represent some transaction in trade, but which were completely fictitious and passed between two people who had agreed to operate the system. It is easy to argue that the system was reprehensible, because it often simply represented an attempt to bolster faltering credit and was frequently started under unwarranted expectations of future profits. One difficulty was that not all banks were willing to discount the bills, certainly not those banks whose conservative lending policies were partly responsible for the more widespread adoption of the system. Such was the background which produced the Ayr Bank (Douglas, Heron and Company), the history of which epitomized the criticism against the established and conservative order. To quote Smith,

'in the midst of this clamour and distress, a new bank was established in Scotland for the express purpose of relieving the distress of the country. The design was generous; but the execution was imprudent, and the nature and causes of the distress which it meant to relieve were not, perhaps, well understood. This bank was more liberal than any other had ever been, both in granting cash accounts, and in discounting bills of exchange. With regard to the latter, it seems to have made scarce any distinction between real and circulating bills, but to have discounted all equally.'[1]

The Ayr Bank was thus engaged in a system which had a cumulative effect on speculation. Yet its wealthy shareholders—among the first rank of the landed proprietors of the south-west of Scotland—assured those who held its notes and the bills it discounted that they could rely on obligations being met, and so the bank was able to expand its activities exceptionally. It stimulated the already speculative conditions of the period.

The Ayr Bank tried to meet the need for discounting facilities, an effort which was allied to the frequent and generous issue of paper money as another way of meeting the need for credit, and one in which the possibilities were so fully exploited that it was the only aspect of Scottish banking subjected to legislative enactment before 1844. A common criticism, from Smith and many others, was the simple one that the note issue was excessive. Two factors aggravated the situation. The first was the tendency to issue notes for very small denominations, a practice frequently adopted by firms to pay their employees, and one encouraged by scarcity of coin in the country. The issue of small notes in itself was not a pernicious practice; it became so only if they could not be honoured. That was the basis of Sir Walter Scott's famous defence of the Scottish note. At this point the second aggravating factor became relevant. A means of enabling banks, or any person who issued notes, to avoid the disastrous effects of over-issue was to insert what was known as the 'optional clause', first adopted by the Bank of Scotland in 1730. The 'optional clause' provided for the payment of a banknote either on demand or, at the option of the issuer, after a period, usually of six months, and so enabled a bank to stave off any exceptional, and sometimes irrational, pressure, as well as providing a long-term precaution against the drain of bullion to England which at times followed deficits on Scotland's balance of payments. But, in spite of such justifications, the system was open to abuse, especially

[1] Smith, *op. cit.*, vol. i, pp. 296–7.

when adopted by the less reputable institutions, which were issuing notes, particularly of small denominations, by the third quarter of the eighteenth century. The problem became pressing in the early 1760's, when the withdrawal of funds to England forced a deflationary policy on the Scottish banks and led many borrowers, deprived of their assistance, to accept more risky ways of raising capital, such as drawing bills or issuing notes. The Bank of Scotland and the Royal Bank, therefore, encouraged the passing of an Act prohibiting the 'optional clause' from 1766 and the issue of notes of less than £1 from 1765. Thereafter those seeking easy credit in Scotland had to rely still more on the drawing and redrawing of bills and so the practice increased in the late 1760's, culminating in the activities of the Ayr Bank from 1769 to 1772.

In one respect contemporary academic commentators on the struggle for financial supremacy made an accurate diagnosis. In 1752 David Hume pointed out that in a country where poverty made the issue of paper money attractive, then, in modern terms, there was a likelihood of over-issue and so of an inflationary tendency, which could lead to a deficit on the balance of payments. On this count Hume doubted some of the supposed advantages of the Scottish banking system. This fear of Hume's Adam Smith came to appreciate, but not at once. In his lectures, probably delivered in the session 1761 to 1762, just as Scotland was moving towards a balance-of-payments crisis, Smith was much less alarmed about the inflationary consequences of a large increase in the circulation than he was later in the *Wealth of Nations*, by the time of the publication of which Scotland had experienced two important financial crises, after the second of which, that of 1772, Hume wrote pointedly to Smith asking if it did not lead him to revise his theories. Both these crises stressed the insecure financial basis of so much of the country's industrial growth. The first was in 1762. Towards the end of the previous year funds had been withdrawn from Scotland for speculation in government securities. Partly these were English funds (one contemporary estimate was that Englishmen had invested about £500,000 in Scotland at that time); but they were also partly Scottish. At this time an important firm of private bankers in Edinburgh, the Fairholmes, became heavily involved in speculation in London and its partners afterwards became bankrupt. In consequence the exchange moved against Scotland, so that by the end of 1761 some of the Scottish banks were experiencing difficulty in maintaining an adequate cash reserve. Restriction of credit was the only solution to some, while

others adopted the 'optional clause' on their notes. The banks weathered
their immediate difficulties, but the fundamental danger of the inflationary pressure led to a continuation of the chronic scarcity of bullion
to 1765. The problem remained and was greater in 1772 when the downfall of the Ayr Bank precipitated the collapse of a number of concerns
connected with it directly or indirectly. The details of the career of the
Ayr Bank are of less importance than its collapse in 1772. The whole
superstructure of credit began to crash with the failure of the London
banking house of Neale, James, Fordyce and Downe and at once
spread to others, including the London correspondent of the Ayr Bank.
The failure of Fordyce, a successful Aberdonian, precipitated a run on
the Ayr Bank, which was quickly forced to suspend payment. Attempts
to save the bank proved fruitless even though some of the leading
landed proprietors who had been its supporters, notably the Dukes of
Buccleuch and Queensberry, announced their continued backing, and
on its behalf approached the Bank of England for further help. Since
the Bank of England held £150,000 of the Ayr Bank's notes, it is not
surprising that the appeal was unsuccessful. The Ayr Bank was never
again in business, though it eventually paid its debts in full, with great
strain on some of those who had to do so. The Ayr Bank was not alone
in its failure. The three chartered institutions, the Bank of Scotland, the
Royal Bank and the British Linen Bank, all survived, but the ranks of
the private banks of Edinburgh were grievously thinned. Only Sir
W. Forbes, J. Hunter and Company, Mansfield, Hunter and Company,
and William Cuming and Sons survived. But, though many suffered
in 1772, others, notably in Glasgow, survived. Hence some have judged
that the crisis of 1793 was more disastrous for the Scottish economy
than was that of 1772. The importance of the crisis of 1772 lay especially
in its impact on financial practices. To some it provided confirmation
of the wisdom of the older banks' pleas for stable policies; to others it
gave confirmation of these banks' failure to provide for expansion.
Whatever the more valid interpretation the structure and policy of
Scottish banking were altered after 1772.

Part Two

ECONOMIC SUCCESS
1780's-1870's

V
TRADE AND TRANSPORT
The changing contribution of trade

THE collapse of the tobacco trade in 1776 provided an opportunity for a fresh start to be made with the capital and ability previously engaged in it. Since most merchants rejected openings then appearing in indigenous economic enterprises, they had to try to re-establish their American connections or exploit still further the West Indian trade in which they had already gained some experience. So long as the war lasted, the latter was the only practical possibility, but the North American connection was not easily supplanted. In the two years from the end of the war in 1783 total imports from the United States increased by over 200 per cent and exports by over 50 per cent. By contrast, during the same period, though imports from the West Indies were rising, exports were falling. The difference stemmed from preferences for American goods and from the struggle of the Glasgow merchants to re-establish trade with the one-time colonists. The latter was not simply a manifestation of conservatism, but an attempt to regain the more profitable venture. After their initial rivalry with others, the Scots obtained a virtual monopoly of the American trade; that with the West Indies became the preserve of Bristol and Liverpool merchants. At any time it could be entered, therefore, only in the face of keen competition, but the Glasgow merchants' attempts to do so coincided with the more risky and speculative years of the beginning of the French Wars. Though the West Indian trade was profitable for the successful, success was not easily gained. But the restrictions on the establishment of an extensive trade with the West Indies proved only temporary. Before the war more than four times as many ships entered Port Glasgow and Greenock from North America as from the West Indies. By 1790 the number from each region was similar and Scottish trade with the West Indies was more important than trade with America.

The change in the direction of Scottish foreign trade in the late eighteenth century was of more than geographical significance. Previously colonial commerce was mainly an entrepot trade, which contributed more to an increase in the influence of Scots throughout the world than to the growth of the Scottish economy, especially the growth of Scottish industry. After the American War the balance began to change. Even the West Indian trade differed significantly from that with America, because, while about one-third of the value of total exports to North America before 1776 were re-exports, chiefly linen goods, re-exports to the West Indies were much less important. Scottish products, such as plain linen, haberdashery and fish, the last of which in 1777–8 accounted for over 20 per cent of total exports and re-exports to the West Indies, provided the basis of that trade. This link between foreign trade and domestic production grew to become the basis for much subsequent industrial expansion,[1] but the relationship whereby the influence of the merchant on the country's internal economic development was slight and much less direct was not eliminated. Though many Scots opened the international markets which led to an extension of trade in the nineteenth century, their activities gave few unique advantages to the Scottish economy. Sometimes there were early benefits, when the exploitation of overseas markets was reflected into a demand for goods at home, as with the pioneering of trade in the east by Kirkman Finlay, or with the trading concerns of William Graham and Company, which sprang from the Lancefield Spinning Company, but in both cases that aspect was eventually dwarfed by wholly external enterprises. In other cases Scottish enterprise overseas did not make even this unique, though marginal, contribution to the growth of the Scottish economy. So it was with the renowned firm of Jardine, Matheson and Company,

[1] See below, p. 82–3.

founded by Scotsmen to pioneer British trade with China and the Far
East, and with the succession of Scottish missionaries and traders who
followed David Livingstone throughout Africa.

Such Scottish enterprise overseas widened during the nineteenth
century, when Scottish financial and shipping interests were added to
the longer-established trading ventures. In the provision of finance
Dundee played a significant part, especially in 1873 when one of the
town's merchants, Robert Fleming, formed the Scottish American
Trust Company, the first, popular investment trust, but capital from
all parts of Scotland contributed to the exploitation of real estate in
both America and Australasia. The Illinois and the Galena Investment
Companies, two early American estate companies, both dating from
the 1840's, were domiciled in Aberdeen, and one contemporary estimate suggested that in the late 1870's and 1880's three-quarters of the
foreign investment in ranching in America came from Scotland. The
Scottish Australian Company, founded, once again in Aberdeen, in
1840, engaged in mortgage business in New South Wales; the Scottish
and New Zealand Company was floated in 1877 to develop Southland;
when the City of Glasgow Bank collapsed in 1878 it had large property
interests in Australia and New Zealand. In the short run such overseas
investment frequently helped to ensure expenditure on Scottish products, especially when it was accompanied by emigrant Scots who had
a loyalty to their country's manufacturers, though in the long run not
all proved beneficial, as when the Bengal jute manufacture, encouraged
by Dundee interests in the 1850's, later proved a major rival. The
expansion of shipping services from Scotland gave more direct assistance to Scottish industry, especially in stimulating the demand for the
increasing tonnage launched from Scottish yards in the later nineteenth
century, but in this case too the effect was frequently limited to the
provision of opportunities for Scotsmen rather than opportunities for
Scottish economic growth. The Peninsular and Oriental Company
was formed by a Scot, who was followed as chairman by a series of
others. The Cunard Company was floated in Glasgow, though Scotland's contribution to its operation was soon confined to building its
ships. Even the many shipping concerns which had their headquarters
in Glasgow until after 1918 had their prime effect on overseas rather
than on home development. The experience of the old Glasgow shipping concern of P. Henderson and Company was typical. Some of its
efforts were unsuccessful, as in attempts to enter the Australian trade
in the 1850's or the river trade of the Plate in the 1880's, but the

failures were more than offset by three notable successes: in the trade to New Zealand, carried out by the Albion line from 1864 until its amalgamation with its old rival, the Shaw Savill, in 1882; in the service to Burma by the British and Burmah Steam Navigation Company and the Burmah Steam Ship Company, and, finally, the river trade on the Irrawaddy by the Irrawaddy Flotilla Company.

In such a diversity of ways Scottish trade, finance and shipping increased Scottish economic influence throughout the world. They provided opportunities for emigration, not for the massive movements which were also characteristic of the nineteenth century, but for movements of key personnel, many of whom never settled abroad, but returned ultimately to Scotland. Nevertheless many of the ventures with which they were associated had only a marginal influence on Scotland's economic evolution, similar to that of much of Scottish trade in the eighteenth century. But in the late eighteenth and in the nineteenth centuries this aspect of Scottish foreign trade was increasingly overshadowed by its importance in ensuring adequate sales of Scottish products overseas. The change was linked to the rise of the textile industries, above all of cotton manufacture. Until the growth of the coal and iron industries gained momentum in the later 1830's, textile goods were an overwhelming part of Scottish exports.[1] The proportion of the output of the heavy industries which was exported was never so high, but throughout the middle decades of the nineteenth century more than half the production of pig iron left Scotland.[2] Imports rose to match the growth in exports. The West Indian trade expanded on the basis of Scotland's need for imports of raw cotton, which rose rapidly to about 2,750,000 lbs. by 1790. The need of the cotton industry for a non-indigenous raw material is obvious. The jute industry had similar requirements. Until the 1840's the raw material was imported through London or Liverpool, but by the 1860's the imports of jute to Dundee were about 65,000 tons annually. Finally, the continuing inadequacy of home supplies of flax forced the less important linen industry to rely on overseas supplies too. On the other hand the natural resources of coal and ironstone were so abundant that Scottish supplies were adequate until the rise of the special demand for hematite ores in the later 1870's for steel-making. But with the increasing variety of Scottish production numerous other commodities had to be imported: Swedish pulp, esparto grass, and rags for paper mills; South American guano and nitrates, mineral phosphates from America

[1] See Chapter 7.   [2] See Chapter 8.

for agricultural fertilizers; Cuban and West Indian sugar for the refineries.

The growth of trade was facilitated by the appearance of more efficient trading agencies and services. Of most direct importance were the increasing port facilities, notably on the Clyde. The success of steam navigation removed the obstacle that the possibility of adverse winds had placed in the way of Glasgow becoming a leading port and in 1840 an Act authorized a scheme for a three-hundred-foot channel with a minimum depth of twenty feet. When the channel reached solid rock in 1854 further progress was delayed until 1869, when, through the expensive expedient of under-water blasting, a channel of fourteen-foot depth was obtained. In consequence the plan authorized in 1840 was realized only in 1886. At the same time demands for more berthage called for increased expenditure as, increasingly, Glasgow began to attract trade away from Port Glasgow and Greenock, where the construction of the James Watt Dock and the Great Harbour in the 1880's and 1890's represented a fruitless attempt to retain trade. Though a wet dock was authorized at Glasgow in 1840, it proved easier to construct temporary timber, and later masonry, wharves downstream; and so by the 1870's the wharves extended to the Kelvin on the north and to Govan on the south, with only Kingston Dock, opened in 1867, providing some relief. The wharves then so encroached on the ship-yards that many of the latter moved to new sites, thus paving the way for further development in the harbour. In 1870 an Act authorized the construction of Queen's Dock and ushered in the period of most active construction of harbour facilities on the Clyde in the last quarter of the nineteenth century.

The improvements on the Clyde, continued throughout the nineteenth century, were accompanied by the commercial fraternity in Glasgow, the achievement of a more formal organization of which included most of the rising traders of Scotland. This not only bore witness to the increasing social and economic importance of the group but also provided a more representative and effective body for deliberation on economic policy than the Convention of Royal Burghs. The West Indian interests were formally organized even before their rise to prominence after 1776, and Glasgow merchants had always gathered as a group for discussion on common problems, as when they met to consider proposals for trade with Ireland in 1778; hence it was an easy step to meet the growing importance of the merchants in Glasgow and of the need for consultation by founding the city's

Chamber of Commerce in 1783. Though the Chamber quickly became as concerned with the problems of manufacturers as with those of merchants, its interests, as reflected in the surviving minutes, bear witness to the influence of the latter, especially of the West Indian interest, in its counsels. Their domination continued throughout most of the nineteenth century, understandably so as long as the cotton industry, with its reliance on foreign trade for both the supply of its raw materials and the sale of its products, was the leading industry in the west of Scotland, but less so with the growth of the heavy industries. Yet any such distinction cannot be pressed too far because the heavy industries relied on exports of pig iron and these in turn were facilitated by a new race of merchants who specialized in dealings in iron on the Glasgow Pig Iron Market, the prices on which were accepted as the standard prices for pig iron throughout the world.

In these ways the commercial fraternity helped to increase the demand for the products of Scottish industry and the supply of raw materials required to meet it. Their prosperity, and that of Scottish manufacturers, became closely interwoven in the nineteenth century. Until the 1780's Scotland's external trade and internal economic development frequently made independent progress, but not afterwards, as the full potential of world-wide markets, which the Union of 1707 had first opened, was fully realized. An economic community, more closely knit than in the past, appeared. It was strengthened still further by the financial contribution of the merchants towards industrial growth in the nineteenth century, as they continued their earlier support to Scottish banks and, through co-operation with the banks, they helped indirectly to finance the manufacturers. The merchant to whom the manufacturer consigned his goods generally issued a bill against them. With the growth of trade and of discount facilities in the late eighteenth century the number of such bills increased, especially in the West Indian trade, and banks, as well as many business houses, became accustomed to holding a considerable quantity of West Indian paper. The system was, however, double-edged. The Scottish manufacturers used it as a means of obtaining credit, but much of the West Indian paper then circulating in London and Edinburgh had been drawn to finance the rapid exploitation of West Indian islands, and so was subject to many speculative influences. Earlier the separate growth and development of the manufacturing and merchanting sectors of the Scottish economy meant that any such speculation in one section (and it was always most notable in foreign trade) could continue in isolation, without any drastic impact on the entire Scottish economy. So it had been in 1776, and, though in reverse, in 1772. It was so no longer. That was the debit side of the closer alliance of the different sectors of the economy.

The greater integration of the economy, resulting from Scotland being drawn increasingly into the nexus of the world economy, meant that from the 1780's to the 1870's the country's prosperity was determined to a considerable degree by external influences, though it was a period when the country's industrial successes in textiles, followed by those in the heavy industries, were so resounding that foreign competition was either entirely absent or still able to effect little damage. Even if the Scottish economy had to face few problems of international economic stagnation, it could not avoid international economic fluctuations. Consequently, while Scottish experience had many exceptional features in 1762, 1772 and 1776, the pattern of the financial crisis of 1793 in Scotland did not differ significantly from elsewhere. The textile industries suffered sharply causing widespread distress, but stocks were quickly reduced and the industries revived. In the first decade of the nineteenth century, war and the consequential restrictions meant a less rapid increase in the crucial cotton exports, culminating in the crisis of 1812, when the relationship between merchant and manufacturer was clearly demonstrated. In 1825 the Scottish economy's experience was again, though for the last time, similar to that of other textile districts. By the crisis of 1836 the industrial structure of Scotland was undergoing a fundamental change, as the iron industry began to over-shadow textiles, but the relationship to foreign markets remained. The iron industry's low costs enabled it to pass through the troubles of 1836 with little adverse effect, but by the next crisis, in 1848, the pattern which had been evident in the cotton industry earlier spread to it. Home demand passed its peak in 1845, but the continuation of a strong overseas demand prevented any collapse in the industry until 1848. The trend continued. In 1857 the failure of cotton merchants led to the closure of the Western Bank of Scotland, with subsequent mercantile and manufacturing distress, and in 1872 all industries, but especially the then dominant iron industry, enjoyed short-lived but very high profits, principally on the basis of foreign demand. Whatever the difficulties raised by such fluctuations, they were small compared with what came later. Until the 1870's the comparative cost of industrial production in Scotland was so favourable that the economy rested on an apparently sure foundation of buoyant foreign demand.

Roads and canals

The rapid expansion of trade depended on contemporary improvements in transport, both internally and externally. The external changes, improvements in shipping and in overseas port facilities, had no particular Scottish connotation, but in the internal improvements Scottish experience was more unique. They fell into two different groups: some aimed at effecting the economic exploitation of a particular area; others, notably in the Highlands, though most striking when judged by a technical or engineering criterion, made relatively little contribution to the country's economic growth.

The most important group of improvements in the second category was in the Highlands. There the need for the military roads declined in the eighteenth century with the increasing pacification of the region and with the restoration of the Forfeited Estates in 1784, and the responsibility for the maintenance of the military roads was transferred to local funds. If the transfer had continued without interruption, the roads would have fallen into disuse through the inadequacy of local funds for their maintenance, but they had other deficiencies which became increasingly evident through contrast with the improvements then taking place in the Lowlands. Virtually none spread beyond the Great Glen, and as the Corrieyairack, rising to two and a half thousand feet, demonstrated, they failed to follow what were technically the best routes. By the end of the eighteenth century, therefore, a completely new road system was required in the Highlands, but, because of the insufficiency of local funds, it could be obtained only by the provision of more direct government encouragement than had been evident in the construction of the military roads. The adoption of such a policy was encouraged at the end of the eighteenth century by the first appearance of a suggestion, much repeated subsequently, that one way of arresting emigration from the Highlands was by providing the area with better communications. In these circumstances George Dempster of Skibo encouraged Pitt to commission Thomas Telford to survey Highland roads in 1801 and again in the following year.

Telford interpreted his remit widely, so that his reports are not concerned simply with the problems involved in surveying or road construction. He recognized the symptoms, even if he failed to provide an accurate diagnosis, of the changed conditions of Highland life. 'The

Lairds have transferred their affections from the people to flocks of sheep and the people have lost their veneration for the Lairds. . . . It is not a pleasant change.' Telford considered he was commissioned not simply to suggest how the best roads could be built in the Highlands, but to suggest how emigration could be stopped, and to him the solution seemed simple: crofting and fishing should be encouraged instead of sheep-farming, and for their successful operation they required a foundation of good communications, a canal through the Great Glen, a network of roads and bridges, and better harbours. Eventually, two official commissions—one for Highland Roads and Bridges and the other for the Caledonian Canal—were appointed with Telford as engineer to both. The state was to pay half the cost of any roads constructed; landowners had to raise the remainder, either voluntarily or by assessment. There followed an immense achievement in civil engineering and, for the time, a notable example of government aid. The Commissioners for Highland Roads and Bridges constructed a total of 920 miles of new roads and 1,117 bridges, notably those over the Dee, Tay, Beauly, Conon and Spey, at a cost of over £500,000, £267,000 of which was contributed by the government. Piers and harbours were also improved by the Commissioners, who contributed about half the total cost of approximately £110,000 from funds which arose from the return of the Forfeited Estates. Then in 1813 they had assigned to their care the remaining military roads, by then only about 300 miles in length, and were given an annual grant of £5,000 for maintenance, which was continued, even when the state's contribution of 50 per cent of the cost of constructional work was withdrawn, until 1862, when the remaining responsibilities of the Commission for Highland Roads and Bridges were transferred to the Commissioners of Supply.

In Telford's view the roads had to be supplemented by the Caledonian Canal, which, like the Forth and Clyde Canal, was suggested by the topography of Scotland. The Caledonian Canal was advocated for some time before it was constructed. James Watt first surveyed the line for the Commissioners of the Forfeited Estates in 1773, was consulted twenty years later by John Rennie, when he prepared a scheme, and yet again by Telford. In the early years of the nineteenth centurys during the French Wars, the construction of the Canal offered the strategic advantage of a safer route for vessels, apart from the economic benefit of making it no longer necessary for ships trading from the Baltic to the west of Scotland, or perhaps to Liverpool, to go north about through the Pentland Firth. The construction of the Canal was financed almost wholly by the state, which had to shoulder a growing burden as unexpected technical difficulties, including damage by floods, and the continual necessity of increasing its size to accommodate larger vessels, required additional expenditure, most of it during a period of rising prices. Telford's original estimate of £474,000 was surpassed, as costs eventually soared beyond £1,000,000. The construction of the Crinan Canal bore many similar features. Initially its construction was in private hands, especially in those of the Duke of Argyll, but the capital expenditure involved necessitated the acceptance of state aid to complete the Canal in 1801. Subsequent difficulties in operation led to further subventions and eventually to the Canal passing under the management of the Commissioners for the Caledonian Canal.

The importance of the work of the two Commissions appointed in 1803 to improve Highland communications cannot be gainsaid, if judged by the sheer magnitude of the work involved, or by the state's contribution to it, but, since the successes were mainly technical, they are less conspicuous if judged by other criteria. Telford had set himself the problem of devising ways and means of diminishing Highland emigration, but the construction of roads, bridges and canals failed to provide a solution. Though the condition of the Highlands did show some improvement in the mid-nineteenth century, and was one factor causing parliament to withdraw its special grant towards road maintenance in 1862, the Highland problem remained, because it was much more complex than Telford imagined. The failure of the Caledonian Canal was the most striking illustration of his miscalculation. When it was officially opened in 1822, the Napoleonic Wars were over, and the strategic reasons which had encouraged its construction no longer applied. Even its supposed economic advantages were less evident. The trade from the Baltic to the west coast, which it was intended the Canal should facilitate, had never been of major importance, and, in any case, a passage through the Pentland Firth became less hazardous with the growing adoption of steam propulsion and the installation of better systems of navigational lights along the coast. The irony of the Caledonian Canal was that, as its cost of construction increased, so its contribution to the economic life of Scotland diminished.

The transport improvements which had an important economic effect lay south of the Highland Line, particularly in the central belt, where many of the industrial changes of the late eighteenth and nineteenth centuries could not progress without them. Frequently attention is concentrated on the contributions of canals and especially of railways, but canals were never of much consequence in many parts of Scotland, while the railways made their contribution only later in the nineteenth century. Hence the road improvements of the late eighteenth and the nineteenth centuries were of major importance. During this period the turnpike trusts made their main contribution. Though many were authorized between the 1750's and the 1780's, this method of road improvement was first used in some areas only in the nineteenth century. Even in Banffshire, where road-making was undertaken under Lord Deskford early in the eighteenth century, the first turnpike trust came only in 1804. Elsewhere, in districts where turnpike trusts had been formed earlier, many were active in improvement only from the last quarter of the eighteenth century. In Ayrshire, which had John Loudon McAdam as one of its road trustees, the effectiveness of the first Turnpike Act of 1766 was limited by the inability of the trustees to borrow on the security of the tolls, but, even when that was remedied in a second Act of 1774, work proceeded slowly. The first turnpike road in the parish of Ardrossan was constructed under the 1766 Act only in 1779; the inland road from Girvan to Ballantrae, constructed under the 1774 Act, was completed only in 1791. In central Scotland, soon to be the centre of much industrial development for which good communications were indispensable, improvements also appeared in the late eighteenth century, as in its last decade, when two new roads (one through Stepps, Falkirk and Linlithgow; the other through Airdrie and Bathgate) joined Glasgow and Edinburgh. Unfortunately the beneficial effects of many of the early roads were limited by imperfect knowledge of road-making, which, according to McAdam, was worse in Scotland than in England, in spite of cheaper raw materials, and by levying so many tolls on the roads (there were ten on the thirty-four miles from Glasgow to Ayr) that traffic was sometimes driven off them. Consequently, though the first mail-coach from London reached Glasgow in 1788, the necessary improvement or the road it had to take from Carlisle exceeded local abilities, both financial and technical. Financial aid came with a parliamentary grant of £50,000; technical aid came from Telford, from whose labours in Lanarkshire more than the Glasgow to Carlisle road benefited. He engineered the branch through Lanark to Cumbernauld; the road which joins the old Edinburgh to Glasgow road from the Calders, across Garrion bridge (built in 1818), to the Ayrshire border at Loudon Hill; and, the most memorable legacy of all, left a series of fine bridges,

built from 1818 to 1830, only one of which, at Fiddler's Gill, near
Carluke, completely failed under modern traffic.

When the surfaces of the newer roads benefited from the work of
McAdam and others, they were far more suitable for fast wheeled
vehicles than were those built earlier in the eighteenth century. They
even made it possible to convey heavy loads in bulk, as from the lead-
mines at Carsphairn and from the ironworks at Dalmellington to the
harbour at Ayr, though never, of course, with the facility and cheapness the canals and railways brought to the areas in which they were
located. It is, therefore, easy to see how frequently the two ministers
who contributed to the first and second statistical accounts of one parish
both recorded major advances in road construction. Those who wrote
in the 1780's and 1790's saw only the beginning of the work of the
turnpike trusts; those who wrote in the 1840's saw its completion and
the extension of minor roads by heritors and others. By then the major
network of roads had been built in many parts of Scotland, frequently
only their surfacing and alignment being changed in later years, until
an Act of 1878, which became effective no later than 1883, finally
abolished the old system of statute labour (compulsorily commuted
to money payments in 1845) and any turnpike trusts that remained.
Thereafter all roads and bridges within a county were administered by
the County Road Board, the executive agency of the County Road
Trustees, who included Commissioners of Supply and representatives
of ratepayers and town councils. In 1889 the newly formed County
Councils assumed responsibility for the roads and provided the members of the County Road Board.

The importance of the road improvements was dimmed only in
those few parts of Scotland where canals were constructed, but Scottish
canals were never extensive and, apart from the Forth and Clyde and
the Caledonian Canals, were of local importance. In another respect
the Forth and Clyde and the Caledonian Canals differed from the
others: the former was first envisaged as providing more convenient
access for west coast merchants to Europe, the latter was conceived as
a means of preventing emigration from the Highlands; the other
canals of any economic importance were intended to assist in the
exploitation of the natural resources of Scotland. Of the last group
the most important was the Monkland Canal, which was aimed at the
opening of the landlocked coalfield of north Lanarkshire in an attempt
to obtain additional sources of supply for the expanding industrial and
domestic demand of Glasgow, estimated by James Watt to be about

70,000 tons annually around 1770, and so break the monopoly of the Glasgow coal merchants, who were thought to be charging extortionate prices because of the increased demand. James Watt was commissioned to survey a possible route in 1769, and, as Smeaton did when he surveyed for the Forth and Clyde Canal, Watt suggested two possibilities. Though the first brought the Canal right into Glasgow, it required a series of locks near the city, and so would have cost about £20,000. Watt, therefore, favoured a cheaper scheme, costing only about half as much, but under which the canal terminated just where the locks began on the first scheme, and the route into the city was then completed by means of a waggon-way down a steep slope. The assumption that the less expensive venture should be accepted reflected the financial stringency in contemporary Scotland and possibly also the same conservative Glasgow interests, which had actively advocated a less elaborate Forth and Clyde Canal. On this occasion, since there was no opposition from those with more ambitious ideas, the minor proposals were more easily accepted. An Act was obtained for the Canal in 1770, but even the restricted conception which had been adopted proved excessively optimistic for Scotland, then embroiled in the financial crisis of 1772, and the project came to a halt until 1784, when at a public sale the largest part of the shares were purchased by the firm of William Stirling and Company. This company which had moved its print-works from Dalsholm to the Vale of Leven and its head from 1777, Andrew Stirling had a direct interest in the development of the Monklands through the purchase of the estate of Drumpellier. Two years later, in 1786, the Stirlings became the sole proprietors of the Canal, which they completed and extended to join the Forth and Clyde Canal at Port Dundas in 1790, the same year in which the Forth and Clyde itself gained access to the sea at Bowling. A third canal, the Union, completed the framework which had been laid by the Forth and Clyde and Monkland Canals for the exploitation of the natural resources of central Scotland. Its aim was to provide a direct link by water between Glasgow and Edinburgh, and, more especially, to enable Edinburgh, and indeed much of Midlothian, to gain from the increased supplies of coal, which, it was hoped, would be encouraged through the junction of the Forth and Clyde and Monkland Canals. Though the conception of the Canal was thus accepted, disputes on the most desirable route delayed its authorization for nearly a quarter of a century. An Act was obtained only in 1817, and the Canal, which ran from lock 16 on the Forth and Clyde Canal to Edinburgh, was finally opened in 1822. With the network provided by the three canals, coal could be sent from the Monkland parishes to Port Dundas on the west or to Port Hopetoun in the east, and so both Glasgow and Edinburgh could be served directly from the coalfields of central Scotland.

A number of other canals were projected towards the end of the eighteenth century, but all did not come to fruition. Of these the most notable was the Glasgow, Paisley and Ardrossan Canal. Its importance lay in the scope of the venture—an attempt to transform Ardrossan into a major port for the increasing shipping traffic from the west of Scotland—and in the problems of its construction. As was not uncommon with canals, the cost considerably exceeded Telford's estimate of over £125,000 and by 1811 the Canal reached its limit of eleven miles from Glasgow to Johnstone. Later a connection to Ardrossan was made by rail. Ardrossan never displaced Port Glasgow and Greenock, or Glasgow itself, but it is impossible to guess what might have happened if the Canal had been completed earlier, before the railways rendered it, and the project it was meant to serve, obsolete. The only other canal of any importance in Scotland was a cut of eighteen miles from Aberdeen to Inverurie, but, since it had a large number of locks, its cost, both in construction and operation, was high. Thus even its local importance, considerable as it was, was diminished.

Railways

Waggon-ways, the direct ancestor of modern railways, became increasingly common around collieries in the late eighteenth century. Originally the rails were of wood, later they were plated with iron and later still they were made entirely of iron. Sometimes, in the most rudimentary instances, waggon-ways were constructed with a slope sufficient to allow the waggons to run along them on their own momentum. More frequently, waggons were horse-drawn until the development of the steam-engine. Examples of such waggon-ways were to be found throughout Scotland. Within the city of Glasgow the present railway line leading into the Central Station on the south side of the river Clyde traverses the line of one from the Govan collieries. But the best known of these early waggon-ways was the line from the Duke of Portland's collieries near Kilmarnock to Troon, whence some of the coal was shipped to Ireland, a line often referred to erroneously as being the first railway in Scotland. Being more than ten miles in length, it was much longer than most, and its construction was more solid and lasting than many others. It had a bridge of four arches, three of them in the river Irvine, and its construction required 70,000 rails of cast iron, manufactured at Glenbuck, at a cost, with carriage added, of about £20,000. But, apart from its scale, the Kilmarnock to Troon railway was of the same type as those waggon-ways which had preceded it.

Like the waggon-ways, the early modern railways were constructed with the direct aim of contributing to the exploitation of the country's natural resources, none more conspicuously than the earliest of the modern type, most of which were in Lanarkshire. The first of the modern group was the Monkland and Kirkintilloch Railway, which in 1824 gave access from Old Monkland to the Forth and Clyde Canal, and enabled coal to go to Port Dundas on the west, to Grangemouth on the east, and, by means of the Union Canal, direct to Edinburgh. The fears of some parties, including the Town Council of Glasgow, that the benefits of cheap coal, made possible by the railway, might be enjoyed by Edinburgh rather than by Glasgow, were apparently justified. As prices fell from the heights of 11s. and 12s. in 1825 to between 5s. 10d. and 6s. 10d. in 1828, at which level they continued until 1834, more coal than ever was sent from the Monklands to try to find a more profitable market in the east. The movement was facilitated further when the Ballochney Railway, approved in 1826 and opened in 1828, connected New Monkland to the Monkland and Kirkintilloch Railway. The Ballochney Railway was therefore a subsidiary or, more accurately, a series of three branches to the Monkland and Kirkintilloch Railway. Much the most important of all these early railways was, however, the Glasgow and Garnkirk Railway which was started in 1827 and opened in 1831. Like the Monkland Canal it was constructed chiefly to break the monopoly of the coal-masters whose power was not diminished because of the continued expansion of demand in Glasgow and district in the 1820's in a way which compared exactly with what had happened in the 1790's, but its importance arose from various factors, all of which indicated the acceptance of new ways and methods. Both the earlier railways used horse-drawn waggons initially; the Glasgow and Garnkirk Railway used steam locomotives from the start: the earlier railways had been integrated into the canal system, and were even simply supplementary to it; the Glasgow and Garnkirk Railway was directly competitive with the canals, following the very line of the Monkland Canal. Two other early railways also made a notable contribution to the exploitation of the resources of central Scotland. First, the Wishaw and Coltness Railway, projected in 1829 and opened in 1833, ran from the Monkland and Kirkintilloch Railway southwards to within a mile of the Omoa ironworks, opened up the area between Holytown and Hamilton, the future site of Carnbroe and Coltness ironworks, and made possible the use of a large field of ironstone which had been found in the coal measures some time previously but which, until the railway was built, had been 'an object scarcely worthy of attention'.[1] Second, the Slammanan Railway, towards which the Ballochney Railway contributed half the capital, gave an outlet from the coal and iron districts of north Lanarkshire to the east without the necessity of using the Forth and Clyde Canal. The line, projected in 1835 and opened in August 1840, ran from Ballochney, where it joined the Ballochney Railway, to the Union Canal. Though it provided direct access from Lanarkshire to the east by rail, the Union Canal was still necessary to obtain contact with Edinburgh. Unlike the Ballochney and the Monkland and Kirkintilloch Railways the Slammanan Railway was not an immediate financial success, perhaps because, by still depending on the canals, it was outmoded. In 1848 all three, the Monkland and Kirkintilloch, the Ballochney, and the Slammanan Railways amalgamated to form the Monkland Railways, later absorbed by the Edinburgh and Glasgow Railway and in turn by the North British Railway.

The railways built until about 1840, and the canals associated with them, were essential to reduce transport costs and so facilitate exploitation of the country's natural resources and its economic advance. Some of the reductions were phenomenal. When the railway was being built the cost of taking rails from Kirkintilloch to Gargill was 6s. 11d., after the railway was in use it was 9d. The immediate outcome, an upsurge in mineral values in the areas being opened up, proved the basis of the success of most of the early railways. Within five years of its opening the shareholders of the Monkland and Kirkintilloch Railway were earning 6 per cent on their capital and their stock stood at 50 per cent above par. The Ballochney Railway was also quickly successful, even though the difficult terrain it traversed so increased its costs of construction that its rates were about double those on the Monkland and Kirkintilloch Railway. To contemporaries such successes highlighted the early financial failure of the Glasgow and Garnkirk Railway, but

[1] *Hamilton Muniments*, Memorandum of William Paterson, 19th January 1831.

the advantages it conferred could not be denied. With its advent, in a period of particular prosperity in the coal and iron industries which it served, the cost of transporting coal from the Monklands to Glasgow fell from 3s. 6d. to 1s. 3d. per ton. Ultimately the Glasgow and Garnkirk Railway became one of the few railways in the country which did not depend on passenger receipts for a large part of its revenue, but other users could not be attracted immediately and the Company made great, and successful, efforts to increase its passenger trade.

The promotion of the early railways was undertaken chiefly by Glasgow merchants and by coalmasters, some of whom afterwards became leading figures in the iron industry. Among them were Alexander Baird, father of the brothers who founded the ironworks, James Merry and William Dixon, all directors of the Glasgow and Garnkirk Railway. James Merry was also on the board of the Monkland and Kirkintilloch Railway, while Dixon played an active part in all railway development. But, apart from the Monkland and Kirkintilloch Railway, most of the directors of which were coal merchants, promotion lay chiefly in the hands of Glasgow merchants and manufacturers. Frequently they were those who earlier had constructed the canals, except that one notable absentee from the group of railway promoters was Kirkman Finlay, who never became fully convinced of the desirability of railways over canals, and who thought, perhaps not surprisingly for the head of the Forth and Clyde Canal Company, that, even as late as 1835, it would be desirable to lead a branch from the Forth and Clyde Canal to Stirling as it would 'be a great matter for the country and for us at Deanston'.[1]

The form of the expansion of the railway network of Scotland from about 1840 was more varied. In some areas the later expansion was aimed, as it had been earlier in central Scotland, at the exploitation of natural advantages. This was so in Ayrshire, where the basis of the system of modern communications was the abortive plan for the canal from Glasgow to Ardrossan. Since for twenty years the canal had not progressed beyond Johnstone, the canal company was authorized to complete the route by railway. The track, starting this time from the coast, reached only Kilwinning, though the line had in addition some useful branches. Then in 1837 the Glasgow, Paisley, Kilmarnock and Ayr Railway was authorized, the five-mile stretch between Ardrossan and Kilwinning was amalgamated into it, and later the bed of the

[1] *Hamilton Muniments*, K. Finlay to R. Brown, 27th October 1835.

moribund canal from Johnstone to Glasgow was filled in to give an alternative line, which, with a later branch from Ayr to Dalmellington, aided mineral development. From the 1840's, however, there appeared other lines, which, though equally important in other fields, did not play such a crucial part in the carriage of minerals. Some, such as the Glasgow, Paisley and Greenock Railway, completed in 1841, were in the south-west of Scotland, but from the 1840's the railways could generally be grouped into two main categories: first, primarily local lines, though not based on Glasgow or other centres of the heavy industries in the south-west of Scotland; second, trunk lines. The railways around Edinburgh and Dundee fell into the first group. In Edinburgh, the railway network began with the Edinburgh and Dalkeith Railway, opened in 1831 for horse-drawn waggons. In Dundee a start was made with the Dundee and Newtyle Railway, opened in 1832, and on which the waggons were pulled up slopes by stationary engines. Others followed to give local networks. The trunk lines of the second group had more distinctive characteristics. Their particular contribution was to the carriage of passengers, but they also provided the means of communication between different parts of Scotland and England, so necessary for the exploitation of foreign demand on which the country's industrial expansion was increasingly dependent. With the wider appearance of trunk lines from the 1840's the Scottish railway system became by mid-century no longer only, or even primarily, concerned with the exploitation of the country's mineral resources.

The expansion of the trunk lines was first demonstrated by the Edinburgh and Glasgow Railway, which represented a direct challenge to the new age, as it was specifically projected to rival the Forth and Clyde Canal. Surveys were made from the 1820's, the Act authorizing the line was obtained in 1838, and the line opened in the spring of 1842. It was followed in the boom in railway promotion in the 1840's by the first appearance of the main railway lines between Scotland and England. Suggestions for them were of long-standing. In 1832 a railway from England to Scotland was first mooted along a line from Newcastle through Jedburgh and Melrose to Edinburgh, a route never exactly followed. The choice between three other routes, each of which became the property of one of the three main railway companies which dominated Scottish railway history in the latter nineteenth century, was the source of much dispute in the 1830's. These were the east coast route through Berwick and Dunbar, the line of the

North British Railway Company; the Annandale route, the line of the Caledonian Railway Company; the Nithsdale route, the line of the Glasgow and South Western Railway Company.

The first line across the border was the North British, east coast, route from Edinburgh to Berwick, opened in 1846. Previously George Stephenson had surveyed two routes from Newcastle to Edinburgh and had greatly favoured the east coast, but the scheme lay dormant until the project was revived by George Hudson in the 1840's. Hudson's energy was responsible for the success of the venture. His Newcastle and Berwick Railway provided the necessary link with the south, his influence was crucial in obtaining the North British Railway Act in 1844, and he invested £50,000 in the North British Railway, shares which were later transferred to the York and North Midland Railway. At the same time as Hudson was extending his interests to the north, the Grand Junction Railway wanted to do likewise, only in their case on the west coast. Accordingly in 1836 Joseph Locke was sent north to survey two possible routes to Glasgow, one through Nithsdale, the other through Annandale. Because of the inclines involved in crossing Beattock summit, Locke chose the former, a preference which seemed even more reasonable when the Glasgow to Kilmarnock Railway was incorporated in the following year and so held out the prospect of a line being constructed part of the way from Glasgow towards Nithsdale. At this stage the Annandale route might have been neglected, but for the enterprise of local landowners. They could stress in its support that Beattock provided only a difficult, not an insurmountable, barrier; that the Annandale route, by leading into Clydesdale, gave access to the developing industrial areas of north Lanarkshire; and that the Annandale line, unlike that through Nithsdale, could provide communications to both Glasgow and Edinburgh. The matter was referred to the Royal Commission then investigating railway communications between London and Scotland. In 1841 it announced its support for the Annandale route, with the addition of a branch to Edinburgh from Symington or Thankerton, and placed least stress on the Nithsdale route, since it was suggested that, if two lines were to be built, they should be the east coast route, with the Annandale route complementary to it. When the east coast route was authorized with Hudson's powerful backing, some of the priority in the claims of the Annandale scheme were removed, but, in spite of opposition from those who favoured Nithsdale and from the Edinburgh and Glasgow Railway which was already associated with the North British Railway, the route was authorized as the Caledonian Railway in 1845 and completed in 1848. Construction of the Nithsdale route was authorized in 1846 and on its completion in 1850 it was amalgamated with the Glasgow, Paisley, Kilmarnock and Ayr Railway to form the Glasgow and South Western Railway.

The railway mania also witnessed expansion to the north. In the 1840's the Scottish Central Railway reached Perth, and the North Eastern Railway completed the Scottish Midland's line from Forfar to Aberdeen. Eventually all became part of the Caledonian Railway. The following decade, the 1850's, saw the beginning of the lines which were ultimately to comprise the two other companies which joined the North British, the Caledonian, and the Glasgow and South Western to form the five great Scottish railway companies. The oldest section of the Great North of Scotland Railway, which was located in the north-east, was the Elgin to Lossiemouth line opened in 1852, and the oldest section of the Highland Railway, which eventually stretched to Thurso, was the line from Inverness to Nairn, opened in 1855. The Scottish railway network was virtually completed in the later nineteenth century by the expansion of the existing companies through amalgamation and through new construction. Of the latter, the work of the North British Railway was most dramatic as it bridged the Tay, first and disastrously in 1878, secondly in 1887, and the Forth in 1890, and at the end of the century carried the railway westwards to Fort William in 1897 (the year in which the Highland Railway completed the ten miles from Strome Ferry to Kyle of Lochalsh) and Mallaig in 1901.

The expansion of the later nineteenth century provided Scotland with some of its more dramatic feats of railway engineering, but its economic influence was not comparable to the construction of the 1840's. The railway mania of the 1840's gave Scotland the nucleus of its railway system. In later years expansion was frequently of branch lines or in rural districts. By the middle of the nineteenth century most of those required for the general exploitation of the country's economic potential had been built. Most important of all the link provided with England in the later 1840's was the greatest step towards economic integration since 1707.

VI
THE TEXTILE INDUSTRIES

The rise of the cotton industry

IN the eighteenth century the progress of the linen industry was retarded by the poor quality and inadequate supply of dressed flax and yarn, obstacles not entirely overcome even by imports of both. The rise of the cotton industry, however, was not so restricted, because the technology on which it was based removed the bottleneck in spinning and enabled yarn to be spun cheaply and efficiently. The new methods of spinning gradually became more effective, and more common, between the invention of the spinning-jenny in the 1760's and the invention of the mule in the 1780's but, though a power-loom was developed by Edmund Cartwright in 1784, a similar revolution in weaving was delayed until after the Napoleonic Wars. The innovations in both spinning and weaving were complemented by the mechanical adaptations which followed Watt's invention of the steam-engine, among them being Watt's own devices to connect the linear motion of the steam-engine into rotary movement. All such developments provided the basis for a new cotton-spinning industry, new in all forms: products, processes, power and location. The origins of the cotton industry in Scotland in the 1780's owes much, therefore, to the new technology of cotton manufacture, which was developed at that time. Yet the new technology is rather the immediate explanation, or the occasion, of the appearance of the new type of industry in Scotland. It provided the renovation which Scottish industry needed so urgently, but found so difficult to achieve, but its application depended on a peculiar combination of circumstances in Scotland in the late eighteenth century. To explain the rise of the industry solely on the basis of the new technology misses the point. The industry depended on the technical inventions, but that it was so successful in Scotland, especially in the west of Scotland, at that time depended on the favourable environment already formed by the linen industry and on two aspects in particular: first, the special skills and abilities, particularly in finer fabrics, of the linen weavers of the west of Scotland, and, second, the

H 97

commercial acumen of the merchants who organized the expansion of the linen industry.

The inadequacies in the supply of yarn placed an effective barrier on a full and satisfactory exploitation of the skill of the linen weavers of the west of Scotland, and one only gradually removed by the new technology, which initially did not provide yarn sufficiently fine for the linen weavers' particular abilities. The yarn spun by the spinning-jenny, which James Hargreaves invented between 1764 and 1767, was soft and suitable only for the weft, while that spun on Richard Arkwright's water-frame, devised in 1768, while sufficiently strong for the warp, was too soft for finer fabrics and was suitable only for cheap cotton calicoes. In spite of its deficiencies, however, the yarn was used for finer fabrics wherever possible and in the late 1760's the weavers of Anderston and Paisley began to use cotton for the weft in an effort to produce muslins, though success was delayed until the 1780's, when James Monteith imported some 'bird-nest' Indian yarn and had the first webs of muslin woven in Scotland. In spite of such efforts to use the new cotton yarn which was still suitable only for coarser fabrics, the textile industry of the west of Scotland was never distracted from its specialization in high-quality fine products. Consequently, the full exploitation in cotton manufacture of the particular abilities the industry had first evolved in the manufacture of linen had to wait until the 1780's, when the invention of Samuel Crompton's mule made possible the spinning of both weft and warp sufficiently strong and fine for high-quality cotton cloth. Thereafter the finest muslins could be woven in Scotland. The new technology gave the Scottish weavers the opportunity they had been seeking.

Though the special skills and abilities of the weavers in the linen industry in the eighteenth century provided a skill essential for the growth of the cotton industry, its successful and continued growth depended on the linen industry's second main contribution, the commercial acumen of the linen merchant, or manufacturer, as he was called indiscriminately. The function of the merchant was superfluous so long as the industry retained its domestic character and depended chiefly on localized raw materials, labour and markets, but by the later eighteenth century the industry was no longer so tied. Spinners were scattered throughout the country, while full-time weavers became concentrated towards the commercial centres of the industry, chiefly in Glasgow, Paisley, and, to a lesser extent, in Dundee, while raw materials came increasingly from overseas and finished products went there.

Unity to the varied industrial complex was given by the merchants, who had resources adequate to finance the rather extended process of production, and who sometimes owned the lint mills or the expensive bleachfields. The establishment of the cotton industry required men with capital, with commercial experience, and with an ability to organize their workers in new places and with new techniques. As it provided the weavers for the cotton industry, so too the linen industry provided the entrepreneurs.

What is reputed to have been Scotland's first cotton mill was built at Penicuik in 1778 and was followed, in 1779, by a more successful one at Rothesay, which, though long disused as a cotton mill, was destroyed by fire only in 1955. The Penicuik and Rothesay mills were exceptional, because Renfrewshire and Lanarkshire were the areas of development even in the earliest phase of the industry's growth. Paisley's existing reputation as a textile centre was confirmed by the foundation of mills, sometimes for hand-operated spinning-jennies, sometimes with the use of oxen as an early means of motive power in them; but the first modern cotton mill in Renfrewshire, and probably the third in Scotland, was just beyond the Paisley parochial boundary, in the parish of Neilston, where an old corn mill, driven by the river Levern, was converted to cotton-spinning in 1780. The first mill in Lanarkshire was founded in 1783 at East Kilbride, and was followed by another at North Woodside, Glasgow, in 1784. The period of greatest construction of cotton mills followed, lasting from the foundation of the Deanston mills in 1785 until the outbreak of the French Wars in 1793, a period of expansion rivalled in Scotland's industrial history only by the growth of the iron industry in the 1830's. In 1787 there were 19 mills driven by water in Scotland (four each in Lanarkshire and Renfrewshire, three in Perthshire, two in Midlothian and six in other places); a decade later there were 39. Until about 1790, relatively few mills were built, but most were of considerable size, and remained the major enterprises of the industry in Scotland; after 1790 began a period of extensive construction of smaller mills. There were also changes in location. Though most of the earliest mills were in the west, the construction of the larger mills from the mid-1780's led to a more haphazard distribution. None were built in Renfrewshire, and only New Lanark and Blantyre in Lanarkshire. Again the smaller mills built in the early 1790's were distributed throughout the country, but in their case with two notable centres: one on the east coast around Dundee, though mills spread southwards to Kinghorn and Dunbar;

another, and more important, cluster was in the west, in north Ayrshire and the adjacent lowlands of Renfrewshire. When the attractions
of some areas diminished in the early nineteenth century through the
use of steam rather than water-power, the erection of new mills nearer
the main centre for importing the raw materials was more feasible, and
so construction became more concentrated in the west of Scotland,
particularly in Glasgow, where new mills were built in Govan and
Bridgeton. The concentration was, however, accompanied by slackening in construction. After the boom of 1825, though expansion was
still undertaken when required by improvements in machinery, the
only spinning-mills built were offshoots of new weaving establishments, as the adoption of power-loom instead of hand-loom weaving
led some merchants, previously concerned only with the organization
of hand-loom weavers, to become power-loom manufacturers and at
the same time to build spinning-mills to supply their own power-
looms with yarn.

The construction of the large mills was usually the result of the work
of a few individuals, frequently linen merchants. Notable among them
was David Dale, better known, perhaps, for his philanthropic than for
his industrial interests. From being a weaver Dale became one of
Glasgow's most important importers of fine foreign yarn for the linen
weavers and controlled a large number of weavers working domestic-
ally throughout the west of Scotland. With the appearance of the new
possibilities of spinning, Dale showed his acumen by his choice of
partners and of sites for his mills. At New Lanark he had Richard
Arkwright, the inventor of the water-frame, as his partner for a short
time; at Blantyre he combined with James Monteith, the pioneer of
the manufacture of muslins in Glasgow, who had similar industrial
interests, mainly in Anderston; at Catrine his partner was Claud
Alexander of Ballochmyle, a laird home from the east with capital to
spare and with land near a good supply of water. Dale's chief rival, the
Buchanan family, had a similar background. Like Dale they imported
the fine yarn the Scottish weavers required, and so, when the new
technology provided the opportunity, were also able to move easily to
cotton-spinning. In 1785 they built the Deanston works in Perthshire
and four years later, in 1789, in partnership with Robert Dunmore,
sometime a Virginian merchant but by then laird of Ballindalloch and
Ballikinrain, they built the Ballindalloch works near Balfron. Few
other mills were established at this time, though among them were
important ventures, such as the Stanley mills in Perthshire, and Dale's

far-flung efforts in partnership with others at Spinningdale, in Sutherland, and at Newton-Stewart. By contrast the smaller mills which
appeared after 1790 were distinguished by continuing a tradition of
local enterprise, evident from the first days of the new technology. The
larger ventures were located on sites which offered special advantages,
such as New Lanark, Deanston, Catrine, Blantyre which offered
adequate water-power, but the smaller mills were located in a particular
area simply because their projectors lived there. The *Old Statistical
Account* frequently refers to such concerns, which ranged in size and
activities from small workshops, in which a number of hand-operated
spinning-jennies were gathered, to water twist mills. The more primitive establishments had a limited life and few survived for long, but the
smaller water twist mills did continue, though primarily only in those
areas which had in any case such special advantages for cotton production that they brought the founders of the larger mills to the same
district.

Though larger mills, Deanston, Catrine, New Lanark and others, were
individually the most evident illustrations of the new Scottish cotton
industry, the numerous smaller mills were more representative of its
development. Many, if not most, of the smaller mills were buildings
converted from other uses, a process which was not always cheap. One
estimate, for example, shows that between £3,000 to £4,000 was
required for the conversion of an old sugar house of seven storeys to
house about 9,360 spindles. The old mill at Neilston, the second in
Scotland, was a conversion of this kind. The spinning of cotton began
in 1780 in what had been originally an old corn mill at Dovecothall on
the banks of the Levern. The old mill was 54 feet long and 24 feet
broad and had three storeys, each being 8 feet high. In 1800 another
mill, 123 feet long and 32½ feet broad, and with five storeys, was
added, and in 1834 yet another, of 113 feet long and 40 feet broad,
until in this way a unit of considerable size was gradually erected. Its
success led to the construction of others: Gateside in 1786; Broadlie
and Arthurlie in 1790; Crofthead in 1792; and Graham's mill in 1801.
The experience of the parish of Lochwinnoch, on the other side of the
Cart Valley, was similar. In the *New Statistical Account*, the parish
minister reported that the old mill, built about 1788, had five storeys
with 8,140 spindles, while the new mill, again with five storeys, had
25,224 spindles. In addition there were two small mills, one of which,
where the jennies were worked by hand, did not last long; the other
was burnt down in 1813. The experience of these two parishes was

common to many in Lanarkshire, Renfrewshire and Ayrshire, indeed wherever there were adequate water supplies, and in them the advent of the mills, of whatever type, effected a transformation by bringing new activities, and new ways of life, into what had been rural parishes, though with a number of the inhabitants already engaged in textile production. Even before the development of cotton-spinning, Lochwinnoch had a linen mill, thread mills and, because of the adequacy of the water supply, a number of bleachfields, as well as a large number of weavers working for Glasgow merchants, on linen cloths, silk gauze, and, from the 1780's, on muslins. But the importance of all was eclipsed by the cotton mills.

A mill converted to other uses in an old community never had the same dramatic effect as a completely new construction or settlement, but of these early major enterprises so little now remains that it is difficult to envisage what they meant to contemporaries. At Anderston, once a centre of the industry, and in the territory of the Monteiths and the Houldsworths, only names remain, as of Carding Lane and Warp Lane, which run from Stobcross Street to Argyle Street near Anderston Cross in the heart of Glasgow. Similarly Bridgeton has its Muslin Street, Dale Street and Monteith Row. At Blantyre more substantial evidence remains, especially through the preservation of a good example of the tenements in which the cotton operatives lived as the centre of the David Livingstone Memorial. On the other hand at New Lanark, and to a lesser extent at Catrine, the complete transformation wrought on virgin sites is still evident, partly because both communities are still maintained by cotton manufacture. The proposal for a cotton mill at New Lanark may have originated with either Dale or Arkwright, as the latter visited Scotland in 1783; but in the following year it was Dale who feued a low-lying and marshy stretch of land, with, however, the supreme advantage of access to ample supplies of water from the Clyde. The barrenness of the site, combined with the difficulty of securing adequate supplies of labour, required the construction of a completely new settlement. Since the building area was limited, the dwelling-houses had of necessity to be built upwards, much higher than was common in most of the textile areas of Scotland at that time, and more in keeping with the traditions of building in some of the older Scottish towns and in the new and overcrowded cities. The building of the first mill started in 1785. Spinning began the following year. A second mill, started in 1788, was destroyed by fire, but expansion continued until there were four mills, with ancillary offices, each mill being 160 feet long and 40 feet wide and with seven storeys. The history of Catrine is similar. It was not such a barren site as was New Lanark, but its general attraction was that Claud Alexander, with his fortune made in the service of the East India Company, lived at adjacent Ballochmyle. Its specific attraction, as at New Lanark, was the presence of an adequate supply of water from the river Ayr. Again as with New Lanark, Catrine was an ideal example of a planned factory town. The local quarries provided the red sandstone with which the town was built in a regular pattern. Subsidiary roads led into a main street, down the centre of which flowed the lade from the mill, a massive five-storeyed building with attics, containing 5,240 spindles and standing in the centre of a square. This pattern remained virtually untouched for many years. It is still easy to trace the lade along an aqueduct from the river Ayr at the bleaching works to the site of the two giant Catrine wheels (12 feet wide, 50 feet in diameter), used from 1828 until 1945, and then along the street back to the river.

The increased output of yarn produced by the new spinning-mills from the 1780's transferred the bottleneck in production from spinning to weaving, especially when the widespread use of the power-loom was delayed after its invention by Cartwright until the end of the Napoleonic Wars, partly because the loom required adjustment and improvement, partly because of the general restriction on capital investment at the time. The power-loom, as improved by Horrocks and Radcliffe, was, however, used successfully at Catrine in 1807; and after the end of the war, and especially in the boom of 1825, such investment as took place in the cotton industry was mainly in power-weaving. The existence from the 1780's to 1800, and even up to 1815, of a bottleneck at the weaving of cotton cloth provided a temporary increase in demand for the services of the hand-loom weavers, many of whom had begun to use imported yarn and to produce for a wider market earlier in the eighteenth century. They then ceased to work on a part-time basis and were encouraged to do so in those areas where new roads enabled merchants to penetrate, but elsewhere too the same tendency towards full-time specialization was evident, even in more remote areas where weavers manufactured linen and woollen cloth from local materials for local consumption. The delay in the application of power to the looms retained the weavers in their cottages, though by then, virtually without exception, they were full-time workers. The output of yarn from the spinning-mills increased the demand for their services. Consequently, numerous villages in

Renfrewshire, Stirlingshire, Ayrshire and Lanarkshire, which until then had been only agricultural hamlets clustering round a parish church, began to acquire additional housing: the cottages, sometimes of two storeys (or one and an attic), or sometimes with a common close between them and a weaver's shed in the garden, have in many cases only recently been demolished, though at Kilbarchan some weavers' cottages have been preserved. These were primarily the villages which often acquired a few larger buildings, long since converted to other uses, in which small-scale establishments carried on spinning and weaving. In some of these a few hand-looms, probably only about six, were gathered together and the weavers employed by a master, in contrast to the majority of their fellows who operated independently on commission for merchants or large manufacturers.

Success and decline in the cotton industry

In the nineteenth century the contributions of the founders of the cotton industry were quickly overshadowed by those of others. Of this second generation perhaps the best known, because of his social ideas and schemes, was David Dale's son-in-law Robert Owen, whose experiments were renowned far beyond Scotland. A more permanent contribution to the growth of the Scottish cotton industry in the nineteenth century came from Kirkman Finlay, the background of whose father, James Finlay, was similar to those of Dale and the Buchanans. The father's firm, James Finlay and Company, specialized in exporting textile goods to the Continent and from this position Kirkman Finlay easily acquired control of a major part of the Scottish cotton industry. By entering into partnership with the Buchanans he gained a share of Deanston, and later added to his interests the mills at Catrine and those at Ballindalloch which the Buchanans had sold when they entered the partnership with Finlay. James Finlay and Company thus became, and has remained, the major concern in the Scottish cotton industry. Kirkman Finlay's views on the state of the Scottish cotton industry in the early nineteenth century have, therefore, a particular pertinence.

The most striking feature of the industry during the years when it was dominated by Finlay was an irrepressible buoyancy. No statistics of output are available, but imports of cotton wool rose sharply at the end of the eighteenth century: in 1778, over 200,000 lbs.; in 1788, over 1,500,000 lbs.; in 1798, over 2,800,000 lbs.; in 1801, nearly 7,550,000 lbs. The confidence of the period of rapid mill construction from the 1780's to the early nineteenth century continued, and the industry was able to withstand the interruptions of the outbreak of war and years of declining demand such as 1788, 1789, 1803 and 1810. In evidence before the Select Committee on Manufactures, Commerce and Shipping in 1833, Kirkman Finlay explained the resiliency of the industry by the absence of foreign competition, an accurate general evaluation, if one that erred in some particulars:

'When I first entered into business extensively, which was in 1792, there was no manufacture of cotton of any importance in any part out of Great Britain. There were, perhaps, some domestic cotton manufactures carried on abroad, but there were no finer fabrics of any kind. I believe my house was among the first that ever exported cotton manufacture of fine fabrics generally to the continent of Europe, to Germany, to Italy, to France and to Switzerland. In those times there was no cotton manufacture in France at all; none in Switzerland worth speaking of; none in any part of Germany. Then the practice came to export cotton twist, and I think it was about the year 1794 or 1795 when we first began to export a good deal of cotton twist. At that time there was no cotton twist spun in any part of Germany.'[1]

To the favourable environment, engendered by the absence of any effective foreign competition, the industry made its own contribution towards resiliency by maintaining the cheapness of its products. The new technology enabled the cotton industry to reduce prices even with higher labour and raw material costs during the war, while at the end of the eighteenth century the fall in raw material prices following the introduction of the cotton-gin in the United States enabled the reduction to be continued.

The expansion of the industry, and especially the growth of its export trade, was encouraged still further by the willingness of the Scottish banks to provide ready finance for exports. Goods were sent overseas on consignment and the bills drawn on the purchaser discounted more readily by banks in Glasgow than by those in Manchester, or even in London. In addition, while in England bills were generally not discountable unless drawn for goods sold, the Scottish banks were willing to discount bills issued to cover intermediate

[1] *Select Committee on Manufactures, Commerce and Shipping, 1833. Q. 652.*

transactions, such as, for instance, those granted by manufacturers to spinners for yarn. Still more generously they were willing to discount even what were virtually accommodation bills, provided the drawer and the endorser were of good credit standing. The Scottish cotton industry gained, therefore, from the availability of additional and special credit facilities. The export trade depended for its growth on this extended credit base, but a corollary was the resulting difficulty of maintaining exports when monetary derangements supervened, even though Scottish banks continued ready to grant discounts when losing heavily on some of them. An example of such difficulties came in 1812. Initially the embargoes and restrictions which culminated in the Continental System in 1810 were circumvented and new markets, as in South America, were developed hopefully, so a strong recovery began in 1808 and was halted only with the stringent restrictions of 1810. With the collapse of many of their markets, especially those in South America, exporting merchants could not meet the bills due to manufacturers, while the banks, many of which had advanced money on them, were unable to increase their advances when the bills returned on the manufacturers. The whole structure of credit in Glasgow collapsed in a series of bankruptcies in the summer of 1812, with repercussions beyond the cotton industry, as for some time the banks adopted a more stringent policy towards all advances. Recovery, on the basis of a revival of exports to the United States, was interrupted by the outbreak of war with America and by the end of 1816 Glasgow was reported to be suffering from an unparalleled distress, relieved only by general charitable subscriptions, while the manager of Catrine held that profits in the seven years previous had failed even to provide an adequate return on capital. By that year, 1816, the Scottish cotton industry had reached the end of its phase of unqualified successful development. Thereafter it experienced increased competition, from both home and foreign producers.

In the long run the appearance of foreign competition was the source of much greater trouble, because the Scots, and the English manufacturers too, had gained from their virtual monopoly of foreign markets. Once again Kirkman Finlay from his wide experience was able to give the most striking picture of the changed environment in which the industry operated after the end of the war in 1815.

'Now there is not a single country in which there is not a great manufacture of cotton carried on. There is a very extensive spinning carried on in Switzerland; there is a very extensive spinning carried on in Austria, and a large cotton manufacture carried on there. By the recent accounts it appears that the Government has relaxed a little the prohibition against cotton twist, and that it may be induced in future on the payment of a moderate duty. Their manufacture has, in my recollection, entirely grown up. The French manufacture, which did not exist at all at the conclusion of the peace in 1814, when I was in France and saw it, has become of late very formidable; and by the means that are taken, as I understand, by the regulation of the drawback, by which the manufacturer receives more amount of drawback than he pays of duty, there is a very formidable advantage given to the French manufacturers by that fiscal regulation.'[1]

In general Finlay was right. Since large sectors of the Scottish industry were dependent on export markets, the undermining of the favourable comparative cost position of the Scottish cotton industry through the development of native industries was bound to have adverse repercussions. Two other developments confirmed even more clearly the weakness and insecurity of the Scottish position. First, competition arose from some of the new producers entering markets in other countries which had not as yet developed any domestic production, but which had previously been Scottish preserves. A Glasgow cotton spinner, William Graham, discussing this topic in 1833, demonstrated the extensive incidence of such competition from the United States.

'In Mexico for the last five or six years largely, to the Brazils considerably, Buenos Ayres and Cape Horn also considerably, and at Valparaiso; I think their imports of the stouter manufactures are larger than ours; and in Marseilles and in Singapore they have also made their appearance. Also from St. Domingo, where we have done considerable business, we have lately had letters expressing great surprise that the Americans should be competing with us.'[2]

Second, and perhaps even more alarming for the industry's long-term prospects, were signs that its competitive position was being weakened within Great Britain. In such circumstances increasing competition in foreign markets brought even greater losses to the Scots than to the Lancashire producers. To some, including Kirkman Finlay, Lancashire was superior only in those branches of cotton production in which it

---

[1] *Select Committee on Manufactures, Commerce and Shipping*, 1833. Q. 652.
[2] *Select Committee on Manufactures, Commerce and Shipping*, 1833. Q. 5451.

had always specialized, but, even if Finlay's interpretation were true, and so Scottish failures in one field could be offset by successes in others, problems were still liable to emerge in the long run if demand for the special products of Scotland proved less stable. Others, among them Henry Houldsworth, a Mancunian long resident in Glasgow, were much less self-satisfied and held that Lancashire led in all fields. Perhaps Finlay and Houldsworth were prejudiced in their respective ways, but others, among them some of the operatives who gave evidence to various parliamentary commissioners on their conditions of employment, believed that by the 1830's the rate of profit was less high in Scotland than in England. Lastly, it was undeniable that in the introduction of mechanized and improved methods of production the Scots quickly became dependent on Manchester. In this field Lancashire gained a lead which it never surrendered except in some innovations to the United States until years later.

In only one period after the Napoleonic Wars, the boom of 1825, was the Scottish cotton industry as buoyant as ever before. A slight increase in economic activity in 1818 had little effect on the industry and had indeed only arrested the downward movement in prices, which had been evident since the end of the war. On the other hand the speculation of 1825 led to a rapid expansion of industrial capacity, most notably in the number of power-looms, which increased throughout the 1820's from 2,000 to 10,000, and was sufficient in some minds to lead to excess capacity in the industry. Kirkman Finlay shared this opinion and characterized the period as 'one of great extension, of a rapid sale and activity, but making very moderate returns of profit'; 'stocks on hand are inconsiderable; the payments are good'. While his large, well-established firm was in good shape, others with limited capital resources found survival less easy in the period of lessened profit margins. In desperation some sent goods abroad, discounted the bills on London, and used short-term finance to expand their capacity yet further. The industry never regained the prosperity, speculative as it was, of 1825. It shared in the boom which began in 1833 and which lasted until 1836, but much less so in the boom of 1845. From 1825 there were few signs of overall buoyancy in the Scottish cotton industry; from 1845 it stagnated. In 1831 1,652 bales of raw cotton were used weekly in Scotland; in 1835 2,035 bales were used; in 1840 consumption was 2,364 bales.[1] Thereafter the trend, though it fluctu-

[1] With the end of the Scottish Board of Customs, separate information on imports of cotton wool to Scotland cease. The figures used in this paragraph

ated until the American Civil War according to the state of trade, was stable. An apparent resurgence of production came in 1866, after the Civil War, when 2,500 bales of raw cotton were used weekly in Scotland, but the quantity fell to 1,700 bales weekly in the following year. For the next decade the average weekly consumption in Scotland varied from 1,500 to 2,000 bales. Stocks of raw cotton in Glasgow, which in the 1830's were normally over 20,000 packets, and in the 1840's normally twice as much, even touching 80,000 packets in 1845, collapsed in the mid-1850's and were never again of any significance. Scotland obtained all the cotton it required from Liverpool. As it stagnated, the industry became more concentrated. In 1838 198 cotton mills employed over 35,500 people; in 1850 168 mills, with 1,683,000 spindles and over 23,500 power-looms, employed 36,325 people; in 1856 152 mills, with over 2,041,000 spindles and over 21,600 power-looms, employed 34,698 people; in 1861 163 mills, with nearly 1,915,400 spindles and over 30,100 power-looms, employed 41,237 people. After 1861 the number of mills decreased still further. Lanark-shire and Renfrewshire continued to be the most important centres of the industry. In 1838 of the 198 mills Lanarkshire had 111 and Renfrew-shire had 60. In 1861 Lanarkshire had 96 and Renfrewshire 44 of the 163 mills.

The cotton industry provides one of the earliest examples in modern Scotland of an industry entering a phase of stagnation. Unlike other industries which decayed later, its decline was less disastrous for the Scottish economy largely because the industry was virtually elimin-ated.[1] In the 1830's and 1840's the rising heavy industries meant more for the future of the Scottish economy than the decline in textiles. That decline, however, cannot be explained simply by the production of cotton being overshadowed by more dramatic developments in other fields. Though the relative ease with which those who became redundant were absorbed in other industries gives the impression of industrial displacement, it was not completely so. A more satisfactory explanation of the industry's decline can be found in the reasons for its successful rise. The Scottish cotton industry reaped its early successes through specializing in the production of finer fabrics which provided the basis for an export trade. Severe competition was experienced first

come from the Clyde Sugar Market Reports in the Mitchell Library, Glasgow. The terms 'bales' and 'packets' are not satisfactorily explained, but were used consistently, and so give a reasonable indication of relative movements.

[1] For the subsequent history of the industry see below, pp. 236 and 250–1.

of all in the 1830's in the markets for coarser goods, especially in those in South America which were accessible to the manufacturers in the United States, and so the Scots were forced to rely increasingly on their traditional specialization in fine fabrics, in which they still made profits in the early 1850's, though by then they could do so no longer in the production of coarser cloths. During the first half of the nineteenth century the specialization moved from being a factor favouring growth to being one that did not. Lancashire, which had always concentrated more on the production of coarser goods, was able to gain by the expansion in the demand for them in markets in the east later in the century, but the majority of Scottish firms could not benefit in the same way. Throughout the traditional Scottish markets of Europe and the United States, where sales had been of finer fabrics, competition appeared from native industries, helped, as often as not, by protection.

The financial crisis of 1857 precipitated the collapse of the industry. Its effects were most severe in the west of Scotland through the failure of the Western Bank of Scotland and the temporary closure of the City of Glasgow Bank. Though many regarded the entire history of the Western Bank as an example of profligate banking, its immediate collapse was precipitated by the failure of four cotton firms to which it had granted liberal credit. The financial history of these firms, particularly that of the Western Bank's chief creditor, demonstrated that their collapse was not the product of adverse conditions beyond their control, but of a policy of financial recklessness followed for some time in a desperate endeavour to stave off disaster. Consequently, the cotton famine which followed the American Civil War in the early 1860's simply worsened the existing difficulties and did not cause the end of the days of prosperity of the Scottish cotton industry. Decline and stagnation had become increasingly evident for a quarter of a century before, from the days of the depression which followed the rapid introduction of power-looms around 1825 and the last phase of high prosperity in the industry. Even in the short run the effects of the cotton famine were not unique; the fatal blow was delivered by the 1857 crisis.

It is easier to explain than to justify the collapse of the Scottish cotton industry. Was it inevitable? Could it have been avoided? Were the Scots to blame? Such questions were frequently avoided, because the rise of the heavy industries prevented the decline of the cotton industry from having any obvious detrimental effect on the Scottish economy in the long run and so gave the impression of industrial displacement.

But one factor is evident. The Scottish cotton manufacturers themselves did not transfer to the new and developing industries, with the partial exception of the Houldsworths. If they had done so, no accusation of lack of enterprise could have been levelled against them. Their actions would have demonstrated an ability to move into the developing sectors of the economy. On the other hand the Scottish cotton manufacturers, unlike their rivals in Lancashire, did suffer from competition for labour from the newer industries, but it is impossible to say that such competition for resources from the heavy industries accounts for the failure, and ultimate collapse, of the cotton industry in Scotland. It does seem possible, however, that the growth of the heavy industries in the west of Scotland at that time probably made a certain lack of enterprise on the part of the cotton manufacturers less evident. Scottish producers were slower to adopt newer mechanized methods and frequently depended on Lancashire for the machinery they used. But such factors were of minor importance. The industry was too strongly tied to fine products, and would have found difficulty in breaking into Lancashire's preserves. Scotland's particular specializations no longer paid.

Other textile industries

The rise of the cotton industry encouraged the growth of many subsidiary processes, some of which first appeared when linen production increased in the eighteenth century. The cloth had to be finished through bleaching, printing and embroidery, or sometimes the yarn was woven into specialized goods, notably the Paisley shawl. In addition to the cotton industry and its subsidiaries, Scotland possessed other branches of textile production in the nineteenth century, particularly the manufacture of jute and woollen goods.

Bleaching was concentrated in the Vale of Leven in Dunbartonshire and in the Cart Valley in Renfrewshire. Both had adequate supplies of lime-free water, but the Vale of Leven was especially fortunate in being able to draw from Loch Lomond. The Board of Trustees assisted there in the eighteenth century and used the Dutch bleachers it introduced to teach the art to the natives, many of whom were Highlanders who had originally come to the area during the summer as seasonal migrants, but who had settled there permanently later in the eighteenth century. The greatest drawback to the satisfactory bleaching of cloth, and the reason why the process had to be helped by the Board of Trustees, was its expense. It required large areas of land, which had to be laid out and suitably watered; the process was lengthy, the cloth requiring about eight months' exposure, reduced later to only about four months; it was only a seasonal occupation, which required a considerable temporary labour force. Fortunately, before the large-scale expansion of cotton manufacturing new methods of bleaching by chemical processes were devised. James Watt is reputed to have suggested the first use of Berthollet's method of chlorine bleaching at the Clober bleachfield in Dunbartonshire in 1787, but a further improvement came in 1798 through the introduction by Charles Tennant of the method of bleaching by chloride of lime. Coinciding as it did with the expansion of the cotton industry, the process was quickly adopted, until, shortly after the beginning of the nineteenth century, the west of Scotland had about sixty bleachworks using the chloride of lime method. As a corollary to the development of the new methods of bleaching, the growth of the chemical industry in Scotland was fostered. Charles Tennant founded the St. Rollox works beside the Monkland Canal to manufacture his bleaching powder (chloride of lime) and in due course St. Rollox became the largest chemical works in Europe, but, though the most famous, it was not the only chemical works which grew from the textile industries. Charles Macintosh, whose father had introduced the cudbear dyeing process to Glasgow, discovered that naphtha, obtained from coal tar, dissolved indiarubber. He applied the resulting solution to cloth, thus making it waterproof, and in 1824 founded a company in Glasgow to manufacture waterproof cloth by cementing two folds of cloth together by means of the solution.

The growth of bleaching was partnered by that of printing, the branch of the textile industries to which, more perhaps than to any other, Glasgow merchants made their greatest direct contribution. Calico-printing had a chequered history in the eighteenth century. It was encouraged after 1707 by a prohibition on the importing and use of Eastern prints, but was discouraged in 1712 with the imposition of an excise duty of 3s. a square yard, which was doubled two years later. Then in 1720, when it was felt that the continued popularity of the fabric spelled ruin for the wool and silk industries, the weaving of printed calicoes was forbidden, and linen alone could be printed until 1736, when mixed goods were allowed. Even under such conditions printing was introduced to Scotland, most notably in the foundation of a large works at Pollokshaws in 1742; and so it gained from the more favourable conditions which coincided with the growth of cotton production, especially when any remaining prohibitions on printing were fully removed in 1774 (though the excise duty remained until 1831) and when the technical efficiency of the industry was increased by the invention of cylinder printing by Thomas Bell of Glasgow in 1785. Apart from such general advantages, Renfrewshire and the Vale of Leven had the particular advantages of adequate supplies of water and of labour cheaper than could be obtained nearer Glasgow and so the printworks went to these areas. William Stirling moved his from Dalsholm on the Kelvin to Cordale in the Vale of Leven; the Crums moved from the Gallowgate in Glasgow to Thornliebank in Renfrewshire.

Dyeing was the third subsidiary industry which expanded with the growth of cotton production. Glasgow and Manchester both claimed the distinction of being the first place in Britain to introduce Turkey Red dyeing, but both claims acknowledged French assistance. At Manchester Louis Borelle received a government grant of £2,500, but shortly afterwards another Frenchman, P. J. Papillon, went to Glasgow and, with George Macintosh, father of Charles, was more successful. Since at first colour could be applied only to yarn and thread, expansion was limited, but in 1810 another Frenchman devised a way of dyeing the cloth. Though Scotland was not, therefore, the place where the practice originated, it soon secured a monopoly of Turkey Red dyeing, and, as was only to be expected, the process was most quickly and permanently established in the bleaching-fields of the Vale of Leven, where it was first successfully used at Croftingea in 1827, but the process was soon adopted elsewhere. Thus the Stirlings, who had originally moved into the Vale of Leven from Dalsholm, had their printworks at Cordale, and their dyeworks at Dulquharn, on the next loop of the Leven. Production was soon concentrated in this way in the nineteenth century and most of the Vale of Leven's industry came to be concentrated in eleven works controlled by nine firms.

Lastly, two more specialized products, to which the growth of the textile industries gave a particular stimulus, were, first, sewed muslin, embroidery or tambouring, as the process was sometimes called, after the circular frames on which the cloth was stretched for embroidery, and, second, the Paisley shawl. The former proved exceptionally profitable when sewed muslin became an acceptable substitute for lace

I

at the end of the eighteenth century. Before 1837, the outlines of the
patterns to be sewn were imprinted by blocks, the cost of manufacturing which limited the variety of designs, but after that year printing
by the lithographic press was adopted, so increasing the variety of
designs. Even before this technical change, a few Glasgow firms gave
out work to be done by women in their own homes, mainly in Ayrshire, where schools were set up for the sewers, and where the collapse
of domestic spinning provided a ready supply of female labour. After
the boom of 1825 cheaper Irish domestic workers were also employed,
but the rapid expansion of demand for sewed muslin in the second
quarter of the nineteenth century meant little unemployment for any,
and there was never any tendency for the headquarters of the trade to
move from Glasgow. Indeed one Donaghadee firm, which first introduced the lithographic process of printing the designs, moved its headquarters to Glasgow during this period of most rapid expansion. The
prosperity of the industry was further assured when the reduction in
price after the introduction of the lithographic process led to a rapid
expansion in exports of sewed muslin, especially between 1845 and
1857. The break in the prosperity of the sewed muslin trade came
sharply in the financial crisis of 1857. Expansion was probably too
rapid and unwise after 1845, when cheap domestic labour in Ireland
enabled muslin to be sewn there more cheaply than ever before. The
leading firm in the industry, D. and J. McDonald, though supported in
its increased activities by the Western Bank, was eventually forced to
adopt a variety of dubious expedients to maintain its credit, but to no
avail. In the autumn of 1857 McDonald's collapsed, carrying the
Western Bank with it. Widespread unemployment among muslin
sewers in both Ayrshire and the north of Ireland followed, and from
this blow the Scottish sewed muslin trade never recovered. The manufacture of the Paisley shawl, a similar fashionable product, was established in the early years of the nineteenth century among Paisley's
highly skilled weavers, who found in this occupation a temporary
remedy for their displacement by the power-loom. Though first made
of cotton, the finer shawls were latterly made of spun silk and were,
therefore, so subject to fluctuations of trade and fashion that one local
historian estimated that in the depression of the early 1840's more than
half of the manufacturing concerns in the burgh collapsed.

Though the textile industries were dominated in the nineteenth
century by the cotton industry, the century witnessed the development
of two other branches of textile production, jute and wool, both of

which survived more successfully than cotton production into the twentieth century. The growth of the jute industry in Dundee and district represented an easy transition from the area's older specialization in the manufacture of the coarse baggings of tow and hemp that were used in the packing of cotton wool. Earlier textile production in the area was limited by the absence of water-power, but by the beginning of the nineteenth century steam-driven mills were established and started to spin tow, the waste produced when flax was dressed, instead of flax. Subsequently hemp spinning was introduced, and then in the 1830's depression led the industry into the use of jute, a switch that was especially marked when Dundee obtained the benefit of direct trade with India in 1839, with a consequential reduction in the price of jute. Technical changes provided further encouragement to transfer to the newer fibre. In 1848 James Aytoun of Kirkcaldy devised a method which enabled jute yarns to be woven without sizing and a new method of carding was invented in 1853. When the Crimean and American Civil Wars both provided the stimulus of a sharp increase in demand, Dundee had almost a complete monopoly of world production, and in 1875 imported nearly 114,000 tons of jute, 22,500 tons of flax and 6,500 tons of tow. The expansion of imports was matched by an increase in capacity, especially in the boom of the early 1870's. In 1870 there were 94,520 spindles and 3,744 looms in the Scottish jute industry, virtually all of them in Dundee; in 1874 there were 185,419 spindles and 8,325 looms. During the same period the employment in the industry more than doubled from almost 15,000 to almost 38,000. The industry's expansion had then reached its peak.

The origins of the woollen industry were ancient, but the more vigorous attempts to encourage its growth before 1707 were not clearly surpassed until the early nineteenth century, and throughout most of the previous century the woollen industry, scattered throughout many parts of Scotland, was frequently cited by contemporary commentators as a sector of the economy where increased growth was both feasible and necessary. In the nineteenth century success attended specialization in three branches: the manufacture of tweeds, hosiery and carpets. The growth of the Border tweed industry, centred especially on Galashiels, was aided by the coincidence in time of the use of the power-loom in the manufacture of narrow cloths, the exploitation of fashionable demand through the use of different patterns, and the availability of supplies of wool from Australia, New Zealand and South America. Consequently, many of the Border mills were built in the middle of the nineteenth century. In 1851 72 tweed factories used 329 power-looms and 225 sets of carding engines; in 1862 82 mills used 1,069 power-looms and 305 sets of carding engines. Hosiery work was less prominent though it played an important part in the local economies of Hawick, where the stocking-frame was probably first introduced to Scotland, and, to a lesser extent, of Dumfries. Once again, the increase of the industry was concentrated in the early nineteenth century. In 1791 Hawick had twelve knitting-frames; by 1844 it had about 1,200. The manufacture of carpets grew particularly from the work of Thomas Morton of Kilmarnock, and later of James Templeton of Glasgow, but it also received encouragement from the Board of Trustees for Manufacturers, when by the early nineteenth century it turned its attention from the linen industry to other branches of the economy. By granting various premiums the Board facilitated the introduction into Scotland of the manufacture of carpets comparable to Brussels and Turkish make. Kilmarnock was quickly established as the centre of the industry and by 1839 carpet manufacturing in the town employed about 1,200 persons, who produced goods valued at about £150,000.

VII
THE HEAVY INDUSTRIES

The rise of the iron industry

FOR the past century the heavy industries have so dominated the Scottish economy that it is difficult to realize that their hegemony has not always characterized modern industrial growth in Scotland, not even in the period of great international success by Scottish industry from the 1780's to the 1870's. That period was divided into two phases by the structural changes in the economy, which, around 1830, ushered in the domination of the heavy industries.

The modern Scottish iron industry was pioneered by Carron Company when it was founded in 1759 to smelt with coke and use both the coal and ironstone of Scotland, but its example was not followed quickly. When the Duddon Company came to Loch Fyneside some years later it still smelted with charcoal. When emulation of the new methods did come, Carron Company's example was influential, as the Scottish iron industry's first expansion owed much to Thomas Edington, sometime traveller with Carron Company and later manager of the slitting-mill at Cramond. Edington helped to promote iron-smelting ventures, first, in 1786 at the Clyde ironworks in partnership with William Cadell and, second, in 1789 at Muirkirk, where two of Edington's three partners were John Gillies of the Dalnotter ironworks and William Robertson of the Smithfield works. Muirkirk was thus practically a co-operative venture by Scotland's leading ironmasters, a form of enterprise which was to have a conspicuous, though not wholly successful, record in the Scottish iron industry in the nineteenth century. Though Carron, Clyde and Muirkirk provided the nucleus from which all branches of the Scottish iron industry grew, they had certain features not typical of later developments. Unlike many later firms, they produced more than pig iron. From its inception Carron Company was basically a firm of iron-founders and had forges for the production of bar and malleable iron; Clyde was formed by Edington partly to try to obviate Carron's need to import bar iron from Sweden and Russia; while Muirkirk quickly became the Scottish ironworks which specialized most of all in the manufacture of bar iron for sale. Its produce, according to the almost certainly biased report of the parish minister, was 'little if at all inferior to the best Swedish iron'.[1] Four other ironworks, all less successful, date from the same period of development: Wilsontown (1779), Cleland or Omoa (1789), Glenbuck and Devon (1792). After a short interval Calder, Shotts and Markinch followed at the turn of the century. During the Napoleonic Wars many of these works found themselves in difficulties. Glenbuck, Wilsontown and Markinch became bankrupt, while at Muirkirk a strong effort was made to sell the works to the landlord on moderate terms. Some of these ironworks operated under disadvantageous conditions. The location of Wilsontown was determined by the availability of coal and ironstone, but its inaccessible position meant that iron had to be taken on horse-drawn carts to Bo'ness and to Glasgow and so costs were increased. Again, the failures of the period were not always permanent. Though the Wilsontown works were deserted from 1812 to 1821, Dixon of Govan and Calder continued them thereafter until 1842, during which period the manager, John Condie, made the first satisfactory water-cooled tuyere, an advance necessary for the fullest exploitation of the hot-blast. Nevertheless, in spite of such qualifications, the relative lack of prosperity of the Scottish iron industry cannot be denied. The contrast with conditions in England was striking, or even more so with the resounding successes then being demonstrated at Carron, the one highly successful Scottish concern. Even after the war, at the peak of the boom of 1825, when the iron industry elsewhere in Britain was expanding, the only developments in Scotland were the flotation of the Shotts ironworks as a joint-stock company and the start of the erection of furnaces at Chapelhall by the Monkland Steel Company.

The deficiencies of the Scottish iron industry lay in its high costs of production. In 1829 the cost of production of one ton of pig iron at Clyde was 82s.; at Calder it was 78s. J. B. Neilson could argue that 'unless as much as £6 per ton could be obtained for iron no profit was realized, on account of the heavy expenses attending the furnaces'.[2] Consequently, Scottish iron was priced out of most markets. It was little known in England, Wales or overseas, and could be sold in Scottish markets only because of the cost of transporting iron from

---

[1] *New Statistical Account*, vol. 5, p. 155.

[2] J. B. Neilson, 'On the construction of hot-blast ovens for iron furnaces', quoted in T. B. Mackenzie, *Life of J. B. Neilson* (Glasgow, 1929), p. 13.

England and Wales. Even these sheltered markets were gradually being lost as transport costs fell with improved communications. With the further reduction of transport costs brought by the railways, Scottish iron would almost certainly have been priced out of most of its home markets. Survival lay in lowering production costs. The alternative was to develop specialized finished products such as those on which the success of Carron Company had been built. For a variety of reasons, this was difficult and was not to happen. The production of pig iron was the basis of the modern Scottish iron industry.

The necessary reduction in costs was effected through the utilization of the west of Scotland's natural resources of coal and ironstone. Since their discovery by David Mushet in 1801 the rich and low-rented fields of blackband ironstone had remained almost untouched except for some limited use at Calder and, later, at Clyde, where, however, the blackband was mixed with other ores. At first the use of the blackband ironstone led to little saving, since its advantages were considerably offset by the difficulty of smelting it when using cold air in the small furnaces which were then common. Making possible the profitable, indeed the highly profitable, use of this was the great work of the hot-blast, patented by J. B. Neilson in 1828. The hot-blast and the black-band ironstone provided respectively the technical and the geological bases for the low production costs of the Scottish iron industry. With the introduction of the hot-blast, coal consumption was cut by at least 50 per cent and costs fell rapidly, especially when from 1831 it became general practice to substitute raw coal, especially non-caking splint coal, for coke. At Muirkirk, coal consumption fell from $7\frac{1}{4}$ to $2\frac{1}{4}$ tons per ton of iron produced, and at the works of the Monkland Company it fell from $7\frac{1}{2}$ to 2 tons. This major reduction in costs was helped still further by two other factors operating at the same time. First, mineral royalties were low, since, like many others, the landlords of the west of Scotland failed at first to appreciate the immense economic impor-tance of their ironstone fields and in the early days leased them to the ironmasters for what was later to seem only a nominal royalty. A common lordship for the smaller fields of ironstone was from 1s. to 2s. per calcined ton of $22\frac{1}{2}$ cwt. with a very low annual rental of £100 to £200 in the years when the field was being worked. Second, the price of labour was low. In Scotland many Irishmen and High-landers were used to break strikes and keep wages down. Generally the Irish were preferred and were employed mainly in unskilled jobs, as drawers or roadmen in the pits or as fillers at the furnaces, but, when

Scottish workers went on strike, the Irish were sufficiently skilled to replace them, not only as colliers but sometimes at the furnaces. Since labour and mineral royalties were the chief components of the prime costs of iron production, it is not surprising, therefore, that Scottish firms at this time were reputedly producing at 27s. 6d. a ton. At Muirkirk pig iron was once produced at 25s. per ton, though there the cost of minerals was unusually small, the lordship on coal being only 1d. per ton and that on ironstone being only 3d. per ton. A more representative comparison may be made with conditions at Clyde and Calder. In 1833 at Clyde the normal cost of production was 49s. 6d. per ton; at Calder it was 47s. 6d., coal accounting for only 20 per cent of the total cost. This represented a fall in the cost of production of about 40 per cent from 1829. Such may be taken as representative for the industry.

Just as earlier the Scottish cotton industry had been able to expand on the basis of low costs of production, so in this way the iron industry became able to do likewise. In Scotland the engineering firms and the foundries, working in many cases for overseas customers, could be supplied cheaply, and provided a ready market. In addition, throughout England engineers bought Scottish hot-blast iron for the first time, and found it successful. Previously Scotch pig iron had always been priced higher than Welsh in the Liverpool market, but after the introduction of the hot-blast it was priced lower, and rose to be that market's most important feature. At Liverpool in July 1833 it was quoted at £4 15s. a ton while Staffordshire iron sold at £6. In Sheffield its quality was found to be 'exceedingly good' and the price, even with transport costs added, was so low that at the end of April 1834 the Yorkshire and Derbyshire ironmasters were forced to reduce No. 1 pig iron by 10s. per ton and Nos. 2 and 3 by 7s. 6d. Some criticism appeared. Hot-blast iron was held to be insufficiently strong, especially for large castings, and was disliked by marine engineers. Some specifications, including government ordnance, excluded its use. But those who were doubtful of its strength were convinced by its price. At Muirkirk in 1839, because of complaints about the hot-blast, 221 tons of cold-blast iron were made; Robert Napier took 54 tons and two other customers 29 tons between them, but the rest had to be used in the works itself for malleable iron and castings. At a price which was 30s. a ton higher than the hot-blast iron, it was unsaleable. With its outlook and prospects thus changed the Scottish iron trade moved forward from stagnation towards great prosperity and expansion. By the invention of the hot-blast the trade was 'saved from certain ruin'.[1] More positively, the foundation was then laid for the subsequent rapid expansion of the iron industry. The number of furnaces increased from 27 in 1830 to over 100 in 1844 and the output of pig iron from 37,500 tons to just under 400,000 tons. In the early 1860's the number of furnaces in Scotland reached its peak, though output continued to follow its almost continuous ascent until the record production for the nineteenth century of over 1,200,000 tons in 1870. More strikingly, the increase was not shared by the iron industry of Britain as a whole. Scottish output rose from 5 per cent of the total British output in 1830 to over 25 per cent in the middle 1840's, above which proportion it stayed, almost without a break, for two decades.

During the years from 1830 to 1843 the expansion of the iron industry was comparable only to that in the cotton industry between the 1780's and the 1790's. The pioneers of this phase in the iron industry were undoubtedly the Bairds of Gartsherrie, who put their first furnace into blast in May 1830 and produced 3,100 tons of pig iron in the first year. They built a second furnace in September 1832, and a third in April 1834, when they also decided to build four more. In addition they 'purchased every foot of ground which they can obtain in the neighbourhood and have likewise taken leases of what could not be bought'.[2] Quickly the Bairds became the leading Scottish producers, making 25 per cent of the total output. They took the greatest risk in exploiting the innovation and, as it was successful, made large profits. They cleared almost £270,000 between 1832 and 1840. In 1856 an American described them as 'princely proprietors . . . the richest manufacturers in the world'.[3] By the 1870's they were reputed to be earning £750,000 a year, while in size Gartsherrie was second only to Dowlais. The example of the Bairds was followed by others. Two other works, both involved in early experiments with blackband ironstone, were also active in the first phase of the expansion. Calder had four furnaces in 1830; Chapelhall (the Monkland Iron and Steel Company) had two. These successes encouraged others to extend their capacity. In 1831 the Monkland Steel Company built a third furnace

---

[1] M. Dufrénoy, 'Report on the use of heated air in the Iron Works of Scotland and England' (Paris, 1834). Translated in *Journal of the Franklin Institute*, vol. xv (N.S.), p. 212.

[2] *The Glasgow Herald*, 28th April 1834.

[3] *On the Statistics and Geography of the Production of Iron*. Reprint of anonymous pamphlet in Glasgow University Library.

at Chapelhall; in 1833 Colin Dunlop, from Clyde, and John Wilson started Dundyvan, which was to be Gartsherrie's rival in size, and took a large area near Coatbridge to work for minerals; Wilsontown, which had had a chequered career and disappointed many hopes, was re-opened in April 1834 by Dixon of Calder, who had purchased it some years previously, but had soon closed it down. Omoa, 'which had been a scene of desolation for a number of years',[1] was restarted at the beginning of 1833. In June of that year six furnaces were being built in Scotland by established producers, three at Gartsherrie and one each at Calder, Dundyvan and by the Monkland Company. In November the Shotts Iron Company resolved to build a second furnace but post-poned its operation for two years through a shortage of minerals. The blackband ironstone was leased equally rapidly. On the Hamilton Estates in north Lanarkshire almost all the ironmasters were eagerly prospecting for it, while in central Scotland three pieces of land, which the Duke of Hamilton thought of adding to his possessions, exceeded any price his representative considered worth offering, mainly because of competition from the ironmasters, Dixon and the Houldsworths.

Even a fall in prices and a gradual decline into depression between 1837 and 1843 did not stop the capital investment in the industry. The established producers expanded their operations. The Bairds built two furnaces in 1837, and in 1839 decided to add eight new furnaces to their existing eight. Four of these were in blast by 1840, three more started in 1841, and the last in 1843. Firms of lesser importance also expanded. In 1837 one more furnace appeared at Calderbank (the Monkland Iron and Steel Company); in 1838 there was another at Calderbank, one at Dundyvan and the Shotts Iron Company started a new ironworks at Castlehill; in 1839 one furnace more was added to the existing two at Shotts itself; in 1840 two more appeared at Calder and at Calderbank and three at Dundyvan; and another furnace was erected at Dundyvan in 1841. But the most startling increases, particularly characteristic of the period, were among the new producers or at the new works. In 1837 Summerlee was established and by 1842 had six furnaces. Coltness, started in the same year, had six by 1845. In 1838 Alison, Merry and Cunninghame began at Carnbroe and had built six furnaces by 1843. In 1839 Dixon started at Govan, meaning to build eight furnaces, but by the end of 1843 had only five and added only one more. The foundation stone of the Blair ironworks was laid in August 1839 and three furnaces were built by December 1843. William Galloway

---

[1] *Glasgow Saturday Post*, 26th April 1834.

bought the estate of Househill at Paisley for £45,000 in February and had two furnaces by 1843. At the end of the year the Cessnock Works were established near Galston and by 1843 had two furnaces. In the summer of 1840 the Glasgow and Ayrshire Iron Company was floated to take over Muirkirk. In the same year operations began at Glengarnock and three furnaces were soon built, the works being taken over by Merry and Cunninghame in 1842. Langloan, opened in 1841, acquired three furnaces in the depression years and the Garscube ironworks two. In 1842 no new works were started but the existing ones still expanded. By the time of the railway boom of the 1840's the Scottish iron industry was well established to take advantage of the rising demand for iron.

The disposal of the iron

The rapid expansion of the industry was maintained by an equally rapid expansion of sales. The times were propitious. British demand for iron was rising rapidly in the 1830's and 1840's just as the reduction in their costs of production made the Scottish ironmasters more able to meet it. In general two main methods of disposal of the iron faced the industry. It was possible either to use the pig iron within Scotland, perhaps to produce goods for sale elsewhere, or, alternatively, to export the pig iron without any further processing. Around 1830 the heavy industries of Scotland were in such a rudimentary state of development that home demand could not automatically absorb the increased output. Yet two reasons would have justified an expectation that such home consumption would increase, at least in the long run. First, there were adequate supplies of fuel, especially in Lanarkshire, for the further processing of iron. Second, before 1830 Carron was the only Scottish ironworks with an international reputation which the Company had earned through the sale of finished goods. Yet even such favourable influences were inadequate to lead to the growth of a demand sufficient to absorb the pig iron produced at home, and the disparate rate of growth between the production of pig iron and its use in iron manufacture is one of the most striking features, and failures, of the iron industry in Scotland. While the finishing trade grew, it consumed only from between 30 per cent to 50 per cent of the output of the Scottish furnaces.

The foundries provided the most ready market for pig iron. Though small, they were numerous, about twenty operating in the environs of Glasgow alone in 1830, and when they increased all over Scotland, again more conspicuously in number than in size, the quantity of pig iron used in them increased accordingly. By 1846, the first year for which any statistics are available, they consumed almost 200,000 tons of pig iron. The surprising failure was, however, in the production of malleable iron, in which the early attempts, at Clyde, Muirkirk and elsewhere had been insignificant, though in that they accorded with the state of the entire Scottish iron industry at the time. When smelting increased under the impetus of the hot-blast, puddling still lagged behind. In 1834 the Frenchman Dufrénoy, on his tour of the Scottish ironworks, could report without exception that 'in the works near Glasgow, they make iron for the foundry'.[1] Only in 1836 was puddling properly introduced, but until 1839, though many of the ironworks had foundries attached to them, as at Shotts or at Devon, little bar iron was produced by anyone. Even after the introduction of the hot-blast Muirkirk still remained the exception, but produced only up to 100 tons a week.

Attention was directed towards the development of malleable iron facilities on a comparatively extensive scale only in the depression years of the late 1830's and early 1840's. The Monkland Iron and Steel Company abandoned the making of about 100 tons of steel annually at Calderbank and in 1840 had mills and forges capable of producing about 220 tons of malleable iron a week. Dixon, who had previously started but abandoned the manufacture of malleable iron at St. Rollox, built a bar-iron plant at Govan with 42 puddling furnaces, capable of producing about 200 tons a week. The malleable ironworks at Dundyvan, which also went into operation in 1840, was capable of producing about 300 tons a week. Apart from two small forges, one at Lancefield and one at Gartness, where they puddled a little white iron, there were no other malleable operations in Scotland. Total production could not have been more than about 40,000 tons a year. Yet it is doubtful if at this time such a large quantity was being produced, because at that time Muirkirk was working at less than 50 per cent of its possible capacity. Though greater than anything that had gone before, this investment in malleable ironworks in the early 1840's was not great. Towards the end of that decade came a further burst of investment. By 1845 Neilson had founded Mossend, capable of

[1] Dufrénoy, *op. cit.*, p. 419.

producing about 80 to 100 tons, and total Scottish malleable iron production, of about 40,000 to 50,000 tons annually, probably consumed the output of only about 15 furnaces. At the same time the new and overwhelming demand for railway iron appeared. Consequently more interest was shown in malleable iron production in the 1840's than at any other period and in the middle of the decade three malleable iron companies were floated. They differed from the earlier Scottish practice by not having the malleable ironworks integrated with blast furnaces but aimed at manufacturing the pig iron produced by the blast furnaces in the localities after which the companies took their names: the West of Scotland, the East of Scotland and Ayrshire. These ventures seemed bound to succeed. When Scotland's malleable ironworks absorbed such a small proportion of the output of the country's increasing number of blast furnaces, any expansion in that direction seemed desirable; their location guaranteed plentiful supplies of pig iron; most important of all, the malleable ironworks were owned and directed by the leading Scottish ironmasters. The high hopes they engendered were, however, doomed to disappointment as the lives of all three companies were short. The first to fall was the Ayrshire Iron Company in 1847; the West of Scotland Malleable Iron Company closed its works in 1848; the East of Scotland Malleable Iron Company did likewise in the following year.

The reasons for such abysmal failure, in face of good prospects, are difficult to determine, but two may be suggested. The first reason was the nature and composition of Scotch pig iron, which was highly suitable for the foundry but not for the forge. On this grade the trade built its reputation, so that the Scottish producers had almost a monopoly of the trade in foundry iron and in some works, Gartsherrie for instance, forge pig iron was rarely made. On the other hand the great suitability of Scotch pig iron in the foundry meant that it was less suitable for the forge, where it had frequently to be mixed with other brands, as was done, for instance, in South Wales and even in the United States. But, at least in the early days, the Scots were unwilling to adopt such an arrangement which required the importation of pig iron. The second reason, which may have accounted for failure, was that the two chief phases of relatively unsuccessful investment in Scottish malleable ironworks, in the late 1830's and early 1840's and again in the late 1840's, were periods of depression. Scottish ironmasters turned their attention to the possibilities of manufacturing iron only when profits from the earlier process of iron manufacture declined. During the 1840's, Scottish ironmasters saw others making large profits by producing railway iron; worse still these profits were sometimes earned through the importation of Scotch pig iron, which was then mixed with other brands to be made into railway iron. So long as they were able to sell pig iron at high prices the Scots do not seem to have been greatly alarmed by this state of affairs. When prices fell, they felt able to augment declining profits by producing malleable iron. Almost certainly for this reason the Scottish ironmasters invested in malleable ironworks during years of relative depression. Yet it was hardly the way to achieve profitable production. When the timing of the investment is combined with the comparatively unsuitable nature of the pig iron, the failure of the early attempts at malleable iron production are perhaps explicable, or, it could be held that, if the Scots had combined the production of malleable iron with that of pig iron from the early days of the industry, their chances of success would have been greater. They might still have been forced to import pig iron from England and Wales to use with their native iron, but would have retained part of the malleable trade in their hands. These unsuccessful efforts at malleable iron production ended any large-scale attempts by Scottish ironmasters to emulate the ironworks of England and Wales. Scottish production of malleable iron remained comparatively small. Some individual forges, such as Parkhead and Lancefield, were large and famous, but they used only a proportion of Scotch pig iron to mix with other brands and consequently failed to provide a major outlet for the produce of Scottish furnaces. Indeed some forges were located in Scotland primarily to be near markets in the shipyards rather than to be near the raw material. Their reputation was gained by their skill in such work rather than by the cheapness of their products. The sum of such developments was that home demand for pig iron did not rise as many anticipated. Neither foundries nor malleable ironworks consumed a major part of the pig iron produced in Scotland. When the first satisfactory statistics became available in 1866, the foundries took 300,000 tons and the malleable ironworks nearly 200,000 tons of pig iron. In 1873, reflecting the increasing competition the Scottish pig-iron industry was experiencing, the foundries took only 230,000 tons and the malleable ironworks 143,000 tons.

Since domestic consumption did not absorb even half of Scottish production, the industry quickly relied on sales to external markets. Though those in England and Wales were nearest, the proximity of the Scottish ironworks to the sea enabled iron to be despatched abroad with comparative ease. Statistics of shipments, foreign and coastwise, reflect the relative importance of the two groups, though, since some coastwise shipments later went overseas, the figures for foreign shipments must be regarded as a minimum. In 1846, the first year for which reliable statistics are available, 119,000 tons or 21 per cent of Scottish production was shipped foreign and 257,000 tons or 46 per cent of production was shipped coastwise. By 1873 the position of the two markets had been reversed. In that year nearly 400,000 tons went foreign (though as much as 617,000 tons had gone overseas in 1872) and nearly 300,000 tons, almost the same as the year before, went coastwise. The relative proportions indicate the difference more clearly. In 1873, while total sales were increased beyond the production for that year through a stock decrease of 7 per cent, 37 per cent was used at home, 30 per cent was shipped coastwise and 40 per cent was shipped foreign. Such proportions were fairly representative. Though England and Wales provided ready markets for the industry's output in the early days of its expansion, foreign markets soon became as important, sometimes even more so. In the period of the industry's great prosperity, from the 1830's to the 1870's, roughly one-third was absorbed by each of the three main groups considered. But it was in foreign exports that the Scottish achievement relative to other British producers was most clearly demonstrated. From 1848, when Scottish pig-iron exports increased in the face of falling British exports, until 1854, Scotland sent abroad more than 90 per cent of the total United Kingdom exports of pig iron. Only thereafter did the proportion fall. In 1855 it was 84 per cent and then, except for 1859 when it was 80 per cent, it never rose above 75 per cent of the total. The decline was caused by the increased competition Scotland experienced from the iron industry of the north-east of England, which, after the mid-1850's, encroached on Scottish markets at home and overseas. From the 1850's began the end of the Scots international commercial supremacy in iron production, but a more certain end came only later through competition from producers overseas. Until after the 1870's that could be ignored. Until then the Scots were simply building up the industrial potential of their future competitors.

The coal industry

The growth of the heavy industries rested on the sure foundation of adequate coal supplies, but, even before their fortunes became closely interwoven, the coal and iron industries had experienced a similar pattern of development. Both had ancient antecedents in Scotland, but both were totally transformed in the nineteenth century.

In the eighteenth century, even before the rapid industrial expansion which began in the 1780's, the coal industry found difficulty in meeting an increasing demand from domestic and industrial consumers. Nevertheless, almost till the end of the century, the industry's problems arose less from a rapid increase in demand than from the exceptional problems of increasing supply in the existing organization of the industry. Two particular difficulties arose in production: first, the problem, general to all countries, of ensuring better drainage; and, second, the problem, unique to Scotland, of improving the supply of labour. To deal with the first, mechanical means to lift water from pits were used increasingly instead of drainage by the gravity flow of the day-level, and so the depth of mining was correspondingly extended. Water-engines and horse-gins used different means of power for the same technique of turning a wheel, which, by various methods, propelled an endless chain of buckets up and down a pit shaft, but from the end of the eighteenth century these were supplemented, and later supplanted, by steam-power vertical-cylinder beam engines.

The second problem, of improving the supply of labour, was more peculiar to Scotland, where the conditions of serfdom of the Scottish miners made the occupation repellent to most people.[1] Some of the coalmasters, among them Sir James Clerk of Penicuik in 1772, appreciated the dislike.

'The servitude the Coaliers have now for more than one century been subjected to has not only been the real cause of the present great scarcity of hands We all justly complain of, but which is infinitely of worse consequence, has rais'd such a spirit of national prejudice and total aversion amongst the Inhabitants of this country to that particular business that I am much affraid that even the best regulated schemes we can possibly devise, will prove inefectual, at least for a great number of years, totaly to root out these national prejudices.'[2]

[1] For details of serfdom see below, pp. 188-9.
[2] Scottish Record Office, *Clerk of Penicuik Muniments*, 1,119.

Carron Company experienced the problem immediately after its foundation and tried to resolve it by introducing English colliers, who had the added attraction of being reputed to be more industrious and sober than the Scots, and by recruiting pauper children as 'apprentice' miners. Generally the ironworks offered special inducements to attract the colliers they required to their pits, thus rousing great indignation among the established coalmasters who felt themselves unfairly treated. One writer, almost certainly the 9th Earl of Dundonald, complained that

> 'the very *great profits* they now make on the manufacture of iron, *exclusive* of an extensive consumption and handsome profit on their coal and minerals, enables them at present to give or rather to promise, such wages to colliers, etc. etc. as coal-owners cannot afford to give'.[1]

Hence came attempts by the coalmasters to secure legislative prohibition against ironmasters enticing their colliers. But even the ironmasters were not immune from such problems. The root of the problem was that no one in Scotland was interested in becoming a collier, an attitude which lasted even after final emancipation in 1799, and gave the Irish their great opportunity.

The industry finally broke away from the restrictions on supply when the growth of the heavy industries made the older methods of production no longer viable. Their increasing demand was felt around the Forth in the late eighteenth century, especially since Carron, then the leading ironworks, drew its supply from that locality. During the French Wars its consumption increased sharply, while some of the works which appeared in the fifteen years after the foundation of Wilsontown were, in contrast to those which appeared after 1830, frequently dependent for their coal on the production of the Forth basin. Since it was suggested that each furnace consumed, directly or indirectly, about 9,000 tons of coal annually, the cause of the concern of contemporaries is clear and went some way to justifying the suggestion by one alarmist that 'the ironworks and foundries of Carron and Clyde alone consume as many coals as all the inhabitants of Edinburgh'.[2] But alarm was only over the difficulties of increasing

---

[1] *Description of the Estate of Culross, particularly of the Mineral and Coal Property* (Edinburgh, 1793), p. 63.

[2] *Considerations on the Present Scarcity and High Rise of Coals in Scotland* (Edinburgh, 1793), p. 20.

supply adequately to meet the demand. There were no fears of the absolute exhaustion of mineral supplies which were to be expressed by the 1870's. In the late eighteenth century all saw adequate coal resources simply awaiting efficient exploitation.

The first fear of exhaustion arose from the great demand from the ironworks after 1830, and this time it was a demand concentrated in the west. This represented a change in the experience of the different regions of Scotland. Until the rise of the iron industry the western coalfield was concerned primarily with domestic consumption and with the export trade, especially to the West Indies, America and Ireland, to which the Ayrshire collieries maintained their traditional trade through the many changes of the nineteenth century. Before the 1830's the only industrial demand in the west, though an increasing one, arose from the growing use of steam-engines in the industrial establishments around Glasgow. By contrast in the east, though the collieries around the Forth shipped most of their coal elsewhere, they also met a varied industrial demand from ironworks, distilleries, glass-works and limeworks, while the output from the Lothians was absorbed entirely by the domestic and industrial demand of Edinburgh and district. By the late eighteenth century the eastern coalmasters could not meet the increasing demand and the deficiency was offset by imports of English coal, especially after 1793, when Henry Dundas ensured the removal of a tax on coal shipped coastwise in Scotland, though a similar tax remained on coal shipped coastwise in England until 1831. The relative position of the producers in the east deteriorated still further, when transport improvements, especially the opening of the Union Canal in 1822, facilitated the movement of coal from the west. Coal from the Monklands was despatched to Edinburgh. In 1824 a group of 'West Country Gentlemen' were reported to be planning to bring 60,000 tons of coal to Edinburgh and until the mid-1830's, whenever the price of coal in Edinburgh rose slightly above that in Glasgow, more coal than ever moved east. Thereafter the prosperity of the industry in the west, as it met the demand of the expanding iron industry, limited the competition for some years.

Though part of Scottish output was exported, the proportion rose slowly to about only 10 per cent in the early 1870's. There was no doubt, therefore, that in the previous forty years the coal industry depended for its prosperity on the level of iron production. Indeed the growth of the iron industry changed the form of much of Scottish coal production. Previously, and even up till 1870, mining remained on a small scale. Pits were generally small, though not necessarily shallow, and, in spite of technical advances, many still worked along an outcrop until drainage difficulties caused them to be abandoned. The advent of the ironmasters as coalmasters did not necessarily lead quickly to a new type of individual colliery, but it did introduce a new type of organization to the industry, something much bigger than anything previously known in Scotland. By the 1870's William Baird and Company and Merry and Cunninghame each had more than twice the number of collieries of any other company and, since they were concentrated in the iron-producing districts, their influence on colliery organization and management was increased. As the importance of the ironmasters in the coal industry grew, so the importance of noble coalmasters, who had frequently determined the industry's growth in the eighteenth century, declined. Consequently many of the organizational and social problems of the whole Scottish coal industry at this time were determined by the policies of the ironmasters. Their aims and actions helped to produce the environment typical initially of the west of Scotland but ultimately of the industry in the whole of Scotland in the nineteenth century.

The policies of the ironmasters were not only social but also economic determinants. Yet care must be taken not to exaggerate what this means. Unfortunately statistics of coal production are not available before 1854, by which time the proportion of total coal output consumed by the ironworks had almost certainly declined, but was still approximately one-third of Scotland's production of 7,448,000 tons. Consequently, though the ironworks were undoubtedly the most important single consumer, overall the consumption of other industrial users, and of domestic demand, is obvious. Nevertheless, since the rapid expansion of the coal industry had been brought about by the ironmasters, the relative decline of their demand posed special problems in the industry. By the 1870's the extent of the decline could not be denied as in 1873 only about 16 per cent of Scotland's coal production of almost 16,855,000 tons was used in the ironworks. The basic reason for this changing relationship was the increasing competition which the iron industry itself was beginning to experience especially after 1866. It was in the late 1860's, after the crisis of 1866, that the coal industry's difficulties first became evident. They were increased through a number of pits, which had been sunk in the years of prosperity, only then coming into operation, and were made most evident by the ironmasters beginning to sell their own coal. The appearance of the ironmasters as salesmasters gave rise to a dichotomy of interests within the trade, and one which was not easily resolved.

The basic requirement of the coal industry from the late 1860's was to obtain new markets to offset the declining consumption of the furnaces. The proportion of total production absorbed by overseas demand doubled between 1854 and the early 1870's but was only partial compensation. The position of the coal industry in the 1870's was, therefore, similar to the iron industry. In the boom which culminated in 1872 and 1873 it was very profitable, but inadequate transport facilities on the railways and deliberate restriction of output led to a fall in production in the face of high prices. At the end of the boom the uncertain position of the coal industry was abundantly demonstrated, when, while iron prices were maintained, coal prices were not. The most important consumer of coal in Scotland was finding difficulty in meeting international competition, a difficulty which grew more evident in later years. The coal industry could not easily find a substitute, even before the years of increasing international competition which came after 1873. The industry which had brought about its earlier rise was becoming increasingly less able to support it.

VIII

FINANCE

Banking policy

THE reorganization of Scottish banking after the collapse of the Ayr Bank in 1772 gave rise to a structure which remained reasonably stable throughout the nineteenth century, and in which, variegated as it was, three different groups of banking institutions may be distinguished.

The first, and best-known group consisted of the chartered banks, led by the two oldest, the Bank of Scotland and the Royal Bank. Though the British Linen Bank quickly began to concentrate on banking, it was nominally authorized to do so only in 1849. The incorporation of these three banks became a privilege envied by others, especially as the charters,[2] since they contained no provision to the contrary, were assumed to confer limited liability. Two other banks, the Commercial Bank of Scotland and the National Bank of Scotland, were granted charters in the nineteenth century, but their liability remained unlimited until they were registered under the Companies' Act of 1879. The distinction within the ranks of the chartered banks is important for another reason. While the Commercial and National Banks were originally critics of the older institutions, all chartered banks later became the targets of criticism from others.

The second identifiable group of banking institutions were the private banks, which were simple partnerships, distinguished from other banking enterprises by being located in Edinburgh and, consequently, by maintaining a closely knit relationship with the capital's chartered banks. The origins of such bankers were diverse and many first entered banking only incidentally from other pursuits. The background of the firm of John Coutts and Company of Edinburgh indicates the form of development. Coutts laid the foundations of his fortunes as a merchant in Edinburgh, but the firm's connections widened and, even before his death, one of his sons was connected with a Rotterdam merchant house, which supplied tea, spirits, and other goods for smugglers on the east and north coasts of Scotland.

---

[1] The Act of Parliament in the case of the Bank of Scotland.

The corn dealings, which had been the basis of the Coutts family fortunes even in the seventeenth century, led to widespread connections. They acquired an agent in Northumberland, who also made purchases in Berwickshire; agents in Dundee, Aberdeen and Portsoy who purchased from the Mearns to the Moray Firth; landed proprietors who made joint purchases for them at Toftingall in Caithness and Rosehall in Ross-shire. The trade was not confined to Scotland. Shipments came from Yarm and Stockton in north-east England; from King's Lynn, Fakenham and Yarmouth in East Anglia; from Haverfordwest in South Wales; from Drogheda and Belfast in Ireland; from Dantzig and Königsberg. Inevitably these various transactions involved the need to negotiate bills of exchange, on Holland, France, Italy, Spain and Portugal, as well as on London, but in the early eighteenth century the need was not met by the chartered banks, since the Bank of Scotland, after an early and unsatisfactory venture, had temporarily deserted the field. The way was left open for merchant houses, which required such a service, to perform it for themselves and then for some to specialize in doing so. Other early private bankers had a similar background to Coutts: among them were Adam and Thomas Fairholme; Fordyce, Malcolm and Company; Arbuthnot and Guthrie; Gibson and Hogg. Then in the middle of the eighteenth century some firms were formed specifically for such monetary transactions, though sometimes in combination with other trading activities, which were often more diverse than those of their forerunners, most of whom started as corn factors. Of this group the two most permanent were Mansfield and Company and William Cumming, firms which originated from a draper's and from a cloth shop respectively. Others included Seton and Houston, who originally manufactured woollen goods; Thomas Kinnear, originally an insurance broker before his sons started their banking business; and William Alexander and Sons who were chiefly employed as purchasers of tobacco for the Farmers-General of the French customs.

The chartered banks and the Edinburgh private bankers are easily identified groups; the third group is more difficult to identify and is indeed the residual element. It was, therefore, much bigger than the two others, since it included both joint-stock companies and private partnerships, and even, during the earlier part of their history before they were chartered, the Commercial and National Banks. Unity was given to this diversity by a common criticism of the two other groups, especially when the two co-operated in a refusal to follow the policies advocated by their rivals. Normally the dispute centred round the adequacy of credit facilities.

The financial crisis of 1772 apparently vindicated the policies of the more conservative bankers and certainly eliminated those of their fellows most willing to assist more risky enterprises, but their triumph does not lead to the further conclusion that stability characterized the Scottish banking system after 1772. A minor factor which did provide a greater degree of stability from 1772 were changes in the Scottish law of bankruptcy which made it less necessary or desirable for any one person to precipitate the bankruptcies always made imminent by any financial crisis and which invariably had an adverse effect on banks, especially since the failure of anyone with an obligation to a bank so easily caused a run on them. In the early eighteenth century the law enabled any creditor who arrested the effects of his debtor to secure for himself the value of the property thus attached to the exclusion of other creditors, even if their arrestments should follow at once. Under this procedure some debtors helped creditors, with whom they were on intimate terms, by informing them privately of an impending bankruptcy, so enabling the favoured creditor to arrest his goods. Apart from the advantages of such advance information, creditors living close to a debtor always had a better chance of making the first arrestments over those living at a distance. Though in 1754 the Court of Session first made an order that all arrestments laid within thirty days of the bankruptcy should be of equal effect, it was not renewed after seven years and a complete change came only in June 1772 with an Act authorizing an equal distribution of a debtor's effects among the creditors. But, while the new provision removed a factor which frequently precipitated bankruptcies, and may have helped to mitigate the repercussions of the crisis of 1772, it did nothing to remove the fundamental causes which led to them.

Important changes in the Scottish economy meant that these fundamental causes had taken on a very different form by 1793, the year of the next major financial collapse in Scotland after 1772. A major difference between these years was that the industrial importance of the west of Scotland had greatly increased, and Glasgow and the west of Scotland suffered much more noticeably in 1793 than it had done two decades earlier. Two financial failures heightened the distress. The effects of the first, of the Glasgow Arms Bank, were lessened by the bank having been struggling for some years; the second, a week later, was more important, as it was of James Dunlop, whose reputation and credit were

second to none, but who, after the collapse of the tobacco trade in
1776, had moved extensively into landed and industrial ventures,
which he could not maintain after the outbreak of the French Wars
in 1793. On the other hand in Edinburgh, in sharp contrast to 1772,
only one bank, Bertram, Gardner and Company failed, though the
survivors experienced difficulties. Thus Sir W. Forbes, J. Hunter and
Company found that, while under normal circumstances in their
business the amount received about equalled the amount paid out, in
the winter of 1792 to 1793 more was being paid out, increasing to an
unfavourable balance of nearly £53,000 in March 1793 and to over
£105,000 in April 1793.

The problems of 1793 were increased in 1797, when the Bank of
England suspended cash payments, whereupon representatives of the
three old chartered banks and of Sir William Forbes' bank met and
agreed to suspend the convertibility of notes into gold likewise, a joint
action then remarkable but which became increasingly common.
Their decision was supported by the leading inhabitants of Edinburgh
and elsewhere and, though there was a popular demand for assistance,
and some real hardship through the gross inadequacy of small change,
especially for the payment of wages, the crisis was in some ways more
easily survived than were those of 1772 and 1793. The system of
mutual support, rather than the wisdom of other policies, began to be
the key to the success and stability of the Scottish banking system. Such
consultation reflected a subtle, if not openly recognized, change in the
organization of Scottish banking towards the end of the eighteenth
and especially at the beginning of the nineteenth centuries, a period
when private and local banking declined before an advancing system of
national banking. Before their decay, indeed partly its cause, the
private banks became increasingly associated with the chartered banks,
and together they followed policies which stimulated such criticism
that new banks appeared to rival them. The early nineteenth century
was a period when two ways of thought on banking practice, similar
to those of the mid-eighteenth century, were evident: the conservative
policy advocating stability and the radical criticism advocating expansion. Consequently, the period of boom in the short peace of 1802 was
one when, among many indices of economic activity in Scotland at
that time, the appearance of a number of banks was among the more
notable. Even the two senior banks, the Bank of Scotland and the
Royal Bank, increased their capitals to £1,500,000, but, more symptomatic of the economic state of the country, was the creation, especially

in 1802, of a number of new institutions outside Edinburgh, in Fife, Renfrew, Falkirk, and elsewhere. The fate of these banks was unfortunate, most notorious of all being the Fife Banking Company, which collapsed in 1829, leaving its shareholders with a liability of £5,500 a share. That disaster was exceptional, but none of these new banks could easily rival the success of their elder competitors, partly because the longer-established banks had more stable and more profitable connections while the newer institutions were often left with the riskiest types of business, partly because the older banks did not tolerate the appearance of the new banks lightly and tried to arrest their progress, as, for instance, by refusing to accept their notes. Both groups could argue that they were entitled to adopt the policies they did. The older banks felt they should refuse the notes because the institutions issuing them were unsound and often insolvent; the newer banks felt that by doing so the older banks were trying to maintain their privileged position and were thus stifling legitimate aspirations in banking. Who was correct? This was the key issue to banking disputes and policy in the first half of the nineteenth century.

The arguments of the critics of the existing system took two forms: first, objections were raised to the organization of the banks, and, in particular, to the relationship between the private and the chartered banks; second, the type of lending policy followed by both groups of banks was criticized.

The source of the unique relationship between the chartered and the private banks lay in the difference between the early activities of the two groups. In contrast to the chartered banks the private banks entered banking in an indirect way, by gradually providing the banking services which as customers they could not easily obtain. The private banks were, therefore, always in the most direct contact with those who wanted banking services; not so the chartered banks. By the beginning of the nineteenth century this dichotomy between the two groups was becoming more rigid. By then the chartered banks dealt rarely with the general public. An individual usually obtained finance only from a private banker, who in turn went to a chartered bank for any assistance he required. Apart from anything else the public paid higher charges through this system. In addition, its growth led to the chartered banks being controlled largely by the private bankers, who had therefore a decisive say in the granting of loans. The system had its advantages to both private and chartered banks. The latter thereby avoided bearing considerable risks and many of the detailed difficulties involved in small deposits and discounts, while the system assured the private bankers custom they might otherwise have lost. That the customer paid more was irrelevant to both sides, so long as they seemed secure in its practice, and certainly the additional cost would have been less oppressive if the private bankers had acted with vision and foresight. They could conceivably have given greater attention to the individual needs of their customers than the chartered banks, especially since the latter's branch system was not extensively developed until later in the nineteenth century. But the private bankers did not operate thus. They occupied a very low place in the public's esteem. To Lord Cockburn:

> 'no men were more devoid of spirit, and even of the proper spirit of their trade, than our old Edinburgh bankers. Respectable men they were, but without talent, general knowledge, or any liberal objects, they were the conspicuous sycophants of existing power.'[1]

Even the favour of a private banker was insufficient to ensure a ready loan because of the lending policies followed by the Scottish banks. This was the second, and more vital, ground of objection to the banking establishment of Scotland. Branch banking reduced the number of possible different policies, while the concentration of control of most of these different units in Edinburgh made for consultation and so for joint action. The organization of banking made the implementation of common policies easy and yet more difficult to breach. The objection to the common lending policy was that inadequate funds were available for the growing demands for industrial investment, chiefly because the largest part of the banks' loanable funds was absorbed in two other outlets: the discounting of bills and investment in government securities.

Earlier, especially in the eighteenth century, the chief means of advancing funds in Scotland was by the discounting of bills, though cash-credits steadily became a more important and widespread means of utilizing funds in the first half of the nineteenth century. The system was, therefore, largely the same as in England, except that in Scotland there was less need for the banks to rediscount bills when the system of branch banking became more fully developed. Then the bill-brokers' importance declined and it became easier to control the rediscount of fictitious bills. Nevertheless, any concentration on bill

[1] Henry Cockburn, *Memorials of His Own Time* (edition by H. A. Cockburn, Edinburgh, 1910), pp. 238–9.

discounting as a means of supplying the necessary funds for business in the late eighteenth century deprived few with a legitimate demand of the finance they required. Since the demand for assistance at that time came dominantly from commerce rather than from industry, most potential borrowers held the necessary trade bills. But concentration on the discounting of bills led others to devise less reputable means of gaining assistance by the method and in the eighteenth century was almost certainly one factor forcing the growth of the issue of accommodation bills.[1] More important, in the nineteenth century the appearance of increasing demands for finance for industrial development produced a group with legitimate demands for financial aid, but without the accepted security. Sometimes advances could be obtained on the security of heritable property, or, as with the pig-iron warrant, a security similar to a trade bill was devised, but often more typical were demands for aid which were not easily met. The bankers' objections to meeting them had, of course, some validity, as these unsatisfied requests were often for finance for fixed capital formation. Advances on the security of trade bills and pig-iron warrants were obviously in a different category. But this was an argument the new industrialists could not readily accept. It seemed to them that the bankers were simply ignoring a new, but entirely legitimate, demand for accommodation through a blind and dogged adherence to outmoded lending policies.

The industrialists' argument was re-enforced by the importance of the second outlet for much of the banks' funds, government securities, probably the more relevant outlet in the first half of the nineteenth century. The Edinburgh banks invested a large proportion of their funds in government stock, which meant, of course, that a smaller proportion was available for lending to industry. The chartered banks first invested heavily in this field during the Napoleonic Wars, when the funds were standing considerably below par, at 60 or even less. Investing at this level gave them a good return and, when prices rose, they made capital gains which were not generally realized since the banks did not sell out. Instead, they continued to hold an amount equal to between one-third to one-quarter of their total deposits in Exchequer bills or government stock. The chartered banks went even further and held that this ratio should be maintained by all banks, some even being willing to support legislation to achieve it, believing that such a large proportion of their assets should be kept in a fairly liquid form in order to meet any emergencies. However, even when it was admitted that

[1] See p. 72–4.

the chartered banks' policy of distributing assets ensured a high degree of liquidity, and so of stability, it was not admitted, as the chartered banks frequently suggested, that any other policy was irresponsible and bound to lead to financial disaster. In complete contrast to the attitudes of the chartered banks, some argued that it was not entirely foolhardy for a bank to use even all its resources in granting cash credits, or in discounting bills of exchange, especially since some very respectable and important English bankers considered ordinary bills of exchange as good security as Exchequer bills. Even some Scottish country bankers who followed the Edinburgh policy agreed with the critics. In any event, whatever the merits of the case, after the Napoleonic Wars new banks found great difficulty in following the precepts of the chartered banks. Owing to its increased price, government stock gave a comparatively low return. In other words, what had proved profitable to the older banks would, in the changed circumstances, have ruined a new one.

The root cause of the objection to the relationship between the private and chartered banks and to their lending policies was because both diminished the funds available for advances to trade and industry. The objections were most vigorous in the first half of the nineteenth century, especially in the earlier period, before there had been many successful attempts to meet them. The first of these attempts, and so the first major attack on the old organization, came with the foundation of the Commercial Banking Company of Scotland in 1810. Even its name was significant. Though the Commercial Bank was not established by public authority, its aim, of providing a national service, was to be characteristic of the new era of banking in Scotland. The private bankers began to decline, especially after the financial crisis of 1825, and were displaced by the large joint-stock banks, which specifically set out to serve the whole country. After the Napoleonic Wars there was, therefore, a decline in local institutions. The Commercial Bank had itself aimed effective blows at the private bankers and in particular at their close connection with the chartered banks by ruling that no private banker could become one of its directors. It also tried to meet the other main objection to the Scottish banking system by trying to ensure a greater flow of funds to commerce and industry. The Commercial Bank's example was followed in subsequent years as new institutions appeared, especially during the period of extensive flotation of joint-stock companies in 1825. In the previous decade only two establishments appeared in Scotland, though banking services were greatly increased through the extension of branches, especially by the Commercial and the British Linen Banks. On the other hand, offsetting the increase, were the closures of a number of other establishments, chiefly private bankers. The year 1825 brought about a new situation with the creation of four banks: the Aberdeen Town and County Banking Company, the Arbroath Banking Company, the Dundee Commercial Bank, and, most important of them all, the National Bank of Scotland, which followed the example of the Commercial Bank by being formed on a national basis.

The protests of the Commercial Bank, and to a lesser extent of the National Bank, against the organization and policies of the older Scottish banks had much success. The relationship between private and chartered banks was broken, and the final decline of the private banks inaugurated. The two banks, following their avowed national coverage, encouraged the growth of branch banking and forced others to follow suit. Hence it was the policy and action of these new banks, as much as those of the older banks, which led to the evolution of some of the features most commonly associated with Scottish banking. But neither the Commercial nor the National Banks were as revolutionary as some institutions which appeared later, and soon they accepted some of the policies of the older banks and worked closely with them. In due course both received royal charters, though they were granted with the liability of shareholders unlimited, a contrast to the position of the older banks, and by about 1830 representatives of the five chartered banks and, generally, a representative of Sir William Forbes and Company held regular meetings to agree on interest rates for both deposits and discounts. A new criticism, similar to that voiced earlier, then began to be heard, because by about 1830 the lending policies of the Commercial and National Banks were similar to those of the three oldest institutions. By then all five chartered banks held that all banks should invest a large part of their assets in government securities. Moreover, to others the agreed rates allowed by them on deposits were so low that the banks' prosperity was notorious. Much of the competitive spirit of earlier years had apparently gone.

Such was the background that led to a further phase of attempted reformation. Significantly, it came from the west of Scotland and may be represented as a reflection of injured local sentiment rather than an objection to more realistic aspects of banking policy. But it did provide the most recent, and also the most striking, illustration of the two interpretations of the development of Scottish banking.

A burst of new activity came in the 1830's. The Ayrshire Banking Company and the Glasgow Union Bank were founded in 1830, the latter growing rapidly through amalgamation to become the Union Bank of Scotland in 1843. In 1834 the Central Bank of Scotland appeared in Perth, in 1836 the North of Scotland Banking Company in Aberdeen, and in 1838 the Clydesdale Bank in Glasgow. But the two most important institutions to appear in this decade were the Western Bank of Scotland in 1832 and the City of Glasgow Bank in 1839, as both actively opposed the chartered banks in Edinburgh before they came to disastrous ends in 1857 and 1878 respectively. The new banks, especially the Western Bank, tried to break the restrictive arrangements imposed on Scottish banking through the system of mutual consultation among the chartered banks with head offices in Edinburgh. The aggressive policy had an early impact on interest policy, previously determined jointly by the Edinburgh banks, as by 1841 even the Bank of Scotland, much against its will, was forced to follow the others and raised its rate on deposit to 3½ per cent. The public benefited greatly from this. They not only received a higher return for deposits, but paid lower rates for discounts. Naturally, the well-established banks suffered. If the Western and its followers had been forced to invest at least a quarter of their deposits in low-yielding government stock, as the Edinburgh banks advocated, they would have been unable to afford to grant such benefits to the public. The old rule of Edinburgh might then have been completely re-established. Not surprisingly, therefore, when the Western Bank opposed the Edinburgh policy on the proportion of assets which should be invested in government stock, it did so with such consistency and strength that it forgot the large element of wisdom in the policy. When, in contrast to the older banks, the Western Bank employed a large part of its resources in discounting ordinary trade bills, it placed itself in a highly dangerous position. Any sudden pressure for funds, perhaps through the failure of some of its clients, was liable to strain the Western's reserves. Nevertheless the bank prospered. Within a decade of its foundation the bank had twenty-six branches, within another, seventy-three, and, by the time of its failure in 1857, over a hundred. At that time it had one of the largest note circulations of any Scottish bank; its paid-up capital of £1,500,000 was the second largest in Scotland and its deposits were over £5,000,000. The extensive system of branches, as well as late-night openings in Glasgow, attracted even more when the Western Bank (as well as the City of Glasgow Bank) gave depositors

½ per cent more on their deposits than the other Scottish banks. The result was that by 1857, of the 42,000 depositors with the Western Bank, 26,000 were for amounts of under £50. The Bank also had the wealthiest of the western industrialists among its proprietors, clients and directors. In 1857 the Baird family (of the Gartsherrie ironworks) held 1,886 shares between them, and from 1839 onwards at least one of the brothers was among the directors. So, too, was either James or George Burns from 1840 and James Dunlop of the Clyde ironworks from 1846. Many other well-known Glasgow men sat with them. Western Bank shares were quoted at a considerable premium on the Glasgow Stock Exchange but rarely entered the market, as few of those who held them ever wanted to sell. As the failure approached, the desire to hold was strengthened, when in 1856 the dividend was raised to 9 per cent. The following year, although profits fell by £20,000, to about £146,000, the rate was maintained and almost £11,000 was carried forward to the reserve.

When four firms which were heavily indebted to the Western Bank collapsed in the crisis of 1857, and so precipitated the Western's downfall, the apprehensions and warnings of the Edinburgh banks seemed at last to be fully justified. Nevertheless much criticism was made of the Edinburgh banks' attitude at the time. With its strong and influential connection in the west of Scotland it is possible that, had the bank been helped over the 1857 crisis, its future might have been bright. Wider considerations, too, re-enforced the desirability of keeping the bank going if possible. The failure of any Scottish bank, but especially that of a major institution such as the Western, was certain to play into the hands of the opponents of Scottish banking and its privileges, particularly its note issue. Moreover, it was clear to everyone that a failure of such magnitude was bound to spread distrust and difficulty throughout the whole Scottish economy. It might have been expected, therefore, that the Edinburgh banks would have done all in their power to support the Western; but this they did not do. It is not entirely uncharitable to suggest that the Edinburgh banks were anxious to seize this opportunity of getting rid of an important and embarrassing rival.

The first offer of help made by the Edinburgh banks seems to suggest they wanted to use this opportunity to end the Western altogether. A condition of their offer of a credit of £500,000 in October 1857 was that the Western should wind up its business. Even when the managers of two other Glasgow banks, the Clydesdale and the Union, went to

Edinburgh and tried to obtain a modification of this condition, no concession was made, and only when it was pointed out that the directors had no legal powers to wind up the Bank, because this required the permission of the shareholders, was the £500,000 advanced unconditionally. The Edinburgh banks, however, ran no risk, because they demanded adequate security for their loan, including a personal guarantee from the directors, among whom were some of the wealthiest men in Scotland. The Union, one of the two leading Glasgow banks which had helped in the negotiations between the Western and Edinburgh, joined in this bargain but the other, the Clydesdale, stood apart. In a more brotherly fashion it advanced £100,000 on its own account with fewer safeguards. The hesitations after the Western appealed to the Edinburgh banks for help caused the negotiations to last for over a week and increased the lack of faith in the bank at the very time when confidence was essential. Moreover, the feeling of mistrust against the Western was intensified by reputed attempts on the part of the Edinburgh banks to secure its customers. This action was not surprising since for some time previously there had been rivalry to increase the number of branches. As the Western and the City of Glasgow had set the pace in this race the local agents of the other banks were naturally glad to gain any ground whenever possible. Certainly, immediately after the failure, the Edinburgh banks, led by the Royal, were quickly at work in the field. Twelve days after the failure, sixteen agents were reported to have transferred their allegiance, twelve to the Royal and one each to the Bank of Scotland, the British Linen, the Commercial and the National. Under such conditions the Western Bank could not easily withstand a run on the bank at the end of October 1857, and on the last day of the month it suggested to Edinburgh that the balances of exchange between the banks for the next few weeks, so far as they arose from the transference of deposits, should be settled by promissory notes at three months' date from the Western to the other banks. These were to be secured by a deposit of bills with the Bank of Scotland and a letter of guarantee. The application met with scant consideration. Even a proposal for an amalgamation with the Clydesdale, an idea canvassed some years before, did not bring forth any offers of help from Edinburgh and the Western Bank was forced to close down in November 1857. After the closure came the most culpable action of the Edinburgh banks when, for two days after the failure, they refused to accept the Western banknotes. Because of the vast resources of some of the proprietors there was no doubt whatever that all the liabilities of the Western would be met in full; and if the stability of Scottish banking and of the Scottish economy had been the only factors that concerned the Edinburgh banks these notes should never have been refused even momentarily. Two of the Glasgow banks sent a deputation to Edinburgh the day after the closure and asked the banks to accept the Western notes but their request was refused. A lead had to be given by others.

It is difficult to form a straightforward opinion on the part played by Edinburgh bankers in the history of the Western Bank. Undoubtedly the two followed different paths in many things. If the Edinburgh bankers were too conservative, there is no doubt that the Western Bank was foolhardy. Much of the dispute hinged round the proportion of assets which should be invested in government stock. It may be argued that the Edinburgh ratio of one-third to one-quarter gave the whole Scottish banking system its high reputation for stability, especially in an age when cash reserves were exceptionally low. But it should also be remembered that other equally stable banks did not adopt this distribution. Moreover, in Scotland many believed that the chartered banks had adopted this ratio in the first place for no other reason than that it was profitable and that Edinburgh wanted the new banks to follow suit in order to prevent them from gaining a dominant position in Scottish banking. Most important of all, it is possible that their policy led the Edinburgh banks to neglect the wider interests involved in the economic development of Scotland: in other words, their emphasis on stability was so excessive that quite legitimate demands from industry and trade, though perhaps of a more risky character, may have been ignored. Certainly, in addition to local sentiment, this belief was a major factor in the origin of the Western Bank and was the cause of the constant disputes between the Western Bank and Edinburgh throughout the former's career. The position adopted by the Edinburgh banks is, of course, justifiable; but a retardation of economic growth may result if, because of such a policy, adequate advances are not made to trade and industry. It is doubtful if this was fully appreciated by the Edinburgh banks. Evidence to support this view may be brought from another field. Less than a year before the stoppage of the Western Bank, when the Scottish banks were asked for their opinion on the Bank Act of 1845, the Edinburgh banks generally gave their approval to the measure. The Glasgow banks objected strongly, because they believed that the restriction placed on their note issues by the Act prevented a legitimate extension of operations to meet the expanding needs of industry and trade. More-over, when the Glasgow banks objected at the same time to the diffi-culties they experienced through not being incorporated, the Edinburgh banks did not support their appeals. In the years after 1830 the newer banks had broken much of the control of Edinburgh and it seems that, though the older banks were interested in maintaining the stability of Scottish banking, they were just as interested in holding their dominant position in it. When some of the Edinburgh banks suggested, in their letter to the Select Committee on the Bank Act of 1857, that it was advisable to prevent a repetition of the competition that had taken place between banks in Scotland before 1844, they perhaps displayed a fear that still more competition might dislodge them entirely from their leading position.

Even if the conduct of the Edinburgh banks is considered blame-worthy, no one could possibly exonerate the Western Bank. However, it is necessary to distinguish between the ideas behind the bank and the failure of its managers or, more inexplicably still, the failure of its group of very able directors. The latter, not the principles of liberal lending alone, caused the failure. The episode is important because it illustrates, as did the failure of the Ayr Bank in the eighteenth century, that the Edinburgh banks did not fully appreciate the desires and aspirations that lay behind the Western Bank. It was perhaps inevitable that the extent of industrial investment in the west of Scotland at that time should lead to unreasonable demands on the banking system, but it is doubtful if the leading Scottish banks were always as reasonable in meeting these requests as they might have been. Had the Edinburgh bankers met the aspirations of the west of Scotland sooner than they did, much misunderstanding and difficulty might have been avoided.

The rise and fall of the Western Bank is in many ways the most interesting of all at that time, as it illustrates the different viewpoints on banking policy. The collapse of the City of Glasgow Bank in 1878 was in a different category. In many ways there was an apparent similarity between the two banks. Though both were critics of the policies of the older banks, both were successful. The City of Glasgow Bank's reputation, like that of the Western, was not of the highest, but, again on the same pattern as the Western, the substantial resources of its shareholders allayed any fear in the minds of the public. The major difference between the two was that in the case of the City of Glasgow, but not of the Western, there was fraud by the directors. Although some of the shareholders of the Western received fairly large advances,

the directors did not do so. It may be that the same kind of mismanage-
ment brought the two banks to a similar position; the difference was
that the leading officials and the directors of the City of Glasgow Bank
covered their actions by systematic falsification of the balance sheets
and tried to boost its standing on the Stock Exchange by purchasing
the shares of the bank. Their action brought the directors of the City
of Glasgow Bank to prison and led the shareholders to meet a deficit
of over £5,000,000. Notably on this occasion, however, the Edinburgh
banks continued to accept City of Glasgow notes.

The failure of the City of Glasgow Bank was the last of the three
great failures in modern Scottish banking. The elements of fraud in it
marked it out as different from those of the Ayr and Western Banks,
but in their origin and action all the banks represented a criticism of
Scottish banking policy. That the critics had such dramatic failures
among their ranks does not necessarily mean that they were completely
erroneous in their views. The line of banking policy most typically
represented by the chartered banks was conservative, and could easily
have become reactionary but for the constant criticism of others. That
was the measure of the contribution, even of the failures. That such
concerns appeared at all was an indication of the continual demand for
financial aid from Scottish industry throughout its period of rapid
growth.

Amalgamation and assimilation

Until the failure of the City of Glasgow bank the most significant
element in Scottish banking was the discussion of the effectiveness of
the banks' contribution to economic growth, a discussion which was
correlative to the phase of industrial history which came to an end
in the 1870's. When industry was growing rapidly, its demands for
finance to assist its rapid expansion led easily to a critical appraisal of
the facilities offered by the Scottish banks. After the 1870's attitudes
and criticism changed, partly a reflection of new policies by the banks,
partly a reflection of different industrial needs. Then Scottish banking
began to assume a more modern, and less uniquely national, form.
With the amalgamations of the banking institutions within Scotland
came a greater assimilation to English ways.

In Scotland only a few new institutions, all of negligible importance,

appeared after the middle of the nineteenth century and the amalgamations took place mainly before its last quarter. The best example is
from the history of the appropriately named Union Bank of Scotland.
In 1836 the Glasgow Union Bank amalgamated with the Thistle Bank
and two years later, in 1838, with Sir William Forbes and Company
and with the Paisley Union Bank Company. In 1843 the designation,
Union Bank of Scotland, was adopted and later in the year amalgamations were effected with Hunters' and Company (which had
merged with the Kilmarnock Banking Company in 1821) and the
Glasgow and Ship Bank (which was formed by the fusion of the
Glasgow Bank Company and the Ship Bank in 1837). Two other
accessions came to the Union Bank in the middle of the nineteenth
century: the Banking Company in Aberdeen in 1849 and in 1857
the Perth Banking Company, which had carried on the business of the
Perth United Company, dissolved in 1787. The classic example of the
Union Bank was followed by other banks, though to a lesser degree:
the Clydesdale Bank amalgamated with the Edinburgh and Glasgow
Bank in 1858 and with the Eastern Bank in 1863; in 1864 the Royal
Bank amalgamated with the Dundee Bank. At the same time others
increased their capital stock. In 1844, the National Bank doubled its
paid-up capital to £1,000,000; in 1850 the British Linen Bank did
likewise; in two stages, in 1859 and in 1864, the Commercial Bank
increased its capital by £400,000 to £1,000,000; in 1864 the City of
Glasgow Bank increased its capital to £850,000.

The timing of the amalgamation movement was such that by the
late nineteenth century there were not the same opportunities for
amalgamation as there then were in England, and from 1868, when
the Bank of Scotland absorbed the Central Bank of Scotland, there
were no more amalgamations among the remaining institutions until
1908, when the Caledonian Banking Company merged with the Bank
of Scotland. Less than a year later two banks, the North of Scotland
and the Town and County Bank, both with head offices in Aberdeen,
also merged, and the number of institutions was thus reduced to eight,
at which number it remained until after the Second World War.

The amalgamations, or more accurately, the affiliations which did
affect the Scottish banks between the wars were of quite a different
type. Then a number of Scottish banks became associated in various
ways with English counterparts. The first instance was in 1918, before
the end of the war, when Lloyds Bank assumed control of the National
Bank. Similar arrangements were effected the following year by

Barclays Bank over the British Linen Bank and by the Midland Bank over the Clydesdale Bank, while the Midland Bank extended its control to the North of Scotland Bank in 1924. In such a way the Scottish banks were brought increasingly within the orbit of English banking and under English control. Only in one case was the role reversed, when the Royal Bank gained control of the English institutions of Williams Deacon's and Glyn, Mills'. By then the trend was irresistible. For all its past Scottish banking was losing its distinctive characteristics.

It was perhaps inevitable that such assimilation should come, and by the second half of the nineteenth century there were unmistakable signs of its imminence. In 1863 the Scottish banks jointly instructed their branches to follow changes in bank rate immediately. In 1865 the banks began to break through the statistical secrecy which until then had surrounded most of their activities by publishing regularly a number of important statistical series. However, to some extent the increasing similarity of banking practice between Scotland and England reflected an increasing approximation of English to Scottish practice. Legal changes enabled the amalgamation movement in English banking to produce a structure of a few large joint-stock banks with branches, similar to that long established in Scotland. Other legal changes tried to force the Scots to approximate to English practice, sometimes to what they considered its less desirable, and sometimes even its erroneous banking principles. The first important attempt to do so was the effort in 1826 to abolish banknotes of under £5, an attempt which produced such an outcry that the proposal to apply the prohibition to Scotland was never implemented. Whatever the provision's merits in England, Scots were so used to small banknotes, and had every justification for their confidence in their convertibility, that the prohibition was quite irrelevant in Scotland. On this occasion the opposition was such that future governments avoided causing similar offence. Thus in 1845 the Bank Act for Scotland left the nineteen issuing banks in Scotland with a legal circulation, determined in the same way as in England, of £3,087,000. The maximum country issue in England was £8,632,000. In two other ways the Scots gained over the English. They were allowed to increase their note issue indefinitely against gold and silver held in their head offices, a privilege restricted in the south to the Bank of England. Further, amalgamations did not affect rights to issue notes in Scotland, though no new banks of issue were permitted. Though the opposition of 1826 was, therefore, sufficiently strong to allow the Scottish banks to remain relatively privileged under the legislation of the 1840's, the note issue did not pass uncriticized. When a bill was introduced into parliament in 1864 to divide the Western Bank's note issue among other Scottish banks in proportion to their existing issues, Gladstone indicated that, while willing to consider the merits of the application on various grounds, he was unwilling to admit it as a legal right. The matter of the note issue arose more dramatically some years later, when the Scottish banks began to open branches in England. The amalgamation movement in Scottish banking was accompanied by an extension of branches, especially when some, notably the Royal Bank, took over many of the branches of the Western Bank after its failure, and subsequently expanded into other areas. After the crisis of 1866 the expansion was especially rapid, helped in Scotland by the effects of the crisis being less severe. From then till the end of the decade the number of branches rose by about 100; in 1873 the number was about 900, 300 more than in 1866; in 1878 there were about 950 branches. The most important repercussions of this expansion came when the branches were in England.

The first move into England was made by the National Bank when it opened a London office in 1864. Others followed, to the indignation of English country bankers who could have taken such action only by losing their note-issuing rights. Eventually all major Scottish banks opened offices in London, the last to do so being the Commercial Bank in 1883. The opposition to this movement increased to a peak in 1874, when the Clydesdale Bank opened three branches in Cumberland, and a much more widespread invasion of England was feared. The excursion to the south cannot be regarded as a victory for the Scots, because the opposition of the English, bankers and politicians, halted it before much had been achieved. That the chief reason for the opposition was jealousy of the note-issuing powers was shown by three different attempts to limit the Scots' activities. The first was in 1875 when Goschen introduced a bill to prohibit the Scottish banks from opening offices in England, a direct attempt to limit the new line of expansion; the second, in 1879, was even more to the point when the bill to grant limited liability to banks at first proposed to exclude from its scope any bank of issue which had offices in a part of the United Kingdom other than that in which its head office was situated; finally, in 1881 the Bank of Scotland, the Royal Bank and the British Linen Bank promoted private bills to enable them to adopt the principle of 'reserve liability', but the government effectively blocked the bills by trying to use them as a means of bargaining over the banks' rights to issue notes.

Though the opposition in England was sufficient to stop the Scots' activities, it itself assumed various forms, as even the opposition of the English bankers was not wholly unanimous. The London bankers were less apprehensive than the country bankers, who were more likely to feel the effect of the new competition and who resented it because of the note-issuing privileges which the Scots were able to retain even with offices in London. The country bankers themselves were not unanimous as some, especially those in areas less likely to be affected by Scottish competition, were apprehensive of opposition to the Scots being pushed to such limits that there would be a general review of the whole position of banks of issue. This was what interested the politicians, none more so than Gladstone. In short the note issue was the topic of greatest interest to all. Their fear of losing their highly prized rights led the Scottish banks to retract from any action which might have jeopardized them. Hence, though the opposition to their entry to England did not lead to any interference with their note-issuing rights, for which some of their opponents hoped, it did effectively end the movement south. Had there not been such opposition it is probable that the Scots would have become more firmly established there. If they had done so, their more concentrated structure might have enabled them to gain considerably in the amalgamation movement in English banking which soon followed.

IX

AGRICULTURE

Prices and production

THE place of agriculture in the Scottish economy changed significantly between the 1780's and the 1870's. In the 1780's the economy was primarily agricultural; in the 1870's, though a large agricultural sector remained, the economy was primarily industrial. But from the 1780's to the 1870's both sectors had one feature in common; both were profitable, because, though the agriculturists, unlike the industrialists, were unable to exploit the rapidly expanding markets of the world, they enjoyed a secure home market. After the end of the Napoleonic Wars there were years of depression, especially between 1820 and 1823, 1826 and 1829, and 1832 and 1836, when lower prices following good harvests plunged less efficient farmers into difficulties, but from the late 1830's prosperity was regained and retained with few interruptions until the last quarter of the nineteenth century. The distortions and distractions caused by the Napoleonic Wars, followed by post-war depression and then by the eventual abolition of the corn laws, ensured that the period was not without change, but it was less dramatic than in the earlier eighteenth century. Its effect differed in the Highlands, especially in the far west and north, and in the Lowlands, through the contrasting experience of the regions during the war itself. Both areas enjoyed the benefits of the high prices of war-time, but, while they encouraged and assisted the pace of agricultural change and improvement in the Lowlands, they provided an opportunity for postponing it in the Highlands. The contrasting response may be explained by differences in natural resources and human initiative, but the implications were far-reaching.

During the wars the experience of agriculture in the Lowlands resembled that in parts of England. Until 1815 the increasing proportion of the population concentrated in urban areas and in industrial employment provided a ready market, which could not easily obtain its supplies from overseas. On the other hand, war-time harvests were generally inadequate in spite of all the improvements of the pre-war years. In only two years could the harvest be described as plentiful, while in about two-thirds of the years it was deficient and in about one-half of these it was grossly inadequate. The rise in agricultural prices was not, therefore, the result only of the general war-time inflation but of crop deficiencies, as in 1795, 1808, 1811, 1812, and above all in the worst years of 1800 and 1801. Fortunately Scotland is uniquely equipped for a study of such phenomena through the records of fiars' prices.[1] The prices for oats at Haddington, though higher than that for many other counties, because of the superior quality of oats in the south-east, indicate sufficiently well the fluctuations, especially under war-time conditions. Between 1707 and 1792 there were only two years, 1762 and 1782, when the price, at 20s. 7¼d. and 24s. 4½d. per imperial quarter respectively, was above 20s. The subsequent price rise was marked:

1793	20s.	8½d.	1805	26s.	10½d.
1794	20s.	4¼d.	1806	30s.	8d.
1795	26s.	8d.	1807	36s.	11d.
1796	20s.	5¾d.	1808	34s.	9½d.
1797	17s.	10¼d.	1809	31s.	9¾d.
1798	19s.	2¾d.	1810	28s.	10d.
1799	39s.	3d.	1811	33s.	5d.
1800	48s.	11¾d.	1812	50s.	9¾d.
1801	23s.	9½d.	1813	30s.	2½d.
1802	21s.	0½d.	1814	27s.	4¼d.
1803	23s.	2¾d.	1815	22s.	5d.
1804	27s.	0d.			

The rise was greatest in 1800, a year of scarcity, when the price of oats was about two and a half times the average of the preceding twenty years, while that of wheat was about three times its average over the same period.

The price rise was reflected in rising rents and property values so that the rental of Scotland at the end of the war, about £6,250,000, stood eight times higher than what it had been in the middle of the eighteenth century. High rents were charged and frequently paid willingly, as the current prosperity seemed soundly based, but the reality behind the prosperity was not the exceptional increase in demand in war-time but the growing demand of the urban population, which remained the basis for prosperity until improved transport led to its being met by greater imports from overseas later in the century.

[1] Fiars' prices are fixed annually for different grains in Scottish counties.

Nevertheless, the exceptional conditions of war-time engendered exceptional expectations, which in turn encouraged a high level of capital investment in agriculture, and so the improvements, introduced in some areas and by some landowners earlier in the eighteenth century, were adopted extensively only during the Napoleonic Wars. When Adam Smith pointed out in 1776 how the country's poverty restricted the widespread application of better ways, the need for capital to effect agricultural improvement was general except in those areas under the control of a wealthy and influential individual. Though the restriction was raised during the wars, it was not wholly removed; but by 1815, while the Lothians and Berwickshire were still most advanced, the north and west of the Highlands were the only areas where agriculture was still functioning on a grossly inefficient basis. In other areas the new and efficient methods were generally adopted, so that the Napoleonic Wars marked the completion of the improving movement in Scottish agriculture. By 1815 agriculture, except in the unimproved remote north and west, was on a modern basis prepared to meet post-war depression.

The war-time price rise varied for different commodities. Fluctuations were most marked in the case of wheat, which was a reflection of both the production and consumption of the cereal in England; but, in spite of an extension of the acreage under wheat, oats still remained the more important crop in Scotland and its price exceeded that of earlier years less frequently. Since, therefore, the prices of the special products of Lowland agriculture did not rise so sharply during the war, the gains accruing to farmers there were less than to their counterparts in the south of England or in the Highlands, where the inflation of incomes by the sharp rise in the prices of their typical products, of wheat in England and of cattle and kelp in the Highlands, gave many landowners and tenants such false impressions of permanent prosperity that their standards of living rose. Since the Lowlands did not specialize in the production of wheat, or of the typical Highland products, the same illusions of grandeur, and especially the assumption of its permanence, were not possible, except in the wheat-growing areas of the Lothians, where, during the wars, the younger farmers began to follow a more expensive way of life than had many of their predecessors. But the rise in the price of wheat during the war gave an incentive to follow English specialization, wherever possible, and grow more wheat, some of which was exported to England. All Scottish farmers, even in areas considered unsuitable for its cultivation, as in Sutherland, tried to gain from growing the grain, as the high prices offset the natural disadvantages of more northerly regions, and so provided a distortion in Scottish agricultural production. But the natural determinants remained, and in Scotland only the Lothians were naturally well endowed for the cultivation of wheat, so that when the end of the war and the repeal of the corn laws removed the exceptional circumstances, the tendency to expand agricultural enterprises for which Scotland was less suited was removed and a pattern of production more appropriate to the natural resources of the country was reasserted. Lack of specialization, particularly in the production of wheat, prevented Scotland from gaining the full benefits of its high price before 1815 and, to a lesser extent, even later. After 1815 the mixed nature of Scottish farming was an advantage, as the main price fall was concentrated, as was the rise, in wheat. English farmers, many of whom had leased additional lands at high rents, and often on borrowed capital, found that, with the fall of prices, they frequently had difficulty in meeting their commitments. Their Scottish counterparts were more favourably placed. The trend, though interrupted, continued in the middle of the nineteenth century, especially when in the 1850's the price of wheat fell absolutely and relative to oats and barley, so that by the 1870's less than 4 per cent of Scotland's arable acreage was under wheat, or only 10 per cent of the acreage under barley. By then only the Lothians retained wheat in a normal rotation though to a diminished extent.

Variations between agricultural enterprises were easier in Scotland, where only the grazing farms of the Highlands and Southern Uplands and a restricted arable belt in the Lothians and the Merse of Berwickshire were highly specialized. In other districts, especially the southwest and the north-east, the move from the cultivation of wheat was most marked as the relative profitability of livestock production increased in the middle of the nineteenth century. In the south-west grain production was much less important than the need for good pasture for stock-rearing, and the change from wheat to temporary leys, enforced by the end of war and of protection, was to the district's long-term benefit, especially since it coincided with the growth of an adjacent urban market and with the improvement of the transport system, both necessary prerequisites of successful dairying. The markets of the Clyde Valley absorbed the produce of Ayrshire, and steamships helped convey the dairy products and cattle of Galloway to Liverpool and other English markets as well. To these attractions the farmers of the south-west added their own contribution in the late eighteenth and early nineteenth centuries by developing Ayrshire cattle, which, apart from the unimportant Shetland, is Scotland's only dairy breed. It originated from a cross between carefully chosen cattle, imported mainly from England and sometimes from overseas, and had the great merit of suiting the climate of the south-west. It could survive damp; it needed little nourishment; it produced much milk. The Ayrshire cow became the basis of the success of the dairy farmers of the south-west and of other parts of Scotland, and of cattle-breeders in the district in which it originated.

The north-east had a more varied pattern of agricultural production, but was divided into two distinct areas lying roughly on either side of the Buchan Ness. The lands to the west along the shore of the Moray Firth rose quickly to the hills in the south, and the latitude was northerly, but the shelter from the east winds, and the full benefit of such sunshine as there was, made the narrow coastal strip suitable for the production of grain of the hardier varieties. Some of the surplus grain from the region was exported to the south, but a large part was consumed locally in the nearby Highlands, in the fishing areas along the coast and in the distilleries. Moreover, though the fertile areas, such as the Black Isle, Ferintosh and the Laigh o' Moray, were few, and somewhat isolated, they proved complementary to the encircling hill areas by providing good pasture for the fattening of cattle. By contrast, the lands of Aberdeenshire to the south of the Buchan Ness were exposed to the east winds, and, being therefore unsuitable for arable cultivation, were used for cattle-rearing. In this region, above all others, the transport improvements of the nineteenth century encouraged the specialization which had been common in that area even in the eighteenth century, because Aberdeenshire breeders could then exploit wider markets without incurring the deterioration in the condition of animals which accompanied their traditional method of walking to market. They became pioneers of scientific breeding, especially when the use of bone meal increased the cultivation of turnips and so provided adequate winter feeding. As early as 1779 Udny of Udny was reported to have an English 'shorthorned' bull on his farm, one of the vanguard of many improved English animals to be introduced to Scotland. Then throughout the 1840's and 1850's two brothers, the Cruickshanks of Sittyton, tried to breed a bull which, when crossed with native cattle, would produce an animal which would fatten quickly and so be suitable for the London market. They succeeded with the beef Shorthorn, which, as breeding stock, became especially popular in America. But more characteristic of the area, and probably better known, was its own breed, the Aberdeen-Angus, which, unlike the beef Shorthorn, owed nothing to English stock. Its first success came at the Smithfield Show in 1829 with animals from the herd of a Cupar Angus farmer, Hugh Watson. Against opposition from the Shorthorn breeders, William McCombie of Tillyfour continued Watson's work successfully until by about 1870 his animals were achieving both national and international success and the Aberdeen-Angus had joined the beef Shorthorn and the Hereford as the world's leading beef breeds.

The transition to new branches of agricultural production, especially after the end of war and of protection, was encouraged by two factors which were more effective in Scotland than in parts of England, especially in the south, and by two technical changes which were appropriate for the agricultural developments then taking place in Scotland.

The first of the two factors which eased the transition was the reduction in rents which accompanied it. The reduction was not peculiarly Scottish and brought its benefits, of course, only to those who were tenant farmers. Even in some areas, such as the Highlands, where nominal rents were not reduced, effective rents were through the simple expedient of tenants not paying them. In such a position the landlord had really no alternative but to accept the situation, since he stood little chance of being able to obtain another tenant willing to pay an adequate rent. The most important consequence of the adjustment of rents downwards was that it removed the assumption, so easily encouraged by inflation, that rents should only be adjustable upwards, and they, therefore, became more flexible. Thereafter there was a greater correlation between the movement of rent and of prices, sometimes explicitly, as in the Lothians, where the adoption of 'corn rents' ensured that rents depended on the price of corn. Such flexibility encouraged a similar flexibility, or adaptability, among the various enterprises in the mixed farming of Scotland. The transition in agriculture was facilitated still further in Scotland through the country's different poor law. Scotland, therefore, avoided the heavy burden of poor rates, which fell on some English agriculturists, especially in the south, through the adoption of the Speenhamland system of supplementing labourers' wages. In Scotland the heritors had to support the poor, but, even with an assessment, which was not universal, the burden was not grievous. Nor did the Scottish system lead to the same demoralization of the labour force as took place elsewhere; labour never became so cheap as in southern England.

The benefits of flexible rents and a lighter poor law favoured all Scottish farmers. The two, more strictly technical, developments in Scottish agriculture in the nineteenth century, both of which encouraged those following the country's specializations, were the practice of putting land down to temporary leys, of which Scottish agriculture still has a higher proportion than English, and the use of under-drainage, especially on heavier soils.

The use of temporary leys was essential in Scotland, where wheat could be cultivated with impunity only in the south-east. Elsewhere the maintenance of fertility required that the land be laid down to grass for periods of two or more years. During the Napoleonic Wars Scottish farmers did not adhere to this practice and their failure to do so combined with the natural unsuitability of much of the soil to ensure low yields of wheat. With the removal of the exceptional inducements which high war-time prices gave to wheat production, the incentive to grow such relatively unsuitable crops was removed. The mixtures of artificial grasses then sown—some combinations of rye-grass and the clovers were most popular—were not always the most appropriate, but their increasing use in temporary leys in the early nineteenth century ensured that rotations in which temporary grasses played an important part were introduced in Scotland. Temporary leys not only conserved the heart of the pasture, they were one of the means whereby certain districts were encouraged to change from excessive concern with the cultivation of wheat to other forms of production, for which temporary leys were essential, and for which these areas were more suited. Ayrshire is a case in point. When the cultivation of wheat became unprofitable, land was laid down to temporary grass, so facilitating the breeding of dairy cattle and the production of milk, butter and cheese, and it is significant that in a farm report from Ayrshire about 1830 a seed mixture of cocksfoot, timothy and rib-grass was recommended, this being far in advance of the customary rye-grass and clovers. Though not all were as far-sighted, and, therefore, though not all mixtures were so suitable, the increasing use of temporary leys led Scottish farmers generally to realize that they were not rivals, or even alternatives, to arable cultivation but complementary to it, as they prevented over-cropping, helped to clear the profusion of weeds, which was the main contribution of the method of 'natural' fallowing of the older system of cropping the outfield, and provided a more even distribution of the farm work throughout the year.

The increasing use of under-drainage was beneficial to those districts which transferred less to grazing and dairying, but remained chiefly arable, and which had fewer advantages in arable cultivation than the areas in the south with which they were competitive. For them arable cultivation was profitable only with inflated prices. Even in such a famous farm as Fenton Barns in East Lothian, grain production could be retained when prices fell only with further improvements, but the fall in prices itself made further improvements less practicable. The developments in drainage were just such an improvement and one which reached Scotland extensively only in the nineteenth century.

Whatever their disadvantages, the old ridges provided a primitive form of drainage. With their removal a substitute became essential, except on sloping ground which had reasonable natural drainage. By the late eighteenth century such substitutes were appearing; sometimes they were channels formed by small stones; sometimes flat stones were inverted against each other to form a channel; sometimes stones formed a box for the drain; but none of these methods was satisfactory on heavy land where surface water was retained. A solution was only gradually approached. Various kinds of tiles were devised, such as the horseshoe tile of Sir James Graham of Netherby, just across the Border from Canonbie, and tile drainage was introduced to Scotland. But a major advance was delayed until the work of James Smith, who began to farm Deanston in Perthshire in 1823 and who, by his various drainage schemes, transformed it into a productive unit. Smith's success rested on a combination of two methods. First, following methods used successfully in Essex, he installed a system with a variety of drains of different depths leading into main drains at the lowest level. Second, Smith realized that such an elaborate system would be effective only if the water could penetrate the subsoil. In achieving this hand trenching and trench ploughs both turned up unsatisfactory soil and the former was expensive. Smith made his original contribution in devising his subsoil plough, which could follow in the furrow made by an ordinary plough. In the 1830's his methods spread throughout Scotland, though their application was limited by their cost. Even with the utmost economy, which was not always practised, drainage was necessarily more expensive in Scotland, as it frequently required larger pipes, though they were not placed at the same depth as in England. The cost of drainage schemes, and the probability that they would benefit areas greater than one farm, normally placed the responsibility for them on the landlords, who were encouraged to undertake improvements by grants of £4,000,000 in the 1840's and by the authorization of private companies for land drainage.

The technical improvements helped to increase the efficiency of the various specializations common to Scottish agriculture and to ensure that by about 1870 Scottish agriculture was mainly concerned with livestock production, which in turn depended on certain arable successes, notably the provision of adequate supplies of turnips and oat straw as supplements to oil-cake and oats for winter fodder. They enabled the more rapid fattening of animals, and sometimes of much younger ones, to be guaranteed. But the arable successes and the consequential expansion of livestock production would have been much less effective without better transport facilities by road, rail and by steamship. Lime and artificial manures, which were being used increasingly, could then be distributed more widely; sheep could be sent for wintering, and all animals despatched for marketing in better condition. In short, arable successes and transport improvements enabled the potentialities of livestock production to be fully exploited.

One last point must be remembered. It is only partly true to regard the specialization in livestock production in Scotland as a response to the diminished attractiveness of grain production as prices fell after the Napoleonic Wars and the abolition of the corn laws. The Scots certainly devoted increased attention to livestock production in the nineteenth century, but partly because they were being encouraged to do so by certain other improvements, not always strictly agricultural, as transport developments showed. But the fundamental cause of the specialization was quite simply that, as always, Scotland was naturally more suited for it. The point must be stressed because of later events. Since the concentration on livestock production in Scotland was a reflection of the country's comparative advantages, Scottish agriculture, except for a few areas, notably the south-east, stood to suffer much less by international competition in grain. Many districts in Scotland were attracted to the production of grain only by the exceptional circumstances of war and protection, and, once these exceptional circumstances were removed, reverted to the production of commodities for which they were naturally more suited. Such a reversion in the case of Scotland was not, therefore, a change forced by the necessity of international competition. Consequently, though in the short run Scottish agriculture stood to lose by the end of war and protection, in the long run their end ensured that the country specialized on lines where success was more lasting. This was to be of even greater importance after the 1870's.

Landlord and tenant

The variations in agricultural production in the middle of the nineteenth century took place in a period of social change, from which arose a relationship between landlord and tenant which lasted, even through years of comparative depression, until the First World War. Sinclair detailed clearly what was expected from the landlords at the beginning of the nineteenth century.

> 'There are various improvements . . . which in a peculiar manner are in the province of proprietors. . . . The erection of substantial and convenient farm-houses and offices is of this description. The making of extensive drains, which reach over a variety of farms, cannot, and ought not to be executed by tenants. Embankments, and straightening of rivers, are of the same nature. . . . Inclosing, planting, trenching and clearing the land of stones and rubbish, as well as reclaiming moors and mosses, are all operations, more appropriate to a landlord, than to a tenant.'[1]

Such responsibilities placed a barrier between landlords and others. Its extent was determined chiefly by the greater capital resources of the landlords themselves but was strengthened by the landlords' ability to gain readier access to bank credit. Tenant farmers were frequently regarded as poor credit risks, but not landlords, not even when their estates were entailed. It may be that the landed interest was given a higher standing, in this case a higher credit standing, than could be justified on rational grounds, especially since some of the capital so obtained was spent in ostentatious living, including the construction of large houses and of decorative parks, but much went into agricultural improvements. Ostentatious living was, therefore, a rival to agricultural improvement, but another possible claimant on the landlord's capital resources was much less pressing in Scotland in the nineteenth century. This was the demand for resources for industrial investment. Though in the early nineteenth century industrial growth rested greatly on the exploitation of natural resources, which were frequently in the

[1] Sinclair, *op. cit.*, vol. iii, p. 376.

M

possession of the landed interest, few landlords showed much interest in developing these with their own capital. In this they differed from their counterparts in the eighteenth century, but they were not thereby necessarily failing in any social obligations, because many diagnosed the problem in the same way as the Minister of Kilsyth.

'It is far from being intended to insinuate, that the whole capital of this kingdom should be vested in agricultural improvements; far less that commercial industry should be discountenanced. On the contrary, these two united, are the strength of Scotland; and, like twin brothers, should be equally cherished. But surely agriculture is the most natural and beneficial employment of the landed interest; and were their whole capital and exertions employed on agricultural improvement, the soil would be rendered more productive; and Great Britain would soon become independent of strangers or enemies, for the necessaries of life.'[1]

The willingness of the landlords to use their resources in agricultural development provided an opportunity to men of ability, and so offered a solution to the problem of the poverty of the country and of the individual in agriculture. Yet, in spite of its benefits, the relationship was subject to strain. The landlord's concern over good farming coincided with his tenant's, but the social power and assumptions of the landlords were as strong through most of the nineteenth century as they had been earlier and, wherever the interests conflicted, the landlord assumed that his way should be followed, an assumption rarely modified in recognition of other compensating qualities the tenant may have possessed.

A classic instance of such conflict arose over the game laws, especially when the landlords' hands were strengthened around 1830. Because the Scottish game laws had been more liberal, their renewed enforcement caused greater conflict in Scotland than in England, even though the worst excesses were avoided. In Scots law trespass was an offence only as contempt of court against a civil interdict, or if special damages could be proved, and, in spite of the increasing power granted to the landlords by legislation, the courts were reluctant to grant them unqualified authority. In 1832, for instance, they recognized a tenant's right to compensation for an excessive increase in game since the date of a lease, if the landlord had failed to keep the game down. On the other hand, though Scots law against the poacher had traditionally

[1] Sinclair, *op. cit.*, vol. iii, pp. 376–7.

been much more stringent, it was surpassed by the English law built up in the first quarter of the nineteenth century. Thus in 1827 the courts decided that man-traps were illegal and that fatal accidents from them were murder. Thereafter Scottish law was assimilated to English practice and the measures against poaching of around 1830 were applied to Scotland. Convictions for poaching in Scotland, which had been much lower than in England, rose, and the sympathy already given to tenants was then extended to poachers. But the game laws were not the only causes of friction; others were numerous. The right of hypothec, or the security of rent by the right to a tenant's goods, is a peculiarly Scottish legal doctrine which gives a landlord a general right over a tenant's moveable property as security of payment of the rent, the general right being converted by a legal process into a real right over certain goods, which may then be sold, and the proceeds used for payment of the rent. In 1867 the operation of this right over land held for agricultural purposes was restricted and in 1880 it was virtually abolished. Other more general social influences led to further tension. Two were notable: the Disruption in 1843 and the growth of Liberalism. In 1843 very few landlords joined the Free Church and the majority actively disapproved of those of their tenants who did, especially when the Free Church became the landlords' critic. The growth of Liberalism was suspect for the same reason. It represented the political criticism, which complemented the ecclesiastical criticism of the Free Church, of the established rights of property and patronage. The common remedy of refusal to renew leases was applied in a number of cases, though most dramatically, and with great effect, in the case of George Hope, third of his family to tenant the world-renowned farm of Fenton Barns in the Lothians. Eight years after he stood as a Liberal candidate, a renewal of his tenancy was refused. By favouring the repeal of the corn laws, Hope followed the wrong side in the symbolic class conflict between industrialists and landlords.

The gulf between the landlord and the tenant was repeated between the tenant and the farm labourer. A tenant, no matter how lowly, was at least on the ladder of social promotion, even if he might never ascend far. Though the structure of landownership, and the provision of credit facilities, offered the prospects of social and economic progress to the farm labourer, he was regarded by the tenant farmer as belonging to a different group until he made the first move. Some tenant farmers drew a social distinction between themselves and their workers as rigid as that drawn by the landlords between themselves and their tenants. Neither was easily breached. The more responsible farm worker, the grieve or manager, was normally employed only by the larger tenant farmers and was himself likely to become at best a small-scale, rather struggling tenant farmer. If before the transformation he had been employed by a man of similar standing the change would have been less drastic, even imperceptible, and the difference between the two social groups would, consequently, have been much less. As his employer was generally among the more successful, the transformation failed to remove the social distinction.

The rigidity of social distinctions varied throughout the country. It was strongest in areas of high specialization and where farms were large and therefore found its classic exposition in the grain-growing districts of the Lothians. There the key farm labourer was the hind, who was capable of performing every agricultural operation efficiently. The hind provided the stable element in rural society in the Lothians and, through the efforts of his wife and family, or of a female servant who lived in his cottage, he was able to supply much of the seasonal labour required. By guaranteeing his employer a supply of labour adequate for permanent and seasonal needs, the farmer was relieved of one of the more intractable problems of agricultural operations. Some benefit fell to the hind too, because, since he had a tied house, and received about two-thirds of his income in kind, he escaped the repercussions of many fluctuations of employment and income. By contrast the other main group of agricultural employees in the Lothians, the regular agricultural labourer, suffered from these uncertainties, as well as from excessive physical labour and consequential ill-health. Though the labourer gained from war-time conditions when, in spite of the inflation, his real income increased, after 1815 he could maintain a reasonable standard of living only when in continuous employment. When they were so employed, some of the labourers were able to maintain standards only slightly less than that of the hinds; when they were not, especially in the Lothians, where there were relatively few opportunities for non-agricultural employment, the standard of living of the labourers sank to a squalor and degradation matched only in the new industrial areas.

Though the structure of rural society in the Lothians in the nineteenth century was perhaps more rigid than elsewhere in Scotland, it provided a basic pattern which other areas frequently tried to approximate. Since the Lothians gave birth to many of the improvements of the eighteenth and nineteenth centuries, its influence, both socially and economically, was heightened. To many it seemed to hold the agricultural and social pattern towards which they had to struggle. Nevertheless since farms were generally neither so large nor so specialized in other parts of Scotland, and since elsewhere there was much greater diversity of ownership, of agricultural practice, and of employment, social conditions inevitably varied. Only in the cattle-rearing northeast and in the dairying south-west was there uniformity in organization through the importance of the family farm. Wherever the family unit was important, the hired labourer was correspondingly much less important than in the Lothians, especially since any increase in demand for hired labour through a particular specialization, as for potato lifting in Ayrshire, was generally only seasonal and could be met by Highland labour, or, as in the south-west, by an increase in its longstanding use of seasonal labour from Ireland. When a labourer was permanently employed on a family farm, he was frequently a farmer's son, preparing himself, technically and financially, to become a tenant farmer. Consequently in areas such as the north-east and south-west, in contrast to the Lothians, there could not be the same social distinction between the tenants and their few employees. In some districts, the south-west among them, social distinctions were even further obliterated through the existence of many small-scale proprietors, who were active workers on their land, and could not readily be distinguished from the tenants on the larger estates. If the south-west represented one extreme, as did the Lothians another, east and central Scotland, from Fife and the Howe of the Mearns through Strathmore and Strathearn to Mentieth, illustrated a variety of social patterns, which reflected its variety of agricultural activities. The larger units required a supply of labour similar to that in the Lothians, but the system never operated successfully in any other area. In central Scotland the young unmarried ploughman was the grade of labour most commonly used. Another factor marked its labour supply as different from other areas. Since hinds were not employed, there was no reserve of seasonal labour from his family, nor was the area favoured, as was the south-west, by close proximity to Ireland, the main reservoir of seasonal labour for Scottish agricultural operations in the nineteenth century. Hence, as a further feature distinguishing this area from others in Scotland, there appeared in it a number of smallholders, given pieces of land, generally to enable them to grow potatoes, in return for help when required on the larger farms.

Whatever the exact position of the various ranks of rural society, the new methods of agricultural production made novel demands on it and, though alternative opportunities were appearing in other sectors of the economy, the supply of rural labourers remained sufficiently ample to provide a continuing inducement to retain labour-consuming methods of production on some farms even when alternatives were being pioneered in Scotland. Meikle's threshing-machine, first produced in 1786, was in its early days more commonly used in Scotland than in England, but the most successful implement devised in Scotland in this period was the reaper, developed by a divinity student, Patrick Bell, in the late 1820's. Since it was inefficiently manufactured by country blacksmiths, few were used. Though the American, McCormick, invented his reaper on the same principles as Bell's in the following decade, neither was exploited until the 1850's, when improved models, combining the best of both, were produced. However, it was only in 1868 that the Highland and Agricultural Society officially recognized Bell's as 'the first efficient reaping-machine'.

Though such pioneering activity did not displace the labour-consuming methods of production followed on many Scottish farms, the new order adopted generally brought extensive social change into the lives of the agricultural workers. It was seen most clearly in the farm-buildings. As the improving movement was completed the old farm-towns were gradually replaced by modern farm-buildings. A typical transformation to the old structure began by making the barn a separate building, running at right angles to the original house, and so forming two sides of a square. The stack-yard was placed behind it. The next stage was to add a third side to the square, with a line of cattle-houses running from the other side of the dwelling-house, and so opposite the barn, but, perhaps as a sign that the transformation was not complete, the midden remained in the middle of the square which was being formed. Later improvements made the whole steading bigger, as, for example, by adding a fourth side to the buildings, but, because the midden frequently remained in the square, the house was set down away from it with its front facing the garden and with its back, with as few windows as possible, facing the steading.

Such structural changes affected the provision of housing for the new groups of agricultural workers. Wherever the new order produced a dominance of family farms, as in much of the south-west, the change was not drastic. There the majority of agriculturists continued to live in the new farm steading much as they had lived in the old and the need to supply new types of housing for the employed labourers was less important. The need for new housing was greatest in the large, specialized, and mainly arable farms of the Lothians and of central and east Scotland. In the east, where the young unmarried worker was employed most extensively, the labourers were normally left to look after themselves, in whatever conditions of squalor they wished, in the bothy, though sometimes they were accommodated and fed in the farm-house. In areas such as the Lothians, where the married worker was employed, some form of housing had to be provided, though it varied greatly from farm to farm and at different times. During wartime prosperity some improvements were made and the hinds' position improved, but the deterioration in his position after 1815 was most obvious in his housing, especially so on the farms of the tenants, where the hinds were normally employed. The tenant had no money to spare on the improvement of the hinds' dwellings, and was reluctant to press his landlord to do so at a time when he was often seeking expenditure in other directions and sometimes even a reduction in rent. Though housing conditions deteriorated, something had to be provided and, as many of the other payments he received were in kind, the hind became an isolated element in an economy increasingly on a cash basis. His isolation, and relative immobility, kept him so until after the middle of the nineteenth century. Then the increasing commutation of his payments in kind gradually led him to consider the possibilities of other occupations. However, no matter how bad the housing of the hinds, it was better than the bothies, where the social degradation of the Scottish agricultural worker was complete. Cobbett was accurate in suggesting, when he saw one near Dunfermline, that cattle were housed as well as the men and that the young pigs fed better.

'I found the "bothie" to be a shed, with a fire-place in it to burn coals in, with one doorway, and one little window. The floor was the ground. There were three wooden bedsteads nailed together like the berths in a barrack-room, with boards for the bottom of them. The bedding seemed to be very coarse sheeting with coarse woollen things at the top; and all seemed to be such as similar things must be when there is nobody but men to look after them. . . . There were ten or twelve bushels of coals lying in a heap in one corner of the place, which was, as nearly as I could guess, about sixteen or eighteen feet square. There was no back-door to the place, and no privy. There were some loose potatoes lying under one of the berths.

'Now for the wages of these men. In the first place the average wages of these single farming men are about ten pounds a year, or not quite four shillings a week. Then, they are found provisions in the following manner: each has allowed him two pecks of coarse oatmeal a week, and three "*choppins*" of milk a day, and a "*choppin*" is, I believe, equal to an English quart. They have to use this meal, which weighs about seventeen pounds, either by mixing it with cold water or with hot, they put some of it into a bowl, pour some boiling water upon it, then stir it about and eat it; and they call this BROSE; and you will be sure to remember that name. When they use milk with the meal, they use it in the same way as they do the water. . . . These men are not troubled with cooking utensils. They had a large iron saucepan and five or six brose-bowls; and are never troubled with those clattering things, knives, forks, plates, vinegar-cruets, salt-cellars, pepper-boxes, mustard-pots, table-cloths, or tables.'[1]

The Highlands

The fortunes of the Highland economy contrasted markedly with the experience of the rest of Scotland between the 1780's and the 1870's, but the elements of the Highland problem were the same as in the middle of the eighteenth century. As population grew and agricultural efficiency was increasingly the aim of the landlords, the grinding poverty which already existed was in no way relieved. In such circumstances emigration, on a scale not so far witnessed in the Highlands, was inevitable, but was postponed by the economic effects of the French Wars until later in the nineteenth century. By that time the split in the Highland economy was patently apparent. In the north and west lay the root of the gravest poverty. In the south and east some approach to a new and revived economy had been achieved. Social stress emerged when the small tenants, tenaciously regarding the land as inalienably theirs, could not meet the landlords' demands for higher rents and so had to submit to new forms of land use, which, whatever merits they may have had, ran counter to the rights the tenants assumed were theirs. The old order could have been maintained, and

[1] W. Cobbett, *Rural Rides* (ed. Cole, London, 1930), vol. iii, p. 783.

the landlords' demands met, only by action in two different ways. First, an increase in the subsistence from the land would have released more of the limited cash income available to Highland tenantry from purchasing necessary imports to meet higher rent payments. Second, an increase in cash income from non-agricultural sources would have provided a means of meeting the landlords' demands directly. The disintegration of the Highland economy was arrested temporarily by developments in both directions.

Subsistence from the land was increased through the introduction of the potato, which was generally accepted by 1800 and which was the major crop on some holdings before the middle of the nineteenth century. Yields were often high because of the abundant supply of labour devoted to its cultivation, while the dangers of monoculture appeared only with the potato famine in the 1840's. Until 1815 the only effect was the benefit of increased subsistence from one of the few crops suitable for Highland weather. Additional cash income came from more varied sources, especially from linen manufacture, distilling, fishing, and from kelp-making.

Linen manufacture was unimportant in the Highlands and was never properly established there in spite of the efforts of the Board of Trustees and others after 1745. Its greatest contribution was in the east, though primarily only for the diminishing number who lived on the inland straths, not in the problem areas of the west and north, but even in the areas of partial success linen manufacture in the Highlands remained dependent on the economic life of the Lowlands. Linen merchants from the south brought the flax to the Highlands to have it spun, but took the yarn back to the Lowlands for weaving. The occupation never interfered with any other activities, but remained mainly a part-time activity. In short, it was not an indigenous, independent, industrial growth.

A second source of cash income, though important only locally, lay in distilling whisky, an operation not, of course, confined to the Highlands, but one with a greater influence in a region with few satisfactory alternatives. In the eighteenth century Lowland distillers complained that they were losing local markets to Highland producers and had to seek outlets in England, where, however, Highland whisky was sold too. The importance of such markets was confirmed by legal exports, which rose from 34,000 gallons in the year 1779–80 to over 195,000 gallons in 1788–9, an increase which was possible only by importing barley from England, almost 100,000 quarters being brought into the country in 1781–2.[1] The official figures of exports are, of course, minimum quantities, because a large quantity of whisky was distilled illicitly, not only for domestic consumption, but for sale. In 1782 1,211 illicit stills were seized in the Highlands and 819 in the Lowlands; in 1796, apparently another active year by excisemen, 799 were condemned in the Highlands and 464 in the Lowlands. Illicit distillation was the result of a heavy taxation policy, which dated from the malt tax, increased in 1760, 1779 and 1780, but made more stringent by additional duties levied in the 1780's, partly at the instigation of English rivals, who objected to differential duties in the malt tax which favoured the Scots, and in the 1780's by the continuation of what they regarded as favoured treatment through the Scotch Distillery Act of 1786. This imposed a duty of only 2s. a gallon (raised to 2s. 6d. in 1788) against the English duty on spirit of 2s. 6d. per gallon, an objection which ignored the imposition of a still-licence tax, equivalent to 6d. a gallon, in Scotland. The imposition of the additional taxation in 1786 and 1788 helped to precipitate a number of bankruptcies in the late 1780's, resulting in a sharp fall in legal imports to England, but the fall was due also to the stimulus the still-licence system gave to illicit distilling. When it was abolished in 1817, the number of distilleries trebled, though the rate of duty, common to the whole of Scotland, increased throughout the nineteenth century: 2s. 10d. a proof gallon in 1826, 14s. 9d. in 1914. The policy of increased taxation, combined with such requirements as the insistence on allowing whisky to mature before being passed for human consumption, removed the industry from being a part-time occupation for many to a full-time activity. It continued to be a useful source of employment in the Highlands and Islands, especially in certain areas, such as Islay and Glenlivet, but it did not remain a universal supplement to either subsistence or cash income throughout the region.

Fishing provided a third, and more fruitful, though an intermittent and uncertain source of additional cash income. White fishing was, however, more stable than herring fishing, because it was not seasonal

[1] The export figures are from the Report on Scotch Distillery Duties, 1798. British Parliamentary Papers, 1803, XI, p. 431. In evidence in the same Report two London distillers gave much higher figures of Scottish exports to England (1781–2, 257,544 gallons; 1782–3, 245,700 gallons). Comparison of these with their statistics of production over the same years leads to the improbable conclusion that consumption in Scotland must have declined from 1780 until 1783, when it became negative, a reflection, presumably, of illicit distillation.

and experienced fewer difficulties in curing its catch or in establishing contact with the main markets of the Lowlands. Above all it had the additional attraction of not being a rival occupation to agriculture. Nevertheless, though white fishing was concentrated in a few locations around the Minch, notably in Barra, its contribution to cash income remained small even in these areas. The contribution of herring fishing was, therefore, more important but, for several reasons, its expansion was severely limited. The capital required to fit out a fishing boat, though small, was beyond the resources of most Highlanders; the salt laws hindered curing, because, though drawbacks could be obtained on salt used for curing, they were difficult to collect from the dispersed customs houses in the Highlands; finally, the commercial barriers to sending the herring to markets in the south, essential to obtain cash income, were insuperable. Frequently, therefore, marketing fell into the hands of Lowland merchants, whose importance ensured that the centre of the industry was located in the Clyde and that the greatest benefit from any expansion in demand accrued to those fishing in the lochs opening from the Firth, especially Loch Fyne. Further north the irregularity of maintaining the necessary commercial contacts prevented any consistent growth of the herring fishing beyond that required to meet the very limited local demand.

Attempts to help the fisheries took various forms. A number of fishing villages were constructed in the late eighteenth and early nineteenth centuries in attempts, sometimes by landlords, sometimes by private companies, to provide the necessary centres for commercial activities. Among them were Torridon, Gairloch, Rodel, Lochinver, Plockton and Dornie. In 1786 a more general effort was made to encourage fishing, especially as a means of reviving the Highlands, in the formation of a joint-stock company, the British Fisheries Society. The Society flourished for over a decade, but it has been remembered primarily because of the failure of its settlements on the west coast, at Lochbay, Tobermory and Ullapool, abandoned in 1838, 1844 and 1848 respectively, against which must be set the successful development of Pultneytown (now part of Wick), where, however, there was already a settlement growing before the Society gave it further assistance. Unfortunately, various external factors did not encourage the Society's growth: the Napoleonic Wars brought enemy interference with shipping and rising prices for raw materials, while the west coast, where the failure was more notable, suffered through the centre of the herring fishing moving from the Minch to the Moray Firth, especially after

1797, and through European demand beginning to displace the older West Indian demand for herring. Yet, in spite of the failure of its settlements, the Society had a wider influence on the success of the fisheries, especially through obtaining some amelioration of the restrictive salt laws and by providing a pattern for official action under the Fishery Act of 1808.

The Act of 1808, which brought into being an official organization for the industry, with resident Fishery Officers, did not represent the beginnings of government aid. In the form of bounties it had existed for some time, though it benefited the Highlands but little, as the bounties granted to encourage private ventures in fishing in the middle of the eighteenth century were limited to grants towards the fitting out of vessels above a certain minimum tonnage. Since the Highlanders had inadequate resources for such ventures, they failed to gain from the state aid that was being given until 1787, when the restriction on bounties was altered and all vessels, of whatever size, received them on the basis of the number of barrels caught. Once again it was the Clyde ports that gained, though the direct repercussions on Highland fishings of the larger vessels then sent north varied. An unfavourable effect was that the ability of the southern boats to follow the herring in the various lochs of the west and north reduced part of the benefit which the erratic movements of the herring brought to particular areas from time to time. On the other hand a favourable effect, though until 1787 an illegal one, was that these ships frequently bought the catches of local fishermen and so provided them with the commercial contact with the south which was so desperately needed.

The fourth, and most important, addition to cash income came, especially during the Napoleonic Wars, from the manufacture of kelp, an extraction of an alkaline ash from seaweed, which was used in various industrial processes but particularly in the making of soap and glass. Industrial demand grew during the latter half of the eighteenth century, then, especially during the wars, the interruption to the supply of such foreign substitutes as barilla, and the taxation of salt, which became the basis of the alkali industry in the nineteenth century, all contributed to maintain the rising demand. Prices, though fluctuating, rose sharply, from £2 a ton in the middle of the eighteenth century to a peak of £20 a ton in 1810. Production responded and rose during the Napoleonic Wars. In 1770 in North Uist it was about 400 tons; in 1810 it was about 1,500 tons. Though kelp manufacture was introduced to the Orkneys and to the east coast as early as the 1730's, the great increase in production in the late eighteenth century was concentrated in the areas of greatest poverty on the west coast and in the Islands. Few industrial products require as little skill or capital as kelp. It was, therefore, one of the few industrial commodities which these areas of such poor natural endowments could produce. So long as prices remained high, such districts were blessed. The rise in kelp prices was, however, only the most dramatic illustration of the effect of the war-time price rise in them as they gained more generally through the prices of typical Highland exports, such as cattle and wool, increasing more than that of grain, the most important import. Cash income increased, therefore, even from traditional products.

Since the determining factor of most Highland development at this time was the desire of the landlords for increased rent, they absorbed most of the cash surplus. The most notable effect of the price rise was, therefore, a substantial rise in rentals. In 1774 the total rental of Breadal-bane was £4,914; in 1815 his rental was £23,000. The appropriation was most conspicuous in the kelping areas. Initially some kelping rights were let on reasonable terms, which allowed the tacksmen or tenants to make some profit, but, as the profits from the manufacture increased, the landlords leased land on the understanding that they would obtain high rents. In addition, though kelp manufacture gave birth to a wage-earning class, the wages paid remained fairly steady. From both groups the landlord removed the surplus which appeared. It was then an easy step for the organization of the trade to fall quickly into the hands of the landlords, or their representatives, and the quantity produced and sold on the account of some became very high. Clanranald, who owned the Uists, sold annually about 1,000 tons during the peak of war-time prices. In 1809 he had a gross income from his kelp manufacture of £13,277, leaving a net income of £10,047, and this on a land rental, increased by kelping rights, of £7,500. Early in the eighteenth century his land rental had been less than £1,000.

The appropriation of the surplus cash income by the landlords was less reprehensible than was their failure to put it to productive use. To their action at this time rather than to their action over the clearances should most attention be directed. The clearances could be justified as a method, though an unhappy one, of attempting to improve the estates, and perhaps they could never have been avoided, but, if they ever could, the opportunities opened up by the Napoleonic Wars provided the occasion. Instead, population continued to increase, especially when the landlords encouraged more people to settle in the already overcrowded kelping areas. This was a more culpable action than their later attempts to clear them, as placing more people in areas with resources already inadequate for subsistence exacerbated an already grave social problem, which became acute when kelp prices and profits collapsed. In short, the economy of the kelping regions became precariously dependent on the continuation of certain factors which could only be but temporary. The greatest tragedy of the period was the ignorance of the landlords, and indeed of most of the people, that their prosperity represented only a temporary respite to the problems which had faced them throughout the eighteenth century. Frequently landlords thought the rise in rents to be the outcome of their own improvements rather than of impersonal, and passing, market forces and so more expensive English ways became not only increasingly attractive but increasingly practicable. Nevertheless, in spite of rising cash income, debts accumulated. Clanranald's debts were £52,289 in 1797; in 1811 they were £71,280; in 1812 they were over £100,000. The decisive break in this prosperity came with falling prices especially after 1815. The effect was worst in the peculiarly vulnerable kelping districts, as the price of kelp fell, before the fall in the prices of agricultural products generally, from a peak of £20 a ton in 1810 to £10 a ton, at which level it remained, though generally drifting down, until the excise duty on salt was abolished in 1825. In 1824 the price was £8 a ton; in 1825 it was £7; in 1828 it was £4 15s.; and in 1834 it was £3 a ton. Since costs of production were around £5 a ton, production fell drastically. In 1827 even Clanranald stopped production for the season.

The drop in kelp prices, and the failure of the Highlands to gain any benefit from the expansion of the herring fishing in the Moray Firth, reduced the cash income of the Highlands sharply and substantially. The landlord had then either to reduce rents or increase his tenants' indebtedness. Eviction was no real solution, except as part of the reorganization of estates, because all tenants were similarly placed. As they had often done before, Highland landlords permitted indebtedness to grow, first that of their tenants, then of themselves. Quickly, the only solution became the desperate one of selling the estates. Clanranald sold part of his in the 1820's. In the 1830's his debts began to accumulate once more and the whole estate was sold in 1838.

Such sales represented the final break-up of the old order which had stressed the needs of the family and of strategy rather than economy in the administration of the land. The gulf between smaller and larger owners widened. On the other hand a landless class did not grow pro-portionately. Where they did, as cottars, the scarcity of any form of employment placed them in a precarious position, but the crofters were little better off because of the pitiful size of their holdings. Lack of capital, intensified by the fall in money incomes after the war, inhibited any form of improvement and a high degree of correlation may be postulated between the extent to which internal reforms in various districts met the challenge and the lesser degree of emigration from them. The greatest contribution to emigration came from the problem areas of the north and west, where natural endowments were inferior and population pressure greater. The area was thus placed in a fundamentally difficult and dangerous position. Increasing population alone led to a worsening of the balance of trade between the Highlands and other regions. Imports of meal were continuous and so the need for a supplementary cash income grew. As cash income dropped and cultivation remained poor and primitive only dependence on the potato enabled the increasing population of the Highlands to be main-tained. In the 1840's this last remaining barrier to change collapsed. The population of many Highland areas reached its peak at the 1841 census. In 1845, and more so in 1846, blight in the potato removed the major source of subsistence. Emigration became a matter of necessity, no longer only of choice. A transformation of the Highland economy could no longer be averted.

The collapse of the economy encouraged the extension of sheep-rearing in the Highlands. Sheep-farming as a specialized occupation was introduced to the central Highlands by men from the Southern Uplands in the 1760's until, by about 1800, the counties just north of the Highland line were well stocked, and the spread into the remoter parts of the west and north began. After the Napoleonic Wars the fall in prices called a temporary halt, but from the 1830's to the 1870's prices were sufficiently high to maintain the profits in sheep-farming. The introduction of sheep occasioned some evictions and has roused much anger, partly through concentration on a few areas, where the worst effects were evident, even more through a complete misappre-hension of the grinding poverty which existed before the sheep came and which impelled emigration, sooner or later, unless the Highlands were to be left in squalor with the lowest standard of living in Scotland. Overall only a small proportion of the land, perhaps only 20 per cent, went out of cultivation to make way for sheep, and even where the area was greater, as in the areas of greatest notoriety, such as the straths of Sutherland, the process was more gradual than has sometimes been assumed. Nevertheless the introduction of sheep was an explosive force in the life of the Highlands, because it was a new agricultural enterprise which required new men, as the Highlanders had neither the capital nor the requisite technical knowledge. It also implied bigger farms, restrictions on hill grazing, and fewer people. Thus population pressure was increased still further in those areas where there were no sheep and where fishing was either impossible or inadequate. But sheep-farming was not the cause of the clearances and of emigration. In certain areas there was emigration without sheep. It is the tragedy of some of the clearances, especially of those in Sutherland, which has caused sheep-farming to be blamed. Yet even in Sutherland, the introduction of sheep only occasioned the change. The prime cause was the rejection of the conception that the land should support the largest number of people irrespective of their standard of living. For that reason the stimulus to emigration was there, and took place from certain areas, without the introduction of sheep. In others the new agricultural enterprises simply precipitated it.

X
AN INDUSTRIAL SOCIETY

Population

IN the eighteenth century contact with England produced a new society in Scotland. In the nineteenth century the growing importance of the industrial sector in the Scottish economy also produced a social transformation but one with very different results. In both periods, though in different ways, the quality and character of the way of life of the people was changed; whether for better or worse is not easy to determine. The most striking change in Scottish society in the nineteenth century was in increased numbers. Sinclair's estimate in the *Old Statistical Account* was of a population of 1,526,492 in 1795. From 1801 the census figures provide more reliable data.

POPULATION OF SCOTLAND

		Percentage increase			Percentage increase
1801	1,608,420	—	1841	2,620,184	10·8
1811	1,805,864	12·3	1851	2,888,742	10·2
1821	2,091,521	15·8	1861	3,062,294	6·0
1831	2,364,386	13·0	1871	3,360,018	9·7

It is difficult to discuss the connection between industrial growth and the increase of population with any degree of certainty in any society, but in Scotland it is virtually impossible to do so at all because of the absence of any reliable statistics of birth-rate and death-rate until the introduction of the compulsory registration of births, deaths and marriages in 1855. Only after the census of 1861 can a discussion of demographic change be based on an adequate statistical foundation. Much more reliable, however, is our knowledge of changes in the distribution of the population, which were among the most important social legacies of industrialization. The better statistics from the 1850's help towards an understanding of these changes. When compulsory registration was introduced in 1855 the birth-rate was 31 per thousand and the death-rate 21 per thousand, giving a rate of natural increase of 10 per thousand. If, as a rough measurement, this rate of natural

177

increase is applied to earlier decades, then in all decades in the first half of the nineteenth century actual increase exceeded the natural increase. Hence the emigration, substantial at times, between 1801 and 1851 was more than counterbalanced by immigration. Their causes may be deduced from the changing pattern of distribution of the population between the four divisions followed by the Registrar-General.[1] Between 1801 and 1871 population increased in the Northern division from 741,000 to 1,041,000, in the Southern division from 185,000 to 272,000, in the East Central division from 352,000 to 803,000, and in the West Central division from 331,000 to 1,244,000. Between these years, therefore, the balance of the population was changed.

Percentage Distribution of Population

	West Central	East Central	Southern	Northern
1801	20·5	22	11·5	46
1871	37	24	8	31

Rural depopulation was accompanied by a contemporaneous increase in urban growth. The maximum population was reached in 1831 in the counties of Argyll, Kinross and Perth; in 1841 in Inverness; in 1851 in Kirkcudbright, Ross and Cromarty, Sutherland and Wigtown; in 1861 in Berwick, Caithness, Orkney, Roxburgh, Zetland. Though the contribution of the Highland counties to emigration is clear, it is equally evident that in the first half of the nineteenth century, depopulation in Scotland was a rural rather than simply a Highland problem. The extent of the decline in some of the Highland counties, such as Ross-shire, was matched by that in the south-western county of Wigtown and the Stewartry of Kirkcudbright. The special problems of the Highlands arose only because certain Highland counties, such as Caithness, Sutherland and Argyll, suffered a greater decline. To counterbalance the losses in the rural areas were the sharp increases in some of the counties of the central belt. Lanarkshire's population increased from 81,726 in 1801 to 765,339 in 1871; Ayrshire's from 84,207 to 200,809; Midlothian's from 122,597 to 328,379; Renfrewshire's from 78,501 to 216,947.

Since the place of birth of all inhabitants in Scotland is given from

---

[1] East Central division: Fife, Clackmannan, Stirling, West Lothian, Midlothian, East Lothian, Dundee. West Central division: Dumbarton, Renfrew, Lanark, Ayr. Counties to the north and west of these are in the Northern division, those to the south and east are in the Southern division.

the 1841 census onwards, it becomes possible to demonstrate the course of this movement more clearly thereafter. The statistics derived from the census are not wholly reliable because they give only a minimum measurement of movement. They do not include semi-permanent or seasonal migrants, if they were in the county of birth at the date of the census, nor those who may have made several moves in the decade between the censuses, but the general pattern is not affected. It is certain that at mid-century the main area of departure was the seven crofting counties and that the main area of reception was Glasgow and its neighbouring counties. The only other reception area was Edinburgh and the Lothians, as in Aberdeen and the north-east the population movements counterbalanced each other. In 1851 all other areas in Scotland had sent more of their natives to other parts of Scotland than they had themselves received the natives of other parts. The two reception areas, however, differed from each other. Glasgow gained a net inflow from all other regions, even from Edinburgh, the only instance of such a contribution from the capital. Glasgow also absorbed a significantly greater proportion of emigrants than Edinburgh from all regions except the Borders, though the greater stream provided from that area for Edinburgh was more than counterbalanced by the movement from Edinburgh to Glasgow.

The movements of population within Scotland were supplemented by movements into the country from overseas. Some immigration into Scotland from overseas was necessary to account for the difference between the actual and the natural increases of the population alone, but the emigration of Scots overseas, the amount of which cannot be accurately estimated, required a still greater level of immigration into Scotland. In the nineteenth century the inward movement was almost entirely of Irish. In 1871 6 per cent of the total population, or 207,770, were Irish born, but the proportion varied considerably throughout Scotland. In some counties there were practically none, in others they were particularly concentrated. In Lanarkshire about 14 per cent of the population was Irish born in 1871, in Renfrewshire about 13 per cent.

Though urban growth offset rural depopulation, the movements overseas meant that the two forces were not rigidly correlated. Movement from rural areas was not motivated, therefore, solely by the attractions of industrial growth, which were sufficient only to explain why immigrants moved to particular districts, above all to Glasgow and the west of Scotland, not to explain why the people—from the rural areas of Scotland and from Ireland—were willing to move in the first place.

Seasonal migration within Scotland, especially from the Highlands to the Lowlands, was an old practice, most migrants finding employment in agriculture, though some gained openings in industry, as in the bleachfields of the Vale of Leven in the eighteenth century. In the nineteenth century the Irish displaced the Highlanders as the preponderant element among seasonal migrants except in the north-east, and, at the same time, seasonal migration, while persisting, was overwhelmed in importance by more permanent movement. Until the displacement of the hand-loom weavers by the use of power-driven machinery around the 1820's, such permanent migration, whether within or from Scotland, was generally from the land because of some agricultural development. Until about the 1780's, in both Highlands and Lowlands, the basic factor underlying rural change was the destruction of the old social structure, but from the 1780's a perceptible difference can be noted. Earlier many of those Highlanders, who—numerically at any rate—dominated the movement from Scotland, were not in abject poverty; after about 1780 they were. The Highlands provide the best illustration,[1] but the Highland problem was not unique. Its experience was shared by other areas of rural depopulation, especially by Galloway. Unless a district achieved 'solvency through reform'[2] there was no alternative for an increasing population but emigration. The extent of 'solvency through reform' depended in turn on natural conditions or on industrial development. In the south-east the growth of the woollen industry, combined with the region's traditional fertility, never produced the same pressing problems as in the south-west, troubled by its lack of industry, by the conversion of arable land to sheep-farming, and by a continuous, and occasionally rapid, influx of Irish.

The Irish, more than any other group, determined the changes in the demographic pattern of Scotland in the nineteenth century. Their movement into the country was not the product of the nineteenth century since there had long been traffic, both ways, between Ulster and south-west Scotland, but the first modern movement was initiated by the Irish rebellion of 1798 and the number of Irish-born inhabitants of Scotland increased rapidly after 1815. The Irish potato famine of the 1840's initiated a second phase of migration, quantitatively much

[1] See p. 6 ff.

[2] M. Gray, *The Highland Economy, 1750–1850* (Edinburgh, 1957), p. 223.

greater than anything experienced earlier and also qualitatively different. Until the 1840's the Irish immigrant was comparable to that from rural Scotland. Both were seeking higher standards of living than could be obtained at home. Blight in the potato brought a difference. 'Self-improvement was the impulse that transported him to Scotland in pre-famine days. Self-preservation was the urge that drove him onwards in the black night of pestilence.'[2] The tendency for the Irish immigrant in Scotland to be much poorer and more desperate than his predecessor before the famine was increased by a further factor. Since most aimed, if possible, at going to the United States, for which the fare was £4, only the poorest stayed in Scotland. Most immigrants came from Antrim by the shortest and cheapest route to Portpatrick. At the beginning of the nineteenth century many settled in Galloway, Dumfriesshire, and Ayrshire to work as farm labourers, especially when the improving movement provided adequate employment. By the 1840's, when the type of migrant changed, Galloway had few opportunities left for Irish labourers, and so the new migrants had to seek employment elsewhere, even though they continued to use the traditional route. The way of the majority lay, therefore, across agricultural Galloway and south Ayrshire to the developing industrial areas of north Ayrshire, Renfrewshire and north Lanarkshire, where, except for a small number who reached Dundee, most remained. After 1830, when the heavy industries were established, and especially in the 1840's, when the type of Irish immigrant changed, the drift of the Irish was almost entirely to the ironworks and to the coal-mines, where they could find unskilled, unpleasant tasks, requiring little or no training, which the native Scots were not anxious to accept.

The rapid influx explains why the growth of population could be maintained at a level greater than the natural rate of increase during the first half of the nineteenth century in spite of considerable movement of Scots overseas. Yet during the same period the high rate of natural increase was the more important factor leading to the rise in population. Its contribution cannot, therefore, be ignored. It was concentrated in the areas of industrial development, especially in the new, growing towns, where an industrial society was first formed.

[1] J. F. Handley, *The Irish in Modern Scotland* (Cork, 1945), p. 1.

An industrial society

The first major break with traditional industrial organization—and so the first moves towards the emergence of an industrial society—came with the establishment of the larger cotton mills, which provided a greater contrast to earlier traditions than did the smaller units. Their mere size—New Lanark employed 368 people in 1791 and about 1,700 in 1820—alone made them unique, and, set in their planned communities, their influence on industrial organization was comparable only with the earlier example of Carron Company in the iron industry. Their impact was great because they were unrepresentative, but their problems were shared by others though to a lesser degree. The most intractable, and one which determined much of the subsequent form of development of many, was the inadequacy of the supply of labour. Some of the larger mills were in existing centres of population, as were Brown's in Dundee, Richard's in Montrose, Bannerman's in Aberdeen and Oswald's in Glasgow, but even they were not easily assured of an adequate supply of labour. However, the problem was most acute in the more remote establishments, conspicuously in those larger mills which were located in sparsely populated districts to exploit natural advantages and which, until the advent of steam-power, had no alternative but to remain near adequate water supplies. Once settled, such mills frequently remained even when steam-power was used in them. The labour they required was provided, first, by the use of pauper children supplied by parish poorhouses, and second, by using emigrants, both Highland and Irish. Pauper children were not used extensively in Scotland. Carron Company found them troublesome and New Lanark was one of the few cotton mills in which they made an important contribution to the labour force. Emigrants were, therefore, the major source of supply of labour, especially the Irish, who were not only more numerous than the Highlanders, but were sometimes preferred. In 1833 Henry Houldsworth, who had mills at Anderston and Woodside in Glasgow, commented in 1833 that they were 'almost full of Irish; we can scarcely get a Scotchman for a partner or a watchman'. Houldsworth was highly, almost offensively, critical of some of the local labour which he had first encountered when he had come to Glasgow from Manchester at the beginning of the nineteenth century:

'At that period the spinning trade was extremely limited; there was not, I believe, more than one mill or so at Glasgow; at that time the hands employed were principally highlandmen, and all the attempts that were made to induce those men to work hard and live better were of no avail, and I had to get Englishmen to show them an example of industry before I could stir; for the first six months I could not get them to earn more than 12*s.* to 14*s.* a week; they would rather live upon meal and potatoes than exert themselves, but they were much more sober than they are now.'[1]

It was almost inevitable that overcrowding and squalid conditions should be the offshoots of such rapid concentrations of industrial population, but conditions varied. In larger concerns, as New Lanark, Catrine, Deanston and elsewhere, a new way of life was most conspicuous, yet it was not lived necessarily in increasing squalor, because there the dwellings of the people, though differing from what many had previously experienced, generally represented an advance on earlier standards. In Catrine, for instance, the stone-built, two-storeyed, slated houses were distinctly better than what was common in adjacent country districts. In even sharper contrast with the earlier conditions in both town and country, some attempt was made to organize social services in most of the larger establishments. At Catrine a church, school-house, gardens and pasture for cows were provided, while, in an early effort to supply police measures, even though aimed chiefly at ensuring the security of the mill and the proprietors' property, the gates at both ends of the main street were locked every night. The existence of such social provision, however elementary, contradicts any extreme assumption that greatly increased squalor was introduced by all the larger industrial units, even though they were the most conspicuous examples of the new industrial order. Defects were, indeed, usually worst in the smaller concerns, where squalor was more universal and industrial discipline more harsh. The distinction may be discerned in the reports of the various parliamentary investigations of the time. Various commissioners were often unduly impressed, perhaps by conscious design on the part of the mill-owners, by some of the more dramatic features of the new industrial enterprises, as at Rothesay, where a band of workers 'serenaded us while there, and from the work to the pier, where we reimbarked [sic]',[2] but throughout all their

---

[1] *Select Committee on Manufactures, Commerce and Shipping*, 1833, Q. 5288.
[2] *Factories Inquiry Commission*, 1833. First Report, p. 19.

reports they stressed repeatedly the adverse and inhuman conditions of the smaller mills, especially of those on the east coast, which remained engaged in the manufacture of linen and were not the scene of the successful large-scale developments in cotton production. The excellent reports given by the Factories Inquiry Commissioners in 1833 to Catrine, New Lanark, Deanston, and Stanley were interspersed with criticisms of others. Little favourable was said of the examination of four mills in Dunfermline, of twenty-two spinning-mills in Kirkcaldy and of thirty-five mills in Dundee, nearly all small and engaged in the linen industry. Later, in Perthshire, after fulsome praise of the Stanley mills, the Commissioner visited a number of small flax mills around Blairgowrie, and reported that 'the small mills are uniformly ill-cleaned and ventilated, and there is more dust in the preparing rooms and less attention to the boxing in of the machinery, than in large establishments'. At Stirling a number of woollen and paper factories 'are kept in a very filthy state, ill ventilated, and the machinery is not well boxed'. By contrast criticism of the larger establishments was rare, with one exception. To use the Commissioner's own words,

'The Blantyre works belonging to Messrs. Henry Monteith and Company is the only great establishment which I have seen, situated in the country, away from the population of a town, of which it is impossible to write chiefly in terms of approbation. The buildings are most of them old, the apartments are not well-cleaned, low roofed, the passages narrow, ventilation little attended to, there are no seats for the workers, and occasionally considerable annoyance from the water closets.'[1]

The Commissioner's explanation of the defects of Blantyre—that they arose through the control and direction of the mill being left in the hands of managers rather than retained by the proprietors—was not entirely convincing, but, whatever the explanation, the condition of Blantyre was considered to be exceptional. That was the measure of its importance.

In spite of the advantages most larger mills offered, they had substantial defects, which loomed large in the minds of the workers, though they were frequently ignored, or regarded as examples of irrational prejudice or ignorance, by owners and official investigators. The objections raised were basically to industrial discipline, or to such social discipline as was required for the effective operation of the

[1] *Factories Inquiry Commission.* First Report, 1833. A.1. Northern District, p. 92.

communities. As New Lanark was the leading example of what could be achieved in the new industrial society, its experience was always regarded as of particular importance. Not all thought New Lanark could succeed commercially. When it did, attention was concentrated on the social arrangements which contradicted many of the viewpoints held tenaciously by cotton manufacturers. They delighted in examples of collapse of such arrangements, especially when they arose through the rejection by workers of supposed benefits. Examples, not necessarily representing the view of the majority employed there, especially under Owen's more idealistic regime, do exist and illustrate the opposition of some workers to better social provisions. The Blantyre mill did not provide the best conditions among the larger mills, nor the most enlightened management, but its proprietor alleged in 1816 that a 'good many' workers preferred to move from New Lanark to Blantyre. One such worker stated clearly the opposition to industrial discipline and direction even when well-intentioned.

'They had got a number of dancing-masters, a fidler, a band of music, that there were drills and exercises, and that they were dancing together till they were more fatigued than if they were working.'[1]

In spite of the differences between the larger and the smaller units the application of the new technology brought common experience to all workers in the spinning of cotton and other textiles. On the other hand the relative backwardness in the application of a new technology to weaving led to a distinctive experience in that section of textile production for some time. The increased output of yarn, which resulted from the new methods of spinning adopted around the 1780's and later, heightened the demand for weavers' services until the widespread adoption of the power-loom, which was used successfully at Catrine in 1807 and soon afterwards at other Finlay establishments. The difficulties of increasing weaving capacity, which had limited the full exploitation of the new methods of spinning, were eliminated and the social and economic condition of the hand-loom weavers correspondingly altered. From the 1780's to about 1815, while the demand for their services was high, hand-loom weavers earned as much as 30s. to 40s. a week and became the most prosperous, the most aristocratic, and the most autocratic, of workmen. There was a rapid accession to

[1] *Report of the Select Committee on the State of Children employed in Factories*, 1816, p. 167.

their numbers, but with the introduction of the power-loom, and the collapse of the demand for their services, their distress became well known. While the technological change occasioned the collapse, it does not provide an adequate explanation of the extent of the depression, because the number of hand-looms continued to increase, and with some rapidity, even after the introduction of the power-driven machinery. In 1828 in Scotland south of the Forth and Clyde Canal there were about 48,000 hand-looms, estimated to be considerably more than in 1815. In 1838 there were 52,164 hand-looms and of these over half were weaving cotton goods. The increase in numbers continued too long for it to be the result only of a short-term failure by the weavers to readjust themselves, and their expectations, to the new technology. The apparently perverse reaction arose from hand-loom weaving being an easy trade to learn and, as the labour market was saturated after 1815, especially with the continuing influx of unskilled, poverty-stricken Irish and Highland immigrants, it offered many the only possibility of some form of livelihood. The report of Jellinger Symons, the Assistant Commissioner for the South of Scotland, to the Hand-loom Weavers Commission in 1839, summed up the situation.

'The Irish weavers are a little in advance in the career down hill, for they are the main cause of pulling the Scotch down after them. Of course they are in a slightly better condition than in their own country, which is precisely the reason why they take the lead in the career downwards, having less natural repugnance to privations which they have been previously in some measure inured to; when a manufacturer desires to lower his wages, it is ten to one but the Irish are the first to accept his terms.'[1]

Without such a rapid influx of labour to the trade, the weavers could have effected an easier transition to the new conditions of production, but the appearance of numbers of poverty-stricken Irish in the west of Scotland at that crucial period was the main explanation of the extent of degradation of the hand-loom weavers. The new technology precipated the collapse; the Irish ensured that it was not easily alleviated.

The distress of the hand-loom weavers eventually forced many to enter other occupations. Some at last entered the factories to operate power-looms, others left the textile industries altogether, while others emigrated, sometimes under the auspices of the emigration societies,

[1] *Report of the Assistant Hand-loom Weavers Commissioner*, 1839 (South of Scotland), p. 19.

which were active from the 1820's among hand-loom weavers, though not always most successfully. Nevertheless, in spite of the decline in hand-loom weaving, the occupation did not collapse entirely but remained, especially in the woollen industry. In Paisley and district the manufacture of woollen goods, which had been introduced about 1840, when the hand-loom weavers were experiencing a decline in demand from their traditional customers, relied extensively on hand-loom work, and from it emerged the most persistent centre of hand-loom weaving of woollen goods at Kilbarchan, which around 1870 still had about 800 hand-loom weavers. At the same time, 1870, the woollen manufacturers of Paisley employed about 2,000 hand-loom weavers in busy seasons. In Glasgow the decline was more noticeable. By 1862, when the Children's Employment Commission investigated conditions, the largest factory in Glasgow using hand-looms only—about 300 of them—was Laird and Thompson's at Mile End. However, even in those areas where employment remained, as in Paisley, the wages of hand-loom weavers were much reduced. Around 1870 they were about 8s. or 9s. a week. And in all, whether in the workshop, which continued to exist in the towns, or in those country districts where individual weavers were still able to make a living of sorts, conditions were shocking. In 1862 one hand-loom weaver, who stated that a regular day for a weaver was from 6 a.m. to 10 p.m., and frequently till midnight or 1 a.m., summed up the situation.

'In town a room and kitchen above, and a four-loom shop below is the most universal system, sometimes a six-loom shop, but in country districts "a but and ben", i.e. a room with part divided off for a loom or two, is very common. Some of the shops are so damp that a fire has no effect upon them; I have seen some quite wet.'[1]

By then most hand-loom weavers found it almost impossible to continue to exist independently, and the opportunities of hand-loom weaving in factories were rapidly declining too. By the late nineteenth century the hand-loom weaver could continue to exist only if, as in Kilbarchan, he was able to work for a very high-quality market which was anxious to obtain woollen goods simply because they had been hand-woven. The mass market, on which most of the Scottish textile industries depended, gave decreasing scope for the activities of the hand-loom weavers after 1815.

[1] *Children's Employment Commission*, 1864. Second Report, p. 227.

The heavy industries and housing

The advent of the domination of the Scottish economy by the heavy industries brought yet another way of life to many people. Though perhaps equally obnoxious to that introduced by modern textile production, it was quite distinct. The existing tendency for industry to be localized, or concentrated, was maintained. In the eighteenth century the availability of water supplies determined the location of the cotton mills; in the nineteenth century the increasing use of steam and the large consumption of coal in the ironworks took industry to the coal measures. As well as being an age of concentration, it was the period of filth and of the destruction of the landscape. Of itself the use of water-power created neither smoke nor dirt, nor did the mills using it produce great quantities of waste. A change came only with the steam-engine, not generally applied in industry until the nineteenth century. With the spread of coalmining and iron-working came the bings, the pit-shafts, with their desolate buildings and coke-ovens, the criss-cross of mineral railways; all the features which still disfigure parts of the Scottish countryside. The transformation was mainly on the coal measures of north Lanarkshire and north Ayrshire. In some parishes, notably the Monklands, existing hamlets grew rapidly and sometimes towns, such as Coatbridge, appeared from nothing. Other towns which had first appeared, or grown to significance, on the basis of textiles were undergoing a complete transformation by the middle of the nineteenth century as a new phase of constructional activity, which is still evident, appeared in them. That part of the town which had been tacked on to the old agricultural community, when domestic weaving expanded, was interspersed and increased by Victorian tenements, while Presbyterian disputation and Irish immigration frequently brought an accession to ecclesiastical buildings.

The social problems raised by the extension of the heavy industries were not completely novel. The mining areas had a long-standing tradition of harshness, which owed much to the ancient serfdom of the Scottish miners, who until 1775 were bound for life to a certain colliery. An Act of 1775 offered freedom through a Sheriff Court process to those who, after a period, were able to provide apprentices to follow them. An Act of 1799 finally freed Scottish colliers completely. Information on the practice before 1775 is sparse, but the law may not always have been stringently enforced. Certainly colliery owners did not always readily unite in attempts to claim bound colliers, but were more annoyed when English colliers, whom they had introduced to Scotland, and who were not, of course, subject to the law of Scotland, absconded. On the surface, the masters usually made a pretence of unity, and some were willing to support each other's actions. Whenever a bound collier fled, possible employers were frequently warned to refuse to engage him, while any who had actually engaged such a man were asked to dismiss him. Nevertheless, in spite of such co-operation against the man, it seems that, beneath the surface, there was much squabbling, and that many attempts were made to attract colliers from one pit to another. Sometimes such disputes arose through doubts over the legal ownership of the man. More important were cases where the overseers in charge of the mines did not follow the policy of their masters even when the latter favoured strict adherence to the law. Generally, however, the law was applied rigidly only when any large-scale trouble or defection among colliers was feared, and, therefore, of course, only when the need to apply it was greatest. In sum, the recall of bound miners probably depended both on who was being recalled and on who was recalling. Thus, if a collier who departed was generally regarded as troublesome, fairly persistent efforts were usually made to have him returned to his lawful owner. The Act of 1775 lessened the number of actions for recall. Only the masters who had previously been most stringent in enforcement continued to try to exercise their powers. Personalities, both on the side of the masters and on the side of the man, were important before 1775; they were much more so afterwards.

In this way mining society was degraded even before the expansion of the heavy industries in the nineteenth century. Whatever the reprehensible legacy of that later expansion, it made the maintenance of the old system of serfdom no longer tenable. The serfdom of the Scottish miners could continue only with the backward condition of coalmining until the middle of the eighteenth century and in so far as they disrupted this social structure, the changes of the nineteenth century were beneficial. The legacy of the old society remained, however, notably in the east, where the restrictions of the old social order were most felt, most resented and lingered longest, even when in the eighteenth century the demand from the domestic consumers in Edinburgh and from the salt trade in the Forth ensured a greater demand for coal in the east than in the west, while the accessibility of collieries to the sea, on both sides of the Forth, facilitated their exploitation. On the other hand in the west of Scotland, when the coal industry first expanded rapidly, it did so with a more modern, typically nineteenth-century, social organization. The difference was made most explicit in the investigations which formed the basis of the Report of 1842 into the employment of women and children in collieries. In the east the condition of women and children was as bad as in any other area; in the west of Scotland, judged by the low standards then current, conditions were better. Thus the employment of women was common in the east, but unknown in the west, and continued, though not always with the consent or knowledge of the colliery owner, even after the Act which forbade their employment. Again, in the east of Scotland before the legislation of 1842 the age of children employed in the pits was generally two or three years younger than that of those employed in the west. Conditions were no better in the west, they were only different. While the remnants of the old social order lingered in the east, the west possessed the most dramatic examples of a different social order, but one equally characterized by brutality and vice. The reason for the distinction is quite simple. The coalfield of the west witnessed the most rapid expansion of the nineteenth century. It suffered, therefore, from the worst effects of rapid immigration and concentration of population in what had previously been only agricultural communities. In these areas, especially in parts of north Lanarkshire and north Ayrshire, the harshness and inadequate social provision of the new settlements was evident. To Thomas Tancred, visiting the Monklands parishes, it seemed that:

'This vast and sudden accession of population consisting for the most part of irregular and dissolute characters from all parts—from Wales, England, Scotland and Ireland—has produced a state of society, upon the existence of which, in a civilized country, we cannot reflect without a deep feeling that it manifests something essentially defective in our religious and educational institutions.

'Everything that meets the eye or ear tells of slavish labour united to brutal intemperance. At night, ascending to the hill on which the Established Church stands, the group of blast-furnaces on all sides might be imagined to be blazing volcanoes, at most of which the smelting is continued Sundays and weekdays, by day and night, without intermission. By day a perpetual steam arises from the blast-engines on both sides of it; and railroads, traversed by long trains of waggons drawn by locomotive engines, intersect the country in all directions, and are the cause of frequent accidents, into which, by the law of Scotland, no inquiry is made.'[1]

The most lasting single legacy of this phase of expansion of mining was the miners' row, which gives the best example of the decline in housing standards in some areas between 1830 and 1880. The miners' row was squalid and remained so. Even during the First World War the Royal Commission on Scottish Housing could still refer to 'the present foul congeries of middens, ashpits and coal-sheds'[2] in front of the older rows, and to the 'ramshackle brick survivals of the mining outbursts of seventy years ago in the mining fields, monotonous miners' rows flung down without a vestige of town-plan or any effort to secure modern conditions of sanitation'.[3] 'Flung down' was the most appropriate description of their planning. The exact location of a row was determined by the need to have it convenient to the mine. As is obvious from even a cursory glance at those which remain, rarely was any attention paid to the nature of the soil or the subsoil, amenities or exposure. Moreover, the possibly short life of a mine, and the tendency to regard the houses as an unproductive form of capital investment, absorbing resources which might well have gone into the mine itself, militated against good construction. For long the proportion of small houses—of one or of two rooms—was higher in the mining areas than elsewhere. Improvement was not easy because of the reluctance of many miners to pay a large part of their income in rent. In the expansion of mining after about 1830 housing was frequently a perquisite. Latterly, when this changed, miners seem to have paid out a smaller proportion of their income in rent than did other groups of workers. Even if the rents paid were all that the houses were worth—as may well have been so—a solution to this social problem required in the nineteenth century not only the provision of better houses, but the occupation of these houses by tenants willing to pay a higher rent. Unfortunately the tradition of poor housing became so ingrained in all Scots, but especially in the miners, that they became satisfied with poor conditions and unwilling to pay for improvements. The problem could

[1] *Report of Commissioners to Children's Employment Commission on Employment of Children in Mines and Colleries*, vol. ii, 1842, pp. 311 ff., paras. 12 and 13.

[2] *Report of the Royal Commission on the Housing of the Industrial Population of Scotland Rural and Urban*, 1918 (Cd. 8731), para. 882.

[3] *Ibid.*, para. 2232.

be solved only by official action, which meant that in practice little could be achieved in the nineteenth century.

To many contemporaries an even more effective barrier to improvement, and the cause of the degradation being most marked in the mining communities, was the advent of the Irish in them. One contemporary writer commented:

'they have . . . eaten up our public charities, filled our prisons, crowded the calendar of crime, and destroyed the appearance and character of many an old Scots village. Dark shadows marked the advent of the Irish among those scenes of peace and prosperity— shadows, which have darkened into sullen, gloomy clouds.'[1]

More accurately the explanation was the rapid influx of people into an area with no, or inadequate, social provision. Hence came overcrowding. Many of those who came to such areas were, of course, Irish, but their numbers, rather than their nationality, was the prime cause of the problem. But the criticism of the Irish was not simply exaggeration or an example of racial intolerance, especially after the appearance of the post-famine immigrant. To these later immigrants squalor was, if possible, less obnoxious than it was to many native Scots, since, as the minister of Whithorn dramatically and precisely recorded, 'they are possessed of nothing but a number of naked, starving children'.[2] Their abject poverty rendered them more docile and so more ready to accept worse conditions than the Scots. Only to this extent had their nationality any effect on the degradation.

One remarkable feature of the mining areas was that their squalor and filth had a less devastating effect on public health than might have been expected, though it was still considerable. The presence of ample fresh air was a chief preventive of many pulmonary diseases, just as the same factor was taken to explain the relative mildness of the incidence of tuberculosis in Edinburgh and Leith compared with other towns, and its supply was certainly ample in the exposed situation of many of the rows, as in the villages south and east of Shotts, such as Breich, or in another area, the valley of the Doon, where the miners, especially if they were Irish, were 'balloted out among the hills in distinct communities by themselves',[3] to mitigate their baneful social influence on

---

[1] R. Wylie, *Ayrshire Streams* (London, 1851), p. 15.

[2] *New Statistical Account*, vol. iv (Wigtownshire), p. 60.

[3] Wylie, *op. cit.*, p. 92.

others. Even today the desolate ruins of some of the mining villages yield a useful insight into the social fabric of nineteenth-century Scotland. The degradation and squalor of the rows reflect the position the miners occupied in Scottish society for years after their legal emancipation. The ethos of the mining community can be realized only if the extent of their physical segregation and desolation is first understood. Their living alone led the miners, in common with most of the agricultural community, to regard themselves as a race apart, as a gathered community, which, of course, they were. A tour of the old settlements, in all their bleakness and primitiveness, makes it easy to understand how such sentiments could continue even when the grounds for them had gone.

Though the housing of miners may have been the worst of all in the nineteenth century, other sectors of the population suffered similarly. The *Reports on the Sanitary Conditions of the Labouring Population* of 1842, while concluding that colliers were worst housed, demonstrated the general nature of the problem; but some thought that even the Reports of 1842 were too favourable. In the same year, while some of the Reports, especially that on Tranent, suggested that the condition of the houses of the hinds was superior, a description of the housing of the same type of rural labourer in the Borders adopted quite a different position.[1] The difference, which was admitted by all to exist between the collier and the rural labourer, and it was a material one, was that, while the miner did little to improve his squalid position, the rural labourers, especially the permanently employed hind, did so. Hence in the countryside condemnation could be passed much more unequivocally on those who provided the houses, but conditions varied and it was only in the more backward parts that the housing conditions of the eighteenth century remained unimproved into the nineteenth. However, whatever the improvements in some areas, there was no doubt that, in sum, in the nineteenth century thoughout Scotland, in the new industrial areas and in the old rural communities, there was overcrowding, and that it became worse. In 1801 there were 546 persons to every 100 houses, most of which were extremely small; in 1851 there were 780 persons to every 100 houses. In the following census, that of 1861, fuller information was requested to ascertain Scottish conditions. It was then revealed that 226,723 families, or one-third of Scotland's population, were living in houses of one room; 7,964 of them were in single rooms without windows. The worst illustrations

---

[1] W. S. Gilly, *The Peasantry of the Border* (London, 1842), pp. 6 ff.

of such overcrowding were to be found in the towns, where the population was increased through migration, than in the country as a whole. It was in the towns too that other factors worsened the already abominable conditions. Houses and tenements were frequently subdivided, an ominous sign indicating that an area had fallen on evil days, and one which, because it did not affect the exterior, did not come under the control of the Dean of Guild until 1891. Even thereafter the inability to determine when an alteration was taking place, when the structure was unaffected, made it difficult to control the practice. And, wherever they went, the post-famine Irish immigrants, having been accustomed to squalor, took in lodgers, though not on a scale sufficiently large to provide for all who required accommodation, and so the number of lodging-houses, virulent sources of infection, grew as their quality declined.

Much of the inadequacy of housing, arising from a rapid accession and concentration of population, was not uniquely Scottish; but one problem more peculiar to Scotland was the rapid multiplication of the tenement, especially in the spreading towns of the mid-nineteenth century. Though the tenement had advantages, many of those erected in the nineteenth century were inadequately lit and ventilated. Worst of all, they had the common stair, which, being no one's responsibility, was, in the words of Glasgow's first medical officer of health, 'just simply a mass of chaos and confusion, with no one to keep order'.[1] The effect was worse when the landings had long passages or, worst of all, a T-passage, off which the doors to the various houses branched. Frequently, too, the tenements produced other defects, such as underground dwellings, which at best was the lowest flat of a good tenement built on sloping ground. But the defects of the tenement lay less in its construction than in the gross overcrowding of so many of them. Hence came the almost indefinite proliferation in them of box-beds, 'cubicles of consumption', and the widespread sub-letting and subdivision. Overcrowding rather than construction had to be controlled, as was indeed recognized after an outbreak of typhus in Glasgow in 1866, when an attempt was made to control the numbers occupying a house by the system of 'ticketing'. The ticket stated how many people could be accommodated in a house, but gave rise to obvious difficulties in enforcement. Its use as a means of preventing overcrowding lay only in a later period.

[1] W. T. Gairdner, *Proceedings of the Philosophical Society of Glasgow*, vol. vii (1870–1), p. 254.

Disease and destitution

The social conditions had a direct influence on the incidence of disease, attributed by one Glasgow doctor

> 'to the total want of cleanliness among the lower orders of the community; to the absence of ventilation in the more densely peopled districts; and to the accumulation, for weeks or months together, of filth of every description in our private and public dunghills; to the over-crowded state of the lodging-houses resorted to by the lowest classes; and to many other circumstances unnecessary to mention'.[1]

The only remedy was to be rid of such filthy, squalid conditions; a palliative, which did not exist, were better medical facilities. The rudimentary beginnings of a hospital system had been provided in the eighteenth century with the foundation of the Edinburgh Infirmary in 1729, of the Aberdeen Infirmary in 1742, of the Dumfries and Galloway Infirmary in 1776 and of the Glasgow Royal Infirmary in 1794. Asylums for the insane were founded somewhat later—in Montrose in 1779, in Aberdeen in 1798, in Edinburgh in 1807, and in Glasgow in 1814. The first public dispensary was in Edinburgh in 1776. The impact of such institutions in curing patients was but slight. It could not have been otherwise when the Edinburgh Infirmary started with accommodation for only six patients, while a new building, opened in 1741, had accommodation for only 228. The Glasgow Royal Infirmary had originally 150 beds, increased in 1816 to 230. In any case the cures for a vast number of diseases—among them the most deadly—simply were not known. The greatest contribution of the new hospitals was, therefore, to the training of doctors.

The inadequacy and general ineffectiveness of hospital provision was highlighted during periods of epidemic, as, for instance, in the cholera outbreaks of 1832, 1848 and 1855. Public dispensaries had to bear the brunt of combating epidemic disease, but, since they were ill-organized and inadequate, general hospitals had to supplement their services, with disastrous consequences to the general hospitals' primary functions, especially through the possibility of the infection being passed to others. The public authorities acted only when a particular

[1] R. Cowan, *Vital Statistics of Glasgow* (Glasgow, 1838), p. 12.

epidemic had become virulent, and consequently when it was too late for any action to be fully effective. The position in Glasgow was typical. In emergencies the magistrates set up a Board of Health and the parochial authorities opened special premises. Thus in Glasgow during an outbreak of typhus a temporary fever hospital for 200 patients was opened in March 1818 and closed in July 1819; in 1827 the infirmary re-opened this hospital for five months; in 1828 a 'temporary booth' was erected for 68 patients in the infirmary grounds; in 1832 a fever hospital was opened and closed at Mile End. Though they could never be effective, it was long before such short-term expedients were superseded as the Town Council of Glasgow provided a permanent municipal fever hospital only in 1865, while acceptance of patients remained subject to qualification until 1881, when the corporation at last accepted full responsibility.

Reliance on such temporary and inadequate provision for the victims of an epidemic placed a greater strain on normal hospital facilities. The strain was greater in Edinburgh, where the temporary provision was less than in Glasgow. But even in Glasgow the sudden increase in the proportion of fever cases treated at the infirmary during periods of epidemic was marked.

PATIENTS TREATED IN GLASGOW ROYAL INFIRMARY,
1816 TO 1836

	Total	Fever		Total	Fever
1816	1,511	399	1827	2,725	1,084
1817	1,886	714	1828	3,133	1,511
1818	2,289	1,371	1829	2,321	865
1819	1,861	630	1830	2,010	729
1820	1,570	289	1831	3,183	1,657
1821	1,454	234	1832	2,974	1,589
1822	1,596	229	1833	3,082	1,288
1823	1,759	269	1834	3,879	2,003
1824	2,091	523	1835	3,260	1,359
1825	2,438	897	1836	5,130	3,125
1826	2,317	926			

Source: Cowan, op. cit., p. 8.

Even those sent to the infirmary, or accommodated in the temporary provision, did not represent the total number of cases. That many remained at home, so spreading the infection still further, is clear from the cases of paupers treated by the District Surgeons in Glasgow.

CASES OF FEVER TREATED BY DISTRICT SURGEONS
IN GLASGOW, 1827 TO 1836

	Total	Sent to infirmary
1827–28	1,281	281
1828–29	1,730	390
1829–30	485	135
1830–31	898	306
1831–32	1,428	336
1833	681	294
1834	936	538
1835	542	215
1836	1,359	643

Source: Cowan, op. cit., p. 10.

The major obstacle to any improvement in public health was that virtually no one had any real conception of the necessity of preventive medicine. It was, therefore, difficult to make any real headway with the eradication of disease, as one usually replaced another. The history of smallpox provides an illustration. The first attempt to combat it was not as successful as some of the sweeping claims made on its behalf suggested.[1] The position changed with the introduction of vaccination with calf lymph, though probably not so dramatically as to suggest that

'up to the very moment of small-pox inoculation being superseded by cow-pox the mortality is immense, and the instant the latter is employed, the mortality becomes trifling in comparison.'[2]

Vaccination was adopted on a widespread scale in the nineteenth century. In Glasgow in 1801 the Faculty of Physicians and Surgeons began vaccinating the children of the poor free of charge and in the next ten years vaccinated 14,500. In 1818 others not connected with the Faculty began vaccinating at the Cow Pock Institution. The effect was undoubtedly beneficial. The low incidence of smallpox among the Irish, which contrasted with the high incidence of typhus, was attributed, at least in part, to the prevalence of vaccination among them, especially when it was discovered that the reverse incidence prevailed among the city's Highlanders, a group which tended to neglect vaccination or which had been vaccinated in the Highlands with

[1] See p. 16.   [2] Cowan, op. cit., p. 28.

impure lymph. But the failure of such successes to lead to a marked improvement in public health was demonstrated in two ways. First, the place of smallpox as a killing disease among children under ten was taken by measles. In short, given the inadequate concern with preventive medicine another disease simply took the place of the one being eradicated. Second, smallpox itself was not wholly eliminated, but remained an important disease among children, especially during periods of industrial distress. It appeared among children in the same way and at the same times as typhus did among adolescents and adults.

CAUSES OF DEATH OF CHILDREN UNDER 10 IN GLASGOW,
1801 TO 1812

	Total	Smallpox	Measles
1801	1,434	245	8
1802	1,770	156	168
1803	1,860	194	45
1804	1,670	213	27
1805	1,671	56	90
1806	1,629	28	56
1807	1,806	97	16
1808	2,623	51	787
1809	2,124	159	44
1810	2,111	28	19
1811	2,342	109	267
1812	2,348	78	304

Source: R. Watt, Treatise on Chincough (Glasgow, 1813),
pp. 375 ff.

Under such conditions little improvement in public health was possible. Even where a specific cure for, or means of preventing, a disease was known, as was the case with smallpox, a noticeable reduction in the death-rate could not be achieved. Thus, in spite of vaccination and other advances, the death-rate in the cities rose in the early nineteenth century. In Edinburgh the death-rate per thousand was 29·1 in the 1780's. In the first two decades of the nineteenth century it was just over 25 per thousand, but in the 1830's had risen again to 29 per thousand. Even the high birth-rate, which the immigrant population of many of the cities, such as Glasgow, implied, was insufficient to offset the higher death-rate, and so the maintenance of growth depended on further immigration.

BIRTHS AND DEATHS IN GLASGOW, 1800 TO 1819

	Births	Deaths		Births	Deaths
1800	1,493	2,096	1810	1,423	2,367
1801	1,350	1,928	1811	1,429	2,622
1802	1,616	2,325	1812	1,300	2,716
1803	1,753	2,438	1813	1,507	2,704
1804	1,592	2,224	1814	1,419	3,254
1805	1,604	2,389	1815	1,714	2,717
1806	1,559	2,280	1816	1,509	3,278
1807	1,456	2,463	1817	1,694	2,757
1808	1,401	3,265	1818	1,520	4,192
1809	1,401	2,368	1819	1,692	3,158

Source: J. Cleland, *Enumeration of the Inhabitants of Glasgow* (Glasgow, 1820), p. 19.

Preventive medicine dictated the need for some of the elementary measures required for public health, such as better water supplies and better drains. As late as 1842 it could still be said of the Old Town of Edinburgh that 'a want of tributary drains and water is a fundamental cause of the uncleanly condition of the town',[1] especially since it effectively limited the introduction of water-closets. The really effective form of preventive medicine most required was, however, of quite a different type. Basically the people of Scotland required even better nutrition than they were receiving. Very pertinently the writer of the sanitary report on Inveresk commented in 1842, 'where fever is prevalent it will often pass by those who are in the habit of being well fed, well clothed, and particularly if they are cleanly in their habits'.[2] An analysis of deaths by social class in Edinburgh in the early nineteenth century confirmed this point of view.[3] For every 1,000 deaths in the highest class only 72 took place under one year of age; in the lowest class there were 241 deaths in the same group. In the highest class the mean age of death was 47·22 years; in the lowest it was 25·88. Half the highest class died before 51·5 years of age; half the lowest before 17·5 years of age. Frequently the high death-rate in the lowest

[1] *Sanitary Reports*, 1842, p. 154.

[2] *Ibid.*, p. 133.

[3] J. Stark, *Contribution to the Vital Statistics of Scotland* (London, 1851), p. 44. For a trenchant elaboration of this theme see the evidence of W. P. Alison to the Royal Commission on the Poor Laws, 1844, Appendix to Report, Part III, pp. 901–14.

social classes, and especially its tendency to rise again in the nineteenth century, was explained by the influx of the Irish, but this viewpoint was sometimes challenged, and, most important of all, by medical opinion. The challenge was justified because the death-rate was highest, not among the immigrants themselves, but among their children and the children of others of similar social status. It was in this group, especially among the children, that the need for better nutrition was greatest. More conventional, and more strictly sanitary, aspects of preventive medicine were less important in leading to improved health, and to a reduction in the death-rate.

The high death-rate, especially among children, was only the most dramatic outcome of the prevailing destitution. The entire fabric of Scottish industrial society provided indicators of its existence, notably in the incidence of drunkenness and in the need for credit.

In the eighteenth century with the imposition of the malt tax the consumption of ale declined and helped the growth of Scotland's reputation for whisky drinking. In the nineteenth century the enormous consumption of alcohol, especially by those who could ill afford it, became a most degrading factor of Scottish social life. The worst effects were in the mining districts, where the excessive number of licensed premises has continued to be a notable feature. Though educational methods achieved considerable success, the beginning of the legislative attack on drink started with the Forbes Mackenzie Act, which came into force in 1854, and which abolished the sale of alcohol in grocers' shops for consumption on the premises, closed public houses, though not specially licensed hotels, from 11 p.m. to 8 a.m., and stopped Sunday drinking except in hotels to lodgers and bona fide travellers.

The excessive consumption of alcohol was partly the cause of the clamant need for credit, so accepted as a social institution that, in the words of J. Hill Burton, 'credit is a national peculiarity from the banknote and cash credit system, down to the grocers' passbook held by the mechanic'.[1] This peculiarity persisted even though, from the foundation of a savings bank in the rural parish of Ruthwell by the minister, Henry Duncan, in 1810, Scotland was the scene of a successful growth of similar ventures and had in the City of Glasgow Savings Bank an institution with the rare distinction, especially significant in an industrial area such as the west of Scotland, of having a wide range of social and economic classes represented among its depositors. Nevertheless,

[1] *Report on the Arrestment of Wages*, 1854, p. 43.

of the chronic need of so many of the lower-income groups for credit —always a sure sign of destitution—there were many examples. Pawnshops grew rapidly in the nineteenth century. The first was opened in 1806 and from the 1830's the numbers increased quickly. In 1865 in Edinburgh alone there were 33 licensed pawnshops and 219 'wee pawns' or brokers, who were unlicensed and so not subject to control. The 33 licensed shops had 1,381,200 pledges in the year, and of pledges under 10s. 12 per cent (165,744) were forfeited. Once again, reflecting the destitution common in them, the most striking, and socially the most harmful, need for credit was in the mining areas. In the nineteenth century in most Scottish collieries and ironworks, but especially in the developing areas of the west, the time between pays was commonly two weeks to a month, though exceptionally, as at the lead mines at Wanlockhead, it was a year. With such a practice many workers had to obtain credit in some form, generally through an advance in wages. The most satisfactory solution would have been to increase the frequency of pay-days, as had long been the practice of some of the older Scottish coalmasters, but even with long-pays there would probably have been little complaint if a worker had been able to obtain a cash advance as and when he wanted it. The real dispute was over the conditions normally attached to them. In Scotland these took two forms. When some colliery owners advanced cash they charged 'poundage', a fee of approximately 1s. in the £. Ostensibly this was to cover the additional costs incurred. In almost every case the employee was then free to spend the remainder where he wished. More commonly an advance was given on condition that at least part was spent in the stores, which the mining companies had of necessity to start in the rural areas in which they operated, though in some cases all employees were expected to spend their total earnings there. This was the crucial point. The employers argued that the men were free to spend their advances where they pleased; the men disagreed; and it is clear that pressure—ultimately of dismissal—was exerted to force them to the store, where goods were sometimes inferior and more expensive than elsewhere.

The employers' objections to more frequent pays, which were recommended by such independent observers as the Inspectors of Mines, as well as by the miners' leaders, were, first, the supposed administrative difficulties involved, and, second, that, by lengthening the period between pays, the absenteeism which resulted from drunkenness on the Mondays after pay-days was reduced, while forcing the workmen to spend any advances in the stores reduced their consumption of alcohol. To some this seemed specious reasoning when some stores sold alcohol too, but these arguments provided the basis for the suggestion that the system was the only means by which the pattern of expenditure of the profligate and the drunkard could be determined in a more desirable fashion. But the group which required advances was not composed wholly of such people. As the Truck Commissioners pointed out in 1871, 'large families, ill health, bad times, accidental misfortunes, swell its numbers'. The truck system made the unfortunate still more so. It increased rather than mitigated destitution.

The truck system declined quickly only in the 1870's so that, when further legislation against it came in 1887, it was really unnecessary. If its ill effects weighed heavily against the miners, they suffered less than others from the effects of the law by which wages could be arrested or attached to meet debts due to third parties. Indeed one reason advanced in favour of truck or of the company store was just that it did prevent such arrestment. Proceedings for arrestment were instituted mostly by the agents of menages (clubs), which were most common in Glasgow and district, and among colliers on the east coast, where the truck system did not operate. Such agents generally issued tickets against which goods could be obtained on credit and any failure to meet the payments due, an extremely common occurrence, led to actions for arrestment. In Glasgow at any time in the middle of the nineteenth century about 6,000 actions for arrestment were being prosecuted by menages, in addition to similar prosecutions by small traders, particularly by grocers. Since the payment of the sum advanced through the issue of the tickets by the agents of the menages was often jointly and severally guaranteed by others, any failure to meet the appropriate payments involved even those who had not received the goods. Though from 1838 workers had to be left with a sum sufficient for subsistence before wages could be arrested, the allowance was grossly inadequate to provide the margin above subsistence so urgently required to eliminate, or even simply to palliate, the prevailing destitution.

Drunkenness, pawnshops, truck and arrestment were but symptoms of destitution. There is little doubt that its main cause in the industrial society of nineteenth-century Scotland was unemployment. In the industrial system, of which for the first time many were finding that they were a part, a trade depression inevitably left many operatives without any means of support, and frequently in a large town, where there was no possibility whatever of any subsistence, as there very often was in the country. Hence came the crying need for credit. These cyclical depressions had the worst influence on health and death. Robert Cowan, the Glasgow doctor whose careful researches provided posterity with a number of valuable statistical series, always supported the connection between good trade and good health, and between bad trade and bad health. He felt the relationship between changing economic conditions and the death-rate from fever was most adequately demonstrated in the boom which culminated in the spring and summer of 1836.

DEATHS IN GLASGOW FROM FEVER, 1835 TO 1837

	Total	To total deaths	To total population
1835	412	1 to 15	1 to 570
1836	841	1 to 10	1 to 290
1837	2,180	1 to 5	1 to 116

So he concluded that

'the mortality bill of 1837 exhibits a rate of mortality inferring an intensity of misery and suffering unequalled in Britain; and not surpassed in any city we are acquainted with on the continent of Europe.'[1]

Such were the conditions of life endured in the industrial society which appeared in Scotland in the nineteenth century. Urgent action to reform them was required.

[1] Cowan, *op. cit.*, pp. 37 and 45.

XI
SOCIAL REFORM

The poor law

EFFECTIVE action to combat the problems raised by the new industrial society took various forms. First, the traditional methods of the poor law were adapted, with varying degrees of success, to the new society; second, medical reform tried to eliminate the worst effects of ill-health and disease; third, those who suffered raised their own protests.

The Scottish poor law had two distinct features, both of which governed its effectiveness in dealing with destitution in an industrial society. The first was that, though assessment was legal by an Act of 1574, the poor should be supported by voluntary contributions in the parish churches and by such subsidiary sources of income as fees for the hire of the parish mortcloth and from mortifications. The second characteristic was that relief should not be given to the able-bodied.

Though the stringency of funds which the voluntary system implied placed an obvious limit on the effectiveness of the poor law, criticism of its success, or suggestions that it was harshly administered, could be levelled more accurately against the rigid interpretation of those who were entitled to relief, and in particular against the law's failure to provide for the destitution which arose from unemployment. The earlier statutes had adopted a most rigid interpretation of those entitled to relief, but by the end of the seventeenth century a looser interpretation, which, with some modification, would have gone some way to meeting the problems of an industrial society, was appearing. It arose from a distinction drawn between the regular and the occasional poor by a proclamation of 1693, which also allowed one-half of church collections to be applied to the relief of the occasional poor. The regular poor were those recognized by an Act of 1579 as entitled to relief—all 'poor, aged, sick, lame and impotent persons, who (of themselves) have not to maintain them, nor are able to work for their living, as also all orphans and other poor children, who are left destitute of all help';[1] the occasional poor were those who were suffering from some

[1] *Acts of the Parliament of Scotland*, III, pp. 139–42.

particular but temporary and exceptional misfortune. The regular poor were granted periodical allowances permanently and as of right; the occasional poor were to be relieved only out of the charity of the parish. The difference here was in the right to relief rather than in the relief given. Though the distinction drawn was important, it could be suggested that in a properly administered parish, where each case was considered on its individual merits, all deserving cases would be met. Failure arose from deficiencies in the implementation of the system rather than from the system itself.

The problem of the provision of help to the able-bodied poor cannot, however, be separated from the other main problem of cost. A general concern over cost is neither surprising nor particularly Scottish, but, when it was combined, as in Scotland, with an extreme reluctance to levy an assessment, a strong economic stimulus strengthened the existing moral stimulus to refuse to grant any help to the able-bodied. But even such a combination was insufficiently strong to ensure complete neglect of their plight, especially with the onset of depression in the manufacturing districts. In 1839 the General Assembly reported 'that the situation of people destitute of employment was not to be overlooked, and that many cases might occur in which men of this class ought to obtain temporary relief in times of occasional sickness or unusual calamity, although not as a matter of right'.[1] However, though with each period of depression the more affluent public was encouraged to augment their existing poor law contributions with further help,[2] such assistance was usually inadequate and, in any case, it was spasmodic. Destitution was not relieved. Hence in 1843, following depression in the manufacturing districts, a Commission was appointed to review the system of poor relief in Scotland.

The Commissioners interpreted their terms of reference stringently, holding that they were not asked to suggest anything completely new but only to devise ways of making the existing laws work more efficiently. Typically, on the leading issues of the granting of help to the able-bodied poor and of assessment, the Commissioners were unwilling to recommend any changes of consequence, and in Lowland rural parishes judged it 'the veriest wantonness of innovation to interfere'.[3] They were optimistic, believing that, even in industrial areas,

[1] Report by a Committee of the General Assembly on the Management of the Poor in Scotland, 1839, p. 7.
[2] Some details of the assistance given are in the Sanitary Reports, 1842, pp. 166–7.
[3] Report of the Royal Commission on the Poor Laws, 1844, p. xlviii.

'Unless . . . it is held, that the experience of late years has proved that the destitution arising in times of great commercial and manufacturing distress, cannot safely be left to be supplied by the spontaneous efforts of public and private benevolence, which the recurrence of such times may be expected to call forth, we must deprecate recourse to any less provisional fund of relief. But no such proof has been given; for if we except the individual cases of hardship incident to the commencement of periods of depression, for the relief of which a temporary assessment is obviously as inadequate as a voluntary contribution, no evidence from medical men, as well as others, countenances an opposite conclusion.'[1]

Not surprisingly, therefore, section 68 of the Act of 1845, which followed the Commission's report, reiterated the existing Scottish practice by declaring that, while permitting the use of all assessment levied for the relief of the occasional as well as of the regular poor, this was always 'provided that nothing herein contained shall be held to confer a right to demand relief on able-bodied persons out of employment'. Though it was utterly unrealistic in an industrial society, the restriction proved less harmful than might have been anticipated. In its third report, in 1848, the Board of Supervision, which had been instituted to control poor law administration, initiated a major change —probably because the exigencies of the potato famine had rendered any other action impossible—and, after taking legal advice, argued that section 68, while maintaining that the able-bodied poor had no right to assistance, did not preclude granting them occasional aid. This interpretation—exactly comparable to that adopted by the General Assembly in its Report of 1839—caused the Board of Supervision to issue instructions that parishes might use funds raised by assessment, and half the collections at the church door, for the temporary relief of the destitute able-bodied unemployed.

In this way the administration of the Scottish poor law was forced to adapt itself to a new environment, but such a reluctant approach to new problems could not produce satisfactory solutions. Some of those most concerned with the administration of the poor law failed to take account of the social and economic changes that had taken place; others, in haste to avoid English practice, favoured retaining Scottish ways, irrespective of their merits; others uncritically advocated the adoption of the new English system. There was unanimity only in the

[1] *Ibid.*, p. lviii.

analysis of the situation. The example of the old English poor law, which under the Speenhamland system had supplemented wages, and above all the warnings of Malthus, brought most people to the same position. Where Malthus was accepted, any proposals which placed the poor in better conditions were unlikely to command widespread acceptance, especially in a society wed to the principles of voluntary contributions. Under such conditions legal assessment was regarded as a means of making provision for, indeed encouraging, a larger population. But for many Scottish parishes the possibility of continuing to rely only on voluntary contributions was an academic question, and no matter how distasteful it was, legal assessment was increasingly adopted, particularly in areas of industrialization and immigration or in those adjacent to England. Though cost seemed high, especially when legal assessment was introduced, it was much lower in Scotland than in other countries. In England, even under its new poor law after 1834, a greater proportion of the population was being relieved, and at a greater cost per head of the population. The international comparison failed to satisfy all critics. Some reiterated the basic assumption of the Scottish poor law, that the aid it authorized was only intended as a supplement to the assistance given from other sources, which were encouraged to be generous by the absence of legal assessment. To them, as to the General Assembly in its Report of 1818, legal assessment would be 'a national calamity'. In short, most people still judged the success of the poor law solely by the degree of economy achieved and so their interest in the effectiveness of its administration too easily gave way to complacency.

The upholders of the voluntary principle found their task most formidable in the industrial areas, where the principle was early and quickly overthrown. By the middle of the eighteenth century an *ad hoc* administration had to be erected in the larger cities. In Edinburgh after 1740 a special committee managed the affairs of the poor and a Poors' Hospital was built. In Glasgow the Town Council, the Merchants' House and the General Kirk Session provided a Town's Hospital in 1733. Though the aim of the hospital was the optimistic one of the gradual extinction of pauperism by the profitable employment, virtuous education and frugal maintenance of the inmates, outdoor relief of an allowance of meal was granted from 1774 and was later converted to cash. The hospital benefited from such assessments as were made, but it required additional voluntary contributions to make ends meet. Its resources, therefore, were continually under strain, especially during any period of extensive or prolonged depression, when many could no longer subsist even on the highest pensions granted by their kirk sessions and so came under the hospital's care. Critics of the voluntary principle could not see its survival under such conditions. They saw defects even in the ways the sessions administered the funds, but when the sessions had to receive additional help through assessment, the need for some reorganization seemed even more pressing.

Though some supported the voluntary principle simply to cover defects in their own ministrations towards the poor, others advocated its retention through their acceptance of the moral obligation that Christian charity had to care for the poor without any support from assessments, whether voluntary or legal. The greatest adherent of this point of view was Thomas Chalmers, who supplemented his general belief with a detailed scheme to make it effective. His proposals were well summarized by the directors of Glasgow's Town's Hospital:

> 'to confine the legal assessment to the existing generation of paupers; to apply the disengaged fund to the establishment of churches,—and then, to invigorate the impulse of voluntary collections for the new cases; to multiply the number of parishes; to narrow the field of superintendence; to cement the intercourse between the administrators and recipients of charity; to increase the personal influence of the ecclesiastical overseers; and to extend the benefits of moral and religious information.'[1]

The crucial point in Chalmers' analysis was that he hoped to provide an incentive for the development or increase of Christian charity. He appreciated that his proposals could not be implemented at once, but, more important, he recognized that to be acceptable his scheme had to meet the problem of destitution in times of industrial depression. Chalmers feared that compulsory assessment would be the worst possible solution. 'What in fact is the best defence of a people against the evils of a state of fluctuation? Their own providential habits, and these are what a compulsory provision goes directly to extinguish.'[2] He also believed that a compulsory assessment would increase the number of regular poor so increasing the difficulty of providing for the occasional poor, in which category fell the victims of unemployment. Lastly, he thought compulsory assessment made the wealthy less willing

---

[1] *Report of the Directors of the Town's Hospital of Glasgow on the Management of the City Poor* (Glasgow, 1818), p. 39.

[2] *Ibid.*, p. 45, quoting reply by Chalmers to the directors.

to support special appeals in times of depression. 'The distress arising from fluctuations of trade ought in fact to be committed to those impulses of public benevolence, which the occurrence of such fluctuations is ever sure to awaken.'[1]

Another stream of criticism produced an analysis of the existing situation, not unlike Chalmers', but, by advocating a compulsory legal assessment, proposed a radically different solution. Such critics envied the greater expenditure on the poor in England, or in countries overseas, and held that in countries where a legal assessment was in force, the poor, far from being demoralized, were of a better type, even if only because they were cleaner. The chief exponent of this school of thought was W. P. Alison. While Alison accepted many of Chalmers' recommendations, two of his comments show the force and pertinence of his standpoint. Negatively, he pointed out that

> 'while there has been much disposition to relieve the sick poor, there has been a very general discouragement of institutions for the relief of *mere poverty*,—of the unemployed poor, the aged or permanently disabled poor, and the widows and orphans of the poor.'

Positively he suggested that

> 'the kind of assistance to the poor, which all medical men know to be of the utmost importance for the *prevention* of many of their most formidable diseases, has been as much as possible withheld.'[2]

Where Alison gained over Chalmers was in the way in which he had acquired his knowledge of the condition of the poor. So many of Chalmers' ideas had been formed in his earlier years in the intimate society of a rural parish, where the traditional method of poor relief could operate successfully. He wanted to apply these ideas to the city. Alison appreciated the benefits of the ideal rural parish which Chalmers wished to see transplanted to the cities, but he believed that such a policy was impracticable. His experience was more bitter. 'These repeated and severe visitations of fever . . . are not merely the occasions of much and widely spread suffering and destitution but . . . *the indication and test* of much previous misery and destitution.'[3] To Alison, and to other pioneers of social medicine, sheer practical considerations

---

[1] *Ibid.*, p. 47.

[2] W. P. Alison, *Observations on the Management of the Poor in Scotland* (Edinburgh, 1840), pp. 21–2.

[3] *Ibid.*, p. 10.

P

of self-preservation, apart from any demands of Christian charity, demanded action. But the strength of Alison's position and achievement lay in his refusal in practice to accept the conclusions of Malthus, whatever he may have said about their theoretical importance. To him

> 'the whole secret of the preventive check appears to me to consist in the growth and support of *artificial wants* among the poor.'[1]

Or again, realizing the importance of a higher standard of living in limiting population,

> 'nothing short of a legal enactment can be relied on for uniformly and permanently securing such comforts during youth, as are essential to sustain these habits; and counteract that real *bounty of population* which accidents and misfortunes, and consequent destitution and degradation, would otherwise continually and inevitably bring on numerous families in every season and in every district of the country.'[2]

To many, Alison's propositions, especially his advocacy of legal assessment, savoured of the new English poor law. There were, however, differences, notably in Alison's sympathy for the 'deserving poor', for whom he advocated outdoor relief; but where he fell into the worst error of the English system was in failing to understand fully the nature of industrial unemployment, which could produce a large number of deserving able-bodied poor. Chalmers at least recognized the existence of such people and made provision for them—inadequate though it may have been—through exceptional private charity. Alison feared the growth of a large number of work-shy people and so, punitively, broke from the Scottish tradition of outdoor relief by advocating relief for such able-bodied only in the workhouse. By adopting this position Alison failed to provide for large-scale help to the able-bodied poor and so virtually failed to provide a solution to the main problem which had led him to consider the need for amendments to the poor law, the problem of how the destitution, disease and epidemics, to which depressions gave rise, could be alleviated. The greatest tragedy of all is that the two points of view could not be reconciled, as the individual care and inspired service of Chalmers on the one hand, when allied with the more generous financial provisions of Alison on the other, would have produced a system of social provision in Scotland far in advance of its time. Yet the failure by both to provide an

[1] *Ibid.*, p. 54.   [2] *Ibid.*, p. 55.

analysis which accepted the new poor of the industrial unemployed within the framework of the old Scottish poor law left a gap in social provision that became increasingly important and dangerous. It was one which, not surprisingly in view of the presuppositions of its members, the Poor Law Commission of 1844 did little to fill. These various failures then left the way open for the infiltration of, and eventual domination by, the ideas of the English poor law.

The early reports of the Board of Supervision illustrate the gradual infiltration of English ideas. Most conspicuously, the long-standing tradition of outdoor relief, with all its advantages, declined. Though in its first report the Board of Supervision stated that it 'had no power to sanction the abolition of outdoor relief in any parish, and that they must judge of the propriety of refusing to relieve a pauper otherwise than by admitting him into the poorhouse', in a few years' time the Board's report, its fifth, contained a perfect exposition, with commendation, of the function of the English workhouse as a means of testing the genuine nature of applicants for relief. Not only were the numbers of unassessed parishes declining; all traces of the Scottish poor law were being removed. The extent of the problem was too great to be met any longer by private philanthropy even before the Disruption finally made the system unworkable, but it was still possible to carry on the Chalmers tradition of service, and it was in the Free Church that this was most noticeably done.

The result of the protracted and learned controversy over the poor law might seem negligible. Yet the complacency, which so long inhibited any action, except over cost, was eventually roused by the medical arguments raised in the poor law controversy. Provision for the sick poor had always been approved and encouraged in Scotland. Indeed, partly for this reason, partly reflecting the force of current medical criticism, the most interesting and effective conclusions of the Poor Law Commission of 1844 were in the medical provisions it suggested. Even this had a flaw. Whatever success the Board of Supervision made of these provisions later, they failed to stress the relevance of preventive rather than of curative medicine. A change of opinion, forced in large measure by the desire for self-preservation induced by epidemic, was necessary. In helping to achieve this change the controversy over the poor law made a major and vital contribution.

Sanitary reform

In England the reform of the poor law after 1834 freed Chadwick and those of like mind from other preoccupations and enabled them to concentrate on sanitary reform. The delay in effecting any reform of the poor law in Scotland in itself produced a unique situation but one made more so by the distinct traditions of relief leading the reformers, even the medical sanitary reformers, to approach their problems in an individual way. The difference was revealed in 1842 in the reports on Scottish sanitary conditions. They were compiled to satisfy a request for information from the English Poor Law Commissioners and showed that the majority of Scottish reporters, while admitting and deploring the disgraceful sanitary conditions of the towns and country-side, suggested that they could be improved only by a prior removal of destitution. Such concern produced a notable race of humane medical reformers, possessed of what may have been a correct scale of values, with strict sanitary reform placed in a secondary position in their activities. Any comparative lack of achievement in that field arose from the reformers diverting their energies to a more important, though less easily solved, problem.

The main barrier to sanitary reform in Scotland was not, however, the diversion of the interests of medical reformers but public and private opposition or lethargy. Until their reform in 1834 the town councils were rarely amenable to any projects for reform, but, in any case, in the late eighteenth and early nineteenth centuries the expansion of towns beyond the original burgh boundaries meant that many councils' political authority was not always coextensive with the need for sanitary supervision. Nevertheless, as sanitary reform remained in the hands of local authorities until the 1860's, they had to take the necessary action if much was to be achieved. The first attempts were made through local acts appointing police commissioners to deal with sanitary problems. The first, for the southern suburbs of Edinburgh, was in 1771 and the first for Glasgow in 1800. But, even where a Town Council, or a Police Commission, wanted to act, it was usually obstructed by private opposition. Scots law placed difficulties in the path of the sanitary reformer through a corporate body, such as a town council, being unable to bring an action for the abatement of a nuisance. Action had to be taken by a private individual, who had to prove personal damage. Worse still, it was possible to achieve a permanent right to create a nuisance, through its use during the period of prescription. The classic impasse created by such a legal situation was the case of the Edinburgh meadows which were irrigated by sewage. Though it was undoubtedly a nuisance, it proved impossible to have it stopped through a right to create such a nuisance having been obtained by its exercise during the period of prescription. The only way of having it stopped seemed to be because the meadows, being near Holyrood, might have been harmful to the Queen, who was excluded from the rule of prescription. In the face of strong protection for property the town councils had a hard task to achieve any satisfactory improvement, even when they became conscious of the problem and active in its solution. The need for sanitary reform was so great and so widespread that any attempt to meet it immediately ran foul of a variety of vested interests. Again Edinburgh provided a conspicuous example when in 1846 the Town Council promoted a Sanitary Improvement Bill, which was opposed, successfully, by some of the groups whose interests would have been affected: the owners of the irrigated meadows to the east of the city; the mill-owners on the Water of Leith; the spirit trade; the owners of private slaughterhouses; the pawnbrokers; the dealers in second-hand goods; and others.

The extension of sanitary reform rested essentially on the wider acceptance of preventive medicine, which was not appreciated since of its efficacy there was little evidence in the eighteenth century. Then the various classes lived together and, since all were subject to the same physical or sanitary conditions, there was little distinction in the incidence of disease. In the late eighteenth century, when the movement of different classes into different areas began, each had then its own location with peculiar physical and sanitary conditions. The distinction between the old and the new towns of Edinburgh is a striking illustration.[1] Such moves represented an acceptance of the belief that refinement was not a luxury but a necessity, even though initially it was thought it need be confined to only one class. The adoption of more spacious surroundings, which alone indicated the evils of concentration, then required only a demonstration from epidemics, the social importance of which cannot be minimized, that even removal to the New Town could not obtain immunity from the filth of the Old Town, and so there appeared a realization of the need to improve the lot of those who remained. The motives behind the actions inspired

[1] See pp. 11–12.

by the epidemics were often blatantly selfish; they were probably more effective for being so.

The cholera epidemic of 1832 first broke through much of the indifference to sanitary reform, but the breach was made effective only in mid-century by an outbreak of typhus in 1847 and by the two subsequent cholera epidemics of 1848 and 1854. The effective reform movement may, therefore, be dated from the passing of the Glasgow Corporation Water Works Act in 1855. It marked the approval, after twenty years' opposition, of an early proposal of the reformed Town Council of 1834 that it should take over the private suppliers of water, one of whom used the Clyde as the source of supply. The way was then opened for the step, most fruitful for posterity, of inaugurating the waterworks at Loch Katrine. Thereafter sanitary reform spread. The Nuisances Removal (Scotland) Act, 1856, enabled Glasgow Corporation to form a Committee of Nuisances. In 1859 the Corporation produced a scheme for the sanitary reform of the city and its proper inspection and enforcement, which was authorized in the Glasgow Police Act, 1862. In the following year the city's first medical officer of health, W. T. Gairdner, was appointed. The Glasgow Improvement Act, 1866, gave the necessary powers for the removal of the worst slums in the city.[1] Action in Edinburgh came more slowly, but was precipitated more dramatically, through the collapse in 1861 of an old tenement in the High Street, resulting in the deaths of 35 people. The following year Henry Littlejohn was appointed the city's first medical officer of health. His work led to the Edinburgh Improvement Act, 1867.

In spite of opposition and inadequate financial support, a new era in public health was beginning by the 1870's. It was aided by administrative changes as, increasingly, initiative became central rather than local, especially with the passing of the Public Health (Scotland) Act, 1867, which ensured that the earlier spasmodic action, both local and central, was replaced by bodies responsible for continuous supervision, a prerequisite of any successful public health measures. By about 1870, therefore, public health measures were accepted in Scotland, even though they were not always acceptable in all circles. Preventive medicine was at last accorded a place. Its achievements, however, still lay before it.

[1] For details see pp. 304–6.

The workers' protests

Changes in the poor law and sanitary reform represented attempts to provide a system of social provision capable of meeting the defects of the new industrial society. Those who suffered from these defects advanced their own remedies, ranging from attempts to change the whole fabric of the new industrial society to attempts to escape from it.

Though many of the remedies advocated were similar to those being suggested in England, they were conditioned by the peculiarities of Scottish society. The most evident distinctions arose from the different legal systems, as in the poor laws of the two countries. An alteration in the Scottish poor law was postponed for a decade after the change in England, and there was a lapse of almost another decade before Scottish practice approximated that in England. Moreover, since the old Scottish poor law had always treated the poor much less generously, the imposition of a harsher, more stringent system of poor relief did not breed the same resentment. Certain aspects, conspicuously the rise of the workhouse, engendered opposition, but its use as a test did not imply losses of outdoor relief on the scale which the Speenhamland system had provided in parts of England. The resentment which followed the adoption of the new system was not present in Scotland. More subtle distinctions arose between the two countries because of their contrasting economic development. In Scotland the boundaries of pronounced social discontent were more limited, sometimes geographically, sometimes occupationally. Without any question the major area of distress in Scotland was the Highlands, where the remedy adopted, the simple one of emigration, did not give rise to any consequential problems. The Highlanders moved to other parts of Scotland and overseas, but, having adopted the simple remedy of leaving the adverse social conditions in which they lived, they made no further contribution to attempts to solve the problems of the new society. The Highlanders were displaced by factors operating geographically or regionally. The hand-loom weavers were the only important group displaced by factors operating industrially. They too tried to adopt the same despairing remedy of emigration, though with less success. However, few other distressed groups emulated the example of the Highlanders or the hand-loom weavers and sought a remedy in emigration, partly because many of those who suffered most acutely in the new industrial society of Scotland in the nineteenth century had already emigrated there from Ireland and, though many cherished the hope of ultimately gaining a passage to the United States, and were in Scotland in the first place only because they were in the poorest classes, they rarely achieved their aim. In sum, the helplessness and discontent bred in the new economic society was not generally remedied by emigration.

The acceptance of the new way of life was made easier for most members of the new industrial society in Scotland by one factor of overriding importance. Their economic prosperity was dependent on the success of a complex of industries, which, fortunately for Scotland, were buoyant until the last quarter of the nineteenth century. The decline of the cotton industry was offset by the rise of the heavy industries, and both offered employment opportunities of some kind in roughly the same areas. In the centre of industrial Scotland there was no long-term stagnation of employment and, apart from the Highlands and the hand-loom weavers, there were no depressed areas or industries in the middle of the nineteenth century in Scotland. Yet distress, notably cyclical, was sufficient to justify much protest, and even if from time to time a high level of demand alleviated, or perhaps entirely removed, much of the economic unrest temporarily, social stress still remained and was most conspicuous in areas of high concentration, nowhere more than in mining districts. The better conditions experienced by most Scottish workers compared with what they had previously known; the presence of the Irish; the peculiar conditions of degradation and depression of the mining areas; all helped to give certain characteristics to the workers' own protests in Scotland in the nineteenth century. First, the Scottish working-class movement experienced phases of violence, as in Glasgow among the weavers between 1815 and the attempt to call a general strike in 1820 or among the cotton spinners in the 1830's, but it was also marked by orderly activity and at times by elements of idealism, so that even some of the more militant organizations, such as the Society of the Friends of the People of the 1790's, were forced from law-abiding activities chiefly by embittered repression. Second, the miners made a major contribution to various social protests, above all to the organization of the trade union movement, through the existence in their ranks of a number of able leaders.

Orderly activity and idealism were demonstrated by the contrast between Scottish and English Chartism and by the development of the movement in Scotland when it came under the control of Irish

immigrants. Until 1848 the English movement was characterized by
spasmodic violent agitations, sufficiently antagonistic to the ownership
of property to alienate some of its erstwhile supporters, while others
were alienated by the movement's religious unorthodoxy. By contrast in
Scotland, even while the movement remained under English leadership
and inspiration, the advocacy of physical force found little support
and, with the collapse of the Convention in 1839, the moral-force
adherents gained ascendancy in Scotland and began to make their own
independent contribution. Since the movement never had a central
organization in Scotland, but rested on the diverse contributions of
local organizations, the strength of the advocates of moral persuasion
varied, but there are several examples of their power. Combined with
the desire to disprove the common charge of unorthodoxy in religion,
their influence led to the institution of Chartists' churches by many of
the local associations, particularly by those in the west of Scotland;
moderation led to the acceptance of middle-class support in Scotland
in contrast to England; lastly, refusal to follow wholeheartedly in the
plan of O'Connor Chartists for strike action in the early 1840's stemmed
partly from the depression being less severe in Scotland but also partly
from more fundamental disquiet over such action on moral principles.
The distinctively Scottish phase of Chartism was brought to an end by
a number of ill-organized strikes without leaving any lasting legacy to
the strength of the adherents of moral persuasion. Thereafter, before
the collapse of the Chartist movement in 1848, the influence of the
Irish, strengthened by the influx of immigrants following the famine,
grew in importance. Their earlier resignation, born of illiteracy and of
poverty less stringent than had been experienced in Ireland, was overshadowed by a desperation engendered by the adverse economic conditions which the 1840's brought even to those industries in which
most of them were employed in Scotland, and, as their influence grew,
the Irish introduced a brand of semi-republicanism to Chartism in
Scotland. By the mid-1840's it rivalled the traditional supremacy of the
advocacy of moral persuasion. Though the culmination and collapse
of the movement in Scotland were, therefore, marked by such Irish
nationalist and republican influences gaining greater control, the
traditional Scottish moderation was never entirely removed and, when
the collapse did come, brought its own rewards by leading to a much
less severe repression of Chartist activities.

The co-operative movement was the other main field of social protest in which idealism, allied in this case with hard practical economic

calculation, was evident. The first co-operative venture (it cannot properly be dignified by the name of a society) was formed in 1769 at Fenwick where the weavers bought oatmeal jointly and where the sum invested in provisions rose from four guineas in 1770 to £40 in 1800. As far as is known, the first organization to which the designation of a society could properly be given was the Govan Victualling Society, which carried on business from 1777 to 1909. Next, in 1812, came the still-extant Lennoxtown Victualling Society. Once again, both the Govan and the Lennoxtown Societies were founded by weavers. These pioneers, precursors of the more famous Rochdale society, differed from it chiefly in the method of paying dividend, as in the early Scottish societies the dividend was not related as strictly as at Rochdale to the purchases made. Tradition claims that the Cambuslang society paid dividends according to purchases made even before Rochdale, and Alexander Campbell, one of the chief advocates of Owenite co-operation in Scotland, claimed that he devised the system at least as early as 1822. Their claims cannot be fully substantiated and, in any case, the Rochdale society gave the method its greatest publicity.

The degree of idealism behind these early ventures is difficult to determine. Though three of the twelve Fenwick weavers who signed their original agreement in 1769 were unable to write their names, the early societies were the product of action by the highest grade of labour in contemporary Scotland. But it is difficult to conclude that the founders were motivated by ideals any more lofty than the desire to meet economic difficulties caused by increasing prices. This was specifically so in Lennoxtown, where war-time inflation, combined with the attraction of selling goods on the neighbouring Glasgow market, kept prices at a level as high as in Glasgow, even though wages were lower in Lennoxtown than in the city. Since the weavers were generally more intelligent, independent and enterprising workers, they attempted to meet this problem. They were the pioneers, less because of their idealism than because, unlike so many in the new industries that were developing, they were not immediately sunk in such squalor that they could not, or would not, make the effort to ameliorate their position.

The second strand of co-operative thought, the idealism, was easily grafted into this environment. Its great advocate in Scotland was Robert Owen, who was so much more concerned with the establishment of a co-operative community rather than simply a co-operative store that there was no co-operative store in his plan at New Lanark.

A co-operative store was merely a palliative of the existing social system. Owen devised schemes which led to its total reformation. There is little evidence that the co-operative movement in Scotland was a similar protest against the entire social order, because such an interpretation stresses the idealism to the neglect of the hard economic realism which lay at the roots of so many of the early Scottish co-operative ventures. Even the similarity to the idealism which triumphed when Scots controlled the Chartist movement does not give rise to any contradiction. In Chartism the preference for moral persuasion was not only a moral issue, but was as much a preference for a method considered likely to lead to its acceptance by middle-class opinion and so to the granting of greater concessions. Owen's idealism was too revolutionary to appeal even to the idealists in Scottish society at the time. Another reason ensured Owen's own contribution to the co-operative movement in Scotland was slight. At New Lanark he was a paternalist employer. Whatever the achievements, and whatever the benefits the workers gained there, Owen did not surrender control to his workers in any way. The ideals of the society at New Lanark were imposed from above; the employer knew best what actions should be followed.

Owen's actions at New Lanark were restricted by his fellow partners, and, in light of his attitude towards the only major attempt to implement his principles, at Orbiston, near Motherwell, it is, in any case, difficult to judge either how far New Lanark was conducted in accordance with his views or whether his views were simply less far advanced at that time than they became later. Though he had first purchased Orbiston, Owen did not participate in the experiment therefor he had become attracted by ventures in the United States, and because he considered the views of the chief promoters—James Hamilton, younger of Dalziel, and Abram Combe, a wealthy Edinburgh tanner—too restricted, especially in their refusal to recognize equality and community of property between members. The scheme continued without Owen and was a failure, chiefly because the idealism of its promoters was not shared by its members. Consequently, though Owen carried out some of his most notable work in Scotland, his brand of revolutionary co-operative idealism made little permanent impression on the practical growth of the co-operative movement in Scotland. His idealism received greater and more successful publicity in Scotland from the work of his disciple, Alexander Campbell, who, unlike the master, was able to work through the existing societies, even though he strove to infuse them with his ideals. His most conspicuous achievement was in the first Glasgow society in 1830, when he instituted a bazaar, at which goods were received from the workers who had produced them, their value being determined by the cost of the raw materials and the time spent on producing them. The goods were exchanged by what was in effect a system of barter for goods of equal value, estimated in the same way, or for notes issued by the co-operative society, and which were accepted in exchange for groceries and other goods by the store. The scheme was not acceptable to many members and the Glasgow Bazaar's existence was as brief as that of the Orbiston community, but though Campbell's attempts to infuse Owenite idealism were not conspicuously successful, he continued to make a major contribution to the existing societies, especially by encouraging their formation in the west of Scotland.

The early societies were pioneers and, as with many of their kind, the casualty rate was high, especially from 1840 to the mid-1850's, when the total number of societies declined. Even the first Glasgow society foundered, when rent by disputes between those who favoured Owenite idealism and those who did not. The limited nature of social protest, typical of much of Scotland at that time, deprived the co-operative movement of much necessary initiative. Revival came between the mid-1850's and the mid-1860's with the foundation of a number of societies which provided the basis for the new and modern co-operative movement in Scotland. The heart of the new movement was Glasgow, where Alexander Campbell again appeared in the 1850's as leader of the second Glasgow society, and in Edinburgh, where St. Cuthbert's Society, founded in 1859, became one of the most successful societies in the east of Scotland. From these two centres, in west and east, branches spread into surrounding districts until the culmination of the successful movement came in the 1860's with the beginning of a national movement, indicative of a new-found unity. In 1863 the first co-operative journal, *The Scottish Co-operator*, was published and the Glasgow Society proposed the institution of a wholesale society for Scotland, similar to that being formed in England, but progress was arrested in 1864 by the collapse of the Glasgow Society, even though some of its branches were able to carry on as independent societies. The proposals for a wholesale society did not die, and, after suggestions for some form of union with the Co-operative Wholesale Society were rejected, the Scottish Co-operative Wholesale Society was formed in 1868. To it were quickly added other ventures in co-operative production, such as the United Co-operative Baking Society, founded in 1869. Thereafter, the successful trend in consumers' co-operation, which had been temporarily interrupted by the failure of the second Glasgow Society in 1864, was reasserted by the formation in Glasgow of the Kinning Park and the St. George's Societies in 1871. By the 1870's the Scottish co-operative movement was well established in all its branches.

Trade unions differed from Chartism and the co-operative movement by representing an attempt to remedy the problems of the new industrial society through action within industry itself. As much of the strength of the co-operative movement stemmed from the problems, thoughts and aspirations of the weavers, so much of the strength and initiative in the trade union movement in Scotland in the nineteenth century came from the miners. They were among the most degraded elements in Scottish society. When the majority of Scottish workers were receiving a share, though perhaps inadequate, of the gains of the country's economic successes in the mid-nineteenth century, the miners were frequently less favoured. In such conditions the introduction of the Irish was not always a passive factor. But if the degraded position of the miners called for an exceptional protest, the extent of that degradation made the protest still more difficult, and produced examples of violence not typical of Chartism or co-operation.

One factor which was relevant to the early attempts at association was the state of the law and its interpretation in the courts. Repression was at its worst in the 1790's, perhaps most conspicuously in the sentencing of Thomas Muir, the radical advocate, to fourteen years' transportation, but by the end of the decade it was moderating. The Combination Acts of 1799 and 1800 brought several associations, such as the United Scotsmen, which had been demanding independence, to an end, but it may be doubted if the Acts were as applicable in practice as they were in legal theory. Indeed in Scotland it is doubtful if the Acts were wholly applicable at all. Though they undermined the law of Scotland on combination, some of the older common law principles still survived to be applied even at the time of greatest restriction. Further, especially as Whig ideas infiltrated among Edinburgh lawyers in the early nineteenth century, the Scottish courts were frequently much more lenient in their treatment of offenders than were those in England, so that the greater charity shown to the Chartists was not entirely exceptional. But a more favourable legal environment could not lead to a major growth of trade unionism in Scotland and, though most of the early industrial activities in Scotland produced some form of union, few lasted. Even though Owen's early attempts at general union provided a pattern which contained the nucleus of effective action, inadequate communications and poor leadership led to the disintegration of much of the effort of the unions into local ventures. Of these early attempts perhaps the best-known and most representative was the Association of Cotton Spinners of Glasgow and neighbourhood, the activities of which were illustrated in 1838 in the trial for violence and sedition of Glasgow cotton spinners, who, though acquitted on the major charge, were transported for seven years for the minor offence. The aims of the union were simply to retain as secure a monopoly of labour as was possible, especially since Glasgow spinners were generally paid higher rates than operatives elsewhere. In consequence others were attracted to Glasgow, where, because of the restrictive actions of the Glasgow men, they were preferred by employers. From this explosive situation violence, such as the throwing of vitriol, of which the spinners were accused, could easily arise. Though the Glasgow union was the leader in the neighbourhood, there were also other, more local unions elsewhere, as at Campsie, where the block printers had a union with funds of over £6,000. Opposition to all these unions was so strong that, whenever they risked their resources in action, be it strike or not, defeat was certain, and inevitably they stagnated thereafter. Moreover, since many of the activities of the cotton industry were widespread, Glasgow alone had a sufficient concentration of operatives, employed by relatively few firms, to make an effective union possible, but in Glasgow the work of any association was greatly weakened by the trial of the cotton spinners in 1838, and thereafter by the beginnings of decline in the cotton industry.

A variety of similar local unions appeared—notably in the building trade—but the success of the miners lay in producing the best-organized association of the period. The first attempt to do so on a national scale was in the Miners' Association of Great Britain and Ireland, formed at Wakefield in 1841 and active in Scotland in the 1840's, but as the strikes it called had little success, the movement collapsed, with so much similar activity, in 1848. Thereafter, the achievement of constructing the miners' organization belonged chiefly to Alexander McDonald, who, from entering the pits at the age of eight, earned for himself a university education and became the leader of the Scottish, and of the British, miners. McDonald's first attempt to build a general association was in 1855, when, on the basis of a successful strike by Lanarkshire

miners, he was able to persuade other areas to join in a wider amalgamation. An unsuccessful strike, which collapsed in 1856, provided
a major trial for the new association, but one which led McDonald to
appreciate the dangers of the local unions still more, and so to stress
the need for greater centralization both of funds and organization.
McDonald's efforts did not achieve conspicuous success at that time,
because, as the 1850's were years of depression, the time was not ripe
for the growth of unionism, especially on the national model which
McDonald consistently advocated. Even his attempts to obtain legislative improvements in the condition of the miners, and his tireless
advocacy to the miners to continue to press for them, failed to attract
much interest at the time. The next movement towards greater organization came from the local level, though McDonald was able to build
on it. First, in the 1860's unique institutions, Lodges of Free Colliers,
modelled in ceremonial and procedure on masonic lodges, came into
being, but they opened their ranks to masters as well as men and were
mainly social in character. Second, and more important, in 1870 the
Fife district union won an eight-hour day, and, since the great mid-
Victorian boom was an easy period in which to consolidate union
organization, the success of the Fife union was followed by attempts
to create similar associations elsewhere. Building on such local initiative,
McDonald began to move towards the ultimate goal of federation, and
in October 1873 a Scottish Federation was accepted, though it was
never fully exploited. When in the following year, 1874, McDonald
was elected Member of Parliament for North Staffordshire, his parliamentary duties absorbed an increasing share of his time and he had to
leave much of the subsequent growth of the Scottish miners' movement to other hands, but his insistence on the need for a centralization
of organization and finance, combined with his insistence on the value
of propaganda and of parliamentary action, were lessons which the
miners and other associations of Scottish workers appreciated increasingly as methods of making their protests more effective.

Though in the middle of the nineteenth century Scottish trade
unionists had, therefore, still to learn the value of unity at a national
level, its merits locally had long been appreciated in what were in
effect nascent trades councils. They expressed the views of members
on a variety of topics, ranging from the strictly industrial to the social,
philanthropic and political. Glasgow led in their growth, but such
associations, which existed at least from about 1830, had only a
shadowy existence and were frequently called into being only to deal

with a specific problem, as to assist the accused in the cotton spinners' trial. A permanent body was formed in Glasgow only in 1858. In Edinburgh, though a small body, the United Trades Delegates' Association, had existed from 1849, the Trades Council was formally constituted only in 1867. In Aberdeen and Dundee the history of the trades councils was similar: earlier associations gave way to modern councils in 1868 and 1885 respectively.

Part Three

ECONOMIC PRESSURE
1870's-1939

XII
INDUSTRY TO 1914
Shipbuilding

FROM the 1780's to the 1870's the cotton and iron industries were the chief determinants of the progress of the Scottish economy; from the 1870's until 1914 the key to the continuing prosperity and security of the Scottish economy lay in the progress of shipbuilding and of the related industries of steelmaking and marine engineering. Though shipbuilding was common in Scotland, and increased in importance throughout the nineteenth century, its major contribution to the country's economic development came only from the 1870's. Its growth was the consequence of the rise of the industry on the Clyde. Initially the Clyde had no special advantages over any other similar waterway. A small point confirms this. Glasgow's earliest trade with America was conducted in vessels built elsewhere, first in Holland, then latterly in America. Though the link with America was broken by the War of Independence, the main rise of the industry came later, when certain factors specially favoured the Clyde. The favourable influences fell mainly into two groups: changes in methods of construction (wood, iron and steel) and changes in methods of propulsion (sail, steam, diesel). Frequently those in the first group are regarded as more important in the growth of shipbuilding, and, following this reasoning,

it becomes possible to suggest that the rise of the iron and steel industries in the west of Scotland adequately explains the rise of shipbuilding
on the Clyde. On the other hand a contrasting position may be adopted
by suggesting that changes in methods of propulsion were of even
greater importance, and on this reasoning the adoption of new constructional materials was made more effective through the prior gains
from engineering abilities. If the second interpretation is more valid,
the rise of the iron and steel industries becomes a second, though not
necessarily a secondary, factor in the growth of Scottish shipbuilding.

The contribution of Scottish marine engineers to the development
of the three chief methods of propulsion (the steam-engine, developed
from Watt's ideas, the steam-turbine and the diesel engine) varied. The
earliest experiments in steam navigation took place in 1788 on the loch
at Dalswinton in Dumfriesshire under the supervision of the inventive
laird, Patrick Miller, the patron of Burns, and with technical assistance,
though of disputed importance, from William Symington, the engineer
from the mines at Wanlockhead. In spite of further successful experiments by Symington with the *Charlotte Dundas* on the Forth and
Clyde Canal, full success in Scotland came only in 1812, when Henry
Bell launched his *Comet*, built by Woods of Port Glasgow, and engined
by John Robertson of Glasgow, but with the engines made in the
foundry of David Napier, who later made a signal contribution to
Clyde shipbuilding. The *Comet*'s success was limited. Though David
Napier, after experiments with models on the Molendinar, made some
minor changes in design, few were made for some years after the
Comet's success. Nor was there any spectacular increase in output.
According to one estimate the annual average tonnage of steamships
launched on the Clyde from 1812 to 1830 was only about 250 tons.
Even as late as the mid-century it was only about 20,000 tons a year.
So initially the use of steamboats was confined to the Clyde, the pre-
cursors of its pleasure steamers, until in 1818 the first steamship navi-
gated the open sea of the Irish Channel.

The widespread adoption of the steamship rested on the work of
marine engineers in the solution of two problems: first, the need to
improve the efficiency of the boilers, frequently limited to as little as
5 lbs. per square inch above atmospheric pressure, as their deficiencies
restricted attempts to gain increased power by increasing steam pressure; second, the need to improve the efficiency of the engines, as the
expansion of higher-pressure steam within one cylinder led to considerable losses in the initial condensation and subsequent re-evaporation

and so led to heavy coal consumption. Improvements in both engine and boiler were complementary to each other until a reasonable degree of success in solving both problems was achieved in the 1860's, when the simple engine, still basically the early adaptation of Watt's design, was superseded by the compound engine, in which the steam was expanded in stages, first satisfactorily devised by McNaught of Bury in 1845. An increase in boiler pressure, sometimes to as high as 100 lbs. per square inch, more commonly around 60 lbs. per square inch, resulted, but progress to this position was not achieved quickly or easily, nor was the achievement even then complete. While pressure was low, boilers were approximately in box form, or tank boilers, but higher pressures could be resisted only by cylindrical-shaped boilers, at first by a type of small diameter, known as 'water-tube' boilers. Progress with the new boilers was sometimes hesitant. In 1857 Scott's, of Greenock, experimented with a water-tube boiler at a pressure of 125 lbs. per square inch, but reverted to half that pressure. More successfully, in 1862, James Howden, who established his firm that year, developed a cylindrical 'tank' boiler, which was the prototype of the 'Scotch boilers' used until the First World War. The next step forward came with an improvement in the engine in the 1870's, when, in response to an order for a boiler to work at a pressure of 150 lbs. per square inch, A. C. Kirk of Napier's devised the triple-expansion engine, which, with its expansion of steam in three stages, could operate with steam at higher pressures without leading to losses similar to those which were experienced earlier with the simple engine. The first triple-expansion engine was unsuccessful, however, and mastery came in the 1880's, again on a prototype of A. C. Kirk, but with a boiler made of steel which, because of its resistance to higher pressures, first made many boiler improvements feasible. Later, the quadruple-expansion engine completed the development of the steam-engine from Watt's model. By then the common practice was to use Scotch boilers working at about 180 lbs. per square inch for triple-expansion engines and at about 220 lbs. per square inch for the less common quadruple-expansion engines.

A second line of development in mechanical propulsion came with the steam-turbine. Though the quadruple-expansion engine marked the culmination of a phase of development, it still left one problem unsolved. Since in the reciprocating engine the transference of the linear motion of a piston within the cylinder to the rotary motion of a shaft results in considerable loss of power through friction, the chief mechanical problem by the end of the nineteenth century was to achieve this rotary motion direct from the engine. It was achieved by C. A. Parsons' steam-turbine, first patented in 1884. The *King Edward*, which plied on the Clyde for half a century, was the first merchant vessel to have the steam-turbine installed in her, with Denny's as builder and Parsons as engineer. The early steam-turbine left another problem to be solved. For maximum efficiency the turbine had to rotate at high speed, while the propeller had to rotate at only a low speed. The solution lay in gearing. Sir John Biles, the Professor of Naval Architecture in the University of Glasgow, claimed that he suggested this innovation to Parsons, and it was in 1912 at Fairfields' that the first ships were designed and built with geared-turbine machinery.

The third major advance in propulsion in the century before 1914 was the invention of the diesel engine, first patented in Britain in 1892, and which is similar in design to the steam-engine. The first sea-going diesel vessels were built in Italy and Holland in 1910 but they were designed for only short voyages. The first ship for long voyages was built in Denmark in 1912, but in that year too Barclay, Curle and Company built its sister ship, the *Jutlandia*. The advent of the diesel engine, therefore, marks a significant change in the history of Clyde shipbuilding. In the development of the steam-engine and, to a less extent, of the steam-turbine, Scottish engineers played a vitally important part, but not in the development of the diesel engine, which was not even a British achievement. Though the Clyde quickly came to build diesel vessels, all the large diesel engines were built under licence. The Clyde never produced its own model, the Doxford from Sunderland being the only large British engine. If the Clyde's shipbuilding fame rested on its engineering abilities, its lead was being lost.

At certain stages the success of marine engineering rested on the prior development of some of the new methods of construction, but the order is significant. Marine engineering came first; shipbuilding came later. When the *Comet* sailed in 1812, twenty years before the rise of the new Scottish iron industry, the first step was taken towards the establishment of the Clyde's reputation. Since ships built elsewhere were then sent to the Clyde to be engined, it was a short step to having them built on the Clyde. In short, it was the substitution of steam vessels for sailing ships that, in the words of John Scott, of Greenock, gave 'a very large impetus' to Clyde shipbuilding.[1] The Clyde was

[1] *Royal Commission on Depression of Trade and Industry*, 1886. Q. 11, 903.

active when other areas were not. In 1833 Alexander Stephen, then still building ships on the east coast, recorded in his diary that ship-building had been remarkably flat apart from the construction of steamboats on the west coast. He was already casting his eyes towards Linthouse, where his firm was later to make its main reputation. Even later, when the Scottish iron industry had grown, and when Clyde yards were building iron ships in increasing numbers, this early contribution of marine engineering was not forgotten. In 1852 the Town Chamberlain of Greenock wrote a report on the past and present of his town for the Town Council. In it he spoke of the increasing demand for Clyde-built ships from foreigners and pointed out that:

> 'our superiority in producing engines has hitherto been the cause of these potentates preferring the work of our artisans to that of any others. But, now that iron is superseding timber and becoming the principal component, not of the engine only, but also of the hull, our power to excel is vastly increased.'[2]

Iron barges first appeared in the later part of the eighteenth century but it was 1816 before Scotland had its first, which continued to ply successfully on the Firth of Clyde for about half a century. The first iron steamship in Scotland was the *Aglaia*, of 30 tons, built by David Napier to sail on Loch Eck. The beginning was hesitant. In 1831 four iron vessels, at least two of which were for the Forth and Clyde Canal, were built, not in Scotland but in Manchester. One was an experimental vessel, the other, the *Lord Dundas*, plied for several years between Port Dundas and Lock 16 on the Forth and Clyde Canal. Also in the year 1831 John Neilson of the Oakbank foundry in Glasgow launched the *Fairy Queen*, the first iron vessel to ply on the Clyde. Some of the engineers, who had previously made a reputation as ship-builders, quickly adopted the new material for their hulls. One of the best known, Robert Napier, launched his first iron vessel, the *Vanguard*, in June 1836. But the most significant development on the Clyde came with the appearance of new firms, formed specifically to build iron ships. The most important was founded by two ex-foremen of Robert Napier, David Tod and John McGregor, who started a yard of their own at Govan to build iron ships, and launched their first vessel, the *Vale of Leven*, in 1835.

Most of the early steamships were built of iron. Of the 247 steam

[1] John Adam, *Greenock as It Was and Is*, p. 18. (Copy in Glasgow University Library.)

vessels launched on the Clyde between 1846 and 1852 only 14 were wooden. The use of iron was restricted by prejudice and by Lloyd's reluctance to produce any insurance provision for iron vessels until 1855; but its economy could not be ignored and was increased when the propeller, with its greater vibration, displaced the paddle-wheel. The 1850's, therefore, saw the virtual extinction of construction by wood. The last wooden Cunarder, the *Arabia*, was built in 1852, and in 1859 the last wooden ship of any considerable size was launched from Scott's of Greenock. For about another decade wood survived as a material in 'composite' construction (that is, wood was placed on iron frames and beams), a method used in the 1860's for the clippers, the best known of which was the *Cutty Sark*, launched at Dumbarton in 1869. Their history demonstrated the ability of sailing vessels to survive even after the victory of iron construction, because, until the opening of the Suez Canal in 1869, the difficulties of coaling vessels enabled them to compete against steamers on the long routes to Australia and China, and thereafter, until the isthmus of Panama was breached in 1915, on the long route round Cape Horn. But their operation was not confined to specialized routes, because in times of depression the cheapness of operating the sailing ship was an obvious advantage over its more expensive, though technically more efficient, steam-propelled rival. Consequently, even after the opening of the Suez Canal, there were times when the proportion of tonnage of sailing vessels launched on the Clyde rose. In 1868 it was 45·1 per cent of the total; in 1871 it was 4·7; in 1877 it was 44·6; in 1879 it was 5·7; in 1885 it was 51·7. The pattern was broken only with the increase in output after the adoption of the steam-turbine in the 1890's. After 1896 the proportion of sailing vessels rapidly became insignificant.

Just as iron displaced wood in shipbuilding, so it was displaced in turn by steel, a change which rested on the adoption of new methods of steel production in the second half of the nineteenth century. The first successful experiments on the Clyde were in the late 1870's. In 1877 John Elder built two steel paddle-steamers at Govan for service on the English Channel. Then, most important of all, in 1879 William Denny, who had previously launched several small steel vessels, built the *Rotomahana*, the first ocean-going vessel to be built of mild steel. Denny's action was an example for others to follow, especially when he became a leading protagonist of the new metal. In 1879 almost half of the 18,000 tons of steel shipping launched on the Clyde came from his yard. At first cost limited the use of steel, but as price fell with the adoption of cheaper methods of production, during a period when prices generally were falling, its use spread. In 1879, when Denny launched the *Rotomahana*, only 10·3 per cent of the tonnage launched on the Clyde was of steel, the remainder being of iron and wood. The position was reversed ten years later when 97·2 per cent of the tonnage launched was of steel. The use of steel in construction and of the steam-turbine in propulsion combined to provide the basis for a stimulus to the Scottish shipbuilding yards at the end of the nineteenth century. From the 1870's output was consistently maintained; from the 1890's it increased, partly through naval orders, into the twentieth century, until in 1913 an all-time record tonnage of 756,976 was launched on the Clyde. From the 1870's until the First World War, shipbuilding was the chief growth point of the Scottish economy.

Steel

The contribution of shipbuilding to the prosperity of the Scottish economy in the late nineteenth and early twentieth centuries was rivalled only by that of steelmaking. For all practical purposes the Scottish steel industry is the creation of the second half of the nineteenth century. Earlier the iron industry always specialized in the production of pig iron with little stress on subsequent processes, and the output of steel was of negligible proportions. Among the older concerns only the Monkland Iron and Steel Company had any reputation as a steel producer, but made only about 100 tons annually, and even that was surrendered for the production of malleable iron in 1840. Steelmaking in Scotland dates, therefore, virtually from the adoption of the new steelmaking processes of the second half of the nineteenth century: the Bessemer converter and the Siemens-Martin open-hearth furnace, with their fundamental defect that they could use only low-phosphorus irons, remedied in the 1880's by the Gilchrist-Thomas basic process.[1] Though the new technology was adopted in Scotland, its success was quickly determined by the strength of the demand for its products

[1] Steel is of two fundamental types, basic and acid, depending on whether the pig iron used in its manufacture has been produced from phosphoric or non-phosphoric (hematite) ore. The different processes of steelmaking, Bessemer converter and open-hearth furnace, manufacture both types, though the former only when combined with the Gilchrist-Thomas process.

from the shipyards. In short, the steel industry failed to have an independent source or stimulus for growth but became an integral part of the complex of industrial specialization which appeared in Scotland at the beginning of the twentieth century.

Two long-term and two short-term determinants of the industry's growth help to explain its dependence on shipbuilding. The first determinant, operating in the long run, was the structure of the older Scottish iron industry which specialized in the production of pig iron and was relatively little concerned with subsequent processes. Consequently, when the new methods of steelmaking appeared, Scottish ironmasters were less interested in their adoption than were those already engaged in the further processing of the pig into malleable iron, especially when, at the time the earliest of the new processes appeared, the Scottish ironmasters were enjoying reasonable profits. Malleable iron manufacturers were less fortunate. Even latterly, when the profit margins of the ironmasters were reduced, pressure on those of the malleable iron manufacturers was greater. The latter had to find new outlets to survive. In sum, there was not the same incentive for Scottish ironmasters to introduce the new steelmaking processes. They were not introduced even in the greatest concern of all, William Baird and Company, though the Baird brothers, who were by then no longer active, were followed in the direction of the firm by men of comparable ability and energy. Eventually their chief rival, Merry and Cunninghame, made the change at Glengarnock.

The second long-term determinant was that the unsuccessful outcome of the first introduction of the new processes in Scotland blighted many thoughts of emulation, especially when the ironmasters were under no great compulsion to adopt the methods to try to ensure their own survival. The first attempt to use the Bessemer process in Scotland was by Thomas Jackson at the Coats Ironworks at Coatbridge, then, more seriously, by Dixon at Govan. Unlike Jackson's home-made plant Dixon's was properly erected and the experiments were under the personal supervision of Bessemer himself. His attempt was, therefore, given every chance of complete success, but, as at the Coats Works, it failed, and Bessemer returned the money paid for the licence. The reason was the common one, which was beginning to show the limited applicability of the Bessemer process, that ordinary Scotch pig iron was an insufficiently low-phosphorus iron and as such was unsuitable for the Bessemer process. Since the difficulty was unexpected, and its cause at first unknown, the disappointment was

greater. Even when it was recognized, and the need to use low-phosphorus or hematite ores understood, other problems remained. Even
though hematite pig iron was used, the introduction of the process at
the Atlas works in 1861 encountered difficulties, though, until the converters were dismantled in 1875, the Atlas works was the only
successful producer of Bessemer iron in Scotland. The next main
technical development in steel production, the Siemens open-hearth
furnace, suffered from the same disadvantage and required low-phosphorus irons for its successful operation. Otherwise there was much to
commend its use, as it provided greater opportunities for control of the
process and it could use scrap, of which Scotland was to have a generous
supply from her shipbreaking yards for many years. Technically,
therefore, it became possible to use ordinary Scotch iron only when the
Gilchrist-Thomas basic process, first developed in the 1880's, could be
applied to either the Bessemer converter or the open-hearth furnace.
Yet it was on the basis of the older, or acid, methods, especially the
open-hearth furnace, that the modern Scottish steel industry was first
erected. It might seem that, if the real difficulties of using these processes were overcome, then their restrictive influence on the ironmasters' failure to move into steel production must be diminished, but
the earliest attempts to use them were the outcome of special factors
which were not universally applicable, and which did not operate,
therefore, to remove the inhibitory effects of the new processes on the
ironmasters.

Such special factors are clearly illustrated by the first attempt at the
large-scale production of steel in Scotland in the establishment of the
Steel Company of Scotland in the early 1870's. Its origins lay in another
line of industrial development, in attempts by Charles Tennant of
St. Rollox and others in the chemical industry to utilize 'Blue Billy',
or 'purple' ore, the residue after copper and silver had been extracted
from the iron pyrites, which was then displacing pure sulphur as a raw
material in the production of sulphuric acid, and of which the Tharsis
Sulphur and Copper Company had acquired a large quantity. Tennant
and his associates envisaged using this 'Blue Billy' in a new process
which Siemens, the inventor of the open-hearth furnace, was then
trying to devise to produce steel direct from ore (in this case it was
hoped direct from the 'Blue Billy') without the necessary intermediary
of the blast furnace. The Company was incorporated in 1872, with
Siemens himself as an important shareholder, and the site of its works
was finally fixed at Hallside. Two furnaces specially designed by

Siemens were erected, but, though good puddled iron was made from
an equal mixture of 'Blue Billy' and ordinary iron, costs were so high
that the process was stopped and standard open-hearth furnaces were
installed. The unusual attempts were terminated and the Steel Company
of Scotland came to rely conventionally on external supplies of pig
iron and scrap. The enterprising efforts indicate, however, the special
reasons why the Steel Company of Scotland made an attempt which
most established ironmasters did not. In the Company's origin it was
hoped that through the utilization of the 'Blue Billy' it would obtain
adequate supplies of a suitable ore, the lack of which was the chief
drawback to the Scottish ironmasters' exploitation of the new processes.

The long-term restrictive influences of the existing, satisfied, position
of the industry and the inadequacy of suitable ore supplies were re-
enforced by two less permanent short-run factors. The first arose from
the lack of contact between Scottish ironmasters and the market to
which many of the earliest steel products went. At first the Steel
Company of Scotland specialized in producing steel rails, for which
demand was strong, but, since Scottish ironmasters had never specialized in the production of that commodity, the first demand for steel
products came from a market with which they did not have a strong
direct link. But the Steel Company of Scotland quickly demonstrated
a more successful specialization, as it soon diversified its output and
began to produce steel for shipbuilding and other constructional
activity. The Company was given its first Admiralty order in 1876 and,
not altogether a coincidence, it then made its first profits. Expansion
followed. Blochairn was purchased in 1880 and was quickly turned to
steel production. The second short-term restrictive influence was that
most of the 1870's, when the opportunities of the new technology
appeared, was a period of depression and low prices, when there was a
natural reluctance on the part of ironmasters and others to venture
from a still reasonably stable position into the risks of new enterprises,
for which they did not think themselves particularly suited. If economic pressure increased, the ironmasters always had the alternative of
renovating their techniques in iron production itself, an alternative they
adopted.

The exceptional nature of the foundation of the Steel Company of
Scotland meant that in its early years in the 1870's it was not in the
main stream of growth of the Scottish iron and steel industry. Absorp-
tion came after about 1880 with the appearance of other Scottish steelmaking concerns in two distinct groups. First, Scotland's relatively few

malleable iron manufacturers transferred to steelmaking. In 1879 William Beardmore began to transform Parkhead Forge into a steel-works. In 1880, as the rate of expansion increased, and as the Steel Company of Scotland bought Blochairn and extended Hallside, David Colville built four Siemens furnaces at his malleable ironworks of Dalziel. From these actions grew the two main steelmaking concerns in Scotland today. Second, an exceptional few of the iron smelters followed the lead of the malleable ironmakers, most notably Merry and Cunninghame, who erected Bessemer converters at Glengarnock in 1884–5. Later they added some Siemens open-hearth furnaces, but Glengarnock soon became, and long remained, the only Scottish works producing Bessemer steel. The consequence of this expansion was that by 1885 Scotland had ten steelmaking firms with 73 open-hearth furnaces producing 240,000 tons, or 42 per cent of the British make of Siemens steel.

The expansion of the early 1880's cannot be explained by any general increase in prosperity, nor by the introduction of a new technology. Existing Scottish producers, of both pig and malleable iron, were attracted to steel production at the time because of the operation of new factors. These may be demonstrated from the early history of the Steel Company of Scotland. It did not simply provide a profitable example for others to follow. It had difficulties and was not especially profitable in its early days. When profits did come, even though only slight, they were in part derived from sales to the shipyards, which had been the traditional markets for many Scottish malleable iron manufacturers. The 1870's witnessed the increasing use of steel in shipbuilding. The Admiralty was satisfied and placed orders with the Steel Company of Scotland. In 1877 Lloyd's issued its first set of rules for steel vessels. The growing demand for steel for shipbuilding was the factor which brought the Scottish steel industry into being in the early 1880's and which continued to maintain it.

The close connection between the two industries explains the Scottish steel industry's preference for the open-hearth furnaces. When in 1887 Lloyd's banned the use of Bessemer steel in shipbuilding, those few Scottish concerns which, like Merry and Cunninghame, had built Bessemer converters were plunged into considerable difficulties and, chiefly for that reason, Merry and Cunninghame built open-hearth furnaces beside their existing, and quite new, Bessemer converters at Glengarnock. The retention of shipbuilding demand was most fortun-ate for Scotland, but it gave rise to the criticism that the industry failed to develop the production of Bessemer steel. So far as the criticism is applied to Scotland, it is misplaced, as it concentrates on one section of the industry alone. In Scotland the production of open-hearth steel did not decline, but, as that of Bessemer steel fell, began to increase in response to demand from the shipyards. Fluctuations there were, but they originated in fluctuations in the demand for ships.

Industrial decline

Success in shipbuilding and steelmaking continued to display the achievement and prosperity which had so characterized Scottish industries before the 1870's. By contrast, from the 1870's some industries in Scotland were in decline, particularly in textiles, and even, though to a lesser extent, in the older heavy industries of coal and iron. Earlier, foreign competition had provided little difficulty to Scottish producers; it became increasingly troublesome to them in the years before 1914. Decline was most conspicuous in the textile industries, which nevertheless still comprised a large part of Scottish industry. At the first census of production in 1907 output and employment in the various textile industries were about half of those for the heavy industries. The least successful of the textile industries was cotton production, where the decline, which had appeared in the 1860's, continued and was completed. The retention of a large textile sector in the economy was due to the continued production of jute and woollen goods. Their experiences and prosperity differed.

The woollen industry retained its competitive position. In 1907 Scotland produced 10 per cent of the United Kingdom's output of woollen cloth. In some specialized fields Scotland's share was even greater: it was 31 per cent of the United Kingdom's output of woollen carpets in 1913. As with most branches of Scotland's textile production, the woollen industry depended on foreign markets, particularly in Europe, but unlike other branches it maintained its position successfully until 1914. By contrast, the jute industry was unable to do so and in the thirty years before 1914 the consumption of jute remained almost stationary. For this there were several explanations, but one was particularly important. The adoption of jute as the staple fibre of the Dundee textile industry arose from successive substitutions of inferior raw materials for the flax originally used, and during subsequent depressions various adulterants (such as tow and hemp) were adopted in efforts to lower costs, but no experiments with new fibres seem to have been made in periods of relative prosperity. While such a short-sighted policy enabled the industry to survive before 1914, it did not lead to expansion and when, in the inter-war years, the policy of substitution could be followed no longer, the range of possible action was severely limited. More than thirty years of stagnation could not easily be overcome.

The woollen and jute industries survived the changed competitive conditions, because they represented independent lines of textile production, but even some of the industries to which cotton production had given rise withstood the decline of the parent industry through the growth of an independent specialization. This was particularly so with the Paisley thread industry which quickly broke free from the cotton industry and met international competition successfully until 1914. Scottish firms pioneered production internationally by setting up mills in the United States in the 1860's, Coats at Pawtucket and Clark at Newark. When the two firms amalgamated in 1896, a large part of the world's thread industry was controlled directly from Paisley, while the remainder was influenced by a central pricing policy. But Coats' Central Agency, which controlled sales and prices, was a commercial achievement, perhaps the most striking of the nineteenth century, rather than a sign of industrial success, and though control of the vast Coats empire continued to be exercised from Glasgow, production in Paisley became increasingly overshadowed by production overseas. Thread manufacture in Scotland was unable to maintain its position internationally. Scottish firms retained their supremacy through their commercial achievements. Calico-printing and dyeing, especially in the Vale of Leven, showed a similar independence in its growth and the same tendency towards amalgamation. By 1868 Turkey Red dyeing in the Vale of Leven was concentrated into three firms, which thereafter gained from the exploitation of the Indian market which the railways made possible. The benefits accruing to calico-printing were less marked. Subsequently, towards the end of the nineteenth century both sectors suffered from extreme competition and price-cutting, while the position of most of the textile-finishing firms in Scotland was worsened by the decline of the cotton industry which had first brought them into being. The implication was that they were forced into international competition during a period when it was becoming more intense. Once again amalgamations followed. In 1898 the three

Turkey Red concerns amalgamated into the United Turkey Red Company and in 1899 the calico-printers formed the Calico Printers' Association. Though the solution adopted was similar to that in the thread industry, the results were not beneficial to Scotland. Even if amalgamation was necessary to ensure that British firms could meet foreign competition, the resulting concentration of the industry, especially when the headquarters of the Calico Printers' Association was in Manchester, led to a neglect of Scottish interests. Scotland gained from the commercial concentration of the thread industry; she lost through the commercial concentration of the finishing trades elsewhere. Thus in spite of a successful record, some concerns in the west of Scotland were closed, and unemployment was high, especially among calico-printers in the Vale of Leven, at the end of the nineteenth century.

The experience of the iron and coal industries from the 1870's confirmed the spread of the less successful industrial sector. Throughout the world came increasing competition as local iron industries grew in countries, especially the United States and Germany, which had previously been among Scotland's leading customers and where indigenous iron industries quickly achieved a high degree of technical competence. At home too, and within their own special field of the production of foundry pig iron, Scottish ironmasters experienced competition from rivals centred in the Cleveland area around Middlesbrough, where iron production increased rapidly between 1850 and 1870 and costs of production were so low that pig iron was delivered in Coatbridge below the price at which local producers found production profitable. Thus from the late 1860's, especially in years of depression, Cleveland pig iron entered Scotland in increasing quantities. The adverse effect of increased competition was heightened by the inevitable diminution of the geological advantages enjoyed by the Scottish iron industry. With the exhaustion of the best seams of blackband ironstone, thinner seams, or the less valuable clayband and slatyband ores, had to be worked at a time when, in any case, the advantages of the native ores had declined because the steelmaking processes, which were used till about 1880, required pig iron from non-phosphoric, or hematite, ores, which were not found in any quantity in Scotland. Scottish ore production, which was 3,000,000 tons and more in the 1870's, was less than 600,000 tons in 1913. Ore had therefore to be imported, chiefly from Spain, and so costs of production rose. Though supplies of coal generally remained adequate, those of particularly valuable grades, such as the important splint coal of Lanarkshire and supplies adjacent to the ironworks, did not. The experience of the iron industry had repercussions on coal-mining. Until the 1870's, though the iron industry had not consumed a major proportion of Scottish coal output, it had provided the demand which led to the industry's first growth and exploitation. From the early 1870's the connection between the two became less close and the coal industry's prosperity grew to be determined by other, and less stable, factors. The great boom in the coal industry between 1872 and 1873 marked the beginning of a new age for it as for so many sectors of the economy.

Between the 1870's and the First World War symptoms of decline were not, however, universal, not even in the older industries, which had provided the stimulus of industrial growth earlier in the nineteenth century. Adaptation to a more competitive international economy was evident in the iron industry. Especially early in the twentieth century it too displayed the tendency to amalgamate which Scottish textile firms used so conspicuously to remedy their problems. In 1900 fifteen Scottish firms amalgamated to form the Rivet, Bolt and Nut Company, which survived subsequent years of depression in shipbuilding, while a concern founded jointly by Clyde shipbuilders as a rival in the same field did not. In 1912 eight tube-making concerns, four of them in Glasgow, joined together to form the Scottish Tube Company Ltd., and thirteen malleable iron and steelmaking concerns merged to form the Scottish Iron and Steel Company. More certain ways of increasing efficiency were followed in the last quarter of the nineteenth century when, though most Scottish ironmasters may be criticized for failing to switch to steel production, they transformed many of their traditional practices in iron-smelting. For such a transformation there was much need, as some believed, with justification, that in the production of iron Britain was technically inferior to foreign countries, while Scottish performance compared unfavourably with other areas in Britain. Natural resources were so abundant that Scottish ironmasters could afford, for a time at any rate, to follow a policy of 'suicidal prodigality'.[1] In Scotland about 30 cwt. of coke (or about 55 cwt. of coal) were required to produce a ton of iron, against about 20 cwt., or under the best practice even less, in Cleveland, and that in spite of the charge with the fuel in the furnace in Scotland being only about 2 tons of ore and limestone, though it was about 4 tons in Cleveland. The average productivity of a furnace in Scotland was accordingly low. In 1872 it was about 165 tons of pig iron a week against nearly 500 tons

[1] F. Kohn, *Iron and Steel Manufacture* (London, 1860), p. 3.

a week in Barrow, where the hematite ore was nearest to the blackband in its iron content.

The most striking features of Scottish blast-furnace technique were the small size of the furnaces, the lowness of the temperature of the blast, and the failure to utilize the waste gases from the furnaces. Heightening the furnaces did not offer an obvious improvement, because, even with furnaces of the normal Scottish height of from forty to sixty feet, considerable difficulty was experienced in keeping the hearth clear of solid matter. For similar reasons raising the temperature seemed impossible; a high temperature softened the materials more and choked the furnace. Even with the splint coal this problem arose, as at Shotts, though admittedly not in other works, for instance Summerlee, where the temperature was raised to some extent. Since a general adoption of increased temperatures required a coal harder than the splint, whatever the future possibilities of improvement along these lines, the most obvious advance in blast-furnace practice in the nineteenth century in Scotland was in the utilization of the gases which escaped from the open-topped furnaces. When raw coal is used as a fuel, as it was in Scotland, the coal is coked near the top of the furnaces and consequently the furnace gases are mixed with coal gas. Instead of trying to conserve and use these gases and their heating power, the ironmasters allowed them to escape and incidentally to pollute the atmosphere. One estimate suggested that a Scottish furnace exuded twice as much fuel into the atmosphere as was usefully consumed. Though some Scottish ironmasters made attempts at conservation in the early 1850's, they were soon abandoned because of the abundance of cheap fuel in Scotland. The need to conserve resources, and consequently the need to conserve gases generally, was taken seriously only in the early 1870's.

The failure to conserve waste gases was symptomatic of a more fundamental defect. The Scottish ironmasters had great commercial acumen but lacked technical ability. Some of the managers, notably Ferrie of Monkland, were technically competent, but, in general, as the Professor of Natural History in the University of Glasgow maintained, 'a very small number indeed' would have passed 'an elementary examination in science'. The masters were little different. Professor Young encountered 'exceptional liberality' in Lanarkshire but 'not a sufficient appreciation of the benefits of scientific education'.[1] Yet their

[1] *Royal Commission on Scientific Instruction and the Advancement of Science*, 1872. Qs. 9603 and 9602.

liberality was insufficient to keep the Mining School in the Andersonian University in Glasgow open for more than five years, even though James Merry, of Merry and Cunninghame, was the chairman of its first committee. The alliance between science and industry, which had been such a conspicuously successful feature of Scottish economic life in the eighteenth century, was ruptured in the nineteenth. Fortunately, later in the nineteenth century, advances in scientific education accompanied the improved practice in the ironworks. In 1887 the chair of metallurgy was founded at the Glasgow and West of Scotland Technical College (now the University of Strathclyde), though the subject had already been taught for three years in the College of Arts and Science by Humboldt Sexton. In 1892 the West of Scotland Iron and Steel Institute was formed at Coatbridge, moving into Glasgow almost at once. Though the accumulated neglect of decades could not easily be remedied, and the lessened comparative advantages could never be regained, the Scottish iron industry moved increasingly in the last quarter of the nineteenth century to an attempt to solve its problems through greater technical efficiency. Whatever benefits that brought, its counterpart, the coal industry, was not absolved from the need for similar measures of adaptation itself.

The necessity for adaptation was not uniform in all sectors of the coal industry because the extent of the severance of the link between the two was not the same throughout Scotland, and indeed a notable feature of the Scottish coal industry was that from the mid-1870's it was increasingly split into two sections, the prosperity of each being differently determined. The first indication of the need for adaptation came in the late 1860's, when the ironmasters first began to sell coal on a large scale. After the boom of the early 1870's, they were forced to do so again, as the prosperity of the iron industry in the west of Scotland declined. By contrast, in the east, and especially in Fife, which was increasingly dependent on export demand, there was no immediate collapse. Export prices for coal were slightly higher and the east coast collieries gained accordingly until 1877 when, for the first time since before the boom of the early 1870's, they began to suffer from a decline in both the value and volume of exports. In 1878 some collieries in Fife were closed. Later still, in the 1880's, it became clear that the appearance of inter-district competition, not only in Scotland but from the north-east of England as well, inhibited revival in any district. In the west the depression in the iron industry forced producers to restrict output; in the east, increased exports, especially in 1885, failed to lead to any increase in price. Lastly, to complete the industry's difficulties, supply began to increase from collieries sunk during the high expectations of the boom of the early 1870's. In short, adaptation in the coal industry in the last quarter of the nineteenth century was difficult because Scottish coalmasters, in trying to find new markets, were simply competing with each other; the one hope for more stable, and more universal, prosperity lay in an expansion of sales overseas into new markets, but that was not easily achieved.

Though coal sales to Ireland, not recorded as exports in trade statistics, absorbed a large part of the output of the west coast collieries, foreign demand was of major importance only in Fife, where nearly half of the output went overseas by the beginning of the twentieth century. The experience of Fife was exceptional, since at the end of the nineteenth century the proportion of Scottish output exported was only slightly higher than for the whole country. From 1895 to 1900 18·88 per cent of Scottish output was exported, against 17·76 per cent of the entire output of the United Kingdom. Though the difference was so marginal that it was insufficient to place the Scottish producers in a unique position in the late nineteenth and early twentieth centuries, it was still the chief variable determining the level of the industry's prosperity, in the same fashion as had the demand from the ironworks in the middle of the nineteenth century. Scottish exports went mainly to a few countries, especially to Denmark, Germany, Norway, Russia and Sweden, and about the turn of the century Scotland generally contributed from 25 per cent to 50 per cent of the coal exported to these countries from the United Kingdom. The growth of Continental production, especially in Germany, and the increasing competition it implied, had a direct effect on the prosperity of the eastern collieries of Scotland, and, indirectly, through inter-district competition, on the prosperity of those in the west. The coal industry was placed, therefore, in an exceptionally difficult position by being forced to rely more on foreign markets during years of increasing international competition. But some attributed the severity of the industry's difficulties to internal characteristics as well as to external competition. Exporters blamed the coalmasters for failing to produce the type of coal required by the overseas customers, and the greatest Glasgow exporter of the day, D. M. Stevenson, asserted that the British consumers encouraged such conservatism. Other criticisms were particularly applicable to Scotland. It was asserted that the tendency of Scottish miners to regulate their output with wage fluctuations, so that they would be assured of a given income, made it difficult for Scottish producers to increase output to meet a rise in demand. Again, it was held that the greater cost of railway transport in Scotland, compared with other parts of the country, and notably with Wales, lessened the competitiveness of Scottish coals in more distant markets. The exact relevance of such criticisms could not easily be measured. Their importance lay more in being symptomatic of the changed position of the coal industry from the 1870's. No longer able to rely on stable demand from the ironworks, it was being forced to a measure of adaptation to the requirements of new, generally foreign, markets. Such adaptation could not easily be achieved, but without it the industry's prosperity was bound to decline.

New industries

In spite of their incomplete adaptation to a new environment, the contribution of the coal and iron industries to the prosperity of the Scottish economy was not reduced so rapidly as was that of the cotton industry, partly because, in spite of the progress of shipbuilding and steelmaking, Scotland did not have the same upsurge of new industries in the late nineteenth century as half a century earlier when the gradual displacement of the cotton industry began. Though it was not then fully appreciated, the need for new industries, distinct from the dominant heavies, appeared in Scotland at the beginning of the twentieth century. The great tragedy of Scottish industrial development was that the need was not met. The basis for much potential achievement in the new industries lay in Scottish engineering which earlier in the nineteenth century was more diversified, with marine engineering occupying a correspondingly less overwhelming position. Some of the earliest engineering establishments in Scotland simply made machinery for their own requirements. The Houldsworths met the mechanical needs of their cotton mills in their own foundry at Anderston. Another group comprised the manufacturers of specialized machinery, generally for export. Blair's, Duncan Stewart and Company, and the Mirrlees Watson Company, founded in the late 1830's, made sugar-manufacturing machinery. Both groups were supplying the machines required for Scottish industrial activities or for the country's overseas trade. The steam-engine introduced independent engineering production through its own demands for means of transport by land and sea. Marine and locomotive engineering were at first frequently combined but from the 1850's began to be separated. Neilson and Company, founded in 1836 by a son of the inventor of the hot-blast, first specialized in this way at the Hyde Park Works by beginning the manufacture of locomotives about 1843 and survived to become one of the three firms which merged to form the North British Locomotive Company in 1903. The use of new metals brought further specialization. Steel led to the growth of structural engineering, especially in bridge-building, which, with shipbuilding, became the main market for open-hearth steel in the west of Scotland, and in which the success of Sir William Arrol and Company in building the Tay and Forth bridges was the greatest achievement.

Though Scotland's modern reputation was built in these fields of heavy engineering, it shared in some of the earliest developments in light engineering at the end of the nineteenth and the beginning of the twentieth centuries. In electrical engineering an important contribution came from the firm of Kelvin and White, later to become Kelvin and Hughes, Ltd., which was founded before mid-century. Through its connection with Lord Kelvin it began the manufacture of electrical instruments and its products made an important contribution to the laying of the first Atlantic cable. Other firms followed its lead until by the beginning of the twentieth century Scottish firms were manufacturing electrical appliances of all kinds and for all purposes of power and lighting. Some began to specialize, among them Mavor and Coulson, which, while still carrying on its general engineering work, increased its output of electrically driven coal-cutting machinery after 1897, and specialized entirely in its manufacture from the 1930's. Lord Kelvin was not the only academic to turn to commercial activities in the nineteenth century. In 1890 Professors Barr and Stroud started the firm which bears their name to produce range-finders, at first by assembling the parts made by others, but from 1895 by their own manufacture. Unfortunately such close contact between science and industry was not universal in Scotland at that time.

The early attempts at the development of the motor-car industry in Scotland were still more important, because, though the possibilities were greatest in that field, the attempts failed. Had they succeeded, the industrial fortunes of Scotland between the wars would have been different. The pioneer of the industry in Scotland was George Johnston, who devised the first all-Scottish car, modelled on the Daimler, and had it put into commercial production in 1896 by the Mo-Car Syndicate, later the Arrol-Johnston Company. In 1901, when the Company's Glasgow works were destroyed by fire, production was transferred to Paisley, and again, just before the First World War, to Dumfries, where it continued until the 1920's. Other concerns followed the lead given by the Arrol-Johnston Company. For years William Beardmore and Company manufactured their car in the old Paisley works of the Arrol-Johnston Company; the A.B.C. Company, with which George Johnston was connected, did likewise in Bridgeton for a few years after 1906; the Bergius Company was more successful when it surrendered car production but used its engine to produce the Kelvin engine for boats. The two concerns which made the most striking contribution to the growth of the car industry in Scotland were, however, the Albion Company, famous and lasting, and the Argyll Company, also famous but not lasting. The Albion Company is the one lasting success from this period in motor-car production in Scotland, but from 1913 it has specialized in the manufacture of commercial vehicles. Consequently, it did not represent an attempt to meet the new mass demand which provided the basis for the success of the modern car industry. In Scotland the main attempt to do so came from the unsuccessful Argyll Company. The Argyll car, designed and engined by Alexander Govan, who had first gained his ideas when assembling the French Darracq car in Bridgeton, was a success and when Govan was still unable to satisfy demand, though producing twenty-five cars a week, he decided to build a new factory at Alexandria in Dunbartonshire. Its opening in 1906 was symbolic of Govan's hopes. He had grasped the modern conception of producing for the mass market, and his new factory, designed after an international study of the latest means of production, was aimed at reaping all possible economies of scale. Unfortunately Govan died, aged only 39, shortly after the opening of the new factory, and its financial burdens led the Argyll Company into partial liquidation in 1908. Subsequently the Company revived but, without Govan's leadership and vision, followed a less revolutionary pattern. It developed the single-sleeve-valve engine, invented by a Glasgow engineer, Peter Burt, whose own firm, the Acme Engineering Company, later became the Acme Wringer Company; but the fruits of this technical achievement were nullified through litigation over patent rights, especially with the inventors of the double-sleeve-valve engine, used by the Daimler Company. Though the Argyll Company won these actions in 1913, the cost of development and litigation forced it into liquidation in 1914. All the Argyll rights and designs were acquired and a new company formed to manufacture the car at the Hozier works in Bridgeton, where Govan had first assembled the Darracq car, but production ceased there too in the 1920's. The collapse of all the attempts to make the Argyll Company the pioneer of modern methods of industrial production in Scotland came to an end. It was not an unrealistic venture, simply one as risky and as speculative as any revolutionary plan, but one which required a man of Govan's vision to ensure its successful prosecution.

In aeronautical engineering there was a similar pattern of development, with a failure to continue early advances into large-scale industrial production. In this case the early successes were sporadic. First, in 1895 Percy Pilcher, a lecturer in naval architecture at the University of Glasgow, made the first glider flight in Britain at Cardross in a glider built by himself, and was far advanced in the development of a power-driven aeroplane, when he was killed while demonstrating a glider in 1899. Second, on the basis of Burt's sleeve-valve engine the Argyll Company designed an aero-engine, which won a prize at Farnborough in 1914, in spite of the crankshaft's breaking. Finally, Beardmore's pioneered aero-engines before 1914 and during the first three years of the war the Royal Flying Corps flew more hours with Beardmore engines than with any other type.

In one other field of modern industrial development, chemicals and allied manufactures, where the need for technical expertise was as important as in light engineering, Scotland had to meet exceptional problems through the loss of important natural advantages. First, from the 1870's the Leblanc method was superseded by the Solvay process in alkali production. Since the Solvay process depended on the action of ammonium bicarbonate solution on strong brine, it was more appropriate to the natural resources of Cheshire, where brine could be pumped direct from the salt-beds, than to Scotland, where, indeed, the Solvay method was never adopted. Second, the electrolytic process for the direct conversion of common salt into caustic soda and chlorine operated similarly against alkali manufacture in Scotland. Thereafter alkali production suffered from amalgamations which led, as in the dyeing and calico-printing industries, to the closure of Scottish establishments. About 1890 the Irvine Chemical Company, the Eglinton Chemical Company, and the St. Rollox works joined with others to form the United Alkali Company. The outcome was the end of alkali production in all Scottish works of the combine, while only one

Scottish concern manufactured caustic soda. The decline of alkali production was not unique; iodine production suffered similarly. A factory
for processing tangle ash was built on Tiree in 1863, but, because of the
difficulties of obtaining adequate fuel, it was removed to Clydebank,
where the Whitecrook Chemical Works had been started about 1864
for the extraction of iodine, bromine and potash salts. There a bewilder-
ing range was produced, and the whole of Britain's iodine production was confined to Scotland. Success was fleeting, because in the
late nineteenth century the working of foreign deposits led to a fall
in the value of potash salts, and Scottish output fell in face of competition.

The loss of natural advantages increased the urgency of using fully
the knowledge of the country's scientists and technologists in the way
which had proved such a conspicuously successful factor in industrial
development in the eighteenth century. Though technical ability was
applied to the problems of the modern industries, as in the work of
Kelvin, Barr and Stroud, much more than to those of the heavy
industries in the nineteenth century, its contribution was to specialized
forms of production, not to large-scale industrial development. Yet in
the later nineteenth century there were at least two successful examples
in the chemical and allied industries of what technical ability could
achieve. The first, the shale-oil industry, originated earlier in the nineteenth century in the work of James Young, who pioneered the preparation of paraffin as a commercial article from mineral sources at
Bathgate in the 1850's and later at Addiewell. Young defended his
patent vigorously against interlopers, but, when it expired in 1864,
others entered the industry and by the 1870's it was estimated that the
Scottish industry produced annually about 1,000,000 gallons of refined
burning oil in addition to crude solid paraffin, naphtha, lubricating oils
and other products and employed about 6,500 men. The second began
in 1873 when Alfred Nobel established his works for the production
of nitroglycerine and dynamite at Ardeer in Ayrshire. It grew to be
among the world's largest explosive works and produced a wide range
of other chemicals too.

Nobel's entry into Scottish industry was significant. Other foreigners
were also doing so and, ominously for Scotland, some of the more
successful branches of modern industrial growth originated in foreign
enterprise. In 1856 the North British Rubber Company established
Scotland's first vulcanized-rubber factory in Edinburgh with American
capital, management, machinery and workers. Even after ownership

passed to British interests in the late 1860's Americans remained influential in company policy. In the early 1880's Singer's, which had shortly before had a factory in Glasgow, established their large sewing-machine factory at Clydebank. Lastly, the British Babcock and Wilcox Company, formed by its American parent in 1891, started their first British works at Renfrew in 1895 and from there spread to other parts of Britain, notably starting production at Dumbarton in 1915 in a factory it had taken over five years earlier.

The failure to exploit the growing industries of the twentieth century excited little comment in Scotland before the First World War. Until then the country's economic prospects seemed bright. It wore the air of prosperity and expansion which to many people in Scotland has been so obliterated by the experiences between the two world wars that they regard Scotland as having been permanently a depressed area. But from the 1870's there were ominous portents. With the growth of shipbuilding, especially after the widespread adoption of steel in construction, the industrial complex of the west of Scotland began to assume its modern form, greatly dependent for its entire prosperity on that of shipbuilding. In short, it is possible to see from the 1870's the growth of the specialized economy which experienced such dire distress from that very fact in the 1930's. The avoidance of such difficulties before 1914 was hardly due to the diversity of the economy, as that was fully marked only for the quarter of a century from the appearance of the heavy industries in their modern form after about 1830 until the end of the increasing prosperity of the cotton industry about 1860. During that halcyon period Scotland had many industries with leading international reputations. Though some remained important until 1914, even in decline, the impetus to the growth of the economy from the 1870's was more specialized, but the impetus continued to ensure prosperity because it was an expanding one. Consequently, Scotland was probably less depressed, or at any rate the periods of depression were neither so intense nor so protracted, than in other parts of Britain from 1875 until 1914. Scotland had more than its share of the rapidly developing industry of shipbuilding and its ancillary branches. Whatever unfortunate effects that was later to bring, its influence was favourable until 1914.

XIII
INDUSTRY, 1914 to 1939

Industry under pressure

THE most memorable feature of Scottish economic life between the wars was the severity of unemployment. The incidence varied, but was marked in the west, which had witnessed the most conspicuous industrial growth before 1914. By contrast in the 1930's the unemployment rates of every southern and eastern county, from Aberdeen to Wigtown, were, with the exception of that for Dundee, below the national average. By the 1930's, when the contraction of the coal industry had removed some of the more persistent pockets of unemployment on the east coast, certain districts, especially those near Edinburgh, which had a high proportion of service and light industries, had unemployment rates as low as in the Midlands. The east and south were not immune from depression, but, though sometimes intense, it was more localized, as in the jute industry of Dundee, the linen industry of Dunfermline, the fishing and granite trades of Aberdeen, and the herring fishing in the Moray Firth. Further west, in West Lothian, dependent on such heavy industries as engineering, ironfounding, coal- and shale-mining, conditions changed, as theirs was the industrial structure which suffered most in the inter-war years and which was so characteristic of the western counties of Lanark, Dunbarton, Ayr and Renfrew.

The collapse of the basic Scottish industries was thought by some to be the consequence of the post-war disorganization of foreign trade. It seemed plausible that Scotland's earlier industrial success had rested on sales in overseas markets and so that the severity of the depression arose from Scottish industry being more dependent on foreign customers than was the industry of the entire United Kingdom. Though plausible, the suggestion is misleading. First, export demand did not absorb a major part of Scottish industrial output. About 20 per cent of the output of Scottish coal, slightly less of that of new ships, and about 35 per cent of that of whisky was exported from Scottish ports.[1]

---

[1] Exports from Scottish ports are the only statistics available. They are almost certainly minimum figures as English goods exported from Scottish ports would

Second, though exports from Scottish ports amounted to 16·3 per cent of the Scottish national income, while total exports from the United Kingdom equalled only 15·4 per cent of its national income, the figures are too close—especially in view of their possible error—to substantiate the suggestion. Whatever the degree of dependence, however, there is no doubt that the volume of Scottish exports between the wars tended to fall earlier, fall to a greater extent and rise again more slowly than that of the entire United Kingdom. For example, the volume of exports from the United Kingdom rose by 29 per cent from its lowest point in 1931 to 1938; the volume of exports from Scottish ports, probably, of course, a minimum figure, rose by 13 per cent. The lack of buoyancy is evident from an examination of the figures for the individual heavy industries on which so much of Scotland's prosperity depended. In 1930 243,000 tons of new ships, or 46 per cent of the total Scottish output, were exported; in 1933 it was 9,000 tons of new ships, or 16 per cent of total Scottish output. In 1929 650,000 tons of iron and steel goods were exported; in 1933 it was 234,000 tons; in 1937 it was 339,000 tons. The performance of different industries varied, but generally there was a heavy fall. Taken together, the proportion of output exported by these three groups—ships, iron and steel products and textiles—was 23 per cent before the depression; it fell to 21 per cent in 1932; at the peak of the national recovery of trade in the 1930's it fell to as low as 17 per cent. In brief, the basic Scottish export industries were not recovering.

Though stagnation was common, total collapse was not, and was most closely approached only in the textile industries, in which, however, among Scotland's three major textile sectors, the cotton, jute and woollen industries, experience varied. The worst affected was the cotton industry. After 1918 the only reasonably successful survivors of this once flourishing sector of Scotland's industrial past were exceptional mills, such as those at Deanston and Catrine, or specialized production, such as the thread industry of Paisley. Generally, between the wars the Scottish cotton industry enjoyed no respite from foreign competition and little from that of Lancashire. Its costs were too high and by the end of 1922 only those producers of the highest-quality coloured cotton goods were well employed. Others could only strive for higher-quality production to try to obtain a similar prosperity. In

probably be more than offset by Scottish goods exported through English ports. I am indebted to Mr. M. W. Flinn for permission to use unpublished material on Scottish foreign trade in this section.

the mid-1920's, when the manufacturers of white cotton goods found they could no longer meet competition from India, China and Lancashire, they tried to diversify output by introducing fabrics of varied colours and designs and by using artificial silk with cotton. Quality adequate to offset higher costs could not easily be achieved and between the wars the final liquidation of the industry, at least as it had been known in Glasgow and the west of Scotland, became inevitable. Amalgamations, useful before 1914, became increasingly necessary after 1918. Small-scale producers with limited resources could not withstand the pressure on profit margins and gradually disappeared, among them the job weavers, once common in Glasgow's east end, and to whom merchants had given material to be woven according to certain specifications, and many small firms which had specialized in one process of production, such as warping.

Stagnation in the manufacture of jute was less complete, because periodically between the wars special factors enabled the industry to meet overseas competition, especially from India. But such phases of greater prosperity stemmed more from the removal of foreign competition for special reasons than from any successful internal changes in the industry. Two examples from the years after the immediate post-war boom of the 1920's illustrate the position. In 1922 Indian manufacturers could not meet the demand for bags from the Cuban sugar trade or from importers on the river Plate. Accordingly the demand was transferred to Dundee, but only by default of the overseas competitors. In 1927 the situation was virtually repeated, when low stocks of hessian in Calcutta encouraged such speculation that prices in India rose. When restricted purchasing by importers on the river Plate failed to obtain any reduction, demand was diverted once more to Dundee, which was able to meet the demand, and at even lower prices. The inadequate basis for the occasional prosperity of the 1920's was confirmed after 1929, when such occasions of prosperity became even rarer. In 1932 the demand for jute products was so depressed that even a small jute crop failed to lead to any increase in the prices of the raw materials. Though the industry's prosperity remained determined mainly by events in Calcutta, it was less by those occasions, typical of the 1920's, when Indian manufacturers were unable to meet demand because their output was fully absorbed elsewhere, than by their inability to do so because mills were closed, sometimes by agreement, sometimes by strike. Yet the inter-war years did not provide radically new conditions for the jute industry, because foreign competition was operative before

1914, even though it was then less pronounced. From 1896 to 1913 retained imports of raw jute to Dundee remained stable, thereafter they declined steadily. Output of jute yarn was greater than it had been in 1912 only in 1938. Moreover, just as the industry's difficulties had accumulated over years, so the possibilities of remedying them were limited by the industry's own action in earlier years of combating depressions by substituting various adulterants for jute. The crux of the depression of the 1930's in the Dundee jute industry was that, in the face of Indian competition, there was no inferior fibre which could be used to produce a cheaper, coarser article. In the 1930's Dundee's method of meeting depressions had reached its limit, a situation not without its disadvantages as it brought an increasing awareness of the need to tackle the industry's problems in a different direction by attempting to reorganize its mills.

The record of the textile industries between the wars was not entirely unsuccessful. Though the woollen industry never fully recovered from after the war, Scottish woollen goods and carpets were exported throughout the inter-war years. The pattern of distribution of exports changed. Before 1914 the most important overseas market was Germany; after the war it was surpassed by the United States and new Continental markets until by 1928 the United States absorbed 35 per cent of all direct exports of Scottish tweeds. Specialization in high-quality products was the key to such success, just as it was a feature which distinguished the woollen industry from the cotton and jute industries, with their dependence on poorer-quality goods. Ironically, such specialization and such success made the woollen industry more vulnerable than other branches of textile production to tariff changes and, chiefly for that reason, the 1930's were less prosperous than the 1920's. Though foreign markets, especially those in Italy, Holland and Austria, were lost, the woollen industry provided relatively stable employment for its workers in both decades. The numbers employed in the industry at the Censuses of Production in 1907 and 1924 were almost identical, at just under 28,000; in 1930 the total fell to 24,000, but in 1935 it rose once again to 25,000. The manufacture of carpets was a specially successful branch of the woollen industry, and one which illustrates the adverse influence of tariffs in the 1930's. Overseas markets were the basis of the industry's buoyancy in the 1920's, but after 1930 increased tariffs in the United States and Canada, and financial difficulties in Australia, which had become the largest overseas market for British carpets, all limited exports and led some factories to work at less than full capacity. The industry had high hopes of the Ottawa conference on imperial preference in 1932 but was disappointed, particularly when the Canadian market was not re-opened and a special tariff was not imposed on Indian carpets, the main source of competition. Consequently, in spite of considerable exports to Australia and South Africa, an improvement in the industry's prosperity from 1933 to 1937 was based mainly on increased demand at home; but home consumption could not easily replace the buoyancy which had come from overseas markets and at the end of 1937 some carpet factories in Scotland were working short-time once more. Exports, which had increased since 1933, fell in 1938 and, with falling prices, Scottish carpet manufacturers estimated that their net return was the lowest since 1916.

In the industrial group of coal and iron, which had followed the textile industries in providing the basis of Scottish industrial prosperity in the nineteenth century, decline was less complete between the wars. Though the connection between the two industries of coal and iron was breaking before 1914, and so the coal industry was being forced to rely increasingly on more volatile markets overseas, the ironworks continued to provide a major source of demand, especially for the collieries in the west of Scotland. But the coal industry was not absolved from the effects of the continued decline in the national and international competitiveness of the iron industry. The relationship was not, however, entirely one-sided, because a fundamental cause of the increased costs of production of Scottish iron arose from the wastage of some of the best of Scotland's geological resources of iron ore and coal. After the First World War Scottish ore production became negligible; in 1913 less than 600,000 tons were mined, in 1920 less than 280,000 tons, in 1929 a mere 25,000 tons, against the 3,000,000 tons and more in the 1870's. Since after the war the blast furnaces produced mainly hematite pig iron for the acid process in the steelworks, the exhaustion of home supplies of phosphoric ores was less important than it might have been and the major geological concern of the iron industry between the wars was over the supplies of coal, particularly good coking coal, which were so limited that the Balfour Committee in 1928 sweepingly decided that 'Scotland has no good coking coal'. This dictum was disputed by the Scottish ironmasters and steelmakers, because there were adequate supplies of semi-coking varieties, which could be utilized, but only at increased cost. The consequences of the worsened position of the iron industry were widespread. Production of pig iron declined to just over 600,000 tons in 1929 and to less than 500,000 tons in 1937. Thus after the First World War the character of the Scottish pig iron trade was completely changed. The decline in its international importance, which had started before 1913, continued after 1918, and by 1930 foreign shipments of pig iron were negligible. The closing of the Glasgow Pig Iron Ring in 1916 is significant as the end not only of a remarkable produce market but of a Scottish industry of international repute.

The problem of the coal industry after the First World War was not, therefore, only that of regaining the markets lost through the reduction of exports to half the pre-war level, but of finding additional markets to compensate for the continued decline of the traditional consumption of the ironworks. Unfortunately, as became abundantly clear in the 1920's, such markets could be entered easily only when, for one reason or another, foreign competitors were unable to meet their needs. As in the jute industry, Scottish coal producers sold abroad after the First World War more by default of their competitors than by their own achievements. By implication, the need for a renovation of the industry for the maintenance of more stable exports was demonstrated. Before the strike of 1926, the water-shed of so much in the industry's history, two periods of relative prosperity confirmed this post-war weakness. The first began in 1919, when restocking at home and overseas carried export prices to 115s. a ton against a domestic price of 36s. 7d. The gains accrued mainly to the eastern collieries, above all to those in Fife, from which nearly 30 per cent of the output was exported in 1919, rather than to the collieries in the west, such as in Ayrshire, from which only 4 per cent of the output was exported. The prosperity at this time was more apparent than real, because the competitive weakness of the coal industry in Scotland in comparison with other districts of Britain was partly hidden by the system of government control which survived the war and which ensured in its last phase that Scottish coalfields were supported by the surpluses of the exporting districts. Even in the prosperous year of 1920, Scotland incurred a deficit of over £5,250,000 (allowing 2s. 8d. per ton for guaranteed profit, depreciation and interest). The Scottish coalfield's staggering losses, which had always to be offset by surpluses elsewhere, so long as control lasted, explain, if they do not justify, decontrol. In January 1921 the loss was £1,023,700; in February it was £918,723; in March it was £1,155,800. The weakness of the Scottish coal industry in a competitive world market was thus made clear, though less so its implications for the industry's prosperity and for its industrial relations. A strike in 1921 was a harbinger of many. A second similar instance of relative prosperity began in late 1921, by which time the Scottish coal industry could no longer gain from the pooling of earnings which had served it so well immediately after the war. In the last four months of the year coal exports from Scottish ports increased by about seven times over those in the same period of the previous year. The peak came in 1923 and was a direct result of the political dislocations following the French occupation of the Ruhr. In sum, once again prosperity came to the industry from exceptional conditions overseas. Consequently, collapse was inevitable and came in 1924 with political stabilization in Europe. Prices fell sharply, and the downward trend continued into 1925. Shipments fell by about 20 per cent, revenue from them by nearly twice as much.

Since such periods of easy access to foreign markets were fleeting, the Scottish coal industry was engaged throughout the inter-war years in a fierce competitive struggle to replace the stagnant, if not declining demand from the heavy industries. For some years after the General Strike, when foreign producers were able to displace British coal in overseas markets, and even to send it to Britain, Scottish exports lagged behind those from the rest of the United Kingdom. The rewards in the struggle did not always seem inviting. The average price of Scottish coal free on board in 1925 was 16s. 8·92d. per ton; in 1927 it was only 15s. 6·89d., the lowest since 1914. The greatest difficulty centred around gaining access to the traditionally important Scandinavian markets, which were entered in the late 1920's by Polish Silesian coal-owners, who had previously sent most of their output to mid-Germany. As a result between 1930 and 1931 British exports to Norway fell by 50 per cent and those to Sweden by 45 per cent. Some improvement came in 1932, when greater consumption of British coal in Scandinavia led to an increase in the volume and value of exports from Scotland, while those from the United Kingdom as a whole fell, but the confidence of producers was even less easily regained. Scottish output continued to fall and in 1932 was the lowest since 1897. Fortunately pessimism was belied. Exports were maintained, not only to Scandinavia, where they were facilitated by an agreement on marketing between British and Polish coal-owners, but to Canada, after the Ottawa agreements of 1932, and to the Irish Free State, after the conclusion of the coal-cattle agreement. In 1934, the peak year for the 1930's, exports reached almost 6,000,000 tons, of which over 4,500,000 tons went from the east coast.

Fortunately Scotland suffered much less than England and Wales from interruptions to the coal trade in the 1930's, as trade agreements with Scandinavian and Baltic countries ensured readier access to the markets in which the country had long concentrated. The dislocations following the Spanish Civil War, and the imposition of quotas on imports to France, fell more heavily on England and Wales. But in spite of the importance of the export trade in the 1930's, especially to the eastern collieries, its contribution to the improvement in the industry's fortunes could not outweigh the contribution of increased home demand, and fundamentally the increase in production, to over 32,350,000 tons in 1937, was a response to greater domestic consumption. When production fell in 1938, it reflected the failure of home industrial demand rather than of overseas sales. By the end of the 1930's, in spite of some successes, especially in Scandinavia and the Baltic, the Scottish coal industry had still not broken free from that link. What happened in shipbuilding and steel production remained the major determinant of what happened in the coal industry. One consequence of the continuation of this link was that the incidence of depression was not spread evenly over the whole of Scotland between the wars. In no area in Scotland did the numbers employed in the industry increase between 1913 and 1931, but in some the fall in numbers was drastic, notably in Lanarkshire, where the labour force was reduced by about 50 per cent. The pattern of production was similar, though in Clackmannan and the Lothians output increased between the two years. In brief, the decline was most conspicuous in the older areas, where the link with the heavy industries was closest; the areas of expansion were in the east, in the Lothians and Fife, where success depended on foreign sales and where the only expansion and capital investment of the 1920's and early 1930's was recorded.

The history of shipbuilding, and of the closely related steel industry, is important for reasons other than their influence in determining the prosperity of other sectors of the economy. They were the leading representatives of the industrial structure which had grown in Scotland from the 1870's, and after 1918 they were the industries which had gone into decline, most conspicuously, if not most drastically.

Two factors—one favourable, the other unfavourable—distinguished shipbuilding from many other Scottish industries. In its favour Scottish shipbuilding remained competitive with that in other parts of Britain, and stood to gain from any increase of demand at home or overseas.

Unfortunately this advantage was nullified by the unfavourable consequence of the shipbuilding industry's home market being less sheltered
between the wars than before 1914, especially when many foreign
yards offered British shipowners more attractive terms than they had
done before 1914. But in any case, British shipowners had themselves
to face fierce competition, sometimes against subsidized foreign shipping. Freights were often so low that it required great confidence to
build. Hence demand for new ships, from yards at home or overseas,
was severely curtailed. The pressure of the unfavourable factor was less
evident throughout the 1920's, when Scottish shipyards were active
generally, not only when some fortuitous events overseas diverted
more orders to Scotland. But, in contrast to the years before the First
World War, fear of foreign competition was a live possibility immediately the war was over, especially fear of competition from American
yards, with their superior methods and apparent absence of demarca-
tion. Such forebodings were submerged in the immediate post-war
boom, when the Clyde in particular gained from a replacement
demand for tramp ships. Of the 422 vessels of 646,154 tons launched in
1919, 90 were cargo steamers of 378,512 tons. The high demand continued into the early months of 1920, when many hoped the tonnage
launched would exceed that of 1913.

The post-war boom was ephemeral, not the beginning of a new age.
Few new orders were placed later in 1920; in 1921 Clyde yards were
working at only about half of their capacity; output fell until 1923.
That the industry could not easily achieve a new level of stability
became clear in the later 1920's, especially in the unsatisfactory basis to
the increased output of 1924 and 1927. An increase in output for 1924
became assured late in 1923, when work was restarted on some vessels
on the Clyde and three yards, which had been closed for periods of up
to two years, were re-opened. The revived activity raised the Clyde's
output for 1924 to about three times over that of the previous year.
The weakness of this achievement lay in the continued violent fluctuations of shipping freights, which showed no real change from their
earlier depressed state. The increased orders, especially on the Clyde
in late 1923 and 1924, were therefore orders which could no longer
be delayed, or which were, at best, a recognition of the reduction of
shipbuilding costs to a level which, many thought, could only be
temporary. In consequence, in 1925 output was lower in all Scottish
shipbuilding areas except the Tay, where there was a slight increase.
In the same year orders fell off sharply and the Clyde was left without

S

a liner on the stocks. The unsatisfactory nature of the prosperity was even more evident in 1927. Output continued its downward trend into 1926, when a reduced tonnage was launched in all Scottish shipbuilding areas except the Forth, where the increased output was explained wholly by the good performance of the Burntisland yard. The reduction was occasioned partly by the difficulty of obtaining adequate supplies of steel during the coal strike, so the tonnage launched in 1927 and in 1928 (with the exception of the Aberdeen area) was greater than that of 1926. In short, the boom of 1927 was largely the result of the completion of work held up in 1926 and by the end of 1928 there were few signs of more orders. In the early months of the year ship-owners were reluctant to place orders for new vessels. Their lack of confidence, engendered basically by depression in the freight market, was further enhanced by uncertainty over the most appropriate form of steam propulsion to adopt. By the end of the year the absence of orders for new tankers was almost complete. Fortunately, the delay of some owners of cargo vessels to place orders, a delay which lasted until September, gave way towards the end of the year with the ordering of some general-cargo steamers, but not, notably, of motor-ships. Such inability to postpone orders any longer enabled the tonnage launched in Scotland in 1929 to be almost the same as in the previous year and the number of vessels launched to be maintained.

Though the shipbuilding industry was markedly less stable than before 1914 its relative prosperity in the 1920's was reflected in steel production, which did not match the pronounced decline in that of pig iron. In some years it was greater than in 1913, being 1,582,000 and 1,895,000 tons in the two relatively prosperous years of 1929 and 1937, but these figures represented a lower proportion of the total United Kingdom's supplies than before the war. In the 1920's the Scottish steel industry was so dependent on shipbuilding that the fluctuations of the two industries showed a high degree of correlation. Because of the immediate post-war boom in shipbuilding Scottish steelmakers were able to charge a higher price than their English rivals in 1920. Thereafter prices fell, forced down especially in 1921 by a suspension of battleship orders. For the next decade Scottish steel producers were engaged in a price war, especially against foreign rivals, whose products ensured that reductions in costs of coal, transport and scrap in 1922 failed to stimulate demand with the result that the industry did not benefit from the mild revival in shipbuilding in 1924. Further reductions in price did not provide any remedy. In March 1925 a cut (of 5s.

in plates and 10s. in angles), aimed at attracting orders from the shipbuilders, brought little response, nor did the freeing of prices in the
following month in an effort to meet complaints from shipbuilders that
the prices of their raw materials were still too high. Thereafter, in a
period of keen competition, the weaknesses of the steel industry were
made evident. As prices fell, many steelworks were closed rather than
operated at prices considered unremunerative, though it was only at
such prices that home-produced steel was competitive with imports
from the Continent. Significantly, though imports of foreign steel continued, Scottish steelworks were active once more in 1927 when the
shipyards were meeting the orders accumulated during the General
Strike, and again in 1929 with another revival of shipbuilding, the
progress of which was affected adversely only by difficulties of ensuring
adequate and cheap raw materials, especially scrap.

The activity in the shipyards in 1929 was the culmination of the
decade's relative prosperity. Thereafter shipbuilding, and with it steelmaking, entered a period of collapse as complete as that already experienced by some of the longer-established industries. Shipbuilding's
fortunes after 1929 must, therefore, be examined closely.

The year 1930 marked the change to the years of undoubted and
drastic depression. The figures of tonnage launched during the year
are misleading because they represent launchings which took place in
the last quarter of the year. There was a complete absence of new
orders, except for the new Cunarder from John Brown's, but that
success was ephemeral, as work was suspended on the vessel in 1931.
The unfinished hull of what was to become the *Queen Mary* became
symbolic of the state of Scottish industry, and of Clyde shipbuilding
in particular, and it was long felt that confidence would return only
with the resumption of work on the vessel. Certainly, until then, the
overall output of ships continued to plunge downwards. Only high
output from a few yards, generally for exceptional reasons, prevented
the entire industry from experiencing a complete collapse. In 1932,
when foreign yards were also suffering from a reduction in the orders
which had kept them engaged longer than British yards, the tonnage
launched on the Forth increased, entirely through the achievements of
the Burntisland Shipbuilding Company, which also obtained ten
orders in the year. On the Clyde, Lithgow's output, especially of
vessels for J. and C. Harrison, prevented a total disaster there. Such
varying performances by different yards was typical of the 1930's.
Orders were so sparse that one or two could affect output tremendously.

In 1930 Barclay, Curle and Company, topped the output figures for Scottish yards by launching ten vessels of 64,714 tons, but in 1931 it launched only two vessels of 3,226 tons. In 1931, two P. and O. liners, the *Corfu* and the *Carthage*, kept Stephen's of Linthouse moderately well employed. Thereafter depression was intense on the upper reaches of the Clyde. At the end of 1932 the only boat on the stocks at Govan was a small steamer being built by Harland and Wolff, Ltd., for Bombay owners; on the north bank, between Pointhouse and Whiteinch, Barclay, Curle's had the only vessel on the stocks, a small motorship; at Scotstoun the Blythswood Shipbuilding Company were building a small tanker; Yarrow and Company were constructing two Portuguese destroyers. Generally such prosperity as the Clyde enjoyed in the early 1930's was concentrated in the lower reaches, especially at Lithgow's at Port Glasgow. In turn Lithgow's prosperity owed much to the orders they received for Harrison vessels. A good example of this trend came in 1933, when only five firms in the world launched vessels of more than 320,000 tons in total. Lithgow's was the only British yard among them. Four out of the five vessels were for Harrison's, these four being the only vessels of over 5,000 tons gross launched on the Clyde that year.

In 1933 the decision to give government help towards the completion of the Cunarder (No. 534) marked the trough of the industry's depression. In 1934 its launch, as the *Queen Mary*, increased the Clyde's output sharply, but the performance was impressive more by comparison with the very low level to which output had fallen in earlier years. More ominously, the type of work was exceptional, and was not that to which the Clyde was entirely accustomed. The *Queen Mary*, the *Orion*, and a few tankers and refrigerator motor-vessels accounted for more than 40 per cent of the shipbuilding; warships in the larger yards explained about 20 per cent more; the remainder consisted of trawlers, coastal and other small vessels. Consequently, the revival on the Clyde in 1934 was accompanied by the continued absence of orders for general cargo steamers and tramp tonnage. Without a revival of this demand, on which the Clyde had so often relied, a lasting recovery did not seem possible. The government's scrap-and-build policy provided little incentive to British shipbuilders to place new orders, but in 1935 an increase did emerge later for vessels of around 9,000 tons, but not for high-class liners. That year the reduction in output on the Clyde, though not on other Scottish rivers, was misleading, being the result of the launch of the *Queen Mary* in the previous year, and though Brown's launched nothing in 1935, the fitting-out of the *Queen Mary* made it one of the busiest yards on the Clyde. More ominously, in 1935 Britain launched only 35 per cent of the world's tonnage, against 50 per cent in 1934. The timing of the launch of the *Queen Mary* was part of the explanation, but so too was foreign competition. Not only were foreigners ceasing to order from British yards, British shipowners were also ordering overseas, especially when for some that became the only method of obtaining a return on debts due to them from Germany. For that reason Aberdeen trawlers were built on the Elbe rather than on the Dee.

Though orders from foreign shipowners remained absent, those from British owners spread in 1936 to other fields, including passenger vessels. Government policy, in a variety of different aids to the ship-building industry, and, more important, in increased expenditure on naval construction, was responsible. Without the increased naval work —which occupied about 20 per cent of the berths, and which con-tinued to provide a basis for activity in the shipyards throughout the later 1930's—the reduction in foreign orders would have had more severe repercussions. But once again, in 1938, though output remained high, especially because of the launching of the *Queen Elizabeth*, orders were so reduced that it was estimated that only one merchant ship was ordered for every four launched. The position was as in 1930. The industry was exhausting its order book and there were no new orders to follow. British costs were too high, and so many British orders were going to Continental yards that there was an adverse balance of ship-building orders in 1938. It was too soon for the output to reflect the adverse position. It would have done so later, as orders were completed, but, before that position had been reached, Admiralty orders increased with war-time demand, so that any excess capacity was fully absorbed.

Disputes and remedies

The collapse of shipbuilding, and especially its inability to meet foreign competition any longer, typified the toils of much of Scottish industry between the wars. The competition may have been unfair, but the effects on industries, and on an economy which had depended heavily for a century or more on foreign trade, could not be ignored. Briefly the problem was that, since Scottish industries were less able to compete against rivals in other countries, and even those in other parts of the United Kingdom, they had either to be renovated and re-equipped to withstand that competition or be reorientated and diversified to produce more for the home market. Though the latter was not necessarily the more difficult course, it did provide additional problems in that it implied some surrender of the traditional role of being an important supplier of world demand. This fundamental problem applied to industry in other parts of Britain, but it was particularly pressing in Scotland where, apart from shipbuilding and steelmaking, the staple industries had been stagnant since about the 1870's, and where the relative sparseness of population and the absence of certain necessary raw materials, or semi-processed goods, limited the range of industrial developments aimed at satisfying the home market. Unfortunately, in the 1920's the extent of the adaptation required was not always appreciated; in the 1930's such adaptation as took place was frequently restrictionist rather than expansionist.

The problem first became acute in coalmining, which gave rise to the main industrial and social unrest of the 1920's. In the 1930's the collapse of shipbuilding and steelmaking, the growing industries of the pre-war years, underlined the need for adaptation. The dilemma which faced coalmining after the First World War was more easily stated than were any remedies for its solution. Given the level of demand, costs had to be reduced or the industry had to contract. The dilemma assumed an even more acute form in Scotland where the more marked decline of coalmining was indicated by the size of the losses incurred before the industry was decontrolled. Immediately after decontrol the dispute between employers and employees flared up as the employers attempted to remedy Scotland's adverse competitive position by cutting wages. Given the dilemma which faced the industry, the masters considered this the only way of cutting costs. To the men, who looked for salvation in improved methods and efficiency, it was the least satisfactory. The men pointed to the lowness of their wages; the masters to how, even at these low wages, they were failing to make a profit. Both were correct between 1920 and 1923. It was agreed in 1921 that wages in Scotland were not to fall below a minimum of 110 per cent above the level of 1888. The minimum was reached in March 1922, when the level of wages, though not of earnings, was down to 8s. 4·8d. per shift. An increase of 2½d. was granted in April, but the minimum returned the following month and continued until December. By any standards the rate was sufficiently low to explain the miners' grievances. On the other hand the masters pointed out that from the resumption of work after the strike on 1st July 1921 until October 1922 the average profit per ton of coal sold was only 5·44*d*. In 1913 it had been 1*s*. 8*d*. per ton, and when Lord Sankey had proposed 1*s*. 2*d*. as reasonable profit, the coal-owners had rejected his suggested figure as inadequate.

Such standpoints remained and were not reconciled by subsequent negotiations. After an exceptional increase in wages and employment following the occupation of the Ruhr, a new wages agreement was concluded in 1924. Under the wages agreement of 1921 every £100 of proceeds was distributed in the ratio of £84 6*s*. to wages and £15 14*s*. to profits; in the 1924 agreement the distribution was £87 8*s*. 9·6*d*. to wages and £12 11*s*. 2·4*d*. to profits. At the same time the minimum wage was raised from 20 per cent to 33⅓ per cent above the pre-war standard. The gain to the men was minimal by any standards, but in the masters' eyes was enough to explain the reversal in their fortunes. The fall in prices after the occupation of the Ruhr was a more accurate explanation of the loss per ton[1] incurred in Scotland in the first month of the agreement, May 1924, a loss which became the normal practice. In April 1925, at the end of the first year of the agreement, the total loss in Scotland was £348,934, or 2·51*d*. per ton, while, if various interest payments were added, it became £765,434 or 5·51*d*. per ton. When the agreement came to an end in July 1925, the aggregate loss, for 15 months, was £1,346,254 or 7·96*d*. per ton. Apart from a temporary break in 1927 the position was unchanged after the long-protracted strike of 1926. In 1928 there was a debit balance per ton in Scotland every quarter and in 1929 a credit balance only in the first quarter. The cumulative deficiency under the wages agreement continued to rise, to £6,175,374 in September 1929 and to £7,663,718 in September 1930. In such circumstances there was no cessation of the pressure by the masters to reduce wages. In November 1926 work was resumed on the basis of an eight-hour instead of a six-hour day and a temporary agreement divided proceeds in the ratio of £87 to wages and £13 to profits, with a minimum wage of 9*s*. 4*d*. a day. A permanent agreement, which came into force in April 1927, accepted the same distribution, but with a minimum wage of only 8*s*. 4·8*d*. The strike brought no benefit.

The wages dispute in the coal industry in the 1920's reflected basically the failure to reduce costs. It was not always realized that it might be

[1] Under the wages agreement independent accountants made the necessary audit. These are their figures.

achieved as effectively, and with much less social unrest, by greater efficiency in methods of production. Fortunately, mechanization of production in Scotland greater than in the rest of the United Kingdom always improved the country's efficiency, but when attempts were made to increase it, they led generally to the advocacy of the concentration of production on more efficient units. Too easily such a policy was interpreted as an attempt to restrict output. Restriction of output, or controlled marketing, was adopted more extensively in the coal industry than in others in the 1930's. By then two factors made the problem easier to tackle than in the 1920's. First, voluntary movement from the industry had left fewer people to be displaced through any schemes of amalgamation and restriction. The average number employed in 1920 was 147,323; in 1930 it was 96,649; in 1933 it was only 80,350. Second, in the 1930's the government began to assist in the reorganization of the industry. The attitude of the masters then seemed to indicate that, having failed to achieve a reduction in costs through lowering wages, the only alternative left was to reduce output. As a result, though the coal-owners and the government agreed on the aim, they frequently disagreed on the means. The coalmasters first suggested that inland prices should be 20 per cent higher than export prices, the surplus being used to help exporters, a scheme aimed at controlling marketing without any provision for ensuring greater efficiency, not even through the then popular method of amalgamating coal-mines. The coalmasters opposed any large-scale amalgamation, even when aimed at obtaining some limited improvements in marketing. The only amalgamations acceptable were those of individual firms, with their interests concentrated in certain areas, as when the coal interests of William Baird and Company and the Dalmellington Iron Company were merged into Bairds and Dalmellington, Ltd., in 1931. Consequently the industry was split in its approach to the two parts of the Coal Mines Act of 1930. The first part, which attempted to introduce a quota system to restrict production, and so, it was hoped, lead to a rise in price, was acceptable to the owners; the second part, which set up a Coal Mines Reorganization Commission to assist in amalgamation schemes, was not.

That the coal-owners' aim was to maintain prices, which they justified as the only method by which wages and profits could be maintained at a reasonable level, was confirmed in the operation of the Act of 1930. Its effect became increasingly restrictive. By the quota scheme it established, an allocation was made for each district in Great Britain by a Central Committee, while the distribution of the quantities rested

with the District Executive Board. The Central Council had no power
to co-ordinate inter-district prices. Fierce competition ensued between
districts, especially between those dependent on foreign and those
dependent on home sales, until an agreement was reached for co-
ordination of inter-district minimum prices and for a separation of
inland and export allocations in 1934. Two years later, in 1936, each
district set up central selling organizations, while at the same time the
Central Council was given additional powers to supervise district
schemes. Scotland was organized as a single district, but in 1936 opted,
with eleven other districts, for a district selling scheme which allowed
each owner to sell his coal to his customers, though he received instructions from a sales committee on tonnage, destination and minimum
prices. The evidence for deliberate restriction of output, one of the
most critical features of the scheme, is difficult to evaluate. The Scottish
allocation was not raised significantly, though actual output was consistently below it by from 2 to 5 per cent until the last quarter of 1933.
At the same time employment in the Scottish coal industry fell. In
1927 it was 109,000; in 1931, 88,000; in 1933, 81,600. Coal prices fell
much less between 1930 and their lowest in 1933 than did the general
price level, but it is improbable that the maintenance of prices limited
demand. When revival in the coal industry came, from 1933 onwards,
it confirmed that the fall in production rested on the fall in demand,
both from home and from abroad, which no practicable fall in price
could have arrested. There is much less doubt on the ineffectiveness of
Part II of the Coal Mines Act, 1930. In effect the Coal Mines Reorganization Commission was charged with bringing into operation a
scheme of large rationalized concerns which, it was hoped, would
make the various schemes of market control superfluous. It achieved
virtually nothing, sometimes it was suggested because of the difficult
problem of royalties, which were nationalized only in 1938. In Scotland its ineffectiveness was quickly apparent. In 1932 the Fife coalmasters were asked to produce a scheme by the beginning of the following year, but failed to do so through opposition from the Wemyss,
Balgonie and Fordell collieries. In the Lothians the coal-owners proved
to be equally intractable. At most the Commission encouraged a trend
already present towards voluntary amalgamation.

   In shipbuilding and steelmaking a similar, though less extensive, contraction seemed necessary unless costs could be reduced, and as in coalmining, so in shipbuilding, there were suggestions that only reductions
in wages could do so. To James Lithgow in 1921,

'under present conditions suggestions that our prosperity as a ship-building country can be regained at anything like the present level of wages are the purest humbug, and those who make them are doing our men an ill-service in fostering hopes which the hard logic of events is bound to blast.'[1]

A year later Lord Maclay, writing as a shipowner, offered a different way of salvation by accusing the shipbuilders of failing to adopt the most efficient production.

'There has been very little improvement on the tramp type of steamer since the introduction of triple expansion engines over thirty years ago. Many orders would be immediately forthcoming if ship-builders and engineers could produce a steamer which would show any real economy over old vessels. There are many owners anxious to build if they could see reasonable hope of a very modest return for their money.'[2]

The words of Lithgow and Maclay represent two different points of view. While Maclay looked to greater economy in operation through the construction of a more efficient vessel, Lithgow was more con-cerned with reducing costs for vessels of a given construction. In the 1920's neither interpretation seemed wholly valid, because then the industry did not seem inherently uncompetitive, it simply seemed to be trying to obtain too large a share of the market to use the additional capacity which its expansion, especially during the war, had produced. After the boom in shipbuilding in 1924 arguments were advanced in favour of rationalization, generally accompanied by the counsel of despair, that British shipyards could never again expect to build the tonnage of former years. In 1930 came the first definite move towards rationalization with the formation of the National Shipbuilders Security, Ltd., by shipbuilders themselves. The closure of a number of famous Scottish yards, such as Caird's of Greenock, followed. It is practically impossible to determine whether the avowed aim of redu-cing costs was thereby achieved, but the plan did not lead to any revival in activity in the industry. In due course that came from other factors. But the British shipbuilders were convinced of the rectitude of their policy and in 1937 were instrumental in the establishment of the International Shipbuilding Conference to try to obtain some collabora-tion and control of international competition.

[1] *The Glasgow Herald Trade Review*, 1921, p. 36.   [2] *Ibid.*, 1922.

Scottish steelmakers faced exceptional adversities through the exhaustion of plentiful natural endowments. As pig-iron production in Scotland declined while that of steel rose, the supplies of pig iron from the Scottish blast furnaces were inadequate to meet the needs of the steelworks and the steelmakers faced the effects of Scotland's diminished advantages in iron production. The problem was intensified for the basic steel producers since the Scottish ironworks continued to specialize in the production of hematite iron, though after the war the improvement in the quality of basic steel led to an increase in its manufacture in Scotland. Thus even in 1937, 198,000 tons of hematite pig iron were produced against 117,000 tons of basic iron (also 182,000 tons of foundry and forge pig), while only 466,000 tons of acid open-hearth steel were made against 1,392,000 of basic open hearth (also 37,000 tons by other processes). The problem of bringing supplies of pig iron into Scotland was, therefore, more pronounced for those steelmakers using the basic process. They were placed at a peculiar disadvantage against their Continental competitors with ample supplies of basic ores. The Scottish practice of using a large quantity of scrap in the open-hearth furnaces provided some relief, but it was estimated that Scotland would have had to produce about 1,000,000 tons of pig iron annually, or about double its then current level of production, to be self-sufficient in the inter-war years.

The most striking economies, particularly in fuel consumption, lay in the integration of the various processes of production. Such integration was lacking in Scotland, because the extensive use of scrap, and, though of much less importance, the use of imported pig iron, made cold metal practice the normal method of Scottish steelmaking. As the scrap ratio declined so the need for, and advantages to be derived from, integration increased. If the lack of integration was the most conspicuous example of failure to obtain the highest degree of technical efficiency, it was not the only one. The pig-iron production per furnace in blast in Scotland, which was only 16,000 tons annually in 1915, was only 33,000 tons in 1937, the figure reached by the whole United Kingdom in 1915, while even the United Kingdom's performance compared adversely with that of other countries. The nature and use of uncoked Scottish coal may have been partly responsible for the difference, but can hardly have accounted for such a striking lag in technical efficiency as was apparent in Scotland. But whatever the relative importance of these various possibilities of internal reform through technical change, the steel industry was more concerned after the war with the elimination of the surplus capacity, much of which was the result of expansion undertaken during the war at the behest of the Ministry of Munitions. Consequently, suggestions for modernization were accompanied, and sometimes overwhelmed, by suggestions for the rationalization of the industry and for its grouping into districts with central buying and selling organizations. The two remedies, expansionist and restrictionist, were both first clearly enunciated at the time of the General Strike, but were implemented only later. On balance, the industry was perhaps more active in promoting the restrictionist than the expansionist solutions. By 1928, central buying and selling organizations were set up, and with the collapse of demand from the shipyards in the 1930's, amalgamations became more attractive than ever. A lead was given through the transfer of the plate and section interest of William Beardmore and Company to David Colville and Sons and then through the merger of the interests of the latter with those of James Dunlop and Company to form Colvilles Ltd.

The difficulties of the Scottish steel industry were brought out in 1932 by the decision of Stewarts and Lloyds to move from Mossend to Corby. Stewarts and Lloyds originally used iron-tube hoops and strips and were supplied with necessary materials from the puddling furnaces and rolling mills of the area. Steel tubes and strips used basic steel, because of its suitability for rapid welding. Though basic steel was not made extensively in Scotland, this disadvantage was partly offset by local firms re-rolling Continental billets and slabs. The relief was only temporary and gradually the material was brought direct from the Continent. That supplies were never likely to be obtained again from Scotland was made clear in 1932 when depreciation and protection forced the use of British steel, but not of Scottish steel, which was then unsuitable, as basic Bessemer steel had not been produced in Scotland since the closure of the plant at Glengarnock in 1920. By 1932 it was not available anywhere in Great Britain and acid Bessemer, which could be used, was made only in England. The position facing Stewarts and Lloyds was, therefore, quite simple. They had to supply their works with cheap basic Bessemer steel and that could be done effectively only at Corby. Such advantages as Scotland could offer were no longer adequate to arrest the movement south.

The move of Stewarts and Lloyds to Corby had more implications than being a sign of the loss of Scotland's relative advantages. It emphasized the need to rationalize what remained. Even more so it emphasized that newer and better-organized plant was more likely to improve the competitive efficiency of the industry than were amalgamations. But in Scotland the tendency towards amalgamation, initiated by the formation of Colvilles Ltd., was well established by 1933. In the early 1930's the closure of the Mossend and Calderbank steelworks began to concentrate steelmaking in the hands of Colvilles, who, at the beginning of 1934, also absorbed the steel-plate rolling section of Stewarts and Lloyds. Apart from Colvilles, with works at Motherwell, Cambuslang and Glengarnock, the other main steelmaking concerns in Scotland by then were the Steel Company of Scotland, with works at Blochairn and Newton, the Lanarkshire Steel Company, with works at Motherwell, and the Scottish Iron and Steel Company, mainly engaged in wrought iron, with works at Coatbridge. In 1934, when the government pressed for the completion of the scheme to reorganize steel production, the amalgamation continued with the purchase of the Steel Company of Scotland by Sir James Lithgow, a director of Colvilles, and by 1936 the process was virtually complete. Both the Steel Company of Scotland and the Lanarkshire Steel Company were then controlled by Colvilles.

Thereafter the policy of meeting the depression by expansion, regarded by some as the logical counterpart to the phase of reorganization, became more evident. Towards the end of 1936 a modern wire, rod and bar mill, with appropriate increases in melting capacity, was completed at Motherwell; reorganization at Glengarnock aimed at producing an additional 2,500 tons per week of semi-products and sections; at Parkhead Beardmore's had a scheme in hand to yield another 50,000 tons a year. In the spring of 1937 Colvilles announced their major plan for renovation; a scheme of expansion at Clydebridge and Clyde including the erection of a battery of coke ovens, modern blast furnaces and steelmaking plant, and an additional plate mill, all of which provided the basis for the future by leading to a semi-integrated plant. Yet it still left Scotland without a wholly integrated steelworks. Its establishment, and indeed the whole question of the industry's technical efficiency, cannot be considered apart from the topic of its location, which was a matter of particular concern in the 1930's. As the consumption of fuel in the furnaces fell, the original advantages of their location on the coalfields were considerably diminished. Thus between the wars the industry was faced with a dilemma; to obtain the advantages of integration the furnaces had to be near the steelworks, which were inland; but, on the other hand, to reduce the costs of transporting the ore, the furnaces had to be located on the lower reaches of the Clyde. In 1929 a plan was advanced for a new location downriver. If implemented, it was alleged that the cost of slabs would have been lowered from the then current average of £6 12s. a ton to £5, but, for a variety of reasons, the scheme was not adopted. The problem of location, which was still unsolved when the war began, reappeared briefly at its close to be settled in favour of an inland location at Ravenscraig.

Expansion and new developments

The adaptation of the traditional industries to their changed environment, whether by restrictionist or expansionist methods, was one solution to the adversities of Scottish industry between the wars. Because of the displacement of labour and reduction in output which it frequently involved, it was not a remedy which appealed to the majority of Scots. Many had little expectation of any solution from the development of the traditional heavy industries and looked instead to the expansion of new enterprises. Even some personally active in the heavy industries, and vigorously involved in promoting their reform and renovation through rationalization, thought likewise. So it was with James Lithgow.

'A personal survey of the industrial field in Scotland leads me to the conclusion that we must look forward to a smaller percentage of our population being employed in what have hitherto been regarded as our heavy basic industries, but that without exception those engaged in these industries do appreciate that by determined effort on their part they may still maintain a highly efficient industry in Scotland, perhaps on a reduced scale. It is equally apparent that the balance of the population must seek an outlet for their activities in the lighter and more specialised industries associated with articles of domestic consumption, ranging from tinned tomatoes to electric fires.'[1]

The belief that such an infusion of new industries was essential for the country's economic salvation was not extensively adopted until after 1930. Lithgow was writing in 1932, and his was the standpoint of the decade. Until 1930 it was hoped that the key to prosperity lay in a revival of the heavy industries. In one sense that was still true, even in the

[1] *Glasgow Herald Trade Review*, 1932.

1930's. The difference between the decades was that in the 1920's there was continual hope of quick revival. After 1930 fatalism smothered hopes of revival in the heavy industries, but had a favourable effect in leading to a greater appreciation of the need for encouragement to the new industries in Scotland. No longer were they regarded as interesting, faintly exotic growths, indeed almost luxuries, but as necessities, as important as the heavy industries in the Scottish economy. Two factors were particularly influential in leading to the adoption of this position. First, the east and south of Scotland were more prosperous than the main industrial belt because of their higher proportion of light industries. The decline in Scotland's major industries understandably overshadowed the successes in a variety of others: papermaking in Aberdeenshire; printing and publishing in Edinburgh, Dundee and elsewhere; the preservation of fruit and vegetables near the Carse of Gowrie; rubber manufacture in Edinburgh; the production of a variety of foodstuffs, especially in Edinburgh. Second, the need for new industrial development was most striking by comparison with England.

'There are . . . important industries in which, between 1924 and 1930, production and employment in England has made great strides but *where no Scottish production exists at all*. Aircraft employed 11,735 in 1924 and 21,322 in 1930. Aircraft are not made in Scotland. In others, Scottish production is trifling. Motors and cycles gave work in England, 185,576 in 1924 and 233,176 in 1930. But in Scotland the numbers at work were only 6,105 and 7,077. Silk and artificial silk; in England, 39,932 in 1924, and 58,905 in 1930; in Scotland, no figure exists for 1924. The employment in 1930 was 971.'[1]

The difference reflected not only advance in England, but decline in Scotland. In 1932, though 20 new factories were opened in Scotland, 36 were closed down. In 1935 22 new factories in Scotland had to be set beside 213 new factories in London.

All this was grist to the mill of those who demanded some measure of political independence for Scotland. Earlier demands for greater independent control of Scottish affairs, especially from the 1880's, were based more on political theories of self-determination. Whatever political or cultural motives may have dominated the leaders of the movement, its popular support, in the 1920's, and especially in the 1930's, was based largely on economic considerations. How far any measure of home rule would have provided an effective answer to the

[1] G. M. Thomson, *Scotland, That Distressed Area* (Edinburgh, 1935), p. 47.

country's economic problems is doubtful. Few believed that the severance of union with England would lead automatically to economic salvation, but more common, and more justifiable, was the belief that, though Scotland was suffering from adverse international economic circumstances, these could be mitigated by the adoption of certain economic policies which a United Kingdom parliament, with its concern for much wider interests, was less likely to adopt than was a parliament in Edinburgh. In short, the basic objection to the existing union with England was that it prevented Scotland adopting the economic policy most suited to the country. Such critics did not desire a complete severance of the union, only whatever was necessary to allow them to implement the economic policies they thought desirable.

The failure of new industrial development in Scotland lent apparent support to their analysis, because it seemed to run counter to the experience of the newer industries in Scotland before 1914. Immediately after the war various developments held out the prospects of further growth. William Beardmore and Company had moved during the war from the production of components for motor-cars to making three models, at Glasgow, Paisley and Coatbridge, and was considering the possibility of adding another plant to these three; a new model of the Argyll car—embodying the famous single-sleeve-valve engine—was planned for marketing early in 1920; at Dumfries Arrol-Johnston specialized in a new model of the 15·9 h.p. car with which they had achieved distinction; earlier, the Albion Motor Car Company produced a new 30 cwt. chassis and Halley's Industrial Motors a six-cylinder engine; Carlaw and Sons planned to market a 20 to 30 cwt. industrial vehicle entirely of their own design and manufacture; the Caledon Company brought out a passenger vehicle chassis fitted with an Argyll-type engine; Barr and Stroud adapted the single-sleeve-valve engine to a motor-cycle. Unfortunately none of these portents bore much fruit in the 1920's. Most of the ventures started after the war continued, with varying degrees of success, throughout the decade, but by the early 1930's all had been eliminated or diverted to other activities except the Albion Company, which continued as an important manufacturer of commercial vehicles. To this collapse was added the decline of some of the lighter industries which were already well-established in Scotland. An example was the boot and shoe industry, where the decline in employment was greater than for the country as a whole. By 1936 the number employed in the industry, 4,500, was only 4·1 per cent of the total employed in it in England.

But the collapse of the early promise in the newer, light industries was more important.

The basic problem of Scottish industry between the wars was therefore a reflection of that which had been emerging for years before 1914. While her major industries were declining, especially in their international standing, no other industrial growth was appearing, and being maintained, as a substitute. The one gleam of hope in Scottish industry after 1930 was that, increasingly, the problem was being analysed and attempts made to find a solution. Yet these attempts had a possible defect. Their analysis led many to the obvious conclusion that new industries should be encouraged in Scotland, and a variety of commendable measures aimed at this end were adopted. On the other hand it is possible that, no matter how successful these industries were (and their success, as it transpired, was not wholly unqualified), they could do little to alter the structural balance of the economy, and so could do little else but touch the fringe of the problem. Consequently, any attempt to alter the balance of the economy could succeed, if at all, only in the long run. If this were true, then more important than the need for diversification was the need that the existing firms should innovate within their own fields; in short that they should attempt reformation through expansionist, not restrictionist, solutions. The *Industrial Survey of the West of Scotland*, compiled by members of the staff of the University of Glasgow in 1932, pointed out that this was the more important policy, but it was one decreasingly accepted with the adoption of special policies for the Depressed Areas. Innovation was especially necessary in one field. The growth of the light industries in Scotland was limited by such exogenous factors as the distance from some of the major markets in the south, and by the heavy industries in Scotland being accustomed to producing the materials required for heavy, rather than for light constructional activity, ship-plates rather than tinplates. But the explanation of their failure was not wholly external. The production of consumers' goods in Scotland was inhibited by the refusal to adopt the mass-production methods essential for success. Before 1939 only the clothing trade had made much progress in that direction. Though according to one estimate, between 80 and 90 per cent of the Scottish demand for cheap furniture, for the manufacture of which mass-production methods were necessary, was met in Scotland, the furniture trade adopted such methods only under enforced war-time standardization. In short, though it might be held that there were two remedies for the problem of Scottish industry,

T

diversification and innovation in the traditional fields, they went together and were complementary; but the relative stress placed on the different remedies, and the changing emphasis over the years, reflected a changing analysis of the problem. The most ardent advocate of diversification, envisaging it taking place to such an extent that there was a change in the entire industrial structure, so great that a new balance emerged, was advocating a policy which was, in effect, a logical consequence of a belief in a permanent labour surplus. On the other hand the less ardent advocates were those who saw it as a useful addition to a policy of increasing the competitive ability of the basic heavy industries, but without leading to a radical change in the industrial balance. On the whole the depressing view of the first group predominated before 1939. Its acceptance led many to look with suspicion on the revival of the heavy industries in 1936 and to regard it as an increase in economic activity which could have no substantial basis. The desire to diversify cannot be criticized in itself; the danger was that undue stress on its importance led to failure to recognize that the encouragements given to the new industries might more appropriately have been given to the old. A broader industrial base was necessary, but that could never have been achieved by the neglect of the older industries. It is striking, however, that in the 1920's much responsible opinion accepted the need for revival in the heavy industries, while in the 1930's their permanent depression was almost accepted. On this account diversification virtually became a means to offset the reduction of certain basic Scottish industries caused by the rationalization considered necessary because of their permanent depression. Such a surplus was accepted by most commentators at the time. The *Industrial Survey* of 1932 envisaged the possibility of a permanent surplus of male labour, an expectation which by 1934 the *Report of the Investigation into Depressed Areas* thought confirmed. Even in 1937, when some revival had come to the heavy industries, Sir Steven Bilsland wrote that 'no conceivable expansion of these industries [the heavy industries] is likely to absorb all the surplus labour which remains'.[1]

The attempts at encouraging diversification had some success but their impact was much greater on the morale of the Scottish industry than in producing a solution to Scotland's worst industrial problems. Attempts at self-help, in the form of encouragement to new industries to settle in Scotland, came in the 1930's. A Development Board for Glasgow and District was set up in 1930. In the following year the

[1] *The Glasgow Herald Trade Review*, 1937.

Scottish Development Council was instituted to encourage and indicate possibilities of industrial development throughout the entire country, and, until 1942, when the Scottish Council on Industry was formed to consider the industrial future of Scotland, remained the most important body assisting the new forms of industry. After the most depressed parts of Scotland were designated as Distressed Areas, the Scottish Development Council co-operated with the Commissioner for them in its most significant contribution towards diversification in the establishment of the industrial estate at Hillington. In 1938 the same idea, which many thought held the greatest opportunity for diversification, was extended to smaller sites at Carfin, Chapelhall and Larkhall. Yet the success of such ventures, which was certainly welcome, was more limited than it might seem at first sight. In isolation it was noteworthy, but much less so when contrasted with the immensity of the problem in the west of Scotland at that time, or, more to the point, with the surplus of male workers with which it was supposed to deal. Thus in 1939, while the industrial estate at Hillington accommodated 75 firms employing about 1,500 workers, it gave employment to only about 3 per cent of the estimated surplus of labour. Moreover, the employment in the new firms was frequently for females, while the surplus labour was chiefly of males. For these reasons the contribution of the new industries towards solving the basic industrial problem of Scotland was more apparent than real, but the reality behind the achievements was the demonstration it provided that light industries could succeed in the west of Scotland in the way many had already succeeded in the east. Remoteness from the main markets in the south, while it always militated against the large-scale expansion of the production of consumers' goods in Scotland, unless the country could offer other compensating advantages, was shown not to place an absolute barrier on that form of industrial growth. But new industrial growth itself required innovation in the heavy industries, not such as would ensure their traditional international competitiveness, but innovation which would also enable them to supply the raw materials required by the consumers' durables industries. That was a problem which had to wait for attempted solutions until after 1945, so that, as with British industry generally, Scottish industry remained beset with many and great difficulties in 1939. The basic dilemma, about which direction industrial development should take, was as unsolved in the 1930's as in the 1920's, but in the later decade more people were aware that such a dilemma existed, even if not of its solution.

XIV
AGRICULTURE, 1870's to 1939

1870 to 1914

In many ways Scottish agriculture changed less dramatically between the 1870's and 1939 than between the 1780's and the 1870's. Remnants of the old order in agriculture were still visible in most parts of the country at the beginning of the earlier period. By the 1870's these had gone and, with the removal of protection, Scottish agriculture had developed various specializations, which continued to provide the basis of its activities until 1939. Scottish agricultural history from the 1870's until the Second World War is, therefore, more one of adaptation of a given pattern to changing international circumstances than of internal revolution and renovation.

The changing environment became evident in the later 1870's. Many current problems could be attributed to the severity of the weather, which reached its climax in the winter of 1878 to 1879, but one significant feature indicated that the problems were not confined to the short-run influence of the vagaries of Scottish weather. The reduced output of some crops—the yield on wheat was down by about 20 per cent—failed to lead to any significant increase in price. The explanation, though simple, had far-reaching repercussions. Imports of foreign produce were beginning to make a major contribution to the British food supply, and in years such as 1879, when American crops were good and British ones were poor, the British farmer could no longer rely on high prices compensating for low yields. The opening of new lands, especially the grain-producing regions of America and Russia, combined with the cheapening in transport costs which the railways and improvements in shipping facilities brought, became the crucial factor determining the prosperity of agriculture from the 1870's and of the policies adopted to combat its decline. In the late nineteenth century, therefore, the determinants of the fortunes of Scottish agriculture became increasingly influenced by what was happening overseas. Scottish agriculture was thus brought to a position similar to that occupied by Scottish industry for a century earlier, but with the difference that the international connections of Scottish industry were

formed through its success in penetrating foreign markets, those of
Scottish agriculture were formed through its inability to prevent
foreign produce entering its markets at home. Comparative international costs of production were in industry's favour, but were against
agriculture. Wherever Scotland retained some measure of international
agricultural leadership from the 1870's, it was only by dint of great
enterprise and ability on the part of the country's farmers.

The incidence of foreign competition did not fall evenly on all
branches of agriculture and from this uneven impact Scotland gained.
The worst effects were felt by wheat producers. In the two decades
from the mid-1870's to the mid-1890's wheat imports to Britain almost
doubled to reach nearly 100,000,000 cwt.; barley imports more than
doubled to 26,000,000 cwt., the increase being concentrated in the
decade from the mid-1880's. But the relative proportions of home to
foreign produce consumed in Britain were more important in determining the prosperity of the home farmer than the absolute level of
imports. The proportion of consumption of wheat met by foreign
supplies rose from about 50 per cent in the mid-1870's to about 75
per cent by the mid-1890's; of barley, from 20 per cent to 45 per cent;
of oats, a constant proportion of about 20 per cent. This was the
differential impact from which Scottish agriculture gained. Except in
the Lothians and parts of the centre and east, Scottish agriculture was
not primarily arable and even among the typical Scottish cash crops—
wheat, barley, oats, potatoes—wheat was least important. Scotland
had no areas so wedded to wheat as were the clay soils of East Anglia
and the Midlands. Even in those districts in the east where wheat
was most commonly grown, its cultivation was always combined with
barley, oats and potatoes, and on many farms it was virtually a joint
product with potatoes, being sown after the potatoes had been lifted
and its straw being used to cover potato pits. Consequently, even on
the arable farms of east Scotland the price of wheat was not the sole
consideration in decisions on whether to cultivate the grain, as it was
in parts of England; the profitability of other crops, of barley, oats
and potatoes, crops which did not suffer so adversely from competition,
was equally relevant. All, of course, suffered some falls in price until
the 1890's, but, while that of wheat fell by about 50 per cent during
these years, those of barley, oats and potatoes fell by only about one-
third and the fall, such as it was, was concentrated in the period after
the early 1880's.

Though the price fall had less drastic effects on arable farming in

Scotland than it had in England, it still provided a similar, though less pronounced, incentive to move away from the less profitable crops. Thus between 1880 and 1914 the acreage under wheat in England and Wales fell by about one-third to just over 1,800,000 acres, but in Scotland it fell during the same period by only about one-fifth to just over 60,000 acres. The Scots had already made their major move away from the production of this crop in earlier years. The fall in the acreage under barley was similar in the two countries. In England it fell by about one-third to just over 1,500,000 acres, in Scotland by about two-sevenths to 194,000 acres. The performance in the production of oats differed significantly once again. The acreage under oats in England and Wales in 1914, almost 1,930,000, was 10 per cent greater than what it had been in 1880; in Scotland during the same period the acreage fell by almost 10 per cent to about 920,000, the level of the mid-1850's. The proportionately greater acreage under oats reflected the traditionally greater emphasis always given to the crop in Scotland, while the increase in the English oats acreage was partly the result of the movement away from the cultivation of wheat to that of other cereal crops, such as oats, which had not become relatively so unprofitable. Though there was a movement from the production of the less profitable cereal crops on the marginal lands in Scotland, such as the less fertile upper reaches of the valleys of the Tay, Dee and Don, into which the improvements earlier in the century had caused cultivation to extend, there was never the same need to surrender the cultivation of wheat, and so never the same pressure to increase the acreage under oats. In both countries the overall effect of the changes in arable cultivation was for a smaller acreage to be cultivated and for more pasture to be laid down to permanent grass. English permanent pasture was nearly 16,116,000 acres in 1914, almost 3,000,000 more than in 1880; in Scotland in 1914 permanent pasture of nearly 1,500,000 acres was 330,000 acres more than in 1880. Though proportionately the alteration is similar, it hides a significant difference. Arable acreage was maintained in England only through the reduction in the cultivation of wheat being partly offset by an increase in that of oats, but in Scotland there was not the same need for a compensating movement. In short the increase in permanent pasture in England would have been greater but for the increased cultivation of a less attractive cereal.

The choice of arable crops in Scotland reflected the continuing importance of livestock husbandry in the country's agriculture, a specialization which proved beneficial in the later nineteenth century in two ways. First, livestock production suffered much less than arable cultivation from foreign competition, and in the one respect in which it did so suffer, Scottish farmers were not affected. Since sheep-grazing was an essential feature of the rotations of many English wheat-growing farms, the decline in the acreage under wheat was accompanied by a decline in their number of sheep, with, in turn, a decline in the acreage of turnips grown to feed the sheep. Because wheat cultivation was never important in Scotland, this connection was never operative there. But foreign competition affected Scottish livestock husbandry in other ways. New methods of preservation, especially the introduction of refrigeration, almost doubled meat imports in the two decades to the 1890's. Dairy farmers also suffered, sometimes directly from competition from the new lands, as from imports of American cheese, more commonly they suffered indirectly, through the exploitation of the grain-producing regions of the new world forcing some European countries, notably Denmark, to specialize in dairy and poultry products, for which the unprotected British market provided a ready demand. Second, a more positive beneficial influence on livestock husbandry came from the changing dietary habits of the British people, as a rising standard of living brought some commodities within the purchasing power of a greater number of people. Wheat consumption dropped slightly from the 1870's. The consumption of potatoes, traditionally a diet associated with a lower standard of living, and therefore popular much longer in the Highlands, as in Ireland, fell more drastically. In Scotland gross production per head of the population was 5·8 cwt. in 1867; in 1939 it was 4·1 cwt. Since a large, almost certainly increasing, proportion of the crop left Scotland as seed, the decline in consumption was even greater. In place of bread and potatoes the British public wanted more meat and dairy products. They also wanted more fruit and green vegetables, but generally over the entire country, and more particularly in Scotland, with its different dietary habits, the preference was for meat and dairy products.

The relative opportunities thus offered by livestock husbandry and by arable cultivation were reflected in the actions of Scottish farmers. Consequently agricultural progress was more apparent in such areas as the dairying south-west or the cattle-rearing north-east, and from these areas farmers moved to succeed, even sometimes as arable farmers, in the areas whence those, used to easier market conditions, had fled. Aberdeenshire breeders moved to the arable areas along the Moray Firth or further south to the Mearns; Ayrshire dairy farmers moved into the Lothians. The migration spread to England, especially in the late nineteenth century when a large number of Ayrshire dairy farmers moved to the Essex clays, on which arable cultivation had been surrendered, but which they transformed into successful dairy farms by exploiting the adjacent urban market and using imported feedingstuffs.

Both north-east and south-west Scotland had enjoyed several favourable factors, which enabled them to confirm their earlier successes based on the Aberdeen-Angus and the Ayrshire breeds. In both the dominance of family farms reduced monetary labour costs to a minimum, though the real costs, always impossible to estimate, were high. Unavoidable cash expenditure was thus kept low, an essential for success in a period of falling prices. Again, the farmers of both districts adapted their activities to the new international economic situation by specializing in quality, rather than cheap, products. As the transactions of the Highland and Agricultural Society testify, farmers in the north-east made many improvements in the Aberdeen-Angus and beef Shorthorn breeds. The best breeding and feeding principles were generally determined by empirical methods, but they were backed by successful arable cultivation, in seed selection and manuring, to ensure an adequate supply of winter fodder, especially of turnips. The result was the production at this time of the highest grade pedigree animals, though in general the north-east breeders were more dependent on producing good commercial animals. In the south-west a permanent dairy school, which eventually became the Dairy School for Scotland, was founded at Kilmarnock in 1889 in an attempt to improve the quality of the produce. At the same time the south-west pioneered better dairy practice by introducing milk recording, by trying to eliminate bovine tuberculosis, and by devising the first satisfactory milking machines. Finally, in both areas success in livestock production depended on the state of grassland husbandry. As permanent pasture increased, many farmers, on both sides of the border, found that an ordinary seeds mixture used in some rotation was inadequate to maintain satisfactory grass for long. The problem was more pressing in England, where the seed was often of short-lived plants suitable for a hay crop for one year, than in Scotland, where the ordinary mixture ensured a reasonable quantity of grasses and clover for two or three years. The result was increased attention to the choice of grass seed and to its cultivation, towards which Scots—and Scots in England—made an important contribution. But the most important discovery of these years, though it yielded its full benefits only between the wars, was the use of wild white clover. It grew better later in the season after being sown for some years, and kept the land cleaner in a way which facilitated the cultivation of subsequent crops in the rotation. Just before 1914 James Cruickshank of Aberdeenshire, who also built the first tower silo in Scotland, became the first Scottish farmer to use it on a large scale.

Better grassland husbandry is strictly an improvement in arable cultivation, though one aimed at supporting livestock. In those branches of arable farming which had no such connection, improvements were less striking and were partly offset by failures. The greatest success was in the cultivation of the potato, the price of which did not fall in the same way as those of most other arable products. The maximum acreage under potatoes in Scotland, 189,161, was reached in 1881. Though it had fallen to 152,318 acres by 1914, the Scottish seed potato trade expanded throughout the world during that period. Scottish seed was acceptable primarily because of its relative freedom from disease, one of the few benefits of the Scottish climate to Scottish farmers, because greenfly, which carry many of the worst diseases to the potato, do not exist so easily in the cooler and windier conditions of Scotland. Even before the 1870's English growers used Scottish seed potatoes and thus throughout most of the nineteenth century Scottish growers held a monopoly of the seed potato trade in Britain. In the 1890's the trade took a notable step forward, when, especially with the introduction of the Up-to-date variety, it began to sell seed potatoes overseas, notably in South Africa. While the seed potato crop was mainly exported, the ware crop was largely consumed in Scotland. The fortunes of the two varied. The seed trade gained from the increased demand which followed the entry into overseas markets; the ware trade supplied a market in which consumption per head was declining in the half-century before 1914. Only the south-west maintained a profitable share in the ware trade by specializing in the production of early potatoes on the Ayrshire and Wigtownshire coasts. 'Boxing', or sprouting of the seed, encouraged the growth of the early potatoes in Ayrshire from the early 1880's, while the Epicure, first marketed in 1897, proved the most successful variety and provided the basis for an export trade in early potatoes, especially to the north of England.

The success of the cultivation of the potato was offset by failures in arable farming in two other directions. First, the period was not one of marked improvements in machinery, in particular in labour-saving devices. There were no innovations comparable to the first development of the milking machine and of cream separators in dairying. It is perhaps significant that in arable farming the most striking improvements were in potato harvesting. The rotary spinner lifter, patented in 1855, was tested, rather unsuccessfully, by the Highland and Agricultural Society in the 1870's and subsequently adapted satisfactorily, but even in potato lifting the adequacy of the labour supply, especially of seasonal labour from Ireland, delayed the development of a more efficient machine until the elevator digger was adopted in the 1920's. In other arable operations the basic form of the implements used remained unaltered, or were simply continuations of those of earlier periods, as in the extension of the use of the reaper, which led to the only noticeable decline in the labour force in grain harvesting. Second, and more important, the yield on grain crops failed to show any marked improvement during the period, even though it was one when land less suited to grain crops went out of cultivation. Yields of most crops seem to have risen in the twenty years before the 1880's, then until 1910 those of hay, oats and barley remained stable, while those of turnips and wheat rose slightly. Some care must be exercised in interpreting these figures. Yields may have failed to increase because many Scottish farmers survived the depression of the 1880's and 1890's less by forcing production to a very high level than by reducing costs. For instance, improved knowledge of manurial practice in turnip husbandry led more to an efficient use of fertilizers to reduce costs than to attempts to increase yields. On the other hand, in potato growing, where the same pressure to reduce costs did not operate, yields did rise, especially after the introduction of the Up-to-date variety in the 1890's.

One notable feature common to the improvements in all branches of agriculture was that they were frequently the work of tenant farmers, or of owner-occupiers, among whom the outstanding leader was probably John Spier of Newton, near Cambuslang. Many of the causes he advocated—notably milk recording—were later accorded international recognition. Such improvers of the late nineteenth century, many of whom have frequently been neglected, came from a different class of society than did the majority of those of the late eighteenth century. In the fifty years before 1914 landlords as a group did not show the interest and ability in agricultural matters which their ancestors had shown in the fifty years before 1815, but they did provide an essential aid to all those who could exploit agricultural opportunities by providing a system of landholding which facilitated the movement of tenant farmers. Its merits would have been reduced if the landlords had been completely inflexible in the rent they charged, but they were not. Though the movement of rents downwards was always slower than the movement upwards, reductions did take place during the depression. More important, throughout Scotland the long-lease, of nineteen years or thereabouts, encouraged tenant farmers to undertake improvements. Though friction emerged over compensation for unexhausted improvements at the end of a lease, it did not arise in its early years, and, in any case, contrasted favourably with the position in England, where tenancies, which could be terminated on six months' notice, gave rise to much greater disputes. It is also significant that two sources of potential dispute between landlord and tenant were removed by statutory provision in the later nineteenth century. First, the possibility of disputes over compensation for improvements increased with the use of newer fertilizers with such long-run effects that, even under a nineteen-years' lease, there were manurial residues; but they were largely avoided by a series of Acts from 1875 to 1906. Second, potentially greater tension could arise from the Game Laws, especially since the assimilation of Scottish and English practice earlier in the century had led to more stringent interpretations in Scotland. That problem too was solved, at least in part, by the Ground Game Acts of 1880, which allowed those who were tenants for periods of more than one year to kill hares and rabbits on their ground. In short, the relationship between landlord and tenant was not such as would inhibit many improvements.

Tenant farmers, or even owner-occupiers, were, however, limited in their improvements through their lack of any of the formal scientific training which was becoming increasingly necessary. Success attended those who, like John Spier of Newton, though without such training, still adopted the rudiments of scientific method in their investigations. So often the work of such empiricists only exploded long-accepted theories but did not provide satisfactory alternatives, a negative approach which did not commend itself to contemporaries, especially when, as was inevitable with pioneers, the advice given to other farmers was not always correct. More formal agricultural education, its extension and dissemination, were necessary. That need was supplemented by another. Scottish farmers could not easily adopt many more advanced agricultural techniques, and more modern implements, because of the small scale of their operations, and for the same reason they could not easily obtain commercial advantages in buying and selling. In this case the remedy suggested was co-operation.

The tradition of agricultural education in Scotland was of long standing. The chair of agriculture was founded in the University of Edinburgh in 1790. The University of Aberdeen planned to have one from the same year, though the intention took effect only in 1840 in the creation of a lectureship. But throughout most of the nineteenth century agricultural education lay mainly with the Highland and Agricultural Society. In 1816 after its attempts to establish veterinary education in the University of Edinburgh were rejected, the Society encouraged William Dick to begin the lectures from which the Edinburgh veterinary school emerged. In research the Society was equally active. In 1848 it appointed a chemist who, with his successors, helped to adapt many experiments to local conditions and in 1858 it instituted examinations for diplomas in dairying and agriculture. On the other hand the Society, though pressed to do so from the days of Sir John Sinclair, was reluctant to establish an experimental farm, but eventually started experimental stations at Pumpherston and Harelaw. On this educational foundation private and public effort built in the later nineteenth century.

The private effort was based on the three traditional centres of higher education at Edinburgh, Glasgow and Aberdeen. Edinburgh instituted a degree in agricultural science which, though it was of little direct relevance to the average Scottish farmer, produced some of the country's leading agricultural scientists. Aberdeen started a full degree course in agriculture in 1895. Glasgow remained backward until in the late 1880's the Technical College assumed responsibility for teaching agriculture. Then in 1899 Glasgow assumed a lead, when, mainly through the efforts of some local directors of the Highland and Agricultural Society, an agricultural college was established there, while experimental work was carried on at the old dairy school at Kilmarnock. Following this example, the East of Scotland Agricultural College was founded in 1901 and the North of Scotland Agricultural College in 1904. All three colleges awarded diplomas and prepared students for the National Diplomas in Dairying and Agriculture, which had been instituted in 1897 and 1900 respectively. The agricultural colleges thus provided a more popular form of agricultural education aimed at the ordinary farmer, education of a type which the universities could not provide. The public efforts for agricultural education began at the end of the century, when local authorities were given grants-in-aid for the provision of technical instruction. The south-west led. Full-time instructors were appointed in Kirkcudbright and Lanark; the dairy school at Kilmarnock received help; the staff of the Glasgow Technical College gave occasional instruction in the area. Such help from public sources remained limited until 1912, when the effectiveness of official interest in Scottish agriculture was increased by the severance of a Scottish Board of Agriculture from the Board of Agriculture which had been founded, for a second time, in 1889.

Co-operation in Scottish agriculture was less successful. It first appeared in the depression of the 1880's, when the Farmers' Supply Association was formed at Leith in 1884. From 1905 the Scottish Agricultural Organization Society encouraged co-operative endeavour, but the movement made slow progress, though by 1910 about fifty societies were in operation. In spite of the closure of a few societies, the movement in Scotland avoided any major catastrophes, its contribution being limited more by the individualism of Scottish farmers. The value of co-operation was outweighed by that of education. Scientific farming rather than new commercial methods brought benefits to Scottish farmers.

1914 to 1939

The First World War provided a temporary interruption to the foreign competition which had determined so much of the history of Scottish agriculture in the later nineteenth century. Its full beneficial effects were not apparent immediately, because until the beginning of 1917 agriculture was not given the high priority it received later. It was, therefore, frequently disorganized, through the inadequacy of labour, fertilizers, implements, and horses, many of the last being commandeered. In 1916 a poor harvest led to low productivity and the acreage under oats in Scotland gave a lower total yield than the smaller acreage of 1914, while the yield of potatoes, then a vitally important food, was just over half a million tons, only about half that of 1914. The announcement that the new administration under Lloyd George intended to guarantee minimum prices for wheat and oats, in an effort to encourage the cultivation of some permanent grassland, was clearly relevant to such a situation. In Scotland the acreage under grain crops was 1,174,000 in 1914; in 1916 it was 1,235,000; in 1918 it was 1,494,000. The acreage under potatoes rose as well, but, reflecting the increased emphasis on the production of food for human consumption, that under turnips declined. The transformation was more easily effected in Scotland than in England. Since no areas in Scotland were so pre-eminently suitable for a particular agricultural operation, as were some of the finest permanent pastures in England, Scottish agriculture always moved more easily between different enterprises. In contrast to conditions in some areas in England, there was no opposition to breaking up permanent pasture in Scotland. Indeed much of the grassland ploughed up in Scotland was only temporary grass, which would in due course have been brought into cultivation in any case, though perhaps not quite so soon. If the process had been continued for long, more drastic adverse repercussions on agricultural practice might have followed, but not in the short run. In England the problem could not be dismissed so lightly.

It was expected that government action would not return to the few tentative efforts at assistance which had been made just before 1914, but remain as active, if not as directive, as during the war. The expectation was given substance by the Agricultural Act of 1920, which seemed to provide a more substantial basis for prosperity than the price rise of 1919 and 1920. The central feature of the Act was its guarantee of the prices of wheat and oats, but its most permanent legacy came from the provision which gave tenants greater security of tenure. The latter marked the beginning of the end of a system of land tenure, which, in spite of its defects, had served Scottish agriculture well in the past.

The expectation that government action would transform the agricultural situation proved to be unfounded. Agricultural prosperity ended suddenly in 1921 and 1922. The price of wool fell first, to be followed quickly by those of wheat and oats, until by 1922 all were at least half, and often less, of what they had been only a short time before. Though livestock prices remained higher, the fall in the price of wool led to a fall in that of sheep. The explanation of the price fall was basically the same as that which had created a similar situation in the 1880's and 1890's: foreign produce again entered the still-unprotected British market in large quantities, exactly the situation from which the farming community, with memories of the earlier decades, expected to be protected by the price guarantees of the Agricultural Act of 1920. The government thought differently, and conceived the Act chiefly as a measure to maintain a high level of grain production rather than as a means of compensating for the effects of a policy of free trade. When the cost of implementing the price guarantees would have amounted to about £20,000,000, the strategic benefits the Act offered no longer seemed worthy of such expenditure, and it was repealed in 1921.

With the removal of the one factor which it was hoped would assure greater prosperity, agriculture returned to the position it had occupied before 1914, except for the retention of the provision of the Act of 1920 which guaranteed greater security of tenure. Once again it was at the mercy of world food prices, and, even more than before 1914, their trends, rather than internal developments, determined the farmers' prosperity. Prices tended to fall until 1923, then steadied until 1929, when there was an even more severe drop. The explanation was simple. After the fall in price in the early years of the 1920's the world stocks of wheat remained around 635 million bushels throughout most of the decade; in 1931 they were 900 million bushels; in 1934 they were 1,140 million bushels. Imports kept British prices in alignment with those elsewhere. In 1931 wheat prices in Britain were only 75 per cent of what they had been before 1914; those of all cereals were down by similar proportions, though the fall in barley was less steep than that of either wheat or oats; the price of store sheep fell by 40 per cent between 1930 and 1931; when there was a very good crop of potatoes, as in 1929 and 1931, they could not all be sold or fed to stock and so often rotted in their pits.

Against such an international background Scottish farmers had to mould their policies. Essentially it did not differ from the international situation which they had met with some success between the 1870's and 1914, except that their short experience of government aid during and immediately after the First World War led many farmers to continue to hope for economic salvation through the reappearance of such action. Since the hope was realized, at least in part, only in the 1930's, the history of agriculture during the inter-war years falls easily into two phases.

During the first period, the ten years following the Corn Production (Repeal) Act of 1921, examples of official aid were sporadic and contributed little towards solving the overriding problem of meeting the continuing danger of more foreign imports. First, afforestation was encouraged in 1919 by the formation of the Forestry Commission, the relationships of which with Scottish farmers were not always amicable, primarily through disputes over the acquisition of land for afforestation. Part of the difficulty arose through differences in the jurisdictions

of the Commission and the Department of Agriculture, but, even
when the Commission's powers of acquiring land were transferred to
the Secretary of State in 1945, the disputes did not end. Second, the
policy of smallholding, also started in 1919, was encouraged still further,
but by the 1930's it had changed from one of setting up small, but
economically viable, farms to one of trying to provide plots to help
the unemployed. Third, four statutes of the 1920's represented the
most important direct governmental contribution to agriculture. Two
of the measures were financial, two were strictly technical or agricultural. For Scotland the former were more important. They were the
Agricultural Rates Act of 1923 which granted some rating relief, but
which was made more influential by the complete derating of agricultural land and buildings in 1926 and 1929 and the Agricultural Credits
(Scotland) Acts of 1925 and 1929, which granted credit to the growing
number of farmers who were purchasing their own farms, as landlords
were forced to dispose of them. The more strictly agricultural assistance came from annual grants on the basis of a percentage of cost for
drainage schemes and from encouragement to the sugar-beet industry
in the British Sugar Subsidy Act of 1925. Of these two schemes the
former was more relevant to Scottish conditions. Though the drainage
schemes were conceived to relieve unemployment as well as to help
agriculture, and though they frequently helped only to patch old
drainage systems rather than create new ones, they gave valuable help
to an agricultural operation, so necessary in many parts of Scotland,
because of the country's climate and soil, and yet one which yields
its returns only over so long a period that it is often neglected in times
of depression. On the other hand the production of sugar beet made
little progress in Scotland, except in Fife. The soil was often too acid,
while the climate prevented the early sowing necessary for a long
period of growth and gave inadequate sun for harvesting. Until the
compulsory growth of sugar beet on many farms during the Second
World War taught some farmers the best techniques for its cultivation,
potatoes were generally considered a more rewarding crop.

The basic defect common to those various measures was that they
failed to deal with the crucial issue of the supplies of foreign produce.
They neither tried to restrict them in some way by accepting a form
of protection, nor, with the exception of the drainage grants, did they
try to make farmers more efficient, and so more able to meet their
foreign competitors. After the Corn Production (Repeal) Act, 1921,
farmers were left to meet their difficulties, as before 1914, on their own

resources and initiative. But one difference from the pre-war situation
was that the landlords were less able to help them to do so. The landlords were the only group in agriculture that lost by the war. Apart
from the heavy incidence of taxation, Scotland's long leases ensured
that landlords were less able to raise rents to match rising expenditure
on lands and buildings. Therefore, in the 1920's, in contrast to the
depression of the 1880's and 1890's, many tenants could not hope to
maintain declining profits through remissions of rents. In any case in
most tenancies started before the years of war-time boom, rents were so
low that landlords were only too anxious to sell when the opportunity
arose. Since before 1914 Scottish tenant farmers had received greater
benefits from the system of land-tenure than had their counterparts in
England, their loss after the First World War was accordingly all the
greater. But the heaviest burden of all was borne by those who had
taken the opportunity offered by the landlords' increased willingness to
sell farms. Many owner-occupiers had to carry a heavy fixed debt
charge, which had to be met in spite of falling prices. This group was
most susceptible to bankruptcy.

Since in the 1920's the farmers' problems were similar to those of
the years before 1914, it is not surprising that their reactions were likewise. The acreage under grain, which had been increased especially
during the last two years of the war, was reduced to make way for
more grass, temporary and permanent, which rose between 1918 and
1932 by 160,000 and 260,000 acres respectively, and by the trough of
the depression of the early 1930's the acreage under most root and
grain crops in Scotland was lower than it had been even in 1914. In
some cases the reduction was drastic. In 1914 194,000 acres were under
barley, but only 67,000 in 1932, and only 60,000 in 1933. As before the
war, the move from arable cultivation to grassland was most pronounced in the traditional arable districts of the east coast. Between the
wars the arable acreage of East Lothian was reduced by 10,000 acres,
3,000 were turned to temporary and 7,000 to permanent grass. But
comparison between the two periods is not wholly exact, because between the wars livestock husbandry did not remain as profitable relative to arable cultivation as it had done in the later nineteenth century.
After 1918 the price fall, which was first felt by the wool-growers,
soon spread to all products, both livestock and arable. The sharp rise in
imports of dairy products from 1919 was as marked as the rise in
imports of grain. Moreover, as some of the grain producers put land
down to grass, they frequently specialized more in livestock husbandry

U

and dairying, providing yet more competition for the traditional producers in these fields.

In such circumstances the need to devise more efficient methods of
breeding and using livestock were as necessary as before 1914. Such
improvements as appeared in arable cultivation were concentrated,
therefore, on producing better fodder, especially in the management
of grasslands, rather than in producing cash crops. In the 1920's two
notable advances were made in the increasing use of wild white clover
in grasslands and in more scientific poultry husbandry. Neither were
new, but their potentialities were only then fully exploited. The increasing use of wild white clover so improved rotation pastures that,
when income from arable cropping failed, the drop could be offset, at
least in part, by keeping more livestock. Its adoption was not, however,
without some disadvantages. In the short run it increased the incidence
of intestinal worms in sheep; in the long run its success may have prevented many Scottish farmers from incurring the additional expense
necessary for some of the more satisfactory changes in grassland
management which were developed between the wars. The improvement in poultry husbandry was in an altogether different category. In
spite of the measure of natural protection from foreign competition
given by the perishability of eggs, poultry farming as such hardly
existed in Scotland before 1914. Few ordinary farmers regarded it as a
serious agricultural enterprise, while the main commercial concern of
specialist breeders was to produce table, not laying, birds. Scientific
poultry farming in Scotland began only in 1906, when a poultry school
was established beside the Scottish Dairy School by the West of Scotland College of Agriculture, but it spread quickly after the war, when
the low prices for grain led many farmers to feed it to poultry instead
of selling it. Thereafter, in the 1920's and 1930's, new methods of
poultry husbandry were introduced, culminating in the 1930's in the
introduction of the battery system, an attempt to ensure the maximum
returns from each bird by eliminating the least productive.

More, and better, grassland and scientific poultry farming were only
palliatives for the main problem of meeting foreign competition. However, government action, the one factor which, until 1921, the farmers
had hoped would provide for their actions an environment different
from that of the pre-war years, increased in the 1930's, and became the
main determinent of the second phase of the history of agriculture
between the wars. The experience of agriculture was similar to that
of industry, when the rejection of free trade enabled Britain to follow

a more independent economic policy, but, as in industry, so in agriculture, the policies adopted with the new opportunities were restrictionist rather than expansionist. A general tariff was impracticable, because all agricultural products did not suffer from foreign competition, and government action assumed mainly two forms, first, the Agricultural Marketing Acts of 1931 and 1933, and, second, a variety of measures aimed at granting specific aid to enterprises in particular adversity.

Generally the marketing acts aimed at satisfying the desire, commonly accepted at the time, that marketing should be orderly. The only Board set up under the first Act was one for hops and it was, therefore, of no account in Scotland, but those which came under the second Act, for potatoes, pigs and bacon, and milk, were. Of these boards the most important for Scottish agriculture was that for milk. Under the Act of 1933 two regional boards, the Aberdeen and District Milk Marketing Board and the North of Scotland Milk Marketing Board, were formed, as well as the main Scottish Milk Marketing Board. They were not the first agencies of their kind in Scotland. In the 1920's the Scottish Agricultural Organization Society and the Scottish National Farmers' Union had tried to organize similar marketing schemes, but, since they could not retain the allegiance of all producers, the schemes collapsed. For their success the compulsion of the marketing acts was clearly necessary, but the operations of the Boards did not go unchallenged by producer-retailers, who in the House of Lords successfully challenged the Boards' right to impose levies on every gallon sold by them. The organization of the Boards, and the effect of their pricing policies on the consumers, were frequently criticized, and the Boards' policies sometimes had quite unexpected repercussions. For example, since a chief aim was to maintain the price of liquid milk, the Scottish Board so flooded the English market with milk that it was given compensation of about £100,000 annually to desist from doing so, but, as more Scottish cream was then sent south, and the Aberdeen Board started dumping its surplus milk in the London market, it is doubtful how effective the measure was for English dairy farmers.

The second form of government help, the miscellaneous provisions, assumed various forms. The Wheat Act of 1932 guaranteed wheat prices by placing an excise duty on flour, which was made mainly from imported wheat, but it was of slight help to the majority of Scottish farmers, who grew little or no wheat. In 1937, partly under pressure from the Scottish National Farmers' Union, the subsidy was extended to oats and barley, though since oats, unlike wheat, was not generally a cash crop, an acreage payment was substituted for a payment on the price deficiency. In 1932 imports of meat were restricted, but proposals to form a Meat Marketing Board were not followed, while subsidies for beef, granted temporarily in 1934, were made permanent in 1937. Also in 1937 the Agriculture Act of that year provided for subsidies on fertilizers and for price guarantees for barley and oats.

These various measures represented a sufficient change in government action to give special character to the 1930's, but they provided only an extraordinary patchwork of assistance, fundamentally defective in that it aimed mainly at preserving the existing structure of agriculture and not at the development of one more in keeping with the modern pattern of international trade in agricultural products. Moreover, some of the measures, such as the guaranteed price on wheat, were more applicable to English than to Scottish conditions. Similarly the Land Fertility Scheme was less effective in Scotland, partly because of the two activities it was supposed to encourage; one, ley farming, had been commonly practised for years, while the other, the reseeding of permanent pastures, was too expensive, even with the subsidy, to be an economic proposition in Scotland. Consequently, because of the particular specializations of Scottish agriculture, the Milk Marketing Board held the greatest prospects for Scottish agriculture, but its actions were insufficiently revolutionary or imaginative to have any great expansionary influence.

In the field of agricultural education and research, action was wholly commendable. The major advances before 1914 had been in the provision of formal instruction in the universities and agricultural colleges; after 1918 the expansion was principally in the number of research stations. Three were of major importance—the Rowett, concerned with nutrition, at Bucksburn; the Macaulay, for Soil Research, at Aberdeen; and the Hannah Dairy Research Institute at Ayr. Though founded earlier, all made their main contribution in the 1930's. Other organizations with similar aims were the Animal Diseases Research Association, the Scottish Society for Research in Plant Breeding and the Edinburgh Centre of Rural Economy. Through these institutes, and through the Agricultural Colleges' Advisory Officers, a system of advice on the latest scientific knowledge, as it could be applied in his own area, was made available to every individual farmer and provided a more permanent basis for the future of agriculture than the marketing schemes, which frequently aimed at the preservation of a given situation, even when it could no longer be retained in the changed international trade in agricultural products in the twentieth century.

The Highlands

Though a major economic assimilation of Highlands and Lowlands came in the forty years before 1914, a solution to the inadequacy of the natural resources of the Highlands was still not found. The Highland problem remained the struggle for an adequate cash income to pay for necessary purchases, both by individuals and by the region, since for most people the natural resources were so inadequate that agriculture could not provide an adequate subsistence income.

From the 1870's to 1914 agricultural change in the Highlands was broadly similar to that elsewhere. Land was converted from arable cultivation to pasture except in areas, such as Lewis, where population pressure was intense. But in the Highlands the switch had wider repercussions than in other parts of the country, because, while the south-west and the north-east were able to exploit the opportunities offered by livestock husbandry, the Highlands were not. The cattle trade, once such an important source of revenue for the area, retained only local customers, and sheep-farming, introduced especially in the century before the 1870's, was no longer so profitable. The decline of the cattle trade had appeared before the 1870's, as the adoption of better and more modern methods elsewhere gave other areas a lead over the Highlands; the loss of the sheep trade was the change which came after the 1870's, especially after the 1890's. The decline in sheep-farming began with the fall in agricultural prices, but several explanations lay behind it. The pastures were able to support fewer sheep than previously. About 1880, for instance, it was estimated that in some areas, such as Sutherland, the grazings were adequate for only about two-thirds of what they had supported forty years earlier, because the grass on the old arable land had become fogged, or choked with weeds, while restrictions placed on heather-burning and the absence of cattle-grazing caused further deterioration. The sheep, too, contributed to the inadequacy of the pastures by spending the nights on the higher and drier pastures, and so removing some of the manure which the lower grazings urgently required. Though a partial remedy for the inadequacy of the sheep-grazings was found in wintering some of the animals on the fertile east coast, the practice was more expensive. Because of the decline in natural advantages, sheep-farming was already in a precarious position, when a further sharp fall in sheep prices after 1890 precipitated a crisis in some areas. Deer-forests then displaced sheep-farming, as the latter had displaced other enterprises, Sheep and deer could not exist together easily, and when sheep-farming became less profitable, many landlords were willing to clear the land to make way for sporting rights, as they commanded a higher return from those to whom the delights of the Highlands had just been revealed by Queen Victoria. Between the early 1880's and 1914 the area of deer-forests rose from 2,000,000 to almost 3,000,000 acres, while the sheep in the Highland counties declined correspondingly, making the maintenance of the sheep total in Scotland during that period the more notable.

On one important aspect of the Highland problem this switch had little effect, as it touched the crofting population only marginally. The Highlanders were more affected by the greater assimilation of Highlands and Lowlands brought about in the late nineteenth and early twentieth centuries by better transport and education. Of this there were numerous examples: though railways did not penetrate the Highlands extensively, their influence, where they did go, was great; government assistance continued to be given to the roads as in the past; shipping was subsidized from 1891, the subsidy being converted into a payment for mails in 1897; better education came after 1872 when the Scottish Education Act placed responsibility for it on the state. The opportunities opened by such assimilation so often attracted the Highlander from his native region. Since he could be more easily assimilated elsewhere, he went there, and so population continued to fall, by about 10 per cent in the crofting counties between 1881 and 1911, and the fall was concentrated in the younger age groups, which contain the potential migrants. The number of children fell most sharply. In short, the Highlands and Islands were becoming increasingly inhabited by an ageing population, not likely to display the initiative and vitality necessary to bring the region into more modern methods and ways.

With landlords and tenants unable or unwilling to take any remedial action, initiative passed increasingly into the hands of the state at the end of the nineteenth century. The entire Highland problem was first fully investigated by a Royal Commission which reported in 1884. In spite of the various factors which for years had encouraged greater assimilation with the Lowlands, the Napier Commission found the Highlanders' position very similar to what it had been about a century earlier. In two respects his condition differed materially from that of the Lowlander. First, tenancies were insecure and, therefore, there was no incentive to improve the land, especially when there were no proper arrangements for compensation. Second, holdings were of an unsuitable size. Their restriction had been enforced by population pressure, which in certain areas was not greatly relieved by emigration, but increasing foreign competition in agricultural products made holdings of a proper size more necessary than ever. Though, like everyone else in Scotland, crofters gained by being able to purchase cheaper grains from overseas, their desire to do so heightened rather than mitigated the existing vital inadequacy of cash income in the Highlands. The Napier Commission suggested remedial action in both directions. First, they recommended leases designed to encourage improvements, for which compensation would be given whenever the lease was terminated. Second, they advocated the legal recognition, and, normally, the perpetuation of the township, as the unit of organization most suitable for encouraging and ensuring improvements. The Commission recognized that within the township it was essential to avoid any further disintegration of holdings and that every effort should be made to increase their size, and recommended, therefore, that, when smaller holdings fell vacant, they should be used for consolidation of others and that further sub-division should be prevented. Finally, one overriding qualification to all the Commission's recommendations was its suggestion that they should be applied only to the minority paying £6 a year or more in rent. Only from this group of the relatively more substantial tenants would any improvements come; the remainder of the tenantry could not be accommodated in an improved and viable economy.

To some the Napier Commission's report was a ruthless document; to others it was realistic in its acceptance of the impossibility of continuing to maintain 'the load of tenantry', with which Highland estates had for so long been burdened. Since the report was not wholly acceptable, the legislation which followed, the Crofters Holdings (Scotland) Act of 1886, failed to implement all its recommendations. Underlying all the suggestions of the Napier Commission was the belief that the Highland economy could survive as a viable unit only with certain drastic changes, but in effect the Act of 1886 rejected this assumption and virtually froze the existing structure, especially through the grant of perpetual tenancy, with the Land Court fixing rents if necessary. Unlike the recommendations of the Napier Commission, the Act of 1886 ensured preservation rather than expansion, except in its creation of the Crofters' Commission, which was given certain powers to enlarge holdings, and later the power to create new ones. Otherwise, the Act accepted the assumption that legislation should protect the position of the individual crofter rather than provide the environment in which more efficient and effective crofting could become possible.

In these circumstances it is not surprising that the problem was not solved and another Royal Commission was appointed in 1892, to be followed in 1897 by legislation in the Congested Districts (Scotland) Act. Though the Act of 1886 granted security of tenure, it failed to provide more land for crofters, except through the very limited powers granted to the Crofters' Commission. The Act of 1897 instituted the Congested Districts Board, charged to provide more land for the enlargement of holdings and for the creation of new ones, and to develop subsidiary industries, such as fishing and weaving, which would supply the necessary cash supplements to the income, mainly in kind, and in itself inadequate, which could be obtained in crofting. Though the second Act helped to remedy some of the deficiencies of the first, the guarantee of individual tenures made an overall renovation of the economy unlikely, since such security made drastic changes, always difficult to achieve in Highland society, even more intractable. Therefore, in spite of the benefits given to crofters, along lines they themselves advocated, depopulation continued. From 1891 to 1911 the population of the crofting counties fell from 360,367 to 341,535. Tillage and livestock in most crofting parishes also fell.

The next statutory attempt to provide a remedy came in 1911 with the passage of the Small Landholders (Scotland) Act. Its most important consequence for the Highlands came later, and indirectly, through a peculiar legal decision of 1917,[1] but until 1914 most of the changes which affected the Highlands were only of minor administrative importance. The Act created the Board of Agriculture for Scotland, which in 1929 became the Department of Agriculture for Scotland, and which assumed the land settlement powers previously vested in the Crofters' Commission and the Congested Districts Board, but the Act was required less through any new attempt to deal with the Highland problem directly than through the belief that the creation of smallholdings, on the model of certain European countries, was a way

[1] See below.

of providing the intensive cultivation which could meet the agricultural depression. In the Highlands it simply encouraged the policy first evolved in 1886. The Highland problem was, therefore, as unsolved in 1914 as it had been a century earlier. Greater security of tenure had been provided, though in the eyes of some who wished to see a drastic enlargement and consolidation of holdings it was much too great, and it certainly failed to arrest emigration. The problem had to be tackled again after 1918, by which time a legal decision under the Act of 1911 had made a solution no easier. The decision was made in 1917 in the case of Rogerson *v.* Chilston. The Act of 1911 provided a new definition of the term crofter and the Courts interpreted it to mean, though the meaning was almost certainly unintentional, that crofters did not need to live on their holdings. The decision introduced a race of absentee crofters into the Highlands. Until then the various statutes and attempts to deal with the Highland problem had aimed at making more land available for the genuine crofter. After 1917 land held by an absentee crofter was not used to give the maximum production, as it was frequently sub-let to a resident crofter only for grazing, and indeed was often not cultivated at all. The decision helped to ensure the continuation of the decline in cultivation in the crofting counties, and, with the exception of sheep, in the number of livestock.

After the First World War such policies as affected the Highlands were concerned less with its peculiar problems than with encouraging land settlement generally, especially smallholding, then considered both an acceptable form of agricultural development and a suitable method of settling ex-servicemen. Under the Land Settlement (Scotland) Act, 1919, 1,344 new holdings were formed, and 1,179 were enlarged in the crofting counties in the 1920's, but in the 1930's only 234 new holdings and 238 enlargements were made. This was a minor, and largely ineffective, attempt to deal with the situation. The continuing decline in tillage and in population, both human and livestock, was a sure indication that the Highland problem was as unsolved in 1939 as it had been in 1914 or even in 1815. In some ways, however, the new statutory provisions of the close of the nineteenth century provided encouragements to Highland development, notably in the improvement of housing, which had long been a disgraceful feature of Highland society. Cattle and people all lived in squalid conditions, practically under the same roof, until security of tenure and compensation for improvements under the Act of 1886 encouraged those who could afford it to improve their own dwellings. Since many, especially among the cottars, could not, the medical officers of health of various crofting counties requested special aid to encourage housing improvements. Though some of their recommendations were elementary precepts of public health, such as that every black house with dwellers infected by various diseases, but especially with typhus, should be burned down and replaced by more sanitary dwellings, towards which the local authorities should grant loans, the Local Government Board finally decided in 1895 that there was no possibility of national funds being made available for such purposes. Eventually only legal action against crofters at the end of the century initiated some more general improvement.

XV
SOCIAL ASSIMILATION

Population

BETWEEN the later nineteenth century and the Second World War, the growth of Scottish population registered two changes from earlier experience: first, at the turn of the two centuries the rate of growth slackened; second, between the two censuses of the inter-war years, those of 1921 and 1931, total population fell.

	Total population	Increase over previous census	Percentage increase
1871	3,360,018	297,724	9·7
1881	3,735,573	375,555	11·2
1891	4,025,647	290,074	7·8
1901	4,472,103	446,456	11·1
1911	4,760,904	288,801	6·5
1921	4,882,497	121,593	2·6
1931	4,842,980	− 39,517	− 0·8
1951	5,095,969	252,989	5·2
1961	5,178,490	82,521	1·6

The overall rate of growth was composed of very different contributions from different regions. Between 1871 and 1931 the population of the counties of Ayr, Bute, Dunbarton and Renfrew increased by 85 per cent; of the three Lothians by 61 per cent; of Stirling and Clackmannan by 62 per cent; of Angus, Fife, Kinross and Perth, by 27 per cent; of Aberdeen, Banff, Kincardine, Moray and Nairn, by 12 per cent. The remaining areas of Scotland registered a decrease in population between these two dates: that of the seven crofting counties fell most sharply of all, by 21 per cent; of Dumfries, Kirkcudbright and Wigtown, by 10 per cent; and of the Border counties of Berwick, Peebles, Selkirk and Roxburgh, by 6 per cent. The increase in population in the later nineteenth century was, therefore, still concentrated in central and west Scotland. The experience of Lanarkshire was, however, most striking, especially since it maintained the increase of its population, though at a substantially diminished rate, until the Second

World War. In 1931 its population of 1,586,047 was 46,605 greater than it had been a decade earlier. In 1931 other adjacent counties, such as Ayrshire, Dunbartonshire and Renfrewshire, all of which had shared in the population rise earlier, registered decreases in population. Lanarkshire was not unique in recording an increase in population between 1921 and 1931, but among the other counties which did so— Dumfries, Midlothian, Roxburgh, Selkirk and Stirling—it was of conspicuous size only in Midlothian, where the population increased between the two censuses by 19,919 to a total of 526,296, and to a lesser extent in Dumfries. In general, therefore, the declining rate of growth of population was common to the whole of Scotland, even though its incidence varied. On the other hand, since the sharpest decreases were registered only in agricultural areas, principally the more remote, especially the Highlands, the declining rate of growth in the industrial areas did not arrest the existing trend for Scots to become urban dwellers, especially dwellers in Scotland's one very large conurbation on Clydeside. Even in the rural areas which were losing population, their small towns frequently continued to grow.

A major factor determining the altered growth of population was a change in the contribution of migration. Throughout the nineteenth century a high outward movement was always partly countered (until towards the end of the nineteenth century) by a high inward movement, especially of Irish. By the end of the nineteenth century the movement into Scotland was slackening. The 1881 census registered 219,000 Irish-born in Scotland, the largest number recorded. By 1931 the Irish had been supplanted by the English as the most important immigrants. At the census of that year 3·4 per cent of the population of Scotland had been born in England, while only 2·6 per cent had been born in Ireland. The Irish had helped to ensure a high natural growth even when there was a net movement of migrants outwards. The 1880's, with a net loss by migration during the decade of 217,000 or 43 per cent of the natural increase for the period, indicated that the possibility of making up the outward movement might not continue to be so easy as in the past, and, though emigration declined in the 1890's, the trend, which had first appeared in the 1880's, was firmly re-established in the twentieth century and accounted for the first significant slackening of population growth. In the first decade the net loss was 254,000, between 1911 and 1921 it was 239,000, or 47 and 66 per cent of the natural increase respectively. After the First World War came another major change, when in the 1920's the net movement outward of 392,000 was not counterbalanced by the natural rate of increase. Hence came the exceptional fall in the population during those years. In the early 1930's an increase in the movement into Scotland caused some expectation of a return of the earlier pattern, but, as this inward movement declined in the later 1930's, the trend of the 1930's seemed to be reappearing just before the Second World War.

Housing

The tendency for Scots to become town dwellers directly influenced the state of their housing, but the need for its improvement was even more pressing in the mining districts, which had suffered from such a rapid concentration of population, and in areas of rural depopulation, such as the Highlands, where the inadequacy of income and employment brought similar dereliction to the existing inferior housing. Its widespread applicability made the improvement of housing standards the leading aspect of social policy in modern Scotland, and one which was in some ways unique, since, unlike most other aspects, where any distinctively Scottish traditions were assimilated to English practice by 1914, housing retained several indigenous features, especially of architecture and law, which ensured a distinctively Scottish problem, even when statutory provisions were determined by the British parliament under the concepts and ideas of an increasingly comprehensive welfare state.

The nature of the problem was evident in many ways. In several building booms before 1914 the tenement of three, four or five storeys was the form of housing most commonly erected and into these the population of the towns was crowded. Since many kept lodgers—23·3 per cent in Glasgow and 23·1 per cent in Edinburgh in 1871—overcrowding increased still more. These tenements continued to have many small houses, or flats, so that in 1871 32·5 per cent of the houses in Scotland had only one room and 37·6 per cent had only two rooms; by 1901 the proportions were 17·6 and 39·9 per cent; by 1911 they were 12·8 and 40·4 per cent. The smaller houses need not necessarily have been overcrowded, but they were. Even in 1911, 56 per cent of one-roomed houses had more than two persons in each room, so had 47 per cent of those with two rooms and 24 per cent of those with three. The deficiencies were more evident when compared with conditions in England, where in the First World War only 7·1 per cent of the population were living in one- and two-roomed houses against 47·9 per cent in Scotland. The difference could not be explained by the average size of room being larger in Scotland, perhaps by as much as 20 per cent, a benefit which was, in any case, offset by most English houses possessing good sculleries. The Royal Commission on Housing of 1918 pointed out that, if the standard of overcrowding adopted by the Registrar-General for England and Wales, more than two persons to a room, were applied in Scotland, 2,077,277 people, or 45·1 per cent of the population, were living in overcrowded conditions. If the excess, as determined by this standard, had been removed from their existing houses, 695,842 people would have required rehousing. The result of such overcrowding was a marked concentration of population, especially in Glasgow, where the density per acre in 1911 was about twice that of Dundee and Edinburgh. Yet between 1871 and 1914 even Glasgow registered some improvement. The peak density, of 94 persons to the acre, was in 1871; in 1881, it was 84; in 1891, it was up again to 93; thereafter there came a sharp change and in 1901 and 1911 the density was 60 persons per acre. Between the wars there were further falls, to densities of 54 and 36 persons to the acre in the two census years of 1921 and 1931, and again a fall to 27 to the acre in 1951.[1]

The worst overcrowding did not arise from the sub-division of houses, typical of areas which had known better days, even though until 1891 alterations could be carried out without any possibility of control by the local authorities so long as the structure was not affected, but from the tenements, which contained all the deplorable, and frequently criticized, features of Scottish building: inadequate light and ventilation, sunk, or basement, flats, box-beds, shared toilets on stairheads, and others. Several factors explain the perpetuation of the tenement, but one frequently forgotten is that it was often the form of housing chosen by many. In his evidence to the Royal Commission of 1918 a Glasgow builder, though personally not in favour of tenements, suggested they had seven main attractions: tenements were substantially constructed and so gave better protection against adverse weather conditions; they enabled their occupants to live nearer to their work; some tenants were further from damp ground and less liable to suffer from choked drains; since tenement flats did not have stairs they were more easily worked; there were fewer burglaries in tenements, and so greater security for those living alone; good-sized apartments,

---

[1] Exact comparison is difficult because of changes in boundaries.

more usual in tenements, could be let more easily; the death-rate among tenement dwellers was as low as among cottage residents. These compensatory advantages ensured the continued adoption in Scotland of a form of building which led inevitably to a high density of people. They also show that the high density, without any qualifications, gives an erroneous impression of the disadvantages of Scottish housing. To some extent density was high by choice.

Partly because of the general acceptance of low standards, concern over the state of Scottish housing became acute only in the twentieth century. A notable early attempt to effect improvement was through co-operative enterprise, which assumed two forms: first, the modern type of building society, more frequently, and more accurately, known in Scotland in the nineteenth century as property investment societies, and, second, associations, more literally deserving the name of building societies, which were concerned not only with the financing of the building of houses, but with their construction, whether for the members of the association or for others. Though Scotland gave birth to early developments in both fields in the middle of the nineteenth century they made little difference to the country's housing requirements. The earliest of the first group, the property investment societies, dated from the early nineteenth century and were often mutual societies lasting only long enough to achieve a certain limited objective. Many were encouraged to become permanent through changes in their legal status later in the nineteenth century, and from the 1870's they prospered through their popularity with Scottish investors. By 1892 Scotland had about 68 societies, with total funds of about £1,000,000, though the trend, which has since continued, for the movement to be dominated by English societies, even in Scotland, was then appearing. Such success was not fully reflected in an improvement in Scottish housing conditions. The societies mobilized small savings to encourage house-ownership rather than house-building, but even that was not normally among those most inadequately housed. The contribution to construction of the second group, the co-operative societies of various kinds, was greater, though their effectiveness was also diminished when they came to be regarded as safe investments for small savers, and so when they ceased to be so concerned with the provision of accommodation for those who needed it most of all. In origin the early societies were mainly philanthropic ventures of the early and mid-nineteenth century and were frequently the means by which such housing reformers as Robert Cranston, or the Free Church leader, the Rev. Dr.

James Begg, implemented their ideas. They could be classified as genuinely co-operative ventures with the registration of the Edinburgh Co-operative Building Company, which erected buildings at Canonmills, Abbeyhill, and in other parts of the city. Similar companies were formed in Edinburgh and elsewhere. Once again the contribution of these concerns to solving the housing shortage lessened as they became property investment societies, and, moreover, since many built houses either for their own subscribers or for sale, they did not provide a major accession to the stock of houses to let, which, because of the Scottish preference for them, was the greatest need of the times.

Scottish public opinion was so inured to the existence of poor housing that it was not easily roused by co-operative ventures, or other action. As early as the 1870's *The Glasgow Herald* campaigned vigorously against housing conditions in the mining districts, and, though the public was impressed, little positive action resulted. Any private inactivity was not offset by official action, since less official concern was expressed over Scottish than over English conditions: the Royal Commission on Housing of 1884 ignored conditions in Scotland; at the end of the nineteenth century official plans for housing agricultural workers placed a bed in the kitchen in the Scottish plans, but not in those for England. The feebleness of official action in Scotland was noticeable, not only by comparison with English conditions, but by comparison with the greater success in dealing with other social problems in Scotland. Worse still, improvements in housing in certain areas in Scotland confirmed the ineffectiveness of action in others. Failure was most striking in the mining districts, where discontent was greatest, and in consequence, at the beginning of the twentieth century, the Scottish Miners' Federation led an agitation for improvement in housing conditions. Deputations met the Secretary of State in 1909 and 1911 and in the following year the Royal Commission on Scottish Housing was appointed. Its investigations, culminating in its report of 1918, made continued complacency difficult.

An explanation of the reluctance to act earlier may be found in the disillusionment which followed the failure of some of the earlier attempts at remedying the adverse influences on public health, especially poor housing. The basis of these early improvements was the Public Health (Scotland) Act of 1867, supplemented by the appropriate powers for remedial action, with which local authorities armed themselves after the example of Glasgow's City Improvement Act of 1866.

Edinburgh obtained an Improvement Act in the following year, 1867, and Dundee in 1871. Among the smaller burghs Greenock led by purchasing land under a Local Housing Act of 1875. The experience of the Glasgow Improvement Trust, the pioneer, and with one of the most difficult situations to tackle, is most instructive. Its activities were limited by two related factors: first, the inadequacy of finance, and, second, the impossibility of integrating a policy of demolition to one of construction and development. Disputes appeared first, and quickly, over finance. In the first year the maximum rate of 6d. authorized by the City Improvement Act of 1867 was imposed and met with strong opposition, which hindered the Trust's effectiveness, especially when, after the first five years of operation, the assessment was limited to 3d. The Trust had to concentrate on less expensive action, and could not, therefore, relate its policy of demolition to the more expensive one of construction. But to demolish without constructing was to provide only half the solution required. Nevertheless, the Trust did clear nearly 15,500 houses between 1870 and 1874. Its efforts were supplemented by the Street Improvements Act of 1873, and by the railway companies' clearance of some areas, such as the widening of the Trongate for Glasgow Cross station. The result was the removal of some of the worst slums in the city. On the other hand, the demolition of a large number of properties, without the provision of adequate substitutes, necessarily increased overcrowding in the remainder. Some of the worst-housed citizens of Glasgow were, therefore, being displaced rather than rehoused. They spread from the old nucleus at Glasgow Cross into the Gorbals, the Cowcaddens and other districts, which then began to decline socially, though, on the favourable side, the move frequently implied better housing, but often only at a higher rent. Worse followed. With inadequate finance, the Trust could not continue even its policy of clearance and so became inactive in that field too, retaining in use some property bought originally for demolition. In this way it came to own some of Glasgow's worst slums, which, because of the anticipated shortness of their life, were not even maintained in the state of decay they had already reached. The limitations imposed by financial stringency became clearer by contrast after 1895, when the Trust became self-supporting for the first time. Since its work could then expand, additional powers were obtained in a new Act of 1897.

For the years of relative failure the unwillingness of some of the wealthier citizens of Glasgow to spend must be blamed, but not entirely, as another factor contributing to the Trust's financial difficulties

x

was the inability, or reluctance, of many of the worst housed in Glasgow to pay higher rents to finance improvements in housing. The problem was not unique to Glasgow, but was common to Scotland, and provided the basic explanation of a striking phenomenon of Scottish housing, that overcrowding was common even when houses were unoccupied. In Glasgow in 1911 more than one house in ten was empty. Such unwillingness to pay more for better housing, with the consequential acceptance of poor living standards, had to be changed before any improvement could be brought about, but doing so was a major social problem, which called forth suggestions for a variety of methods of social amelioration, ranging, for the more intractable, to 'the 'licensed lodging house, the poorhouse, the lunatic asylum, the infirmary, the labour colony, or the jail'. It may have been comforting to the wealthier elements in society to imagine that all those who were badly housed fell into this category, but there were others, the 'decent poor', and some who were anxious to mend their ways, perhaps under supervision, to whom little help was given. Their position became increasingly difficult in the later nineteenth century, when rents did not follow the fall in most prices. Even the poor lodger was given greater help when the Improvement Trust constructed lodging-houses. The demand of poor prospective tenants of decent houses was met only in the 1890's, but not resolutely, since, though Glasgow Corporation had built over 2,000 houses by 1909, only 28 per cent were reserved for the poorest class of tenant. By 1914 houses were being built as well as demolished, but they were not always the type most desperately required socially. The slums were being cleared, but decent and sanitary substitutes were not being provided.

The failure of municipal action in Glasgow was striking because of the immensity of the problem to be tackled there. By comparison most other local authorities were even more backward. As late as 19th June 1914 the Housing Committee of Ayr County Council had only reached the stage of passing a resolution that 'privies should have doors and seats'.[1] All had to face the opposition of those who denied the responsibility, or even right, of local authorities to engage in economic enterprise, but any denial of the right of public bodies to enter into competition with private house builders was applicable in practice only in the provision of houses for those with higher incomes, and even in that field, where the possibilities of profitable construction were greatest, the achievements of private enterprise were not conspicuous.

[1] *Report of the Royal Commission on Housing*, 1918, para. 931.

The majority report of the Royal Commission on Scottish Housing had no doubt on the matter:

> 'private enterprise was practically the only agency that undertook the building of houses, and most of the troubles which we have been investigating are due to the failure of private enterprise to provide and maintain the necessary houses sufficient in quantity and quality'.[1]

The condemnation of the private builders cannot, however, be complete, because to them the provision of working-class dwellings was not an economic proposition. Even though elaborate dwellings were not required, costs could not be lowered excessively, especially when the houses were in cities where land was expensive, which, when combined with the reluctance of many to pay a reasonable rent, made the problem virtually insoluble by the private builder. His fault was only in pretending that he could solve it. On the other hand, even those who advocated public enterprise sometimes failed to see the entire social implications of their policy, as public enterprise could solve the problem only if allowed to levy sufficient rates to make good any deficit which might arise from the reluctance of some to pay an economic rent. Before 1914 the pressure to restrict expenditure made those who were anxious to see better housing for all aware of this reluctance, and so ready to suggest remedies, most of which were neglected after 1918 in favour of more generous financial provisions to subsidize rents. While removing the bottleneck that had inhibited much action before 1914, the adoption of this policy brought new difficulties in its train. Until the 1890's, and even to 1914, slums were being demolished, but inadequate housing provided for their former denizens. After 1918 it is not so certain that the first, and undoubtedly favourable, aspect of this judgement was as applicable.

The dispute over the ability of public and private enterprise to remedy the housing situation appeared in sharp focus in the reports of the Royal Commission on Scottish Housing. Its members split on the issue. The majority held that action mainly by local authorities was necessary; the minority held that all forms of enterprise should be employed, and, in particular, that some form of assistance should be given to private builders. The majority realized, in a way no one had previously fully appreciated, the immensity of the problem to be tackled in Scotland, and that local authorities, though not above criticism themselves, had been armed only with inadequate powers. Since

[1] *Ibid.*, para. 1,937.

they considered that private enterprise had been given the opportunity to provide adequate housing before 1914, the majority, in effect, proposed a new and radical solution. By contrast, the view of the minority was, to say the least, optimistic, especially in their belief that it was possible to live successfully in a one-roomed house, but they did understand more acutely some of the long-run difficulties inherent in the majority's recommendation of relying heavily on the local authorities, and even envisaged the political problems which would arise from the voting powers of the municipal tenants. The difference of opinion revealed by the two reports was significant for the future.

Both majority and minority reports had, however, one defect in common in their almost total failure to recognize the reluctance, or the inability, of Scots to pay higher rents, so that the overcrowded conditions in which so many Scots lived was as much the consequence of their choice as were the tenements in which many lived. Certainly overcrowding did not result from any absolute shortage in the stock of houses as bigger and better, though more expensive, houses were available for working-class families. Though the demand for more house-room fluctuated with economic conditions in an area, a general and permanent improvement in housing could have been obtained by many families if the proportion of 8 per cent of family income spent on rent in Scotland had been increased to the English proportion of 10 per cent. To rely on the efforts of private builders for an improvement in housing under such conditions was unrealistic. There was not a large and unsatisfied effective demand for housing in Scotland, and, more surprising than any failure by private builders to erect houses, was their willingness to continue to do so even in the face of a surplus of unoccupied accommodation. To provide better housing for those unwilling to pay a higher proportion of their incomes in rent, it was necessary that private builders should allow their profit margins to be reduced, or cut altogether, which was impracticable, or that public authorities should build the houses and subsidize rents. The majority report of 1918 failed to appreciate this necessary implication of the policy of public action which it advocated.

In such an environment rent restriction operated still more against the private builder of houses to let. But the peculiar system of Scottish rating, by which rates were paid jointly by owner and by occupier, until placed on the latter in 1957 by the Valuation and Rating (Scotland) Act, 1956, ensured that the Rent Restriction Acts had a more detrimental influence in Scotland than in England. Before 1914 owners' rates were normally passed on to the tenant through an increase in rents. On the other hand, until 1957 the rateable value was determined by the rent charged. Therefore, an owner could achieve a given increase in rent only by raising rent by a sum sufficient to give him both the desired increase in rent *and* an amount sufficient to pay for the rates payment for which he would become liable through the resulting increase in the rateable value of the property. The Rent Restriction Act of 1920 closed even this limited possibility of an increase by fixing the rent of a controlled house (those under £45 rateable value) at 140 per cent of the 1914 rent plus any increase in owner's rates between 1914 and 1920 only. Any later increase in owner's, though not in occupier's rates, lowered the net return to the owner. Through such legislation property owning became a less profitable proposition, and remained so, with only slight relaxations in restrictions, until the Second World War, when the restrictions were imposed on houses with rateable values of up to £90. On the other hand, since the influence of the Scottish rating system operated adversely only after the First World War, its effect on the deficiencies of Scottish housing was limited, because as the Royal Commission of 1918 amply demonstrated, the situation was extremely bad even before 1914. Between the wars rent restriction and the rating system were, therefore, only additional deterrents to private builders of houses to rent. It was, however, a new influence, discouraging the maintenance of existing property in good condition, and any existing tendency on the part of landlords to try to maximize short-run profits was increased by the trend of legislation.

Between the wars, therefore, responsibility for remedial action continued to fall on public authorities. In these years the proportion of houses built by public enterprise in Scotland was greater than in England and Wales, though, per head of population, the total number of houses built in the two areas was only marginally in England's favour. Of the 337,000 houses built in Scotland between the wars 67 per cent were built by public authorities, against only 25 per cent of the 4,194,000 houses built in England and Wales. The field for action by public authorities remained restricted by Scots still giving house-room a relatively low claim on their budgets. According to the Ministry of Labour's investigations into the budgets of working-class households between the wars, 9·1 per cent of the total expenditure of Scottish households was on rent and rates against a proportion of 12·7 per cent for Great Britain as a whole. Under such conditions housing needs, as judged by any reasonable social criterion, could be met only by some form of subsidy. One other effect of the changed responsibility for the construction of houses to let was that the tenement, which had been the chief form of house construction before 1914, was built only occasionally after 1918 and in construction stone gave way to brick. But, even with public action, Scotland remained the worst-housed area of the United Kingdom. By the standards of overcrowding applied under the Housing Act of 1935 almost one in every four of Scottish houses was overcrowded, against only one in every twenty-six in England and Wales. By 1939 housing was still Scotland's major social problem.

After 1945, when responsibility for action was assumed almost wholly by the local authorities, increased construction reached its peak in 1953, with an output of 39,548 houses, an achievement which must be modified by the recognition that it represented only a small addition (about 3 per cent) to the existing stock, much of which was being allowed to deteriorate through rent restriction rendering even the maintenance of property to let by private landlords an uneconomic proposition. Consequently, while the post-war years witnessed remarkable improvements in public health—such as the virtual elimination of diphtheria and a marked reduction in tuberculosis—the state of housing remained a major social problem. Fortunately there were improvements. In 1931 44 per cent of the people of Scotland lived in houses with one or two rooms, but in 1951 it was only 29·7 per cent; in the two badly housed cities of Glasgow and Dundee the reduction between 1931 and 1951 was from 55·4 to 41·5 per cent and 56·2 to 39·4 per cent respectively; to relieve the pressure in the most grossly overcrowded districts new towns were planned at East Kilbride, Glenrothes, Cumbernauld and Livingston, while arrangements were made for the surplus of Glasgow's population to 'overspill' into other towns. Yet in the 1950's all shades of opinion agreed that in this field much progress was still required; how far it was limited by the social attitudes which had hindered earlier plans is a matter of dispute.

The poor law

By the middle of the nineteenth century, the characteristic features of the Scottish poor law were being submerged into English practice and to some it seemed that its administration became less concerned with all aspects of destitution and concentrated instead on a narrower conception of relief. In other words, preventive measures became subsidiary to the relief of destitution, especially when the Public Health (Scotland) Act of 1867 placed responsibility for improving public health on the Board of Supervision, because the Board was more concerned with the relief of actual destitution than with its prevention, or with preventive medicine in general. Its instructions to its officers in 1869, after the passing of the new Public Health Act, confirmed its scale of priorities:

'The Board do not wish you, at present, to make such regular and minute inspection of your district with reference to its sanitary condition, as would seriously interfere with your ordinary duties as General Superintendent of Poor.'

Since the peak of pauperism in Scotland, of nearly 42 paupers per 1,000 of the population, was reached in 1868, the Board's concern may be appreciated, but it ensured that the desire to reduce costs became the leading principle in the administration of the poor law. That attitude, more than the reduction of poverty by better public health, or by improved nutritional standards, explains the sharp reduction in the incidence of pauperism to about 24 per 1,000 of the population, at which level it remained until there was a further drop to about 21 per 1,000 after the removal of those who became entitled to old age pensions in 1911.

Though in the lower rungs of the administration of relief a more generous attitude towards the poor sometimes prevailed, the Board's approach prevented the official adoption of policies to prevent rather than simply relieve destitution. Fortunately, though concern with cost was general, others did adopt a more liberal attitude to relief. The House of Lords finally decided in 1864 that neither an able-bodied man nor his family were entitled to relief under any circumstances, but relief was often given by parochial boards, some of them even advocating a change in the law. Again, until the twentieth century the Board of Supervision opposed granting out-door relief to the mothers of illegitimate children, but its recommendations were often flatly ignored or rejected by the parochial boards, which frequently went so far as to criticize the Board's policy as so deterring mothers from applying for relief that it implied subsequent suffering, and even death, for the children. The great bone of contention was, however, over the use of an offer of admission to the poorhouse as a test of the good faith of an

applicant's request for relief. The rigidity of the Board of Supervision's policy became evident in the circulars it sent to parochial
boards advocating this policy, as in 1878, 1883 and 1887, and in the
Board's officers frequently trying to follow up this pressure more
locally, though not always successfully.

In spite of such differences of opinion the administration of the poor
law in Scotland experienced no major changes in the later half of the
nineteenth century, because, though a number of amending bills were
introduced into parliament in its last quarter, none was passed, and the
parochial boards continued to administer relief under the general sur-
veillance of the Board of Supervision until 1894, when responsibility
was assumed by the parish councils, and the powers of the Board of
Supervision were transferred to the Local Government Board. In
practice the change had little effect. In the nineteenth century, however,
parochial authorities found additional sources of dispute with higher
authorities emerging through the creation of new specialized authorities, charged with the supervision of some aspect of public welfare,
such as the care and isolation of those suffering from infectious diseases.
The general responsibilities of local authorities hindered the effective
discharge of specialized functions, which more modern conceptions of
welfare advocated. The dispute foreshadowed the greater dispute which
emerged in the report of the Royal Commission on the Poor Laws in
1909, when the minority recommended the disintegration of the old
poor law administration into specialized services responsible for different aspects of welfare. By then, though there were a few aspects of the
poor law which still had distinctly Scottish features, its administration,
and the problems of social welfare generally, were cast in a British
mould. With one major exception of housing policy, the rise of the
welfare state cannot be considered only as a Scottish problem.

Trade unions

Even earlier in the nineteenth century it was hard to speak of a strictly
Scottish working-class movement and it soon became possible to say
that 'the Scottish trade union movement is not, nor with a few
possible exceptions, does it wish to be, completely separate and
divided from its counterpart in the rest of the United Kingdom'.[1] Such

[1] A. K. Cairncross (ed.), *The Scottish Economy* (Cambridge, 1954), p. 295.

assimilation became increasingly common with the increasing adoption of political action by the unions, a policy of which the Scots
generally approved.

Until the end of the nineteenth century smaller unions, generally
covering only a restricted geographical area and with limited funds,
were typical of the organization of the Scottish trade union movement,
which was, therefore, disintegrated and so limited in effectiveness. An
illustration of the more general situation arose in the heavy industries
which employed about one-third of all Scottish trade unionists, but
union membership was only 25 per cent of the possible total and was
distributed between small, and so frequently ineffective, societies.
Even the well-organized, such as the shipwrights and ironmoulders,
were inactive, and organizations which co-operated with the employers,
among them the British Steel Smelters Amalgamated Association,
formed in 1888, and the Associated Society of Millmen, formed two
years later, though powerful, failed to achieve many major gains. An
increase in power and strength was accompanied by decreasing control
and direction from Scotland. The British Steel Smelters Amalgamated
Association extended its activities to the north of England and transferred its head office from Motherwell to Manchester, and its leader,
John Hodge, became a national as well as a Scottish figure. Success
implied assimilation with movements south of the border.

Once again many of the struggles, achievements and failures of the
trade union movement in Scotland were illustrated most clearly by
the experience of the miners, who probably made a contribution
greater than any other group to the growth of the national movement.
Just as the Scottish miners gave the British labour movement a leader
of the middle of the nineteenth century in Alexander McDonald, so
towards the end of the century it produced a much greater successor in
James Keir Hardie. Hardie's efforts to build up a national union followed the lines laid down by McDonald, especially when after 1874
the success of the local and county unions waned. Their collapse provided the environment in which Hardie carried out his early work. The
incidence of the collapse of the county organizations varied. In Lanarkshire, where, against the advice of McDonald, there was general
resistance to all wage cuts, the men lost their ground and had to accept
the cuts proposed. By contrast, in Fife a lock-out was defeated, at
least in part, in 1877. But, unlike the miners in Lanarkshire, those in
Fife received outside support and their action was more in accordance
with the organized effort suggested by McDonald to the Lanarkshire

miners, but rejected by them. By 1880 the only county union which survived was the Fife and Kinross Miners' Association.

The first step towards a united organization came in 1866 with the formation of the Scottish Miners' National Federation with Keir Hardie as its secretary. Though the Federation was short-lived, and mainly only a propaganda body, it encouraged the formation of more local unions in addition to the Fife and Kinross Association. Better organization came through following English examples and by uniting with English movements until it led to the formation in 1894 of the Scottish Miners' Federation, immediately affiliated to the Miners' Federation of Great Britain. On the basis of the new-found strength, which came from unity, a strike was called in June 1894. It brought out most Scottish miners, even though only one in three was a member of a union, and ended completely in October, when most returned to work on the employers' terms, but its failure did not interrupt the related trends towards maintenance of contact with the south and towards large-scale organization. Both—and the tendency to use opportunities thus provided for the establishment of more direct socialist representation in political life—were encouraged when Robert Smillie, of the Larkhall Miners' Association, built up the local unions of Lanarkshire, and then of the whole of Scotland, to become by the end of the nineteenth century the first leader of the Scottish miners accepted in any way comparable to his predecessor from Lanarkshire, Alexander McDonald.

In the late nineteenth century the guiding light in the miners' struggle was the attempt to break away from the sliding scale, which related movements in wages to movements in the price of coal, towards a minimum wage. Only on condition that their demand was granted were the miners willing to accept a Conciliation Board in 1899. The Board took wages in 1888 (roughly about 4s. a day) as the standard which it long remained, and accepted a minimum wage of 31¼ per cent above the 1888 basis and a maximum wage of 75 per cent above it, or 5s. 3d. and 7s. The history of the Conciliation Board was not smooth, because the coalmasters sought to have the minimum wage reduced, especially when coal prices began to recede from their peak in 1907, a policy which to the miners amounted to a return to the sliding scale. A further grievance, which foreshadowed the more bitter disputes of the inter-war years, arose from the Scottish Conciliation Board fixing a minimum wage lower than that in England. The differential stimulated trade union organization and activity in Scotland,

and a threatened national strike in favour of the stand taken by the Scottish miners was only just averted and a minimum wage of 50 per cent above the level of 1888 accepted. Thereafter a sliding scale was to be adopted, with the price of coal to which the minimum wage was equated being fixed by an arbiter, and with any 'losses' incurred by the owners through the maintenance of the minimum wage, when prices were lower than that necessary to warrant it, being offset against periods when higher prices would otherwise have warranted an increase in wages above the minimum. In effect the old sliding scale was brought back, the only difference being that its adverse impact was tempered by being spread over longer periods.

Opposition to the sliding scale remained, therefore, the major concern of Scottish miners before 1914. Though they were actively engaged in the strike of 1912, the issue then at stake, the demand for a minimum wage for all miners working at the coalface, was less relevant to conditions in Scotland, where, since most miners worked on a daily basis, exceptional interference with piecework, such as falls of rock, could be met by transferring to another pit elsewhere. Though the Scots supported the general claim, and, proportionately, gave a greater majority than did the rest of the country for the continuation of the strike after the passing of the Miners' Minimum Wage Act, the main consequence was to confirm the suspicion of Scottish miners that they were treated harshly, because the schedule of claims for minimum wages in different districts showed that Scotland's 6s. a day was the lowest. The possibility that the Scottish coalfield was less profitable was hardly ever considered, though it was the root cause of the trouble. Even before 1914 the miners were suffering from the adverse effects of the inter-regional and international competition which increased between the wars.

For all its varied success the growth in numbers in the miners' organization was steady. The Scottish Miners' Federation had about 50,000 members in 1900 and 87,200 members in 1913. Other unions showed comparable growth. According to the estimates made by the Webbs there were 147,000 trade unionists in Scotland in 1892. In the next estimate, made by the Scottish Trades Union Congress in 1924, membership was 536,000. More strikingly, between these two dates, 1892 and 1924, the percentage of trade unionists relative to Scotland's population had risen from 3·7 per cent to 11 per cent, and though the proportions were slightly lower than for the United Kingdom, they showed a tendency to increase at a similar rate. But growth brought assimilation and between the wars it became increasingly difficult to speak of a Scottish trade union movement. Earlier movements to link various local Scottish unions into one gave way to attempts to merge into United Kingdom movements. In coalmining the county unions, which were common before 1914, transformed their loosely-knit Scottish Miners' Federation into the National Union of Scottish Mine Workers, a prelude, it was hoped, to one union, but a prelude which was protracted by the industry's difficulties until the Second World War. In 1944 the county unions were replaced by one union, which retained the old name of the federation, the National Union of Scottish Mine Workers, until it became the National Union of Mineworkers (Scottish Area) a year later. Assimilation was complete.

In spite of the move towards assimilation, important Scottish unions remained. In 1924 out of a total of 227 unions with 536,432 members, 90 unions, with 213,469 members, could be described as purely Scottish. That proportion has declined, especially since some of the bigger unions, such as those of the miners', were even in 1924 seeking wider amalgamations, which have since come to pass. Though the proportion of Scottish unions remained high, and probably still is, the purely Scottish unions became increasingly the smaller, local unions. Only in textiles, in some branches of which, notably jute, Scotland has always had a high stake, did large and powerful unions with a completely Scottish base still remain. The only way, organizationally or administratively, in which Scottish trade unions moved away from greater integration with England towards greater independence after 1870 was in the establishment of the Scottish Trades Union Congress in 1897, but its foundation was forced on the Scottish trade union movement and was not a sign of rising Scottish independence. When trades councils were excluded from the British T.U.C. in 1895 the Aberdeen Trades Council convened a meeting at Dundee to protest against the decision. The following year the Falkirk Trades Council continued the protest by suggesting that a Scottish federation should be formed, and, as a result, the S.T.U.C. came into being in Edinburgh in the following year, when about sixty delegates from both trade unions and trades councils were present. In 1923 the S.T.U.C. followed the example of its British counterpart by adopting a new constitution which, under the secretaryship of William Elger from 1922 to 1946, enabled the Congress to lead not only purely Scottish trade unions but all trade unionists in Scotland, as the Scottish membership of national trade unions is also affiliated to the S.T.U.C. The S.T.U.C. came to lead the trade union movement in Scotland because it became the spearhead of discussion among trade unionists on many major Scottish economic problems, and to that extent an independent Scottish trade union movement has continued. Indeed, one of the peculiarities of trade union history in Scotland in the twentieth century is that the greater administrative assimilation to national bodies has been accompanied by an increasing awareness of the extent to which Scottish trade unionists have to meet problems which are considerably different in degree, if not in kind. Without the existence of the S.T.U.C. and the focus it has given to such discussion, it is doubtful if the development would have taken place, but in the organization of trade unions generally in Scotland, even with the existence of the S.T.U.C., as strengthened after 1923, the dominance of British thought and policy became increasingly evident.

The co-operative movement was the field of working-class activity which remained most distinctly Scottish, though, in contrast to the trade unions, primarily so only in organization. Its problems arose, and had generally to be considered, on a national basis, even though Scottish co-operators often adopted a distinct viewpoint, as when, like their brethren in the trade union movement, they favoured direct political action more than their English counterparts. The Scottish co-operative movement, which was established in its modern form by about 1870, thereafter frequently met opposition from those who disliked its principles, as when, in an attempt to combat co-operative propaganda, the Scottish Traders' Defence Association was formed in 1888 and was especially active in the mid-1890's. One particular instance of opposition was when meat salesmen in the Glasgow Meat Market refused to accept offers by co-operative buyers until the Corporation, as landlords of the Meat Market, insisted that all tenants of public stances should accept the highest offers. Such opposition was generally ineffective as the progress of the co-operative movement in Scotland in the late nineteenth century was virtually uninterrupted. Of its progress there are various examples. The sales of the S.C.W.S. showed a steady trend upwards from its foundation in 1868 to 1914. In 1868 they were worth £9,697; in 1878, £600,590; in 1888, £1,963,854; in 1898, £4,692,330; in 1908, £7,531,126; and in 1914, £9,425,384. In 1886 the S.C.W.S. bought the Shieldhall estate between Glasgow and Renfrew, where it subsequently developed a whole range of manufacturing activities. The retail societies showed a similar growth. Progress came, too, in a different direction in the institution of federal retail societies to provide services which were beyond the resources of the smaller retail societies. In 1886 the Drapery and Furnishing Society was formed by a number of Glasgow societies, when the wholesale society announced that it could no longer deal with the expanding retail trade in these two fields. Such federal societies existed only so long as societies or branches could not maintain their own departments in these fields. Their growth was interrupted as constituent member-societies became able to provide their own departments, but such interruptions were signs of the movement's general growth.

Epilogue

AFTER 1939 many of the pre-war problems of the Scottish economy were submerged in the increase in production which reduced the numbers of unemployed to just over 16,000 people, or about 0·9 per cent of the insured population, in the summer of 1944; but the need for structural adjustment, which had been so pressing a problem before the Second World War, was still the main task in the Scottish economy after 1945. In agriculture and in industry the continuity was evident: how far a solution has been achieved cannot yet be determined.

The war-time expansion of agricultural production was a necessary consequence of the reduction in imports. Arable cultivation increased quickly, and by 1943 the 2,120,700 acres then under crop was an increase of 43 per cent over 1939. In view of the reduction in imports of feeding stuffs, the numbers of livestock were well maintained. Exceptions were pigs and poultry, both of which suffered from lack of feeding-stuffs, and sheep, which in some areas had to be reduced to allow tillage to expand; but the number of dairy cattle increased throughout the period and that of beef cattle, while it declined at first, was fully maintained in later years. Not surprisingly, the war-time expansion in arable acreage was greater than could be justified by the best agricultural practice, but a decline to the unduly low level of pre-war days was arrested by government aid. This had been withdrawn disastrously in the inter-war years, but after the Second World War it placed agriculture in a position which contrasted sharply with its experiences between 1918 and 1939. Its statutory basis lay in Part I of the Agricultural Act of 1947 and in the Agriculture (Scotland) Act, 1948: the former guaranteed prices and markets for the main agricultural products, the latter tried to ensure a degree of agricultural efficiency in return for the stability and guaranteed security of tenure for the efficient tenant, a security which was heritable in Scotland. Following these measures the Agricultural Marketing Act of 1949 provided for the re-establishment of the marketing boards which had been either suspended or carried on in attenuated versions during the war, though with the retention of a greater degree of ministerial discretion.

The statutory provisions placed agriculture in an environment totally different to what had existed before the war. Its response to the different opportunities was accordingly different too. On the favourable side output increased and by about 1957 was more than 50 per cent greater than in pre-war years. The increase in output was notable even within the post-war years themselves. In 1960, 144,000 tons of wheat were produced against 93,000 tons in 1948; in the same years the output of barley was 349,000 tons and 182,000 tons respectively. By contrast, the output of oats fell from 812,000 tons in 1948 to 707,000 tons in 1960. The different pattern reflected the diminished need for home-produced feeding-stuffs, and was evident also, though less conspicuously, in the production of potatoes and turnips. The increase was not only in output; productivity increased between the same years: 21·5 cwt. of wheat were harvested per acre in 1948 and 30·4 in 1960; 21·8 cwt. of barley against 27·5 cwt.; 17·1 cwt. of oats against 20·8 cwt. The greater arable output was maintained, therefore, on a diminished arable acreage, which fell from 1,851,669 in 1948 to 1,548,075 in 1960. With the exception of dairy cattle and poultry the numbers of most livestock were maintained during the same period. Between 1948 and 1960 the number (to the nearest thousand) of beef cattle in Scotland rose from 672,000 to 1,242,000; of sheep, from 6,731,000 to 8,407,000; of pigs, from 184,000 to 403,000. Poultry fell from 9,285,000 to 8,521,000 and dairy cattle from 828,000 to 761,000.

This increase in agricultural output presented a contrast to what had been achieved before the war, but it was subjected to two criticisms, both aimed basically at the statutory provisions which lay behind the agricultural successes of the post-war years. First, apart altogether from the question of whether the guaranteed prices were too high, especially by comparison with world prices, doubts were expressed on whether the system was sufficiently flexible to give the consumer increased supplies of the commodities most in demand. To this a precise answer cannot be given, as it depends on how extensive a switch in output it is considered Scottish agriculture should have made. Scottish farmers did, however, respond in the direction required by government policy, though whether they went far enough or not is another matter; in particular they responded appropriately when policy was altered to encourage an increase in beef cattle and a diminution in dairy animals. The general encouragement of livestock production accorded well with Scottish practice, but the preference for beef provided a much greater opportunity for the north-eastern farmers than for those in the south-west, who were forced to try to adapt themselves to more versatile herds. The second criticism against Scottish agriculture in the post-war years is more intangible. It suggests that the stability or security granted by the post-war acts has not been properly counterbalanced by increased agricultural efficiency. The criticism cannot easily be accepted, because there is no doubt that agricultural productivity did increase, so it must rest, therefore, on doubts as to whether more might still have been achieved. But in one respect at least the criticism is telling. The greater security of tenure which the Agriculture (Scotland) Act of 1948 provided has resulted in farms with vacant possession obtaining much higher prices than those with a sitting tenant, while the inability of landlords to gain control of their farms, apart from exceptional circumstances, has led to an almost complete absence of farms to let. The possibilities of social and economic ascent, which farming frequently offered in the past to those of limited means, was, therefore, effectively brought to an end. But to those already established as farmers these criticisms were relatively unimportant. The government aid for which the farmer had struggled in the inter-war years was given to him and he enjoyed a degree of stable prosperity which had not been his for many years.

As always, the experience of the Highlands and Islands, with their own problems, was unique. They received special aid, notably in the development of hydro-electricity and the adoption of a new approach to crofting. Hydro-electricity was pioneered in the Highlands at the Foyers station, opened in 1896, and at Kinlochleven, opened in 1909, but strong opposition delayed a comprehensive scheme until the North of Scotland Hydro Electric Board was formed in 1943. Since then electric power has been made available to most areas in the Highlands, but at an undoubtedly high capital cost. The legislative attempt to revive crofting, and indeed the entire Highland economy, lay in the Crofters (Scotland) Act of 1955, which instituted a Crofters' Commission, charged with responsibility for making the maximum and most efficient use of land through reorganizing townships, particularly through re-allocating the unworked land of absentee or infirm crofters. Since crofting by itself cannot guarantee an adequate income, additional employment must also be provided, but, in spite of afforestation, weaving, tourism, and pioneering attempts to establish light industries, the achievements in this field have been less notable. Without them, however, a viable crofting economy, and an end to the decline in population, are hardly possible. Unfortunately, one traditional source of additional income, fishing, is likely to be even less helpful than in the past, as fishing is now largely a full-time occupation, dominated by the boats from the north-east, which, however, frequently land catches in the west. Even in the north-east prospects are not wholly reassuring. Though the white-fishing fleet has been modernized, especially through the introduction of seine netters, helped by grants from the White Fish Authority, and is now the more prosperous branch of the industry in Scotland, transport charges have made it difficult for Aberdeen vessels to compete with those of Hull and Grimsby. A greater problem has, however, been faced by the Scottish herring fishing, which before 1914 had the largest output of cured herring in the world, most of which was exported to Continental markets that were never recovered after 1918. Since 1945 the Herring Industry Board, set up before the war and with head offices in Edinburgh, provided a guaranteed market, exported cured herring and gave grants for the construction of new vessels. From all such help the herring fishing has gained but has inevitably contracted sharply from the years of its prosperity.

In many ways the position of Scottish industry was even more interesting than that of agriculture, because, though it suffered the worst effects of the depression before the Second World War, afterwards, unlike agriculture, it was not given the protection of an all-embracing policy of government aid. If government aid was considered to be the remedy to avoid an agricultural depression in the post-war world, so the remedy generally advocated for Scottish industry was the policy of diversification, which had been increasingly accepted before 1939. Its implementation seemed urgent in 1945, when there was a general fear that, shortly after an immediate post-war boom, the heavy industries would relapse once more into the stagnant condition which had characterized them before 1939. Indeed in some ways the position was made worse during the war, since its demands had led to an expansion of the heavy industries, until in July 1945 they employed almost a quarter of the insured population in work, against only just under 16 per cent in July 1939. Since, therefore, the aim of implementing some change in Scotland's industrial structure, which had been the key to so much effort in the immediate pre-war years, was no nearer realization in 1945, it was a major aspect of policy even before the war was over. Two factors were particularly relevant to its prosecution afterwards.

The first was the government's policy, which rested on the Distribution of Industry Acts of 1945 and 1950, under which the Board of Trade was authorized to acquire land for the provision of facilities for industrial development. Scottish Industrial Estates, Ltd., transformed in 1960 into the Industrial Estates Management Corporation for Scotland, acted as agents for the Board of Trade under the Act, and, in addition to expansion on the four pre-war estates at Hillington, Carfin, Chapelhall and Larkhall, acquired a number of areas in the Scottish Development Area, which had taken the place of the old Special Area, and which, with the addition of Dundee and, from 1949, of an area round Inverness, covered most of the industrial belt, including Glasgow, which had been the centre of the pre-war depression. The first of the new estates to be developed was at Newhouse in 1945. The second factor which played a crucial part in encouraging the policy of diversification was the work of the Scottish Council (Development and Industry), which was formed through the merging of the Scottish Development Council and the Scottish Council on Industry. Its voluntary efforts proved to be an invaluable counterpart to the statutory provisions.

The policy of industrial development started after 1945 was chiefly an attempt to broaden Scotland's industrial structure by encouraging a large number of small firms in the light industries to start on the industrial estates and elsewhere, but it was soon diverted from concern solely with this aim through wider considerations of national policy, aimed at fostering industrial development which would save dollars or which was necessary for purposes of defence. A notable consequence was the establishment of a large number of subsidiaries of American concerns in Scotland, a reversal of the process of earlier years when Scottish firms had set up branches in the United States. Considered in isolation the success of such ventures could not be denied, but their contribution towards the provision of a new balance in the structure of the Scottish economy was more doubtful. Two defects were particularly striking. First, too much of the industrial investment rested on either government action, action by overseas industrialists, or on some combination of the two. In short, there was inadequate development by indigenous Scottish concerns. On the industrial estates before the war about two-thirds of the tenants, renting more than half of the floor area, were Scottish concerns; by about 1960 only one-third, renting about 15 per cent of the floor area, were Scottish. Since by the mid-1950's about one-sixth of factory construction in Scotland was government financed, it was not surprising that the restrictions on government expenditure fell particularly heavily on Scotland in 1956 and 1957, when Scottish Industrial Estates, Ltd., were authorized to build factory space of only 172,000 and 250,000 square feet respectively, against 842,000 square feet in 1958, when the restrictions were relaxed, 927,000 square feet in 1959, and 2,014,000 square feet in 1960. The failure of independent, indigenous Scottish enterprise provided a contrast with earlier years as it ensured that the responsibility for development was passed in this way to others. Second, even the policy of the government itself could be criticized; partly because of its inflexibility, which allowed help to be given only within the Development Area until the Local Employment Act of 1960 gave the government power to grant aid to any area of high, or potentially high, and persistent unemployment; partly, and probably more seriously, because the policy remained more concerned with the relief of unemployment than with the promotion of industrial growth. In consequence some projects, necessary not only for the development of particular areas, but for the growth of the entire Scottish economy, were not entitled to aid. That defect had to be set against the achievements, which, in addition to the many American concerns in Scotland, culminated most notably in 1960 in decisions by the British Motor Corporation to establish a plant at Bathgate to manufacture tractors and heavy commercial vehicles and by the Rootes Group to produce motor-cars at Linwood, projects which started production in 1961 and 1963 respectively and which, it was estimated, would each employ more than 5,000 people.

The criticisms of the policy of diversification reflected its failure to lead to any major change in the industrial structure of Scotland, which, by implication, demonstrated the continuing reliance of the Scottish economy on the prosperity of the heavy industries. Fortunately their experience after 1945 differed from that in the inter-war years, and, more than anything else, accounted for the success of the Scottish economy. The contrast could be noted most strikingly in coalmining and shipbuilding. Since after 1945 the inadequacy of supplies of coal placed a major limitation on expansion, the key to the growth of the Scottish economy in the years immediately after the war lay in the development of the coal industry, which had been so stagnant in the 1920's and 1930's. In shipbuilding occasional dearths of orders, as in 1949 and 1953, indicated that the prospects for the industry were not wholly certain, but until the later 1950's the tonnage launched was usually around 500,000 tons. Since Scotland still remained heavily dependent on these industries, their experience was of major importance for continuing prosperity, but their depressed nature between the wars indicated the undesirability of continuing to rely heavily on them. In turn this led to the attempts to diversify the economy, but it was always necessary that the modernization of the basic industries themselves should not be neglected. Since the balance of the industrial structure of Scotland was not altered, even with the efforts directed to that end, the need for modernization and renovation in the basic industries was more pressing than ever.

Progress in modernization was made after 1945, though it was mixed. In spite of the exceptional need for increased supplies of coal after the war, output increased in Scotland only slightly and then declined. In 1946 it was 22,500,000 tons; in 1949, 23,835,000 tons; in 1955, 22,844,000 tons; in 1961, 17,977,000 tons. The richest seams of Lanarkshire, which had been the source of the industry's greatest prosperity, were exhausted, and development lay elsewhere, especially in Fife and Ayrshire, but Scottish costs remained higher than in other districts. The loss per ton of coal (before charging interest) in the Scottish Division of the National Coal Board in 1952 was 3s. 7·4d. against a profit of 6·5d. per ton for the entire United Kingdom; in 1958 the relative figures were a loss of 14s. 5d. in Scotland and a profit of 1s. 2d. for the United Kingdom. Though a modest improvement followed, it was inevitable in these circumstances that the incidence of pit closures should fall heavily on Scotland. In 1961 the National Coal Board announced that 16 Scottish pits would be closed in 1962, among them the Glenochil colliery, which had been opened only in 1955. In coalmining there were, therefore, opportunities for development, especially immediately after the war, but Scotland's diminished natural advantages were one factor which made it less easy to exploit them. The experience of shipbuilding, with its central importance in the industrial complex of the west of Scotland, was equally important. In construction the most important change has been the substitution of welding and prefabrication in place of riveting and piecemeal erection on open hearths, a change reflected in employment—from 1,440 journeymen riveters and holders-on and 452 electric welders in April 1939 to 685 and 1,806 respectively in May 1955. Such a switch was particularly necessary for the Clyde to gain from the increasing demand for tankers, for which the high-quality yards on the Clyde had no particular advantage. In steelmaking, too, there were even more dramatic advances in the years after 1945. The pre-war dispute on the most desirable location for an integrated steelworks, inland or on the coast, was settled when Colville's steelworks at Ravenscraig near Motherwell came into operation in 1957 and when at the same time a new dock installation was constructed at the General Terminus Quay in Glasgow to deal with their imports of ore. An even more significant step towards the modernization of the steel industry began in 1958 when it was announced that a semi-continuous strip mill, the first in Scotland, was to be built at Ravenscraig and a cold strip mill at Gartcosh. At this point the development of the new industries, typified by those of the car industry at Bathgate and Linwood, converged with the modernization in traditional fields. Taken together, the three projects could rightly be described as 'the largest economic advance made in Scotland during the century'.[1]

Such advance, however, represented no more than an indication of changes that might come. Scotland's unemployment still remained higher than that for the entire United Kingdom. Since 1945 it was on average twice as high, a ratio never reached by the much higher pre-war rates. The investigations of the Committee of Inquiry into the Scottish economy (Toothill Committee), appointed by the Scottish Council in 1959, were, therefore, relevant to show the directions in which the Scottish economy should be encouraged to move. Their analysis of the problem confirmed its historical origins: 'Why . . . has growth not been at least as vigorous as in the more congested South? Part of the answer undoubtedly lies in the earlier years of rapid growth in Scotland: these were associated with heavy specialisation which made it inevitable that a period of transition, when it came, would be difficult. The change was delayed by the depression years before the war and by the war itself. . . . The common tendency is to persist in doing what has long been done well and profitably and especially so where innovation requires a wholly different know-how.'[2]

---

[1] Statement by the Executive Committee of the Scottish Council (Development and Industry).

[2] Report of Committee of Inquiry into the Scottish Economy, 1960–1 (Scottish Council Development and Industry), paras. 23.14, 23.15, 23.18.

Bibliography

THE following does not represent a complete bibliography of the works used but a selection of those mainly concerned with Scottish affairs and generally available. A rare work has been included only if considered particularly important. The selection is not, therefore, the ideal but rather the most convenient for the general reader. Those works marked * are considered especially useful.

The following abbreviations have been used:

EHR	*Economic History Review*
JEH	*Journal of Economic History*
J(R)SS	*Journal of the Royal Statistical Society*
SGM	*Scottish Geographical Magazine*
SHR	*Scottish Historical Review*
SHS	*Scottish History Society*
SJPE	*Scottish Journal of Political Economy*
TBR	*Three Banks' Review*
THAS	*Transactions of the Highland and Agricultural Society of Scotland.*

General

a. *Statistical Accounts.* The First, or Old, Statistical Account was written *c.* 1790, the Second, or New, Statistical Account *c.* 1840. The Third Statistical Account is in process of publication. The Accounts give comments on the life of all Scottish parishes at the time they were written, but vary enormously in their value, according to the personal knowledge a minister had of his parish and the strength of his prejudices. An attempt to summarize the first Statistical Account and other material was made by Sir John Sinclair in his *General Report of the Agricultural State and Political Circumstances of Scotland* (1814) and his *Analysis of the Statistical Account of Scotland* (1825). In spite of their defects the parochial accounts are greatly superior to parish histories, especially for economic and social information. Where a parish history does deal with some matter satisfactorily, it is listed in that section.

b. *Agricultural Reports.* The Board of Agriculture carried out two surveys of agriculture in Britain by counties between 1793 and 1816. The Reports are invaluable for information on the improving movement in Scotland. They are generally to be found indexed under the name of the author and bear the title *General View of the Agriculture of the County of....* A list is given in J. A. Symon, *Scottish Farming, Past and Present* (Edinburgh, 1959), pp. 445–7.

c. *Tours.* Accounts of tours are sometimes useful for descriptions of social and economic changes, especially around the end of the eighteenth century. The value of such accounts varies, but a selection from the very large number is given below. The date of the journey is given. Several have appeared in various editions.

W.A., *Journal of a Short Tour from Edinburgh* (1787).
J. Boswell, *Journal of a Tour to the Hebrides* (1773).
A. Campbell, *Journey from Edinburgh* (1802).
D. Defoe, *A Tour through Great Britain* (1727).
B. Faujes de St. Fond, *A Journey through England and Scotland to the Hebrides in 1784.*
J. Hall, *Travels in Scotland* (1807).
R. Heron, *Observations on a Journey through the Western Counties o Scotland* (1799).
S. Johnson, *Journey to the Western Islands of Scotland* (1773).
I. Lettice, *Letters on a Tour through various parts of Scotland in the year 1792.*
J. Macky, *A Journey through Scotland* (1723).
Sir A. Mitchell, *Macfarlane's Geographical Collections*, vols. I, II and III. SHS publications, vols. 51, 52, 53 (First series).
T. Newte, *Prospects and observations on a Tour in England and Scotland* (1785).
T. Pennant, *A Tour in Scotland and Voyage to the Hebrides* (1772).
R. Pococke, *Tours in Scotland, 1747, 1750, 1760* (Edinburgh, 1887). SHS publication, vol. 1 (First series).
H. Skrine, *Tours in the North of England and a great part of Scotland* (1795).
D. Wordsworth, *Recollections of a Tour made in Scotland in A.D. 1803.*

d. *Biographies.* Of these there is a large number of varying merit.

The Old Country Houses of the Old Glasgow Gentry (Glasgow, 1870).

Memoirs and Portraits of One Hundred Glasgow Men (Glasgow, 1886), 2 vols.

A. Carlyle, *Autobiography, 1722–1805* (ed. by J. H. Burton. Edinburgh, 1910).

M. Cole, *Robert Owen of New Lanark, 1771–1858* (London, 1953).

C. Hope, *George Hope of Fenton Barns* (Edinburgh, 1881).

J. S. Jeans, *Gallery of Western Worthies* (Glasgow, 1872).

A. M. Macgeorge, *The Bairds of Gartsherrie* (Glasgow, 1875).

R. Mitchison, *Agricultural Sir John* (Sir John Sinclair) (London, 1962).

J. P. Muirhead, *The Life of James Watt* (London, 1858).

J. Napier, *Life of Robert Napier* (Edinburgh, 1904).

W. Ramsay, *The Life and Letters of Joseph Black, M.D.* (London, 1918).

W. R. Scott, *Adam Smith as student and professor* (Glasgow, 1937).

e. *Periodicals.* The *Scots Magazine* was founded in 1739 and provides thereafter, throughout the eighteenth century, a useful record of, and comment on, economic and social affairs. Newspapers vary in the amount of information they contain, but some indication of their views is given in R. M. W. Cowan, *The Newspaper in Scotland* (Glasgow, 1946).

f. *Bibliographies*

P. D. Hancock, *A Bibliography of Works relating to Scotland, 1916–1950* (Edinburgh, 1959). 2 vols.

W. H. Marwick, 'A bibliography of Scottish economic history.' EHR, vol. V (1935).

'A bibliography of works on Scottish economic history published during the last twenty years.' EHR, (Second series) vol. II (1952).

'A bibliography of Scottish economic history, 1951–1962.' EHR, (Second series) vol. XVI (1963).

Sir Arthur Mitchell and C. G. Cash, *A Contribution to the Bibliography of Scottish Topography* (Edinburgh, 1917), 2 vols. SHS publications, vols. 14 and 15 (Second series).

W. R. Scott, *Scottish Economic Literature to 1800* (Glasgow, 1911).

g. The following are relevant to several periods or subjects:

Books

*D. Bremner, *The Industries of Scotland* (Edinburgh, 1869).

*A. K. Cairncross (ed.), *The Scottish Economy* (Cambridge, 1954).

Sir Reginald Coupland, *Welsh and Scottish Nationalism* (London, 1954).

J. G. Fyfe, *Scottish Diaries and Memoirs, 1550–1746* (Stirling, 1928). *Scottish Diaries and Memoirs, 1746–1843* (Glasgow, 1942).

*H. Hamilton, *The Industrial Revolution in Scotland* (Oxford, 1922). **An Economic History of Scotland in the Eighteenth Century* (Oxford, 1963).

W. H. Marwick, *Economic Developments in Victorian Scotland* (London, 1936).

W. Notestein, *The Scot in History* (London, 1946). (A study of the interplay of character and history.)

A. C. O'Dell and K. Walton, *The Highlands and Islands of Scotland* (London, 1962).

G. C. H. Paton (ed.), *An Introduction to Scottish Legal History* (Edinburgh, 1958), Stair Society publication, vol. 20.

G. S. Pryde, *Scotland from 1603 to the present day* (Edinburgh, 1962).

*J. A. Symon, *Scottish Farming, Past and Present* (Edinburgh, 1959).

Article

H. Hamilton, 'Economic growth in Scotland, 1720–1770.' SJPE, vol. VI (1959).

h. *Unpublished works.* A large number of unpublished sources have been used, the more important, and their custodians, being as follows:

Scottish Record Office

Records of the Board of Trustees for Fisheries and Manufactures
Records of the Scottish Exchequer.
Records of the Scottish Customs Board.
Records of the Court of Session.
Abercairney Muniments.
Carron Company Muniments.
Clerk of Penicuik Muniments.
Hamilton of Pinmore Muniments.
Loch Etive Trading Company Muniments.
Seaforth Muniments.
Shotts Iron Company Minute Books.

National Library of Scotland

Delvine Muniments.
Melville Muniments.

Mitchell Library, Glasgow
Bogle Muniments.
Clyde Market Reports.

Signet Library, Edinburgh
Session Papers.

Duke of Hamilton
Hamilton Muniments.

Theses

T. J. Byers, 'The Scottish Economy during the "Great Depression", 1873–1896, with special reference to the Heavy Industries of the South-west." Glasgow B.Litt., 1962.

W. S. Cormack, 'An Economic History of Shipbuilding and Marine Engineering.' Glasgow Ph.D., 1931.

Jean Dunlop, 'The British Fisheries Society, 1786–1893.' Edinburgh Ph.D., 1952.

D. I. Fagerstrom, 'The American Revolutionary Movement in Scottish Opinion, 1763 to 1783.' Edinburgh Ph.D., 1951.

B. Gaskin, 'The Decline of the Hand-Loom Weaving Industry in Scotland during the years 1815–1845.' Edinburgh Ph.D., 1955.

C. F. Smith, 'The Attitude of the Clergy to the Industrial Revolution as reflected in the First and Second Statistical Accounts.' Glasgow Ph.D., 1953.

T. Soper, 'Monymusk, 1770–1850.' Aberdeen Ph.D., 1954.

A. J. Youngson Brown, 'The Scots Coal Industry, 1854–1886.' Aberdeen D.Litt., 1952.

i. *Parliamentary Papers.* Parliamentary papers have been classified according to subject. The sessional volume number is quoted. A reference to the evidence of a particular witness is given only when a small part of the investigation was concerned with Scotland, or where some part of that evidence is considered particularly important. Only a fraction of those dealing with modern times has been cited.

CHAPTER I. A CHANGING SOCIETY
Books
A. G. Clement and R. H. S. Robertson. *Scotland's Scientific Heritage* (Edinburgh, 1961).

G. E. Davie, *The Democratic Intellect* (Edinburgh, 1961).

W. K. Dickson (ed.), *Memoirs of Ayrshire about 1780 by the Rev. John Mitchell, D.D.* (Edinburgh, 1939). SHS publication, vol. 33 (Miscellany) (Third series).

C. R. Fay, *Adam Smith and the Scotland of his Day* (Cambridge, 1956).

T. Ferguson, *The Dawn of Scottish Social Welfare* (Edinburgh, 1948).

J. Fergusson, *Lowland Lairds* (London, 1946).
John Fergusson, 1727–1750 (London, 1948).

I. C. C. Graham, *Colonists from Scotland: Emigration to North America, 1707–1783* (Oxford, 1956).

*M. Gray, *The Highland Economy, 1750–1850* (Edinburgh, 1957).

J. Y. T. Greig, *The Letters of David Hume* (Oxford, 1932).

*A. Kent (ed.), *An Eighteenth Century Lectureship in Chemistry* (Glasgow, 1950).

*J. G. Kyd, *Scottish Population Statistics* (Edinburgh, 1952). SHS publication, vol. 43 (Third series).

M. Lochhead, *The Scots Household in the Eighteenth Century* (Edinburgh, 1948).

C. A. Malcolm (ed.), *Minutes of the Justices of the Peace for Lanarkshire, 1707–1723* (Edinburgh, 1931). SHS publication, vol. 17 (Third series).

*R. Pares, *The Historian's Business* (Chapter VII) (Oxford, 1961).

*M. Plant, *The Domestic Life of Scotland in the Eighteenth Century* (Edinburgh, 1952).

CHAPTER II. AGRICULTURE

Books

J. Anderson, *An Account of the Present State of the Hebrides and Western Coasts of Scotland* (Edinburgh, 1785).

*A. R. B. Haldane, *The Drove Roads of Scotland* (Edinburgh, 1952).

*J. E. Handley, *Scottish Farming in the Eighteenth Century* (London, 1953).

A. H. Millar (ed.), *Forfeited Estates Papers* (Edinburgh, 1907). SHS publication, vol. 57 (First series).

J. H. Smith (ed.), *The Gordon's Mill Farming Club, 1758–1764* (Edinburgh, 1962).

*A. Wight, *Present State of Husbandry in Scotland* (Edinburgh, 1778 to 1784).

Articles

M. I. Adam, 'The Highland Emigration of 1770.' SHR, vol. 16 (1919).

H. Bone, 'The Ayrshire Breed of Cattle.' *Collections of the Ayrshire Archaeological and Natural History Society*, vol. I (Second series) (1947–9).

R. A. Gailey, 'Settlement and population in Kintyre, 1750–1800.' SGM, vol. 76 (1960).

*I. F. Grant, 'The Highland Openfield System.' *Geographical Teacher*, Autumn, 1926.

J. A. S. Watson and G. D. Amery, 'Early Scottish Agricultural Writers, 1697–1790.' THAS, vol. XLIII (Fifth series) (1931).

One of the best ways of studying agricultural conditions in the eighteenth century is by reading some of the published collections of estate papers or the writings of agricultural improvers.

Estate Papers

R. J. Adam (ed.), *John Home's Survey of Assynt* (Edinburgh, 1960). SHS publication, vol. 52 (Third series).

I. F. Grant, *Everyday Life on an old Highland Farm* (London, 1924).

H. Hamilton (ed.), *Life and labour on an Aberdeenshire Estate, 1735–1750* (Aberdeen, 1946). Third Spalding Club publication.

Monymusk Papers, 1713–1733 (Edinburgh, 1945). SHS publication, vol. 39 (Third series).

M. M. McArthur (ed.), *Survey of Lochtayside, 1769* (Edinburgh, 1936). SHS publication, vol. 27 (Third series).

Agricultural improvers

James Colville (ed.), *J. Cockburn. Letters to his Gardener, 1727–1744* (Edinburgh, 1904). SHS publication, vol. 45.

J. Fergusson (ed.), *Letters of George Dempster of Dunnichen to Sir Adam Fergusson, 1756–1813* (London, 1934).

Lord Kames, *The Gentleman Farmer* (Edinburgh, 1776).

R. Maxwell, *The Practical Husbandman* (Edinburgh, 1757).

CHAPTER III. TRADE AND TRANSPORT

Books

E. Pratt, *Scottish Canals and Waterways* (London, 1922).

James Hopkirk, *Account of the Forth and Clyde Canal Navigation* (Glasgow, 1816).

J. B. Salmond, *Wade in Scotland* (Edinburgh, 1934).

John Smeaton, *Report on the Forth and Clyde Navigation* (1764). Reprinted in *Reports of John Smeaton* (London, 1837).

Scots Magazine, vol. XXX (1768). Contains full reports on much of the discussion on the construction of the Forth and Clyde Canal.

Articles

*B. Crispin, 'Clyde Shipping and the American War.' SHR, vol. 41 (1962).

H. Hamilton, 'The Founding of the Glasgow Chamber of Commerce in 1783.' SJPE, vol. I (1954).

*M. L. Robertson, 'Scottish Commerce and the American War of Independence.' EHR (Second series), vol. IX (1956).

W. R. Scott, 'Economic Resiliency.' EHR, vol. II (1930).

*J. H. Soltow, 'Scottish Traders in Virginia, 1750–1775.' EHR (Second series), vol. XII (1959).

G. Thomson, 'James Watt and the Monkland Canal.' SHR, vol. 29, (1950).

CHAPTER IV. INDUSTRY AND FINANCE

Books

R. H. Campbell, *Carron Company* (Edinburgh, 1961).

A. and N. L. Clow, *The Chemical Revolution* (London, 1952).

H. W. Dickinson, *A Short History of the Steam Engine* (Cambridge, 1939).

*A. Fell, *The Early Iron Industry of Furness and District* (Ulverston, 1908).

*A. W. Kerr, *History of Banking in Scotland* (Glasgow, 4th ed., 1926).

David Murray, *The York Buildings Company* (Glasgow, 1883).

*G. S. Pryde, *The Treaty of Union of Scotland and England, 1707* (Edinburgh, 1950).

*A. J. Warden, *The Linen Trade* (London, 1864).

Articles

*H. Hamilton, 'The Failure of the Ayr Bank, 1772.' EHR (Second series), vol. VIII (1956).

'Scotland's Balance of Payments Problem in 1762.' EHR (Second series), vol. V (1953).

'The Royal Bank and the Scottish Economy, 1727–1780.' TBR, No. 35 (September, 1957).

G. Thomson, 'The Dalnottar Iron Company.' SHR, vol. 35 (1956).

Anon., 'The Bank of England—Agent of the Royal Bank of Scotland.' TBR, No. 39 (September 1958).

The problems involved in the development of the Scottish economy, especially in new fields, can be understood from a consideration of some of the contemporary discussion on economic policy, such as:

James Anderson, *Observations on the means of exciting a spirit of national industry* (Edinburgh, 1777).

John Knox, *A View of the British Empire, more especially Scotland* (London, 1784).

Patrick Lindsay, *The Interest of Scotland* (Edinburgh, 1733).

Reasons for Encouraging the Linen Manufacture of Scotland (London, 1735).

David Loch, *Essay on the Trade, Commerce and Manufactures of Scotland* (Edinburgh, 1775).

CHAPTER V. TRADE AND TRANSPORT

Books

*A. M. Acworth, *The Railways of Scotland* (London, 1890).

G. Buchanan, *Account of the Glasgow and Garnkirk Railway* (Edinburgh, 1832).

J. H. Burton, *The Scot Abroad* (Edinburgh, 1864).

G. Dott, *Early Scottish Colliery Wagon Ways* (London, 1947).

*A. D. Gibb, *Scottish Empire* (Glasgow, 1937).

*A. R. B. Haldane, *New Ways through the Glens* (Edinburgh, 1962).

D. S. Macmillan, *The Debtors' War* (Melbourne, 1960). (Scottish investment in Australia.)

O. S. Nock, *Scottish Railways* (Edinburgh, 1950).

Articles

Anon., 'The Rise of Glasgow's West Indian Trade, 1793–1818.' TBR, No. 38 (June 1958).

J. D. Bailey, 'Australian Borrowing in Scotland.' EHR (Second series), vol. XII (1959).

S. G. Checkland, 'Two Scottish West Indian Liquidations after 1793.' SJPE, vol. IV (1957).

D. S. Macmillan, 'The Scottish Australian Company, 1840–1850.' SHR, vol. 39 (1960).

Parliamentary Papers

★Survey and Reports of the Coasts and Central Highlands of Scotland in Autumn of 1802, by Thomas Telford. In Reports of the Select Committee on the Survey of the Central Highlands of Scotland. 1802–3. IV.

★Report of the Royal Commission for inquiring into matters relating to the public roads of Scotland. 1860. XXXVIII.

The histories of most railways have been written, but generally with a technical emphasis.

Sir Malcolm Barclay-Harvey, *A History of the Great North of Scotland Railway* (1940).

G. Dow, *The First Railway across the Border* (Edinburgh, 1946). (North British Railway.)

O. S. Nock, *The Caledonian Railway* (London, n.d.).

H. A. Vallance, *The Highland Railway* (Dawlish. Revised edition, 1963).

CHAPTER VI. THE TEXTILE INDUSTRIES

Books

M. Blair, *The Paisley Shawl* (Paisley, 1904).
    The Paisley Thread Industry (Paisley, 1907).

Articles

★W. O. Henderson, 'The Cotton Famine in Scotland and the Relief of Distress, 1862–1864.' SHR, vol. 30 (1951).

N. McIntosh, 'Changing Population Distribution in the Cart Basin in the Eighteenth and early Nineteenth Centuries.' *Transactions of the Institute of British Geographers* (1956).

W. H. Marwick, 'The Cotton Industry and the Industrial Revolution in Scotland.' SHR, vol. 21 (1924).

G. M. Mitchell, 'The English and Scottish Cotton Industries.' SHR, vol. 22 (1925).

★J. Strang, 'On the Altered Condition of the Embroidered Muslin Manufactures of Scotland and Ireland since 1857.' JSS, vol. 24 (1861).

Parliamentary Papers

Report of Select Committee appointed to enquire into the State of Commercial Credit, 1810–11. II. And *House of Commons Journal*, vol. 66 (1810–11), Appendix (No. 13).

Report of Select Committee on Children employed in the Manufactories of the United Kingdom, 1816. III. (Evidence of Alexander Buchanan, Robert Owen, Adam Bogle, Henry Houldsworth.)

Report of Select Committee on Children in Mills and Factories in the United Kingdom, 1831–32. XV. (Evidence of William Smith, James McNish, Peter Smart, A. L. Gordon.)

Factories Inquiry Commission, 1833. (1st Report, 1833. XX—reports on factories from Commissioners.) (2nd report, 1833. XXI—medical evidence.) (Supplementary report, 1833. XIX–XX—analysis of answers to questionnaires.)

*Report of Select Committee on Manufacturers, Commerce and Shipping, 1833. VI. (Evidence of Kirkman Finlay, William Graham, junr., Henry Houldsworth.)

Report of Select Committee on Handloom Weavers, 1834. X. (Evidence of James Stewart, James Buik, Lawrence Don, Thomas Malloch, James McEwen, James Grant, John Wilkie.)

Reports of the Assistant Handloom Weavers' Commissioners, 1839. XLII. (Reports by J. C. Symons on the south of Scotland; J. D. Harding on the east of Scotland.)

Children's Employment Commission, 1843. XV. (Reports by Thomas Tancred and Robert Franks in Part II of the Commissioners' reports.)

Children's Employment Commission, 1864. (Second Report, XXII—on textile factories.)

Chapter VII. The Heavy Industries

Books

*R. Bald, *A General View of the Coal Trade of Scotland* (Edinburgh, 1808).

T. B. Mackenzie, *Life of J. B. Neilson* (Glasgow, 1929).

A. Miller, *Rise and Progress of Coatbridge* (Glasgow, 1929).

Articles

R. H. Campbell, 'Investment in the Scottish Pig Iron Trade, 1830–1843.' SJPE, vol. I (1954).

'Developments in the Scottish Pig Iron Trade, 1844–1848.' JEH, vol. XV (1955).

'Fluctuations in Stocks: A Nineteenth Century Case Study.' *Oxford Economic Papers* (new series), vol. 9 (1957).

'Early Malleable Iron Production in Scotland.' *Business History*, vol. IV (1961).

J. H. G. Lebon, 'The Development of the Ayrshire Coalfield.' SGM, vol. 49 (1933).

P. L. Payne, 'The Govan Collieries, 1804–1805.' *Business History*, vol. III (1961).

Parliamentary Papers

Children's Employment Commission, 1842. (Reports by Assistant Commissioners. Part I, 1842, XVI. Part II, 1842, XVII. Report by T. Tancred.)

★Reports of the Inspectors of Mines, from 1844.

Report of Select Committee on Mining Acts, 1865. XII. (Evidence of A. McDonald, R. Moore, W. Burns, J. W. Ormiston, J. Baird.)

★Report of Royal Commission on Coal, 1871. XVII. (Especially report of Committee E.)

★Report of Select Committee on present dearness and scarcity of Coal, 1873. X. (Evidence of William Alexander, Ralph Moore, Alexander McDonald, Andrew Landale, Allan Gilmour.)

CHAPTER VIII. FINANCE

Books

J. S. Fleming, *Scottish Banking: a historical sketch* (Edinburgh, 1877).

★Sir William Forbes, *Memoirs of a Banking-House* (London, 1860).

W. Graham, *The One Pound Note in Scotland* (Edinburgh, 1886).

C. A. Malcolm, *The Bank of Scotland, 1695–1945* (Edinburgh, 1948).
  The History of the British Linen Bank (Edinburgh, 1950).

N. Munro, *The History of the Royal Bank of Scotland, 1727–1927* (Edinburgh, 1928).

R. S. Rait, *The History of the Union Bank of Scotland* (Glasgow, 1930).

J. M. Reid, *The History of the Clydesdale Bank, 1838–1938* (Glasgow, 1938).

★R. Somers, *The Scotch Banks and System of Issue* (Edinburgh, 1873).

Articles

R. H. Campbell, 'Edinburgh Bankers and the Western Bank of Scotland.' SJPE, vol. II (1955).

M. Gaskin, 'Scottish Bankers and the English Banking Laws.' *Bankers' Magazine*, No. 1411 (October 1961).

*'Anglo-Scottish Banking Conflicts, 1874–1881.' EHR, (Second series), vol. XII (1960).

Anon., 'John Coutts, Corn Merchant and Banker.' TBR, No. 26 (June 1955).

*'The Royal Bank and the London–Edinburgh Exchange Rate in the Eighteenth Century.' TBR, No. 38 (June 1958).

Parliamentary Papers

Report of the Select Committee on the State of Commercial Credit, 1793. Parliamentary Papers, 1826. III. And *House of Commons Journal*, vol. 78, p. 702.

Report of the Select Committee on Promissory Notes in Scotland and Ireland, 1826. III.

Second Report of the Select Committee on Banks of Issue, 1841. V.

Second Report of the Committee on Commercial Distress, 1847–8. VIII (Evidence of J. G. Kinnear, J. A. Anderson, R. Bell, J. F. Macfarlan.)

Report of the Select Committee on the Bank Acts, 1857. Session 2. X.

*Report of the Select Committee on the Bank Acts and Causes of the Recent Commercial Distress, 1857–8. V.

Chapter IX. Agriculture

Books

Aliquis, *Landlords, Land Laws and Land Leagues in Scotland* (Edinburgh, 1881).

*W. Cobbett, *Rural Rides* (ed. by G. D. H. and M. Cole), 1930.

W. M. Findlay, *Oats, their cultivation and use from earliest times to the present day* (Edinburgh, 1956).

T. B. Franklin, *A History of Scottish Farming* (Edinburgh, 1951).

I. Grimble, *The Trial of Patrick Sellar* (London, 1962). (An indictment of the Sutherland clearances.)

J. Loch, *Account of the Improvements on the Estates of the Marquess of Stafford* (London, 1820). (A commendation of the Sutherland clearances.)

A. Mackenzie, *The History of the Highland Clearances* (Glasgow, 2nd edition, 1946).

W. McCombie, *Cattle and Cattle-Breeders* (Edinburgh, 4th edition, 1866).

*George Robertson, *Rural Recollections* (Irvine, 1829).

z*

R. Salaman, *The History and Social Influence of the Potato* (Cambridge, 1949).

Sir James Steuart, *Considerations on the Interest of the County of Lanark*. In *Collected Works*, vol. 5 (London, 1805).

J. A. S. Watson and M. E. Hobbs, *Great Farmers* (London, 2nd ed., 1951).

Articles

M. I. Adam, 'Causes of the Highland Emigration, 1783–1803.' SHR, vol. 17 (1920).

'Eighteenth Century Highland Landlords and the Poverty Problem.' SHR, vol. 19 (1922).

A. Birnie, 'Ridge Cultivation.' SHR, vol. 24 (1927).

*J. B. Caird and H. A. Moisley, 'Leadership and Innovation in the Crofting Communities of the Outer Hebrides.' *The Sociological Review*, vol. 9 (new series) (1961).

R. A. Gailey, 'Mobility of Tenants on a Highland Estate in the Early Nineteenth Century.' SHR, vol. 40 (1961).

G. Houston, 'Labour Relations in Scottish Agriculture before 1870.' *Agricultural History Review* (1958).

'Farm Wages in Central Scotland from 1814 to 1870.' J of RSS, vol. 118 (1955).

*'Agricultural Statistics in Scotland before 1866.' *Agricultural History Review*, vol. IX (1961).

*E. H. Whetham, 'Prices and Production in Scottish Farming, 1850–1870.' SJPE, vol. IX (1962).

Parliamentary Papers

Report respecting the Scotch Distillery Duties, 1798. Parliamentary Papers, 1803. XI.

Select Committee on the Depressed State of Agriculture in the United Kingdom, 1821. IX (Evidence of John Brodie of Scoughall and John Brodie of West Fenton.)

Report of the Select Committee on the present State of Agriculture, 1833. V.

Report of the Select Committee on Emigration, Scotland, 1841.

Report of Select Committee on the Law of Hypothec in Scotland, 1868–9. IX.

Return of Owners of Land in Scotland, 1872–3. 1874. LXXII. Part III.

CHAPTER X. AN INDUSTRIAL SOCIETY

Books

*J. H. F. Brotherston, *Observations on the Early Public Health Movement in Scotland* (London, 1952).

A. K. Chalmers (ed.), *Public Health in Glasgow* (Glasgow, 1905).

J. D. Comrie, *History of Scottish Medicine* (London, 1932).

*R. Cowan, *Vital Statistics of Glasgow* (Glasgow, 1838).

A. S. Cunningham, *Mining in Mid and East Lothian* (Edinburgh, 1925).

J. E. Handley, *The Irish in Scotland, 1798–1845* (Cork, 1943).
The Irish in Modern Scotland (Cork, 1947).

G. W. Hilton, *The Truck System* (Cambridge, 1960).

*D. F. Macdonald, *Scotland's Shifting Population, 1770–1850* (Glasgow, 1937).

*L. J. Saunders, *Scottish Democracy, 1815–1840* (Edinburgh, 1950).

J. Stark, *Contribution to the Vital Statistics of Scotland* (London, 1851).

*R. Watt, *Treatise on Chincough* (Glasgow, 1813). (Includes an appendix on 'An Inquiry into the Relative Mortality of the Principal Diseases of Childhood'.)

Articles

J. R. Kellett, 'Property Speculators and the Building of Glasgow 1783–1830.' SJPE, vol. VIII (1961).

A. R. Thompson, 'The Use of Libraries by the Working Class in Scotland.' SHR, vol. 42 (1963).

J. T. Ward, 'The Factory Reform Movement in Scotland.' SHR, vol. 41 (1962).

Parliamentary Papers

Report upon the Boundaries of the Cities, Burghs and Towns of Scotland, 1831–32. XLIII.

Report of Royal Commission on State of the Irish Poor in Great Britain, 1836. XXXIV. (Evidence of George Burns, George Miller, Hugh Logan, William Dixon, Alexander Guthrie.)

Report of Select Committee on Payment of Wages, 1842. IX. (Evidence of J. Smith, W. Dixon, W. Brown, J. Cross.)

*Reports on the Sanitary Conditions of the labouring Population of Scotland, 1842. XXVIII.

Report on the Arrestment of Wages in Scotland, 1854. LXIX.

Report of the Select Committee on the State of the Law affecting the Pawnbroking Trades, 1870. VIII.

Report of Royal Commission on the Truck System, 1871. XXXVI.

CHAPTER XI. SOCIAL REFORM

Books

*R. Page Arnot, *A History of the Scottish Miners* (London, 1955).

A. Briggs, *Chartist Studies* (London, 1959). (Chapter 8, Alex. Wilson: 'Chartism in Glasgow'.)

A. A. Cormack, *Poor Relief in Scotland* (Aberdeen, 1923).

T. Hamilton, *Poor Relief in South Ayrshire, 1700–1845* (Edinburgh, 1942).

*S. Mechie, *The Church and Scottish Social Development, 1780–1870* (London, 1960).

Sir George Nicholls, *A History of the Scotch Poor Laws* (London, 1856).

A. Swinton (ed.), *Report of the Trial of the Glasgow Cotton Spinners* (Edinburgh, 1838).

*L. C. Wright, *Scottish Chartism* (Edinburgh, 1953).

Articles

J. L. Gray, 'The Law of Combination in Scotland.' *Economica*, No. 24 (1928).

A. J. Youngson Brown, 'Trade Union Policy in the Scots Coalfields, 1855–1885.' EHR (Second series), vol. VI.

Parliamentary Papers

Report of Select Committee on the Combination Laws, 1825. IV. (Evidence of G. Taylor, A. Guthrie, W. McAllister.)

Report of Select Committee on Emigration from the U.K., 1826. IV. (Evidence of R. J. Uniacke, W. F. Campbell, Sir Hugh Innes, G. M. Grant, A. Campbell.)

Report of Select Committee on Emigration from the U.K., 1827. V. (Evidence of John Foster, James Little, A. Campbell, T. F. Kennedy, H. H. Drummond, W. S. Northouse.)

Report of Select Committee on Combinations of Workmen, 1838. VIII. (Evidence of A. Alison, J. Houldsworth.)

Report of a Committee of the General Assembly of the Church of Scotland on the Management of the Poor in Scotland, 1839.

Report of the Royal Commission on the Poor Laws of Scotland, 1844. XX.

Report of Select Committee on Master and Servant, 1865 and 1866. XIII. (Evidence of A. McDonald.)

Report on the Royal Commission on Trade Unions, 1867–8. XXXIX. (Evidence of A. Hood, A. McDonald, J. D. Samuda, R. Steel, junr., J. P. Smith, J. McDonald.)

Report of Select Committee on the Poor Laws in Scotland, 1868–9. XI.

CHAPTER XII. INDUSTRY TO 1914

Books

J. L. Carvel, *A Record of 200 Years of Shipbuilding: Stephen of Linthouse, 1750–1950* (Glasgow, 1951).

C. R. Fay, *Round about Industrial Britain, 1830–1860* (Toronto, 1952). (Includes account of early shipbuilding.)

Sir Allan Grant, *Steel and Ships: the history of John Brown's* (London, 1950).

*R. Miller and J. Tivy (edd.), *The Glasgow Region* (Glasgow, 1958). (Especially James and Sarah C. Orr, 'The Growth of the Engineering Industries'.)

J. Williamson, *The Clyde Passenger Steamer, 1812–1901* (Glasgow, 1904).

Articles

*I. F. Gibson, 'The Establishment of the Scottish Steel Industry.' SJPE, vol. V (1958).

S. G. E. Lythe, 'Shipbuilding at Dundee down to 1914.' SJPE, vol. IX (1962).

W. Woodruff, 'The American Origins of a Scottish Industry.' SJPE, vol. II (1955).

Parliamentary Papers

Report of Royal Commission on Scientific Instruction and the Advancement of Science, 1872. XXV. (Evidence of J. Young, J. McClelland.)

Report of Royal Commission on Depression of Trade and Industry, 1886. XXI, XXIII. (Evidence of John Scott in Third Report, 1886. XXIII.)

Second Report of the Royal Commission on Mining Royalties, 1890–91. XLI. (Evidence of R. Brown, R. Smillie, D. Landale.)

Report of Royal Commission on Coal Supplies. Final Report, 1905. XVI. (Evidence of D. M. Stevenson.)

CHAPTER XIII. INDUSTRY, 1914 TO 1939

Books

J. A. Bowie, *The Future of Scotland* (Edinburgh, 1929).

R. M. Findlay, *Scotland at the cross-roads* (Edinburgh, 1937).

Mary J. F. Gregor and Ruth M. Crichton, *From Croft to Factory* (Edinburgh, 1946).

*C. E. V. Leser and A. H. Silvey, *Scottish Industries during the Inter-war Period* (Glasgow, 1950).

*C. E. V. Leser, *Industrial Specialization in Scotland and in regions of England and Wales* (Glasgow, 1949).

Sir Alexander MacEwen, *The Thistle and the Rose* (Edinburgh, 1932).

N. Milnes, *A study of industrial Edinburgh and the surrounding areas, 1923–1934* (Edinburgh, 1936).

C. A. Oakley, *Industrial Map of Scotland* (Edinburgh, 1939).
   Scottish Industry Today (Edinburgh, 1937).

W. R. Scott and J. Cunnison, *The Industries of the Clyde Valley during the War* (Oxford, 1924).

G. M. Thomson, *Scotland, that distressed area* (Edinburgh, 1935).

*A. C. Turner, *Scottish Home Rule* (Oxford, 1951).

Scottish Economic Committee, *Light Industries in Scotland: a case for development* (Glasgow, 1938).

Clydesdale Bank, *Annual Review of Economic Conditions in Scotland*.

Articles

*A. D. Campbell, 'Changes in Scottish Incomes, 1924–49.' *Economic Journal*, vol. 65.

G. S. Pryde, 'The Development of Nationalism in Scotland.' *The Sociological Review*, vol. XXVII (1935).

D. I. Trotman-Dickenson, 'The Scottish Industrial Estates.' SJPE, vol. VIII (1961).

Parliamentary Papers

Industrial Survey of the South-West of Scotland; an industrial survey made for the Board of Trade by the Department of Political Economy, Glasgow University, 1932.

Report of Investigations into the Industrial Conditions in certain Depressed Areas. IV. Scotland. 1933–34. XIII.

Chapter XIV. Agriculture, 1870's to 1939

Books

*A. Collier, *The Crofting Problem* (Cambridge, 1953).

D. J. Jones *et al.*, *Rural Scotland during the War* (London, 1926).

*N. Nicolson, *Lord of the Isles* (London, 1960). (Work of Lord Lever-hulme in the Outer Isles.)

Scottish Economic Committee, *Review of the economic conditions of the Highlands and Islands of Scotland* (Glasgow, 1938).

Horace Plunkett Foundation, *Agricultural Co-operation in Scotland and Wales* (London, 1932).

Articles

T. G. Henderson, 'Agricultural Co-operation in Scotland.' THAS, vol. XLI (Fifth series) (1929).

*J. A. Symon, 'John Spier.' *Scottish Agriculture*, vol. XXX (1950).

Parliamentary Papers

Report of the Royal Commission on Depressed Conditions of the Agricultural Interests, 1881. XVI. (Reports of Assistant Commissioners on Scotland.)

Report of the Royal Commission on the Conditions of Crofters and Cottars in the Highlands and Islands of Scotland, 1884. XXXII–XXXVI. (Napier Commission.)

Reports of the Department of Agriculture for Scotland.

Chapter XV. Social Assimilation

Books

*J. D. M. Bell, *Strength of Trade Unionism in Scotland* (Glasgow, 1950).

K. D. Buckley, *Trade Unionism in Aberdeen, 1878 to 1900* (Edinburgh, 1955).

T. Ferguson, *Scottish Social Welfare, 1884 to 1914* (Edinburgh, 1958).

J. A. Flanagan, *Wholesale Co-operation in Scotland, 1868–1918* (Glasgow, 1920).

*S. C. Gillespie, *A Hundred Years of Progress, 1853–1952* (Glasgow, 1953. (History of the Scottish Typographical Association.)

Articles

R. H. Osborne, 'Scottish Migration Statistics: A Note.' SGM, vol. 72 (1956).

★'The Movements of People in Scotland, 1851–1951.' *Scottish Studies*, vol. 2 (1958).

M. C. Storrie, 'The Census of Scotland as a Source in the Historical Geography of Islay.' SGM, vol. 78 (1962).

Parliamentary Papers

Royal Commission on Labour, Vol. III, 1893. VII. (Evidence of Alexander Wilkie, Alexander Law, John Lindsay, John Inglis, James M. Jack.)

Report of the Royal Commission on Mines. (Committee on Accidents.) Vols. II and III. 1908. XX. (Evidence of J. T. Forgie, James Brown, Peter Muir, John Weir.) Vol. IV. 1909. XXXIV. (Evidence of J. T. Forgie, William Smith, James Allardice.)

★Report of the Royal Commission on the Housing of the Industrial Population of Scotland (Rural and Urban). 1917–18. XIV.

INDEX

347